# READING EARLY MODERN WOMEN'S WRITING

# Reading Early Modern Women's Writing

PAUL SALZMAN

OXFORD
UNIVERSITY PRESS

# OXFORD
UNIVERSITY PRESS

Great Clarendon Street, Oxford OX2 6DP

Oxford University Press is a department of the University of Oxford.
It furthers the University's objective of excellence in research, scholarship,
and education by publishing worldwide in

Oxford New York

Auckland Cape Town Dar es Salaam Hong Kong Karachi
Kuala Lumpur Madrid Melbourne Mexico City Nairobi
New Delhi Shanghai Taipei Toronto

With offices in

Argentina Austria Brazil Chile Czech Republic France Greece
Guatemala Hungary Italy Japan Poland Portugal Singapore
South Korea Switzerland Thailand Turkey Ukraine Vietnam

Oxford is a registered trade mark of Oxford University Press
in the UK and in certain other countries

Published in the United States
by Oxford University Press Inc., New York

© Paul Salzman 2006

The moral rights of the author have been asserted
Database right Oxford University Press (maker)

First published 2006

British Library Cataloguing in Publication Data

Data available

Library of Congress Cataloging in Publication Data

Data available

Typeset by Laserwords Private Limited, Chennai, India
Printed in Great Britain
on acid-free paper by
Biddles Ltd., King's Lynn, Norfolk

ISBN 0–19–926104–0   978–0–19–926104–8

1 3 5 7 9 10 8 6 4 2

For Susan, Imogen, Joseph, and Charles

# Acknowledgements

During the time I have been working on this book, and on other projects in the area of early modern women's writing, I have benefited from the unfailing generosity of other scholars in the field. Here I want especially to thank Margaret Ezell, Elizabeth Hageman, Elaine Hobby, Kate Lilley, Harold Love, Richard McCabe, David Norbrook, Michelle O'Callaghan, Nigel Smith, Mihoko Suzuki, Sophie Tomlinson, Jo Wallwork, and Susan Wiseman.

I am grateful to La Trobe University's Faculty of Humanities and Social Sciences for granting me study leave in 2003, and to colleagues in the English Program for their support. During that time I was assisted by a British Academy Visiting Fellowship, sponsored by Birkbeck College and Susan Wiseman, and by an Oxford Brookes University Visiting Overseas Fellowship. I want to thank all those at Oxford Brookes who helped to organize my visit there; most particularly Michelle O'Callaghan.

During a number of visits to Oxford I have been privileged to be welcomed, in a variety of ways, by Merton College, and I want to thank the Warden and fellows for their hospitality, with special thanks owing to Richard McCabe for helping to make Oxford seem like a second home. I have made extensive use of the Bodleian Library during this project, and have received imaginative assistance from the staff of Duke Humfrey's Library.

At La Trobe University, I have relied on the professional and tireless assistance of the Interlibrary Loan staff at the Borchardt Library. I was also aided, late in this project, by a personal subscription to Early English Books On Line, provided by the NEER project and the Australian and New Zealand Association for Medieval and Early Modern Studies.

Some of the ideas in this book were explored in papers delivered at the following venues: La Trobe University English Program Seminar; Oxford Brookes University School of Arts and Humanities; the Oxford Brookes University/St Hilda's College Renaissance Seminar; the Oxford University Graduate Early Modern Seminar; the London Renaissance Seminar; the 'Old Worlds New Worlds' ANZAMEMS conference held at Auckland University; Loughborough University Department of English and Drama; and the 'Still Kissing the Rod?' conference at St Hilda's College, Oxford University.

The frontispiece from Margaret Cavendish's *Poems and Fancies* is reproduced with the permission of the Huntington Library, San Marino.

# Contents

# Introduction: 'Were They That Name?': Categorizing Early Modern Women's Writing

The title of this introduction pays tribute to Denise Riley's important book *Am I That Name?*—a book in which she interrogates the category of women in history.[1] Here, I want to ponder some of the implications of the rapid establishment in the last few years of early modern women's writing as a body of knowledge, an object of academic scrutiny and a field of pedagogical practice. I want to start with some of Denise Riley's warnings about categorization in relation to the history and practice of humanist feminism, because I think that they can be related quite directly to issues surrounding the category 'early modern women's writing'. Riley warns, at the beginning of her study, that ' "women" is a volatile collectivity in which female persons can be very differently positioned, so that the apparent continuity of the subject of "women" isn't to be relied on' (2). This might seem like an unnecessary caution to scholars working in the area of early modern women's writing, who have, after all, been engaged in a very self-conscious recovery of a series of buried and neglected writers and genres. But I think that, to at least some degree, the excitement of recovery and rapid consolidation of the field has meant rather less self-conscious reflection than the earlier phases of feminist theory have produced.

My two (very different) models for this self-examination are Margaret Ezell and Jonathan Goldberg. Ezell has been addressing some of these issues for the past fifteen years, notably in two books: *The Patriarch's Wife* and *Writing Women's Literary History*.[2] Having established, in *The Patriarch's Wife*, the need for some recognition of the manuscript communities with which early modern women writers were intimately involved in considerable numbers, Ezell, in *Writing Women's Literary History*, produced a cautionary polemic tracing the diminishing presence of early modern women's writing, partly due, in her argument, to the preference for traditional genres in the recovery of women's

---

[1] Denise Riley, *Am I That Name?: Feminism and the Category of 'Women' In History* (London: Macmillan, 1988); further page references in parenthesis.

[2] Margaret Ezell, *The Patriarch's Wife: Literary Evidence and the History of the Family* (Chapel Hill: University of North Carolina Press, 1987); *Writing Women's Literary History* (Baltimore: Johns Hopkins University Press, 1993).

writing by feminist scholars. Ezell uses Quaker women's writing as a test case, pointing out how under-represented it is, and how consideration of it transforms notions of Restoration women's writing. Ezell's criticisms have been answered to at least some degree, given that the kind of attention she asks for is demonstrated in work done over the last twenty years, from Elaine Hobby's *Virtue of Necessity* through to the more detailed accounts of Quaker and other prophetic writing by people like Hilary Hinds (I consider Quaker writing in Chapter 5).[3] This book is in part a continuation of this kind of response to Ezell, in so far as it traces a history of the production, reception, and transmission of the immensely varied writing by early modern women from the 1550s through to the present.

Ezell specifically calls for the breakdown of nineteenth-century assumptions about authorship as a way of unlocking the restricted approach to women's writing before 1700. She traces the representation of women writers in eighteenth- and nineteenth-century biographical compendia and literary anthologies, outlining the way women writers were categorized in increasingly narrow and restrictive ways, so that, by the end of the nineteenth century, they were locked into the limited framework that dominated responses to them, even by feminist critics and anthologizers. Ezell offers an important analysis of George Ballard's biographical compendium, *Memoirs of Several Ladies of Great Britain*, first published in 1752 and relied on for information about women writers by numerous succeeding commentators, down to the twentieth century. (I will be analysing Ballard in more detail myself in Chapter 1.) Ezell points out that Ballard, far from being an objective, antiquarian compiler of information, was intent on endorsing the figure of the moral, learned lady—as opposed to writers like Behn, Pix, or Hannah Woolley (all omitted from his volume).[4] Ezell argues that, following Ballard, in the late eighteenth and nineteenth centuries a limited canon of women's writing grew up, one which served to convince readers, by the end of the nineteenth century, that early modern women writers were limited in number and scope. While I will be offering a more detailed and, in many respects, more positive account of nineteenth-century responses to a number of early modern women writers in my case studies, Ezell certainly offers a convincing account of how limited the image of early modern women writers had become by the publication of the first edition of *The Norton Anthology of Literature by Women* in 1968.

As noted above, this situation has changed quite dramatically over the last twenty years, as editions of early modern women's writing have increased in number and variety, and scholarship in the field has proliferated. There is still, however, considerable fragmentation in the presentation and representation of early modern women's writing. This is partly because of the way in which so many approaches to this field are constrained by the artificial dividing line that is

---

[3] Elaine Hobby, *Virtue of Necessity: English Women's Writing 1649–1688* (London: Virago, 1988); Hilary Hinds, *God's Englishwomen: Seventeenth Century Radical Sectarian Writing and Feminist Criticism* (Manchester: Manchester University Press, 1996).

[4] Ezell, *Writing Women's Literary History*, 78–88.

drawn at 1660, so that seventeenth-century women's writing is followed through from the 'Renaissance' period but halted at the Restoration, or alternatively seen as part of the 'long eighteenth century' and not traced back before 1660. This has had a distorting effect on the approach to many women writers who flourished during the intensely productive period of the Civil War and its aftermath, from the late 1640s until the 1680s. (Elaine Hobby's book, devoted to the period 1649 to 1688, is the notable exception to this.) Similarly, much of the writing itself has been represented (especially for teaching purposes) by way of anthologies. It is important to distinguish here between the small but growing number of scholarly editions of early modern women's writing, and what might generally be called teaching texts (whether in book or electronic form). It is not surprising that the major scholarly editions in this area are of women writing in what we might call conventional literary genres: Aphra Behn, Mary Wroth, Elizabeth Cary, Aemilia Lanyer, Rachel Speght, Lucy Hutchinson, Katherine Philips.[5] There are a few exceptions to this, such as Elaine Hobby's edition of Jane Sharp's *Midwives Book*, Sara Jayne Steen's of the letters of Arbella Stuart, or some examples of Margaret Cavendish, such as James Fitzmaurice's edition of the *Sociable Letters*.[6] However, the Oxford Women Writers in English series, which published the editions of Lanyer, Speght, Sharp, Stuart, and also Anna Weamys, Ann Askew and Mary Chudleigh, has been discontinued. The editions of Behn and Wroth in particular are clearly responsible for a substantial increase in scholarly attention devoted to those two writers, and David Norbrook's edition of Lucy Hutchinson will certainly stimulate similar attention.

Electronic texts are also, there is no doubt, a magnificent resource for scholars. The Brown electronic women writers series reproduces a significant number of printed texts which can be delivered to a desktop in a matter of seconds. The Brown electronic text archive is, at present, a default canon (however randomly compiled) and will remain so until it approaches 'completeness'. So, to take one example, Margaret Cavendish is allotted considerable space, given the daunting length of her books, but far more of her literary works are reproduced than

---

[5] Aphra Behn, *Complete Works*, ed. Janet Todd, 7 vols. (London: Pickering, 1992–6); Mary Wroth, *Poems*, ed. Josephine Roberts (Baton Rouge: Louisiana State University Press, 1983), *Urania Part One*, ed. Josephine Roberts (Binghampton: MRTS, 1995), *Urania Part Two*, ed. Josephine Roberts, Suzanne Gossett, and Janel Mueller (Tempe, Ariz.: RETS, 1999); Elizabeth Cary, *Tragedy of Mariam*, ed. Barry Weller and Margaret W. Ferguson (Berkeley: University of California Press), see also in S. P. Cerasano and Marion Wynne-Davies, eds., *Renaissance Drama by Women: Texts and Documents* (London. Routledge, 1995), and in Diane Purkiss, ed., *Renaissance Women* (London: Pickering, 1994); *The Poems of Aemilia Lanyer*, ed. Susanne Woods (New York: Oxford University Press, 1993); *The Polemics and Poems of Rachel Speght*, ed. Barbara K. Lewalski (New York: Oxford University Press, 1996); *Lucy Hutchinson's Translation of Lucretius, De Rerum Natura* ed. Hugh de Quehen (London: Duckworth, 1996), *Order and Disorder*, ed. David Norbrook (Oxford: Blackwell, 2001); Katherine Philips, poems, ed. Patrick Thomas, translations ed. Germaine Greer and R. Little, in *Collected Works* (Saffron Walden: Stump Cross, 3 vols., 1990–3).

[6] Jane Sharp, *The Midwives Book*, ed. Elaine Hobby (New York: Oxford University Press, 1999); Sara Jayne Steen, ed., *The Letters of Lady Arbella Stuart* (New York: Oxford University Press, 1994); Margaret Cavendish, *Sociable Letters*, ed. James Fitzmaurice (Toronto: Broadview, 2004).

her philosophical works.[7] The Brown database also reproduces printed works, not manuscript texts, and therefore fails to represent the significant function of manuscript circulation for women writing in the sixteenth and seventeenth centuries, both in the form of the scribal publication analysed by Harold Love, and the 'social' or coterie manuscript texts analysed by Margaret Ezell.[8] Texts in a subset of the Brown archive are available with very brief introductions, but they are unlikely to replace books for teaching purposes. The book equivalent of the Brown Electronic texts is the wonderful Scolar Press Early Modern Englishwoman Series, which combines facsimile texts with very useful introductions, and has by now covered an impressive range of printed texts, some of them grouped thematically. The best examples of electronic *teaching* texts are Isabella Whitney's *Sweet Nosegay* and Ephelia's *Poems*, put together by Sara Jayne Steen's students at Montana State University: the electronic revolution might come when there are dozens of such texts.[9] In the meantime, most teaching is done from the increasing number of printed anthologies that have been appearing over the last fifteen years or so. I want to consider these, not in order to assess their individual worth, but in order to consider how they tend to represent early modern women's writing.

The anthologies bear an interesting relationship to the packaging of early modern women's writing in the eighteenth and nineteenth centuries.[10] Inevitably, such is the nature of the anthology, individual writers are presented via titbits, often through works or parts of works that are not necessarily representative of their writing as a whole. (A good example in the past was Aphra Behn, who was generally represented by a small number of poems, though this situation has now changed.) This fragmentation is particularly true of anthologies designed to represent what might be called early modern female experience. Examples of these volumes include Angeline Goreau's *The Whole Duty of a Woman* and Charlotte Otten's *English Women's Voices*.[11] Otten, for example, offers forty-six themed extracts from a wide variety of women writing across a range of genres and styles. Otten mines some interesting and unusual sources (for example, legal testimony), and she deliberately excludes the literary figures who are represented elsewhere.

---

[7] The books reproduced (though individual plays are listed separately in the Brown Women Writers Project contents) are *Plays* (1662); *The Blazing World*; *Poems and Fancies*; *Nature's Pictures*; *Observations Upon Experimental Philosophy*, *The World's Olio*, and *the Life of William Cavendish*; http://www.wwp.brown.edu/texts/wwoentry.html

[8] See Harold Love, *Scribal Publication in Seventeenth-Century England* (Oxford: Clarendon Press, 1993); Ezell, *The Patriarch's Wife* and also her *Social Authorship and the Advent of Print* (Baltimore: Johns Hopkins University Press, 1999).

[9] http://www.montana.edu/wwwhitn/

[10] Some of my caveats are echoed in Ramona Wray's essay, 'Anthologising the Early Modern Female Voice', in which she calls for a feminist editorial intervention in the anthologizing of early modern women's writing, in Andrew Murphy, ed., *The Renaissance Text* (Manchester: Manchester University Press, 2000), 55–72.

[11] Angeline Goreau, *The Whole Duty of a Woman* (New York: Dial Press, 1985); Charlotte Otten, *English Women's Voices 1540–1700* (Miami: Florida International University Press, 1992).

It is true to say that literary anthologies have proliferated in the last decade and in some ways it is more difficult to make generalizations about them. In terms of representative scope, genre-based anthologies are most successful in conveying some sense of the detail of individual works. Cerasano and Wynn-Davies's *Renaissance Drama by Women* is able to be comprehensive because of its time frame and because this is the genre least favoured by women before the Restoration. The pioneering *Her Own Life* collection of autobiographical writing, in contrast, is able to offer some sense of the scope of that genre at the cost of presenting abbreviated texts.[12] Poetry is best served of all the genres, from the groundbreaking *Kissing the Rod* anthology produced by Germaine Greer (and her associates) in 1988, through to the generous selections in Marion Wynne Davies's *Women Poets of the Renaissance* and the fine scholarship on display in the Oxford *Early Modern Women Poets*, which showcases, for the first time for just about all of its readers, verse in Gaelic and Welsh, as well as a remarkable range of English verse.[13] Manuscript poetry is now comprehensively represented in the fine collection *Early Modern Women's Manuscript Verse*, stemming from the Perdita Project.[14] General literary anthologies skirt between representativeness of a wide range of writers via textual extracts, and full, or fuller, texts but a smaller selection of writers.

Despite their differences, all of these anthologies serve to constitute the body of writing attached to 'women', real or imagined.[15] In order to ask how this category, 'early modern women's writing', works, I return to Denise Riley's questions by way of Jonathan Goldberg. In *Desiring Women Writing*, Goldberg reiterates and expands Ezell's point about the canonization of 'worthy women', in the process claiming a double desire: 'the desire that there should be women writers in the Renaissance and that the desires articulated in their texts should be acknowledged' (14).[16] Goldberg questions the constitution of Renaissance women's writing as a category which requires a certain moral stature in the women thus separated out, and notes that the process of creating 'women writers' as a category detached from writers in general occurs during the history of literary canon formation in the eighteenth and nineteenth centuries. In some respects,

[12] Elspeth Graham *et al.*, eds., *Her Own Life* (London: Routledge, 1989).

[13] Germaine Greer *et al.*, eds., *Kissing the Rod* (London: Virago, 1988); Marion Wynne-Davies, ed., *Women Poets of the Renaissance* (London: Dent, 1998); Jane Stevenson and Peter Davidson, eds., *Early Modern Women Poets* (Oxford: Oxford University Press, 2001).

[14] Jill Seal Millman and Gillian Wright, eds., *Early Modern Women's Manuscript Verse* (Manchester: Manchester University Press, 2005).

[15] An interesting exception is Betty S. Travitsky and Anne Lake Prescott's *Female and Male Voices in Early Modern England* (New York: Columbia University Press, 2000), which pairs male and female writers addressing a series of themed issues; the scope is very wide indeed, although once again selections tend to be rather truncated.

[16] Jonathan Goldberg, *Desiring Women Writing: Renaissance Examples* (Stanford, Calif.: Stanford University Press, 1997); I should note here that it is Goldberg who led me to Riley, and Goldberg evokes Riley in some detail as part of his attempt to break down the monolithic identity of the category Renaissance 'women writers'; see esp. 135–40.

Goldberg's strictures, like Ezell's, have been overtaken by the progress of scholarship, in so far as the range of women writers now 'present' is considerable, and so the categorizing them as 'good' and, in some ways, unique, has lost much of its force. Goldberg himself, while admitting that his study is confined to a few examples that can be analysed in detail, produces a curiously limited set of writers who support his case—other writers would, I believe, have pointed to a greater interest in seeing early modern women's writing as transgressive than Goldberg is prepared to allow to the scholars he singles out for reprimand.

Goldberg sets up, I think, a critical position that certainly exists, but that he exaggerates in order to reinforce his claim that we have, as part of our desire *for* Renaissance women writers, overlooked or straightened out the desire *of* Renaissance women writers. His argument depends upon typically ingenious readings of Amelia Lanyer and Aphra Behn. In the case of Lanyer, it is certainly true that many scholars have been intent on claiming her as a 'good' woman; but in Behn's case, Goldberg's argument looks weightier than it actually is because he concentrates on a very limited range of Behn's texts. Even more to the point, I think, is the curious absence of Mary Wroth from the book, except via an aside buried in a footnote. I would want to say here not just that Wroth's writing, in all its enormous detail and variety, offers a perfect example of the kinds of shifting desire that Goldberg looks for, but that Wroth criticism has, over the past twenty years, been quite alert to that issue (see my detailed discussion of Wroth in Chapter 3).[17]

Goldberg represents early modern women's writing via a series of examples which seem, at times, chosen in order to provide a canvas for his dazzling interpretations, rather than as representative of early modern women's writing itself. Of course, Goldberg wants to call into question the certainty implied by the word 'itself', and in some instances he offers a salutary insight into the misleading way in which we tend to collapse the heterogeneity of early modern women's writing into confined categories. This works best in his rescue of women's 'translation' from notions of translation as a secondary, feminized activity. But running through the book, for all its corrective tendencies and its embrace of the unsettling of categories, is, I believe, a different kind of homogenizing, which I might sum up as turning a Renaissance seen in the past as too straight into one that becomes too queer—or, in some ways, not queer enough. When *all* Goldberg's examples—Aemilia Lanyer, Aphra Behn, Margaret Roper, Mary Sidney, Mary Shelton, Elizabeth Cary—are valorized because they disturb sexual categories, one wonders whether difference, far from being allowed for, is not being materialized as a certain sameness.

I want to illustrate this with what might seem like a marginal example, but in doing so I am following Goldberg's own methodology. In his account of

[17] Among many examples, I would cite a number of essays in *Reading Mary Wroth*, ed. Miller and Waller (Knoxville: University of Tennessee Press, 1991); an interesting recent example—published after Goldberg, of course—is Helen Hackett, *Women and Romance Fiction in the English Renaissance* (Cambridge: Cambridge University Press, 2000), ch. 10.

Lanyer, Goldberg very briefly mentions Anne Clifford, the subject along with her mother of Lanyer's now quite well-known country house poem 'The Description of Cookham'.[18] While arguing for the merging of 'hetero- and homoerotics' in a 'bedroom scene' in Lanyer's 'Salve Deus', Goldberg notes Clifford's refusal to follow her mother's advice and sleep in Arbella Stuart's chamber (39). Goldberg then notes that Clifford did, in his words, have 'sex' with her cousin Frances Bourchier (200 n. 27). Goldberg's evidence for this comes from a passage in Clifford's 1603 diary, which reads 'my Mother in her Anger commanded that I should lie in a Chamber alone, which I could not endure. But my Cousin Frances got the Key of my Chamber & lay with me which was the first time I loved her so well'.[19] Goldberg believes that 'the first time I loved her so well' means 'the first time I had sex with her'—this seems patently a case of overlaying a modern mistranslation onto a Renaissance text. Clifford means that Frances's defiance of her mother's punishment, and the offer of her comforting presence in the chamber, marked the beginning of Clifford's love for her cousin. In an earlier passage, Clifford wrote that she 'lay all night with my Cousin & Mrs Mary Carey, which was the first beginning of the greatness between us'.[20] Goldberg admits that this earlier occasion was not a sexual encounter. One might want to note many more counters to Goldberg's claim, including the fact that sharing a chamber does not necessarily mean sharing a bed, and that sharing a bed may well be a sexual experience, but it might not be. For example, Clifford does seem to imply in her diary that when her husband refuses to lie with her in her chamber there are sexual connotations: 'this night my Lord shou'd have layen with me in my Chamber, but he & I fell out about Mathew'.[21] On the other hand, Clifford writes 'Upon the 13th the Childe [i.e. her daughter Margaret, who was 3] came to lye with me which was the first time that ever she lay all night in a bed with me ever since she was born'.[22] Clifford's love for Frances Bourchier is marked out by her mentioning twice, later in her diaries, that Frances lies buried in the family vault at Chenies in Buckinghamshire; this is evidence of love, including, one might want to say, many kinds of desire, but not sex—or at least not claimable as 'sex', whatever that might actually mean, with the certainty that Goldberg manifests.

I have been focusing on this apparently small detail because it seems to run counter in some ways to Goldberg's entire project: Clifford becomes, for Goldberg, a passing example in an argument designed to startle us by turning our expectations on their head. But in doing so, Clifford as a writer disappears; her diary is read (I would say misread) simply for autobiographical information, *it is not read as a woman's writing*. (And, as Chapter 4 will indicate, I would want to

---

[18] See my detailed account of Clifford in Ch. 4.
[19] *The Diaries of Lady Anne Clifford*, ed. D. J. H. Clifford (Stroud: Alan Sutton, 1990), 25.
[20] Ibid. 23.
[21] 23 April 1617, *The Diary of Anne Clifford 1616–1619*, ed. Katherine O. Acheson (New York: Garland, 1995), 80.
[22] 13 May 1617; ibid. 82.

see Clifford as a significant and significantly self-conscious early modern woman writer.) Goldberg's quest to queer everything is not really queer reading, as his notion of Clifford's lesbian sexual encounter with her cousin sees sexual difference in terms of the very binary he is at such pains to dismantle everywhere else. Of course it is true that encounters in bedchambers may be sexual, they may indeed be homosexual, they may be sexual in a multi-valenced way—and they may be something slightly different, and that is a difference that also counts. Similarly, because Goldberg can get so much mileage out of undermining the self-identity of the 'woman' in Renaissance women's writing, he does run the danger of bypassing many examples of women *as writers* in the sixteenth and seventeenth centuries. I want to ask, at this point, how we can steer between the Scylla of homogenizing transparently identifiable early modern women writers, and the Charybdis of deconstructed texts which call any identity into question. (Though to be fair to Goldberg I should note here that many of his readings are acutely conscious of this dilemma and are illuminating in their treatment of the intersection between a 'woman' writing and a textual product.)

This issue has been addressed productively for Renaissance women writers by Danielle Clarke, who stresses the material conditions of women's lives as a significant issue, but who offers a sophisticated account of the political context for a variety of writings by women, including those of sometimes undecidable authorship.[23] I have attempted in this study to follow on from Clarke's aim 'to avoid collapsing of all women into a single gendered category'.[24] One way out is to re-examine how early modern women writers' texts were produced and reproduced; in other words, look at the processing of the texts in order to understand how they intersect with shifting and even conflicting categories, including gender and genre. I am not suggesting that there is anything particularly new in this, but simply that this kind of textual history offers a chance to see the variety of texts produced by early modern women as permeable in all sorts of ways. At the same time, such a study underlines the fact that, while there is no such thing as a homogeneous category of early modern women's writing, many women in the sixteenth and seventeenth centuries did use the category 'women's writing' in relation to the texts they produced (along with many other categories, including, for example, religion), and many readers of those texts also used the category. In terms of authorship, this allows us to 'read' texts ranging from those that are self-conscious about authorship through to those that are undecidable, depending upon how they are transmitted. It is at this point that one could evoke Diane Purkiss's excellent account of the seventeenth-century pamphlet controversy over the nature of women, where she looks at the pseudonymous pamphlets signed

---

[23] See Danielle Clarke, *The Politics of Early Modern Women's Writing* (Harlow: Pearson, 2001), esp. 4–6.
[24] Ibid. 265.

'Jane Anger', 'Esther Sowernam', and so on as 'performance[s] of femininity'.[25] On the other hand, it is important to consider a quite different example, like Mary Wroth's *Urania*, as a way of analysing a woman writer who was extremely conscious of her multiple identities *as* woman writer, and who includes not one but *two* women writers as characters in *Urania* (both of whom may in part be seen as versions of Wroth herself).

In her influential book on the interrelationship between Renaissance publication and gender, Wendy Wall offers a sophisticated account of female authorship, which stresses the complex negotiations required for female entry into print.[26] Wall traces, especially through her examination of Isabella Whitney, Aemilia Lanyer, and Mary Wroth, what might be described as cautious negotiations with the problems of print publication. I would want to suggest that Lanyer and Wroth are more self-assured about publication. In particular, the supposed 'silencing' of Wroth after the publication of *Urania* needs to be tempered by a realization that her 'scandalous' book circulated, even though the continuation remained in manuscript. And, to return to Margaret Ezell's point about the circulation of manuscripts, Wall's sense of the difficulties of print publication needs to be offset with the wide range of manuscript writing by women—something we are now much more conscious of as the Perdita Project achieves wide recognition and the full extent of these manuscripts is taken into account. So, to take an example I will be discussing in detail in Chapter 4, Anne Clifford wrote extensively and had her work preserved in a series of 'great books' which were intended for a very specific, but far from restricted, readership. Similarly the Perdita project as a whole has uncovered an enormous amount of women's poetry by authors who seem destined to join the canon, such as Hester Poulter or Mary Roper.[27] And in terms of the wider range of women's writing, Margaret Ezell has pointed to the category of 'Domestic Papers' as the source for a significant amount of women's manuscript writing in a 'sphere' that has, in the past, been seen as of marginal interest, but will in the future undoubtedly yield material that will add to the recognition, now more firmly established, that a great many women wrote a great deal in the early modern period.[28]

While many women who wrote saw themselves as venturing into dangerous and uncharted territory, many were conscious of their predecessors and saw themselves as 'women writers'. In the course of the seventeenth century, as the diversity of women's writing increased, the category of women's writing may

[25] Diane Purkiss, 'Material Girls: The Seventeenth-Century Woman Debate', in Clare Brant and Diane Purkiss, eds., *Women, Texts and Histories* (London: Routledge, 1992), 85.

[26] Wendy Wall, *The Imprint of Gender: Authorship and Publication in the Renaissance* (Ithaca, NY: Cornell University Press, 1993).

[27] The beginning of this process may be marked by the Millman and Wright anthology.

[28] Margaret Ezell, 'Domestic Papers', keynote address to 'Still Kissing the Rod?' conference, Oxford, July 2005.

be seen as more problematic, but also as a category used by readers and writers themselves. My purpose is to give due deference to the heterogeneity of this writing, while at the same time analysing how it was transmitted and received in a variety of ways, many of which depend upon some sense of it *as* women's writing. The most effective way to do this is to look in detail at a range of case studies, representative, as far as is possible, of the range and diversity of early modern women's writing. After a general outline of the nature of early modern women's writing in Chapter 1, the case studies which follow will examine writing by aristocratic women and those from quite ordinary backgrounds; they will outline writing in a wide variety of genres and forms, transmitted in print and in manuscript. They will also entail histories of reception and later transmission, in order to illuminate what might be called the 'processing' of early modern women's writing both within the period, and in succeeding centuries.

I want to stress here that this book is an analysis of how early modern women's writing has been interpreted by early modern women themselves, and then by those who for a variety of reasons engaged with it in succeeding centuries. I do not, on the whole, emphasize my own readings of individual works, although my own interpretations are evident from time to time. Similarly, I do not address this book to the small group of specialists in this area (although I hope they may find things of interest in it), but to those from a wide variety of fields and disciplines who want to know more about what women wrote in the sixteenth and seventeenth centuries, and how that writing was read, processed, interpreted, rewritten, and often rediscovered, from the time of its writing through to the present day. It is now clear that a considerable number of early modern women wrote a huge range of works in every conceivable genre; this book can offer only an introduction to that rich variety—a variety being added to as more scholarship finds more examples of women's work.

# 1

# The Scope of Early Modern Women's Writing

## THE NATURE OF WOMEN'S WRITING
## FROM 1558 TO 1700

In the past twenty years early modern women's writing, at least in academic conceptions of its scope, has grown from a small group of obscure writings by figures like Mary Sidney or Aphra Behn to what now seems like an ever-expanding body of work. From a focus (by literary scholars, not historians) on genres like poetry or drama, there has been a shift towards the many kinds of writing produced by women in the period: autobiography, diaries, letters, spiritual works of many kinds, translations, advice books, manuals. Women writers were once seen as exceptional; now they are seen as, not exactly commonplace, but far more common than was once thought possible. Of course there are considerable variations to this state of affairs, depending upon the class of woman and the period under consideration. There are comparatively few women writers from lower strata of society until the Civil War, when many more marginalized figures, male and female, burst into print. What I want to offer here is a brief overview, before looking in detail at the way early modern women's writing was circulated and collected together in the seventeenth, eighteenth, and nineteenth centuries. This chapter will then be followed by the case studies of representative writers, or groups of writers, looking in detail at the nature and transmission of their work.

'Early modern' is a loose term taken over from historians by literary scholars. It is difficult to know where one should draw time lines and begin a study such as this one. I have decided to make my starting point the accession of Queen Elizabeth to the throne in 1558, Elizabeth herself being one of my case studies. This means that some women writers from earlier in the sixteenth century—such as, to take perhaps the most prominent examples, the Protestant martyr Anne Askew, or the learned Margaret Roper—fall beyond the scope of this book. I am offering a sample, rather than an exhaustive overview of every woman who wrote, and a certain arbitrariness becomes a necessity. Some compensation for this is provided by my extended end point (compared to many conceptions of the early modern period by literary scholars), which allows me to trace women's writing through to the conclusion of the seventeenth century.

It is possible to view women's writing from 1558 to 1700 as a series of phases, although it is vital to avoid any forced homogenization of what was a very diverse set of practices.[1] In the Elizabethan period, a significant number of aristocratic women up to and including the Queen were well educated, and wrote and (more frequently) translated a variety of works, often, although not exclusively, of a religious nature. There are far fewer examples, in the sixteenth century, of women writing what we might call secular literature, although a few notable instances will be discussed in the next chapter (the poetry of Isabella Whitney, and of Queen Elizabeth). There was a dramatic increase in the amount of writing by non-aristocratic women from early in the seventeenth century, but even in the sixteenth century there are examples. Perhaps the most notable, because her work was published, is Anne Vaughan Lock, who translated a set of sermons by Calvin in 1560, and who published an 'expanded' translation of a theological work by John Taffin in 1590, dedicating the translation to the Countess of Warwick.[2] Lock was born into a merchant family with strong Protestant connections (her first husband, Henry Lock, was an associate of John Knox; her second, Edward Dering, was a Puritan preacher; her third, Richard Prowse, served as Mayor of Exeter as well as in parliament). Anne Lock joined Knox in exile in Geneva in 1557 when Mary Tudor began to make life difficult for active Protestants. On her return to England she published her Calvin translation. At the end of the translation, Lock appended a sonnet sequence, 'A meditation of a Penitent Sinner Written in manner of a paraphrase upon the 51. Psalme of David'.[3] Lock's second translation appeared thirty years later, when she was married to her third husband, and at a time when nonconformist clergy were under attack. The translation of John Taffin's *Of the Markes of the Children of God* is, like Lock's earlier translation, followed by an original poem of Lock's. Micheline White places Lock's translation of Taffin in a political context in the course of an article which corrects the older scholarly notion of translation as 'secondary' literary activity, and therefore able to be undertaken by early modern women with safety and without damage to their modesty.[4] Instead, White notes how early modern translations by women

---

[1] In the case of printed writing, this diversity can be traced through an excellent biographical dictionary of women writers which also offers a useful brief history of published writing in an appendix: *English Women Writers 1580–1720*, ed. Maureen Bell, George Parfitt, and Simon Shepherd (Brighton: Harvester, 1990).

[2] See *The Collected Works of Anne Vaughan Lock*, ed. Susan M. Felch (Tempe, Ariz.: RETS, 1999); the biographical information which follows is taken from Felch's excellent introduction.

[3] While it is not absolutely certain that Lock wrote the sonnets, most scholars now accept them as hers, see Felch's discussion, ibid., pp. liii–iv.

[4] Micheline White, 'Renaissance Englishwomen and Religious Translations: The Case of Anne Lock's *Of the Markes of the Children of God* (1590)', *ELR*, 29 (1999), 375–400; see also Rosalind Smith, ' "In a Mirrour clere": Protestantism and Politics in Anne Lok's Miserere mei Deus', in Danielle Clarke and Elizabeth Clarke, eds., *'This Double Voice': Gendered Writing in Early Modern England* (Basingstoke: Macmillan, 2000), 41–60; and see the revisionist account of women as translators in Jonathan Goldberg, *Desiring Women Writing* (Stanford, Calif.: Stanford University Press, 1997).

(and men) were seen as worthy examples of cultural transmission, and (often) of what might be called ideological moment. In Lock's case, this is seen in the translation of Taffin as, in White's words, a contribution 'to the Puritan cause'.[5] Lock's combative tone can be seen in her dedication of the Taffin translation to the Countess of Warwick, where she boldly states:

Forasmuch as it hath pleased almightie God of his infinite goodnesse, to give unto the glorious Gospell of his eternall sonne, so long and prosperous successe in this our Countrie; it is now time (right Honourable and my verie good Ladie) for everie one that is a true professor of the same, all carnall perswasions of humane reason deluding the soule being set aside, to prepare our selves to the day of trial.[6]

Lock's literary activities can be compared to those of the Cooke sisters, who continued the tradition of educated women within Tudor humanist circles. Lock had a close association with one of the Cooke sisters, and Anne Russell, Countess of Warwick, dedicatee of the Taffin translation, was sister-in-law to Elizabeth Cooke.[7] The daughters of Sir Anthony Cooke, who was a reader to King Edward VI, and who went into exile under Mary Tudor, were educated to read Greek and Latin. This was, once again, a committed Protestant household. The sisters married influential men, notably Mildred, who married William Cecil; Anne, who married Sir Nicholas Bacon and was the mother of Francis Bacon; and Elizabeth, who married Sir Thomas Hoby, and then after his death married John Russell. All the sisters wrote and translated; notable examples include Mildred's translation of a Greek sermon by St Basil; Elizabeth's translation of a Latin theological work by Bishop John Ponet; and Anne's important translation of Bishop Jewel's *Apologia Ecclesiae Anglicanae* (1562).[8] Mary Ellen Lamb has noted how Mildred's, Anne's, and Elizabeth's theological translations can be linked to the ideas about the reformed church promulgated by their husbands, particularly by William Cecil and Nicholas Bacon.[9] Louise Schleiner has discovered a series of poems by the sisters in an elaborate manuscript gift for Queen Elizabeth, which was part of an attempt to get her to reinstate Anne Lock's second husband, Edward Dering.[10] Elizabeth Cooke/Russell also wrote a series of epitaphs, including those for her husband and her son.[11]

---

[5] Ibid. 398.      [6] Ibid. 76.

[7] The translations of the Cooke sisters are discussed by Mary Ellen Lamb in 'The Cooke Sisters: Attitudes Towards Learned Women in the Renaissance', in Margaret Patterson Hannay, *Silent but for the Word: Tudor Women as Patrons, Translators, and Writers of Religious Works* (Kent: Kent State University Press, 1985), 107–25.

[8] There is an excellent account of the Cooke sisters in Louise Schleiner, *Tudor and Stuart Women Writers* (Bloomington: Indiana University Press, 1994), ch. 2; there is a facsimile volume of Anne Cooke/Bacon's translations of Jewel and Ochine with an introduction by Valerie Wayne in The Early Modern Englishwoman facsimile series, Series 1, part 2, vol. 1 (Aldershot: Ashgate, 2000); facsimiles of Elizabeth Cooke/Russell's translation of Ponet, together with Anne Lock's two translations, introduced by Elaine Beilin, make up volume 12 (Aldershot: Ashgate, 2001).

[9] Lamb, 'Cooke Sisters', 111–12.      [10] See Schleiner, *Women Writers*, 39–45.

[11] A selection of the epitaphs is presented, with translations, in ibid.

This tradition of religious and other kinds of translation by women continued into the seventeenth century, where the most notable example is Mary Sidney, Countess of Pembroke, who achieved considerable renown for her metric translations of the psalms (continuing the efforts of her brother, Philip Sidney), and of Robert Garnier's play *Antonie* and Petrarch's 'Trionfo della Morte' (her work will be discussed in more detail in Chapter 2 and Chapter 6). Virtually all of the Countess of Pembroke's writing circulated in manuscript. In 1634 Alice Sutcliffe published *Meditations of Man's Mortalities*.[12] Works such as Sutcliffe's testify to the continuation of original religious writing seen most dramatically in Aemilia Lanyer's now much discussed 1611 volume, *Salve Deus Rex Judaeorum* (combining an elaborate series of dedications to influential women, a highly original religious poem, and a country house poem celebrating Cookham and Anne and Margaret Clifford), which will be examined in more detail in the next chapter. Alice Sutcliffe's volume was published with a considerable apparatus of prefatory material, including dedicatory poems by Ben Jonson, Thomas May, and George Wither. It went through two editions (only the second is extant), noting on the title page that Alice Sutcliffe was the wife of John Sutcliffe, a groom of King Charles's privy chamber. Alice Sutcliffe dedicated the volume to Katherine, Duchess of Buckingham, her sister Susan, Countess Denbigh, and Philip Herbert, Earl of Pembroke and Montgomery. The volume contains a series of prose meditations and a poem on similar themes (the poem being rather pedestrian compared with the work of Lanyer).

While it is often classified with mother's advice books, because it is addressed to her son, Elizabeth Grymestone's *Miscellanea. Meditations. Memoratives* (1604) is not dissimilar to Sutcliffe's volume, containing as it does a series of prose meditations and pieces of advice interspersed with poetry (the poems are not by Grymeston, but are taken from Catholic poets, notably Robert Southwell); it was, like the associated advice books, which will be discussed below, a popular volume, and went through four editions between 1604 and 1618. In a separate but related category we might place Elizabeth Cary's play *The Tragedy of Mariam* (1613), based on the Old Testament (Cary became a Catholic), and the only example of an original play by a woman to be published prior to Margaret Cavendish's first volume of plays in 1662.[13]

---

[12] See Kim Walker, *Women Writers of the English Renaissance* (New York: Tawyne, 1996), 101–14; Walker also discusses the manuscript poem 'Death and Passion of Our Lord Jesus Christ' by Elizabeth Middleton, but this poem has been revealed by Elizabeth Clarke to be essentially a series of slightly altered plagiarisms, notably from a 1622 poem by Ralph Bollukar; see 'Elizabeth Middleton: Early Modern Copyist', *N&Q* 42 (Dec. 1995).

[13] I discuss *Mariam* in more detail in Ch. 6; because of its unique status, *Mariam* has been edited a number of times in recent years: see esp. the editions by Diane Purkiss (London: Pickering, 1994); Barry Weller and Margaret W. Ferguson (Berkeley: University of California Press, 1994); and Stephanie Wright (Keele: Keele University Press, 1996).

Later in the seventeenth century, the political upheaval associated with the
Civil War allowed a significant number of women access to print for more original
religious writing, much of it produced by women who came from a far humbler
background than any of the individuals discussed so far: by mid-century, women
such as Anna Trapnel, Margaret Fell, and many others associated with radical religious sects articulated a variety of challenging religious positions (see the
detailed discussion in Chapter 5). After the Restoration, women continued to
make a substantial contribution to religious writing, particularly Quaker women.

In the area of secular literature, the story is rather more complicated. Owing in
large part to very recent efforts by a number of scholars working on early modern
women, it has become apparent that far more writing circulated in manuscript
than was previously realized.[14] Jane Stevenson has estimated that around fifty
women wrote verse before 1600, and notes that 'a number of women of the rank
of gentlewoman and above participated in the writing of ephemeral poetry as
a social activity'.[15] Since the detailed bibliographical work of the Perdita Project, it has become evident that a significant and increasing amount of women's
poetry circulated in manuscript in the seventeenth century (as well as many other
forms of writing that had manuscript circulation).[16] Women sometimes contributed one or two poems to a manuscript miscellany, manuscript anthology,
or family manuscript collection.[17] Some manuscripts were produced either by a
single woman or a small group; for example, the Cooke sisters' manuscript noted
above. A good example of a commonplace book that contains a large amount
of original poetry is Anne Southwell's commonplace book, recently edited by
Jean Klene.[18] Like many such commonplace books and manuscript miscellanies,
Southwell's contains, not just her own work (though in this particular case it does

---

[14] Access to women's writing in manuscript will be facilitated by the recent completion of
the Perdita Project, which offers a web-based catalogue of manuscripts by (or containing material
by) women: http://human,ntu.ac.uk/research/perdita/index.html, and by a number of publications
stemming from the project, including, to date, the anthology *Early Modern Women's Manuscript
Poetry*, ed. Jill Seal Millman and Gillian Wright (Manchester: Manchester University Press, 2005);
and *The 'Centuries' of Julia Palmer*, ed. Victoria Burke and Elizabeth Clarke (Nottingham: Trent
Editions, 2001); editions planned of the poetry of Hester Poulter and Anne More will undoubtedly
generate work on two fine but hitherto completely unknown poets.

[15] Jane Stevenson, 'Women, Writing and Scribal Publication in the Sixteenth Century', *English
Manuscript Studies*, 9 (2000), 1 and 4.

[16] For a good general account see the collection of essays derived from the Perdita Project: *Early
Modern Women's Manuscript Writing*, ed. Victoria Burke and Jonathan Gibson (Aldershot: Ashgate,
2004).

[17] For manuscript miscellanies in the seventeenth century, see Mary Hobbs, *Early Seventeenth
Century Verse Miscellany Manuscripts* (London: Scolar Press, 1992); see also the more detailed
discussion of women and manuscript poetry collections in Arthur F. Marotti, *Manuscript, Print,
and the English Renaissance Lyric* (Ithaca, NY: Cornell University Press, 1995), 48–60.

[18] Jean Klene, ed., *The Southwell–Sibthorpe Commonplace Book, Folger MS V.b.198* (Tempe,
Ariz.: MRTS, 1997).

predominate), but poems by other writers which, in transcription, are adapted or altered—a common practice notably illustrated in this instance by Southwell's version of Ralegh's famous poem 'The Lie: Go soul, the body's guest', with a number of unique variants pointing to her own adaptation of Ralegh's verses.[19] Another good example of an extensive manuscript collection of poetry is the arresting work produced by Hester Poulter.[20] Publication via manuscript, rather than print, continued with great vigour throughout the seventeenth century, the most notable late seventeenth-century example being Katherine Philips, who will be discussed in detail in a later chapter.[21] As Margaret Ezell has pointed out, a large amount of seventeenth-century women's writing circulated in manuscript within different groups, from families through to coteries of writers.[22] William Cavendish's daughters Elizabeth Brackley and Jane Cheney compiled a collection of miscellaneous writing, including a play entitled 'Concealed Fancies', some time in the 1640s (the most likely date is 1645). The collection is entitled *Poems Songs a Pastorall and a Play by the Honorable the Lady Jane Cavendish and Lady Elizabeth Brackley*.[23] The sisters' manuscript begins with a series of complimentary poems by Jane addressed to their father, William Cavendish, Duke of Newcastle, their uncle Charles, and to their brothers Charles and Henry, followed by a series of bland poems on a variety of subjects and a number of poems by Jane to her sister Elizabeth. These are followed by a pastoral written by both sisters and dedicated to their father, and then *The Concealed Fansyes*, a witty comedy. While the play has attracted all the attention of recent scholars (not surprisingly, given its attractive quality and the fact that it is such a rare example of drama produced by a

---

[19] See ibid. 2–4 and notes; and a detailed and speculative account of Southwell's possible political context by Victoria E. Burke, 'Medium and Meaning in the Manuscripts of Anne, Lady Southwell', in *Women's Writing and the Circulation of Ideas*, ed. George Justice and Nathan Tinker (Cambridge: Cambridge University Press, 2002), 94–120. For a reading that offers a complex view of Southwell's exploration of religious and gender issues, see Erica Longfellow, 'Lady Anne Southwell's Indictment of Adam', in Burke and Gibson, *Manuscript Writing*, 111–33; and see also Elizabeth Clarke, 'Anne Southwell and the Pamphlet Debate', in Cristina Malcomson and Mihoko Suzuki, eds., *Debating Gender in Early Modern England, 1500–1700* (Houndmills: Palgrave, 2002), 37–53.

[20] A selection of Poulter's poems may be found in Millman and Wright, *Manuscript Verse*, 110–27; the complete manuscript of her collection, 'Poems Breathed Forth by the Nobel Hadassas' (Leeds University, Brotherton Library MS Lt q 32) is being edited by Sarah Ross.

[21] On manuscript publication by women in general in the period, see the essays in Justice and Tinker, *Women's Writing and the Circulation of Ideas*.

[22] See Margaret Ezell, *The Patriarch's Wife: Literary Evidence and the History of the Family* (Chapel Hill: University of North Carolina Press, 1987), chs. 3 and 4.

[23] Bodleian Library MS Rawlinson Poet. 16; further references in parentheses. There is a second presentation manuscript, but without *Concealed Fancies*: Yale University Beineke Library Osborn MS b. 233. For a detailed account of these manuscripts in relation to Elizabeth Brackley (Egerton), see the detailed introduction by Betty S. Travitsky to her edition of Elizabeth's 'Loose Papers', a manuscript collection of prayers, meditations, and poems collected together after her death in 1663: Elizabeth Brackley, *Subordination and Authorship in Early Modern England: The Case of Elizabeth Cavendish Egerton and her 'Loose Papers'* (Tempe, Ariz.: MRTS, 1999); Travitsky has a particularly helpful discussion of *Concealed Fancies* and the manuscripts in general, 62–78.

woman at this period), the volume does need to be seen in its entirety as a particularly ambitious and wide-ranging anthology, presided over by the sisters' father, object of so many of their compliments and allusions. Another good example of this kind of literary activity is the family group of Sir Walter Aston, which produced a considerable quantity of correspondence (including poetry) exchanged between Aston's children, Constance Aston Fowler, Gertrude Aston Thimelby, and Katherine Thimelby (who married Henry Aston).[24]

Printed poetry is much scarcer until the middle of the seventeenth century. Individual poems by women were included in a variety of the verse anthologies that were so popular in the late sixteenth and early seventeenth centuries.[25] There were only a handful of single volumes of poetry by women published between 1558 and 1640: Isabella Whitney, Anne Dowriche, Elizabeth Melville, Aemilia Lanyer, Mary Fage, Rachel Speght, and Diana Primrose; one might also wish to include Mary Wroth's poetry published as part of her prose romance *Urania* (see Chapter 3). Isabella Whitney's two small volumes, *The Copy of a Letter* and *A Sweet Nosegay*, were published in 1567 and 1573 respectively; Anne Dowriche's *French History* in 1589; Elizabeth Melville's *A Godly Dreame* in Scottish and English versions in 1604; Lanyer's *Salve Deus Rex Judaeorum* in 1611; Rachel Speght's *Mortalities Memorandum* in 1621; Diana Primrose's *A Chaine of Pearl* in 1630; and Mary Fage's *Fame's Roule* in 1637. These women offer a quite disparate range of poetry, from sharp love poetry (Whitney, Wroth); to religious verse (Lanyer, Melville); historial verse (Dowriche, Primrose); and what we might call philosophical verse (Speght). In the second half of the century, volumes of poetry increased, though not nearly as dramatically as religious writing (though Collins and much of Bradstreet must be classified as part of the religious tradition). Notable examples would include Anne Bradstreet's *Tenth Muse* (1650); Margaret Cavendish's *Poems and Fancies* (1653); and An Collins's *Divine Songs* (1653); and after the Restoration, poetry by Aphra Behn, Katherine Philips, Anne Finch, Anne Killigrew, and others. During this whole period, there was far more women's manuscript poetry than poetry in print.

When we move away from literary genres, the quantity of material written by women is far more substantial, and grows dramatically throughout the seventeenth century. There is considerable overlap between religious writing, religious poetry, books of prayers or meditations, spiritual autobiography, and what have been labelled mother's advice books. Considerable weight was given to religious

---

[24] The material was first edited by Arthur Clifford as *Tixall Poetry* (Edinburgh: Longman, 1813); see also Constance Aston Fowler's commonplace book, which contains family verse but also poems by many other authors, including King and Southwell, edited as *The Verse Miscellany of Constance Aston Fowler*, ed. Deborah Aldrich-Watson (Tempe, Ariz.: MRTS, 2000).

[25] See J. B. Lethbridge, 'Anthological Reading and Writing in Tudor England', who argues that 'everyone in Tudor England read as if what they were reading were an anthology of disparate, unrelated pieces', in Barbara Korte *et al.*, eds., *Anthologies of British Poetry: Critical Perspectives from Literary and Cultural Studies* (Amsterdam: Rodopi, 2000), 57.

writing from the sixteenth century by the royal precedents set by Katherine Parr and Queen Elizabeth. Katherine Parr's *Prayers or Meditacyons* was first published in 1545 but went through some fifteen editions by 1640. The 11-year-old Elizabeth dedicated her translation of Marguerite de Navarre's *Godly meditatcyon of the christen soul* to Katherine Parr in 1544, and it too was reprinted a number of time after its first publication, overseen by John Bale, in 1548. The religious writing of sixteenth-century women received something like encyclopaedic representation in a massive volume edited by Thomas Bentley in 1582, entitled *The Monument of Matrones*.[26] This massive folio is dedicated to Elizabeth, and it contains a series of prayers gathered by Bentley from a large number of women, including (as well as Elizabeth herself) Anne Askew, Anne Bacon, Katherine Parr, Mary Tudor, and the work of Elizabeth Tyrwhit, whose *Morning and Evening Prayers* had been published in 1574. Bentley's work is a monument to what has often been seen as the respectable activity of religious writing by early modern women, and most particularly the production of prayers and hymns—an activity extended throughout the seventeenth century, from Mary Pembroke's psalms through to the radical religious writing of the Civil War period and after.

The mother's advice book is also an eminently respectable genre, which proved to be extremely popular in the seventeenth century.[27] I have already mentioned Elizabeth Grymeston's *Miscellanea. Meditations. Memoratives*, which begins with a posthumous address to her son Bernye—she explains how he is her only surviving child: 'my affectionate loue, which diffused amongst nine children which God did lend me, is now vnited in thee, whom God hath onely left for my comfort' (A4v). Grymeston, who had been fined as a Recusant in the 1590s, draws on a number of Catholic sources. Even more popular than Grymeston, Dorothy Leigh's *A Mothers Blessing* (1616) went through nineteen editions by 1640, making it a genuine early modern best-seller. Leigh dedicated her book to Princess Elizabeth of Bohemia, and her quite forthright, Puritan advice has been characterized by Catherine Gray as a conscious, political engagement with religious debate, 'as close to sermonizing as a woman could get at this early stage in the seventeenth century'.[28] Leigh, like Grymeston, is writing advice for a son—in her case, for her three sons, George, John, and William. But Leigh's book contains far more than just the prayers and meditations of Grymeston: it is explicitly concerned with advice and counsel—even going so far as to prescribe the names the sons should give to their children, when they have them (Philip, Elizabeth,

[26] See Elaine Beilin, *Redeeming Eve: Women Writers of the English Renaissance* (Princeton: Princeton University Press, 1987), 64–7; and on Bentley, Colin and Jo Atkinson, 'The Identity and Life of Thomas Bentley, Compiler of *The Monument of Matrones* (1582)', *Sixteenth Century Journal*, 31 (2000), 323–48.

[27] See the introduction by Betty Travitsky to the facsimile edition of 'Mother's Advice Books', The Early Modern Englishwoman facsimile series, Series 1, part 2, vol. 8 (Aldershot: Ashgate, 2001).

[28] Catherine Gray, '"Feeding on the Seed of the Woman": Dorothy Leigh and the Figure of Maternal Dissent', *ELH* 68 (2001), 574.

James, John, and Susannah)! Leigh explains in the preface that the death of her husband necessitates this didactic manual produced for her sons, but she then also admits that she has published it 'so that heerein I may shew my selfe a louing Mother, and a dutifull Wife' (A7v). Leigh is determined that her sons will follow her essentially Puritan Christianity, which includes the need for them to marry godly women. Indeed, her greatest desire is that some of them might become preachers.

Elizabeth Clinton's short *Countesse of Lincoln's Nursery* (1622), addressed to Clinton's daughter-in-law, is much more a practical guide for motherhood, rather than the spiritual counselling that Leigh provided. Its main purpose is to emphasize the importance of breast-feeding one's own infant—an activity not in favour with most aristocratic women at the time. Finally, Elizabeth Jocelin's *The Mothers Legacie to her Unborne Childe* was almost as popular as Leigh's volume, with five editions between 1624 and 1635, and then two further editions in the early eighteenth century (1722, 1724). Jocelin died nine days after giving birth to her first child, and her treatise was presented in manuscript to her husband before then being published with an admiring preface by Thomas Goad, a clergyman, who explains that Jocelin herself was brought up without a mother, but raised by her father and her grandfather (who was Bishop of Lincoln and Chester, and at one time Master of Queens' College, Cambridge). Jocelin's treatise is a devout manual of instruction written to her unborn child (because, Jocelin states, she had a strong premonition of her death); it prescribes forms of daily prayer and precepts for living a virtuous life, along moderate Puritan lines.

The religious precepts of Leigh and Jocelin can be compared to the outpouring of more radical religious material in the course of the seventeenth century. Most radical of all, in form and intent, was prophecy and theological questioning, which gained momentum as the Civil War took hold. While many men engaged in this activity, there were notable examples produced by women.[29] Indeed, because there were a comparatively large number of women attracted to the Quakers, a group who actively engaged in prophecy, the overall quantity of prophetic utterances by women in the seventeenth century was quite high: Phyllis Mack estimates this as over 400 women engaging in prophecy of some kind (the large majority being Quakers).[30] As well as their strong connection

[29] Christopher Hill's pioneering *The World Turned Upside Down* (Harmondsworth: Penguin, 1975) remains a valuable overview of this activity; the three principal studies of women's prophecy are Phyllis Mack, *Visionary Women: Ecstatic Prophecy in Seventeenth-Century England* (Berkeley: University of California Press, 1992); Diane Watt, *Secretaries of God: Women Prophets in Late Medieval and Early Modern England* (Cambridge: Brewer, 1997); and Hilary Hinds, *God's Englishwomen: Seventeenth-Century Radical Sectarian Writing and Feminist Criticism* (Manchester: Manchester University Press, 1996).

[30] Phyllis Mack quoted in Hilary Hinds, ed., Anna Trapnel, *The Cry of a Stone* (Tempe: Arizona Centre for Medieval and Renaissance Studies, 2000), p. xiv; there were over 7,000 women's signatures on a Quaker petition presented to Parliament in 1659, and purportedly 10,000 on the Leveller Petition of April 1649; see Patricia Higgins, 'The Reactions of Women, with Special

with the Quakers, women became involved in a number of radical sects that proliferated in the 1640s and 1650s, notably Independents, Baptists, and Fifth Monarchists. I will be looking at the prophecies of Anna Trapnel in Chapter 5, along with the more polemical writings of the Quaker Margaret Fell. Another woman who produced an enormous number of prophetical texts is Lady Eleanor Davies/Douglas, discussed in detail in Chapter 5, who did not belong to any religious sect, but who infuriated figures in authority from King Charles and Archbishop Laud through to Cromwell with her complex pamphlets (usually prophesying the downfall of such authority figures) from the 1620s to the 1650s.[31] These kinds of writing range from the opaque and highly allusive work of Davies or Trapnel, through to the plain and direct—a good example of the latter being Priscilla Cotton and Mary Cole's tough warning *To the Priests and People of England* (1655), conveniently edited and discussed at some length by Hilary Hinds.[32] Hinds notes how the notion of an 'ungendered soul', common to all the radical sects, freed women to participate in spiritual expression in dramatic (albeit not unprecedented) fashion.[33] In an important essay on the ways in which this often puzzling material may be interpreted, Sue Wiseman has also noted how these disparate women 'use the space of religious writing to reinvent models of authority, language and control'.[34]

To the significant numbers of prophecies written by women in the seventeenth century we can add a large number of spiritual autobiographies—in fact, the two forms are at times hard to distinguish, given that a prophecy like Anna Trapnel's *The Cry of a Stone* also contains her autobiography. Nevertheless, the more introspective form of spiritual autobiography can be identified in many cases. Notable examples of women's autobiographical writing in the seventeenth century were gathered together in the 1989 anthology *Her Own Life*, which has proven to be extremely influential in bringing these kinds of text to the awareness of students and scholars alike.[35] The editors include autobiographical work in a variety of genres, rather than just the more obvious form of prose autobiography.

---

Reference to Women Petitioners', in Brian Manning, ed., *Politics, Religion and the English Civil War* (London: Edward Arnold, 1973), 179–222.

[31] See Esther S. Cope, *Handmaid of the Holy Spirit: Dame Eleanor Davies* (Ann Arbor: University of Michigan Press, 1992).

[32] See Hinds, *God's Englishwomen*, app. C and ch. 7.

[33] Ibid. 49.

[34] Sue Wiseman, 'Unsilent Instruments and the Devil's Cushions: Authority in Seventeenth-Century Women's Prophetical Discourse', in Isobel Armstrong, ed., *New Feminist Discourses* (London: Routledge, 1992), 178.

[35] Elspeth Graham *et al.*, *Her Own Life: Autobiographical Writings by Seventeenth-Century Englishwomen* (London: Routledge, 1989); a fascinating example of a spiritual autobiography that had manuscript circulation is that of Dionys Fitzherbert: three manuscripts of her story of a spiritual crisis exist and are discussed most cogently in Mary Morrissey, 'Narrative Authority in Spiritual Life Writing: The Example of Dionys Fitzherbert (fl. 1608–41)', *Seventeenth Century*, 15 (2000), 1–17.

Many examples of these spiritual autobiographies written by women could be cited here; for example, the arresting *A Vindication of Anne Wentworth* (1677), in which Wentworth explains how she came to defy her husband and the Baptist congregation of which she had been a member in order to follow Christ (who is, she adamantly declares, her true bridegroom, rather than her earthly husband). Wentworth followed this in 1679 with a more radical, apocalyptic pamphlet detailing the revelations given to her by God, much of them in verse, and including some satisfying promises of dire punishment for her oppressive husband and his supporters in her former congregation.[36] Wentworth, with her fierce certainty, can be contrasted to Jane Turner, whose fascinating spiritual autobiography *Choice experiences of the kind dealings of God* (1653) details her path through a variety of religious possibilities during this period of change and turmoil (she moved between Newcastle and London). Having rejected the established church, Turner seeks the truth amongst Independents, Baptists, and Quakers. Her narrative is written with a firm and impressive control and she intersperses her personal account with tough-minded precepts for godly behaviour.[37] As a final example, one might cite Agnes Beaumont's narrative. Originally circulated in manuscript and published only late in the eighteenth century (but then frequently reprinted), Beaumont's spiritual autobiography attained notoriety because she was a member of John Bunyan's congregation and she and Bunyan were charged by her jealous, rejected suitor with the murder of Beaumont's father (they were acquitted).[38] Beaumont's account of her resistance to her father is written with enormous dramatic flair, placed always in the context of her faith.

A series of more secular autobiographies and biographies have attained greater visibility than many of these religious autobiographies because of their relationship to Civil War history. The most notable is Lucy Hutchinson's account of her husband, the regicide John Hutchinson; of almost equal interest is Margaret Cavendish's biography of her husband, the Royalist General William Cavendish, Duke of Newcastle; both discussed in detail in Chapter 6. There are two further royalist women's autobiographies: Lady Anne Halkett's and Lady Ann Fanshawe's. Long considered to be a valuable source for historians, since its first publication in 1816 (prior to that date the manuscript had remained within the family), Lucy Hutchinson's ambitious account of her husband's life can now be read alongside her impressive achievements in poetry and translation, with the

---

[36] *The Revelation of Jesus Christ* (1679).

[37] See the discussion of Turner in Elaine Hobby, *Virtue of Necessity: English Women's Writing 1649–1688* (London: Virago, 1988), 168–9; Hobby's book remains invaluable for women's writing in the fifty-year period she covers, and it is particularly helpful in the areas of non-literary texts.

[38] See the useful edition by Vera J. Camden, *The Narrative of the Persecutions of Agnes Beaumont* (East Lansing, Mich.: Colleagues Press, 1992).

recent editions of her major poem *Order and Disorder* and of her translation of Lucretius.[39] While Hutchinson will be discussed in detail in Chapter 6, it is worth noting here that her biography does not just contain an extremely detailed account of John Hutchinson's actions in the Civil War, but it is infused with Lucy Hutchinson's highly intelligent and self-reflective Independent Puritanism, and fierce adherence to the Republican cause. It is a polemical account directed to her children (in that sense not entirely unrelated to the mother's advice genre), in an attempt to shore up what in the 1660s seemed like a defeated cause. It also serves to justify the actions of John Hutchinson, who never wavers from his Independent principles. In this sense, it has a mirror image in Margaret Cavendish's Royalist justification of *her* husband's actions. Cavendish published her life of her husband in 1667, characterizing it as a 'short History of the Loyal, Heroick and Prudent Actions of my Noble Lord, as also of his Sufferings, Losses, and ill-Fortunes'.[40] Like Hutchinson, Cavendish represents her own ideas as much as her husband's, although her justifications of William Cavendish's actions are rather less subtle than Hutchinson's reflections. Cavendish's volume was, like the rest of her work, published, and it forms part of her self-construction as public author, while, in contrast, works by Hutchinson, Fanshawe, and Halkett all remained in manuscript.[41] Far less well known than these four examples is Theodosia Alleine's contribution to a collective biography of her husband, the dissenting preacher Joseph Alleine.[42] The work as a whole is introduced by Richard Baxter and Theodosia Alleine's section covers the last stage of her husband's life.

There are, once again, connections that may be made between these biographical and autobiographical works and the diaries which a number of women kept during this period.[43] For example, Anne Bathurst's voluminous diary begins with a brief spiritual autobiography, tracing her religious development back to the age of 12, followed by the vision she had on 17 March 1679.[44] Bathurst was part of an active family of Quaker women who wrote, most notably her sister Elizabeth

[39] Lucy Hutchinson, *Order and Disorder*, ed. David Norbrook (Oxford: Blackwell, 2000); *Lucy Hutchinson's Translation of Lucretius, De rerum natura*, ed. Hugh de Quehen (London: Duckworth, 1996).

[40] Margaret Cavendish, *Life of the Thrice Noble . . . Duke* (1667), sig. C2.

[41] Cavendish published a purely autobiographical account, which she entitled 'A true relation of my birth, breeding and life', as part of her anthology of stories and poems *Natures Pictures drawn by fancy's Pencil to the Life* (1656).

[42] *The Life and Death of . . . Mr Joseph Alleine* (1677).

[43] See the excellent brief account by Sara Heller Mendelson, 'Stuart Women's Diaries and Occasional Memoirs', which includes an annotated bibliography of seventeenth-century diaries, in Mary Prior, ed., *Women in English Society 1500–1800* (London: Methuen, 1985), 181–210; for spiritual diaries in particular see Effie Botonakis, 'Seventeenth-Century Englishwomen's Spiritual Diaries: Self-Examination, Covenanting, and Account Keeping', *Sixteenth Century Journal*, 30 (1999), 3–19.

[44] Anne Bathurst's manuscript diary is in two volumes: Bodleian Library MS Rawlinson D 1262 and D 1263; given a number of retrospective marginal comments and instructions for the insertion of particular passages, these volumes may be transcripts of earlier diaries, although both volumes

Bathurst, who published a number of Quaker texts.[45] Bathurst then became a member of the Philadelphian Society, followers of Boehme and eventually headed by Jane Lead, whose visionary works are similar to Bathurst's (see my detailed discussion of Lead in Chapter 5).[46] Anne Bathurst's diary consists of an astonishingly detailed, day-by-day account of her visions: she is attended by angels, absorbed into the body of Christ, transported to Heaven and Hell—all these mystical visions are outlined (in an impressively clear prose style, with occasional interspersed poems), from 1679 to 1696. At times Bathurst reads rather like a precursor of William Blake (and seems to draw on the same mystical tradition); to take a random example: 'There was opened to me a Similitude of the Mind, it seemed to be of a thin spiritous substance, like a Globe of Glass; and I was placed standing in the midst of it. And this Mind seemed to be the Mind of God, and that God himself was rimmed and incompassed with such a thin misty Light, it was like clear Glass' (vol. i, fo. 279). While it is very repetitive (especially stretched over some 700 pages), the diary is, cumulatively, an extremely powerful, mystical expression.

One can contrast Bathurst's visionary diary with a rather better-known example of a spiritual diary from the beginning of the seventeenth century: the diary kept by Lady Margaret Hoby from 1599 to 1605. Hoby's diary is essentially a sombre account of her day-to-day devotions, although a certain amount of domestic detail is also present. Hoby was married to her third husband when she kept the diary (she had been married to Walter Devereaux, younger brother of the Earl of Essex, and Thomas Sidney, younger brother of Philip Sidney). Here is a typical entry from the earlier (and more detailed) part of the diary, for 23 August 1599:

In the morninge I praied: then I took order for things about the house tell I went to breakfast, and sonne after I took my Coach and went to linton where, after I had salluted my mother, I praied, and then, walkinge a litle and readinge of the bible in my Chamber went to supper: after which I hard the Lector [i.e. a reading from a sermon or the Bible] and sonne after that went to bed.[47]

Over time, Hoby's diary entries become scanter and the diary seems to peter out by July 1605. While there are, not surprisingly, a number of other examples of diaries with what might be called a religious orientation, there are some notable examples of diaries that pay much less attention to spiritual matters and more to

---

are in the same hand, which may be Bathurst's, or possibly scribal, given that it may have been transcribed for the members of the Philadelphian Society after Bathurst's death.

[45] Anne has a brief note at the end of Elizabeth's *An Expostulatory Appeal to the Professors of Christianity Joyned in Community with Samuel Ansley* (no title page, Bathurst states she writes in 1678; Wing B1135A), it would seem from this volume that Anne's visions began soon after her confrontation with Ansley's congregation.

[46] See Mack, *Visionary Women*, 8–9, for a brief discussion of Bathurst.

[47] Joanna Moody, ed., *The Private Life of an Elizabethan Lady: The Diary of Lady Margaret Hoby 1599–1605* (Phoenix Mill: Sutton, 1998), 9.

worldly issues.[48] The most famous of all is that of Lady Anne Clifford, which details her long pursuit of her inheritance, and will be discussed in detail in Chapter 4. Clifford's day-by-day diary for 1616, 1617, and 1619 offers some remarkable insights into her miserable life in what she saw as exile at Knole, when she was wife to Richard Sackville, Earl of Dorset, while we also have a year-by-year diary, stemming from the time when she finally achieved her Westmorland inheritance, that runs from 1650 to 1676. There are some other fascinating secular diaries that have survived from the seventeenth century. That of Mary Rich, Countess of Warwick from 1666 to 1678 parallels her autobiography; the diary is a much more revealing document, recounting the trials of her marriage to Charles Rich and her piety.[49] The diaries of Elizabeth Freke are closer in some ways to those of Anne Clifford. Described by her modern editor as 'long suffering and defiant', Freke wrote extensively of her financial battles with her husband and, in later life, the trials of illness.[50] The diaries cover the years from 1671 to 1714, but exist in two distinct versions, because Freke wrote a revised version of her earlier diary from 1702, after which the diaries seem to have been written in parallel. Freke's differing accounts of her marriage and her husband (the revised version shows considerably more affection for him) are rather like Rich's two versions of her marriage (the more negative view expressed in her diary, rather than her autobiography). Freke offers a series of tart and at times self-pitying comments throughout her diaries; for example, of her disappointing son she writes on 22 December 1702: 'I sent my son fowre hundred pound to purchas Dirryloan with. For which I never had soe much as his thanks for itt. This tis to have butt one child, and him none of the best to me neither, But God forgive him and give patience to me, his unhappy mother, Eliz Frek.'[51]

Women were actively involved in letter-writing throughout this period, and some women produced letters that, gathered together, have a similar effect to that of some of the diaries I have been discussing. In his introduction to a recent collection of essays on early modern women's letters, James Daybell points to the large number of letters by women that are extant (he notes an estimate of 10,000 before 1640).[52] The most famous female seventeenth-century letter writer is Dorothy Osborne, whose letters to William Temple, written between 1652 and 1654, have been edited a number of times and were celebrated by Virginia

---

[48] Amongst the spiritual diaries one can note that of Elizabeth, Viscountess Mordaunt for 1656 to 1678, which only details major family events and is 90% meditations, prayers, and some poems; see *The Private Diary of Elizabeth, Viscountess Mordaunt*, ed. Earl of Roden (n.p.: Duncairn, 1856); and Elizabeth Delavel's large manuscript volume of meditations and some limited diary entries (Bodleian MS Rawlinson D 78).

[49] For a detailed account of Mary Rich, see Sara Heller Mendelson, *The Mental World of Stuart Women* (Brighton: Harvester, 1987), ch. 2; the diary is BL Additional MS 27351-5.

[50] *The Remembrances of Elizabeth Freke 1671–1714* ed. Raymond A. Anselment (Cambridge: Cambridge University Press, 2001), Camden Fifth Series, vol. 18, 3.

[51] Ibid. 241–2.

[52] James Daybell, ed., *Early Modern Women's Letter Writing, 1450–1700* (Houndmills: Palgrave, 2001), 3.

Woolf in her essay 'Dorothy Osborne's Letters'.[53] Osborne's lively, appealing correspondence with the man who she was forbidden to marry is not entirely representative of early modern women's letter-writing, but one would be hard pressed to find a male letter writer who matched her infectious high-spiritedness. There are a number of other early modern women who wrote letters that have been edited either because of their historical interest or because of their inherent literary qualities. Perhaps the most interesting example from earlier in the period is Arbella Stuart, cousin of King James. Given that Arbella Stuart had a strong claim to the throne, she was treated with wariness by both Elizabeth and James. Her complex letters, ably edited and analysed by Sara Jayne Steen, offer a remarkable reflection of her shifting attempts to carve out a space for herself beyond the bounds imposed upon her by those who attempted to control her life (she was ultimately unsuccessful and died in the Tower of London in 1615 after years of imprisonment).[54] Lady Brilliana Harley's letters to her son Edward, written from 1638 to 1643, describe her single-handed defence of Brompton Castle during the early years of the Civil War, while her husband, Robert Harley, was in Parliament, leaving her to manage all the family affairs and preserve their estate from Royalist attacks.[55] The letters of Joan and Maria Thynne also offer a fascinating glimpse into the tense relationships within a family; a more genial set of exchanges is collected in the Tixall letters, produced by the family of Astons and Thimelbys noted above for their poetry.[56]

Throughout the seventeenth century in particular, women wrote (and published) a considerable amount of factual material, ranging from cookery books to midwifery manuals. In manuscript, many women compiled recipes, remedies, and advice of various kinds, as a reflection of their role in running what were often large and complex households. For example, Lady Grace Mildmay compiled a large number of elaborate remedies, reflecting her active role in prescribing and administering medicine.[57] Many household manuals were published by men (such as Gervase Markham, who, for example, produced the extremely popular *A Way to Get Wealth by Approved Rules of Husbandry and Huswifrie*

---

[53] Woolf's essay began as a *TLS* review of G. C. Moore Smith's edition of the letters for Oxford University Press in 1928, and was then expanded into an essay for *The Common Reader, Second Series* (1932). The most recent (and detailed) edition of the letters is by Kenneth Parker, *Dorothy Osborne: Letters to William Temple, 1652–54* (Aldershot: Ashgate, 2002).

[54] *The Letters of Lady Arbella Stuart*, ed. Sara Jayne Steen (New York: Oxford University Press, 1994).

[55] *Letters of the Lady Brilliana Harley*, ed. Thomas Taylor Lewis (London: Camden Society, 1854); see the sophisticated analysis of Harley's letters in Susan Wiseman, *Conspiracy and Virtue: Women, Writing, and Politics in Seventeenth-Century England* (Oxford: Oxford University Press, 2006), ch. 2.

[56] Alison D. Wall, ed., *Two Elizabethan Women: Correspondence of Joan and Maria Thynne 1571–1611* (Devizes: Wiltshire Record Society vol. 38, 1983); *Tixall Letters*, ed. Arthur Clifford (London: Longman, 1815).

[57] See Linda Pollock, *With Faith and Physic: The Life of a Tudor Gentlewoman, Lady Grace Mildmay 1552–1620* (London: Collins and Brown, 1993), which includes a sample of the remedies, as well as Mildmay's autobiographical and spiritual writings.

(1625)), but in the course of the seventeenth century an increasing number of such manuals written by women began to appear in print. The most successful woman to produce such works was Hannah Woolley.[58] For example, in *The Queen-Like Closet* (1670), as the title page indicates, Woolley offers 'Rare receipts for Preserving, Candying and Cookery, Very Pleasant and beneficial to all Ingenious Persons of the Female Sex'. In *The Queen-Like Closet*'s supplement, Woolley offers more discursive advice about such issues as how to deal with servants and how to treat children. She offers a series of model letters for women, noting that 'They many times spend their time in Learning a good Hand; but their English and Language is, The one not easie to understand, The other weak and impertinent.'[59]

During the course of the seventeenth century, midwives were challenged by male doctors. Jane Sharp's *The Midwives Book* (1671) represents perhaps the most elaborate and detailed example of female knowledge of sexuality, conception, and birth.[60] Just as Margaret Fell and other Quaker women defended the right of women to speak in church, to testify, and to proselytize, so there were general defences of female education. The two most notable examples are Bathsua Makin's *An Essay to Revive the Ancient Education of Gentlewomen* (1673) and Mary Astell's *A Serious Proposal to the Ladies* (1694). The dates of these works also point to the significant increase in printed works by women in the second half of the seventeenth century. A number of women clearly saw themselves as writers in this period. While I would want to make that claim for Mary Wroth, she stands alone at the beginning of the century. By the end of the seventeenth century, three women in particular produced calculated *oeuvres* which included a self-consciousness about their roles as writers: Margaret Cavendish, Aphra Behn, and Katherine Philips. Cavendish published her first volumes while in exile on the Continent: *Poems and Fancies* (1653), *Philosophical and Physical Opinions* (1655), and *The World's Olio* (1655), and then a series of folios in the 1660s. Behn's dramatic career began with the performance of *The Forced Marriage* in 1671, and following that she had a large number of plays performed and printed during the 1670s, as well as undertaking translations and editing poetic miscellanies. Later in her career, when the demand for new plays shrank, Behn turned to fiction, although much of this was published posthumously. Philips published her translation of *Pompey* following its performance in 1663, and an authorized edition of her poetry followed an apparently unauthorized one in 1664. All three writers will be considered in detail in later chapters. But before beginning the case studies that form the bulk of this book, I want to offer here a brief account of the main avenues through which early modern women writers were considered in the eighteenth and nineteenth centuries.

---

[58] For an excellent account of Woolley's publications, see Hobby, *Virtue of Necessity*, 166–75.
[59] Hannah Woolley, *A Supplement to the Queen-like Closet* (1674), 104.
[60] See Elaine Hobby's edition of Sharp (New York: Oxford University Press, 1999).

## THE PRESERVATION OF EARLY MODERN WOMEN'S WRITING: 1700–1900

As will be evident in later chapters, a number of Restoration women writers remained visible during the eighteenth century (including some whose output straddled the two centuries). Contrasted as they were in many ways, Behn and Philips (increasingly placed in the roles, respectively, of scandalous and respectable woman writer), remained in print during the course of the eighteenth century.[61] During the seventeenth century, especially after the Restoration, women writers were occasionally singled out for attention. Some women writers remained in view, or at least in partial view, during the immediate period in which they wrote, and for some time afterwards. A good example is Mary Wroth, whose detailed textual transmission and reputation are considered in Chapter 3. But general considerations of women's writing, and of women authors as a category, began to appear in the middle of the seventeenth century, alongside the increasing amount of criticism directed at male writers. This process can be paralleled with the literary self-consciousness mentioned above: one can see Wroth and Cavendish at least as modelling themselves on male writers who were presented to the public, through impressive folio volumes, as 'authors'.

A general interest in encylopaedic reference works from the mid-seventeenth century included some recognition of the position of women. Thomas Heywood published *Gynaikeion; or Nine Bookes of Various History Concerning Women* in 1624; this was reissued in 1657 as *The Generall Historie of Women*. Heywood offers a large number of exemplary histories of women from classical and modern periods. His treatment of women writers is extremely brief, given the size of the work as a whole: after some discussion of ancient female poets, including Sappho, he very briefly mentions Queen Elizabeth, Lady Jane Grey, Arbella Stuart ('who had a great facility in poetry and was elaborately conversant amongst the Muses; as likewise the ingenious Lady, the late composer of our extant *Vrania*'), the Cooke sisters, and Mary, Countess of Pembroke.[62] Later in the century, the Restoration author and publisher Nathaniel Crouch, amongst his large range of popular compilations of worthies, wonders, and sensationalist history, included *The Female Excellency* (1688), a biographical account of nine 'worthy' and 'famous' women.[63] These popular biographical collections celebrate their chosen women

---

[61] Behn's reception in the eighteenth century has been studied in detail in Jane Spencer's excellent *Aphra Behn's Afterlife* (Oxford: Oxford University Press, 2000); see also the detailed account below in Ch. 7.

[62] Thomas Heywood, *The Generall Historie of Women* (1657), 555–6; none of Arbella Stuart's poetry has survived; it is perhaps also worth noting that Heywood apparently knows the Cooke sisters only through Sir John Harington's mentioning them, not through any acquaintance with their writing.

[63] The women in question are Deborah, Judith, Esther, Susanna, Lucretia, Boadicea, Mariamne, Clotilde, and Antigone.

as exemplary; it is difficult to know if they were aimed at a specifically female audience.

Women are placed alongside male writers in Edward Phillips's *Theatrum Poetarum, or A Compleat Collection of the Poets* (1675). Once again, Phillips's volume is an encyclopaedic collection of authors and brief facts and comments about them; it is not a sustained critical work. After his entries on ancient and modern male poets, Phillips offers sections at the end on Ancient and modern 'poetesses'. Phillips is able to name and describe forty-four ancient poetesses, but only twenty-five modern women—and he includes European examples and ventures back as far as medieval authors. Of British early modern women, Phillips mentions Anne Askew, Anne Bradstreet, Arbella Stuart, Aphra Behn, the Cooke sisters, Katherine Philips, Elizabeth Carew, Elizabeth Westonia, Lady Jane Grey, Margaret Cavendish, Mary Morpeth, Mary Sidney, and Mary Wroth.[64] The women writers are, like the men, merely described briefly, in keeping with the nature of this work as essentially a compact biographical dictionary. In her important account of the treatment of women writers by critics and anthologists in the eighteenth and nineteenth centuries, Margaret Ezell notes how the range of women's writing represented diminishes over time.[65] In the Restoration, perhaps because of the prominence of Margaret Cavendish, Aphra Behn, and Katherine Philips, there were some interesting examples of what might be called the self-conscious representation of women writers as a category. This is evident in a number of ways, including the self-presentation of authors who will be considered in detail later in this book, such as Cavendish and Behn. Behn and Philips in particular were (albeit in very different ways) seen as accomplished and significant writers within the general Restoration literary scene, and this resulted in various negotiations of their status as 'women writers'—some of these negotiations are discussed in more detail in Chapter 7.

Behn's and Philips's poetry appeared in a number of Restoration anthologies of verse, including *Poems on Several Occasions by the Duke of Buckingham* (1696).[66] There were also some self-conscious collections of women's writing. For example, Ephelia's *Female Poems on Several Occasions* (1679/1682) announces in its title the sex of the author as, one assumes, something of a selling point (*Poems on Several Occasions* was a title that was used often for anthologies, most notably for Rochester's 1680 collection, which contained poems by a number of authors, including a poem by Ephelia, 'In the Person of a Lady to Bejazet', though it

---

[64] It is possible that the idea of Arbella Stuart as poet derives from Heywood; if there is an independent tradition, it is particularly frustrating that, while her letters are available, the poetry seems to have disappeared.

[65] Ezell, *Writing Women*, ch. 4; see the discussion of Ezell in the Introduction, above.

[66] Their poems appeared in manuscript miscellanies as well; to take one example from many, John Dunton's manuscript collection, Bodleian Library Rawlinson Poet. 173, where they are placed beside poems by Waller, Rochester, Sedley, Dryden, and others.

has also been attributed to Etheredge).[67] Ephelia's poems can be compared to Aphra Behn's, many of which were printed in her anthology *Poems Upon Several Occasions* (1684).[68] Behn's anthology bears some interesting resemblances to Ephelia's, especially in their presentation: both have an engraved portrait, in a very similar style, facing the title page. Ephelia's portrait is more classical in style and includes a coat of arms, but manner of dress and address can easily be compared. One could take this a step further and note some similarities with the engraved self-portraits on many of Margaret Cavendish's volumes—Cavendish's portraits, like her volumes, are much grander, but the decolletage favoured by all three women could be seen as something designed to underline their femininity, while at the same time the portraits elevate them as classically respectable poets (especially true of Ephelia's, which has a classical pedestal, and Cavendish's, which goes so far as to place the figure of Cavendish on a pedestal and crown her with a laurel wreath).

In 1688 Jane Barker's *Poetical Recreations: Consisting of Original Poems, Songs, Odes, &c. with Several New Translations*, was prefaced by a number of poems, one of which, by 'Philaster' at St John's College, Cambridge, proclaims Barker as one who will take over from the recently deceased Katherine Philips:

> Soon as some envious *Angel*'s willing hand
> Snatch's Great *Orinda* from our happy Land;
> The Great *Orinda*, whose *Seraphick* Pen
> Triumph's o'er *Women*, and out-brav's ev'n *Men*:
> Then our Male-*Poets* modestly thought fit,
> To claim the honour'd *Primacy* in *Wit*;
> But, lo, the *Heiress* of that Ladies *Muse*,
> Rivals their Merits, and their *Sence* out-do's. (A5)

Barker, at this stage of her life, was at the centre of a small coterie of young men who were students at St John's; part two of the volume contains a large number of poems by students at both universities, a number of them addressed to Barker.[69] As a coterie poet, Barker bears out the comparison with Philips in a variety of ways (although she does not join Philips in celebrating female friendship, but addresses all but one of her poems to men). Kathryn King points out

---

[67] Ephelia's identity remains uncertain and contested; her editor Maureen Mulvihill has identified her first as Joan Phillips, in her edition of her poetry (Delmar, NY: Scholars' Facsimiles, 1992), 65–88, and more recently as Mary Villiers (dedicatee of the volume, which to my mind makes the identification doubtful), see her later edition for 'The Early Modern Englishwoman' (Aldershot: Ashgate, 2003); Mulvihill also strongly argues for the 'Bejazet' poem as Ephelia's, not Etheredge's. The title was famously used for Waller's extremely popular collection *Poems &c. Written Upon Several Occasions* (1664).

[68] See also my more detailed discussion in Ch 7.

[69] For new, detailed information about Barker's life, see Kathryn R. King and Jeslyn Medoff, 'Jane Barker Her Life: The Documentary Record', *Eighteenth Century Life*, 21 (1997), 16–38.

that Barker is a good example of an early modern woman writer supported by a group of congenial men: a pattern that needs to be set against the kind of misogynistic rivalry more commonly ascribed to the period.[70] Some of the poems also reflect Barker's medical interests: she became well known as a doctor.[71] In the eighteenth century Barker went on to publish a number of novels and was, as a Catholic convert, involved in the Jacobite cause.

In 1700 this sense of the possibility of a female community of poets was marked by the publication of one of a number of volumes marking the death of Dryden. *The Nine Muses* brought together commemorative poems by writers such as Mary Pix, Catherine Trotter, Mary Manley, Mary Egerton, and Susannah Centlivre—writers who marked the transition to a strong gathering of eighteenth-century women poets, as noted by Carol Barash in her important study of women's poetry at this time, where she comments on 'women's strong sense of poetic community in the years immediately preceding Anne's coronation'.[72]

In the eighteenth century the greatest (and still enduring) contribution to the knowledge of early modern women writers was made by a remarkable tailor and amateur antiquarian, George Ballard.[73] In the brief and modest preface to his biographical dictionary, *Memoirs of Several Ladies of Great Britain* (1752), Ballard explains that he has felt the lack of attention paid to women writers in the present age of biography to be an anomaly, which he decided to remedy in the absence of anyone else taking on the task. Ruth Perry, editor of the modern edition of Ballard, notes how Ballard's enthusiastic defence of female accomplishment, evident in the manuscript draft of the *Memoirs*, was toned down for the published version, apparently in response to a number of male scholars who belittled the whole idea of devoting so much antiquarian attention to female achievements.[74] Ballard's efforts to preserve information about the sixty-one women he discusses produced a remarkable work of scholarship. Margaret Ezell has (as noted above in the Introduction) pointed out that Ballard, while appearing to be an objective antiquarian, is in fact helping to establish the notion of the 'worthy' woman writer, by concentrating on women who can easily pass as respectable and ignoring those who, in the mid-eighteenth century, might be seen as disreputable (the most obvious example of an omission on such grounds being Aphra Behn).[75] Ezell also notes how Ballard creates something of an ideal type of woman writer,

---

[70] Kathryn R. King, 'Jane Barker, *Poetical Recreations*, and the Sociable Text', *ELH* 61 (1994), 551–70.

[71] See *The Galesia Trilogy and Selected Manuscript Poems of Jane Barker*, ed. Carol Shiner Wilson (New York: Oxford University Press, 1997), p. xxiv.

[72] *The Nine Muses, or, Poems Written by Nine Severall ladies Upon the Death of the Late Famous John Dryden Esq.* (1700); Carol Barash, *English Women's Poetry 1649–1714* (Oxford: Oxford University Press, 1996), 241.

[73] See the discussion of Ballard in the Introduction, above.

[74] George Ballard, *Memoirs of Several Ladies of Great Britain who have been celebrated for their writings or skill in the learned languages, arts and sciences*, ed. Ruth Perry (Detroit: Wayne State University Press, 1985), 35–6.

[75] See Ezell, *Writing Women*, 85–8.

emphasizing that it is possible to see 'Ballard's entries as composing a didactic narrative of feminine accomplishment' based on a 'role model of the patient, suffering literary lady'.[76] Nevertheless, Ballard supplies a considerable amount of often unique information about the women he includes; of early modern women, he discusses: Anne Askew, Katherine Parr, Lady Jane Grey, Lady Elizabeth Fane, Mary Countess of Arundel, Lady Joanna Lumley, Lady Mary Howard, Queen Mary, Anne, Margaret, and Jane Seymour, Catherine Tishem, Jane Countess of Westmorland, Elizabeth Dancy, Cecilia Heron, Margaret Clement, Mary Roper, Margaret Ascham, Queen Mary of Scotland, Blanch Parry, Lady Burleigh, Lady Bacon, Lady Russell, Katherine Killigrew, Queen Elizabeth, Elizabeth Weston, Arbella Seymour [Stuart], Mary Sidney Countess of Pembroke, Elizabeth Countess of Lincoln, Esther Inglis, Lady Eleanor Davies, Katherine Chidley, Elizabeth Countess of Bridgwater, Katherine Philips, Anne Wharton, Margaret Cavendish Duchess of Newcastle, Anne Clifford Countess of Pembroke, Lady Pakington, Anne Killigrew, Elizabeth Walker, Anne Baynard, Elizabeth Legge, Lady Gethin, Lady Halket, Lady Masham, Susanna Hopton, Elizabeth Burnet, Lady Chudleigh, Mrs Dudley North, Elizabeth Bland, Mrs Monk, Elizabeth Bury, Anne Countess of Winchelsea, Lady Norton, Catherine Bovey, Mary Astell, and Constantia Grierson. This huge list makes the scope of Ballard's researches abundantly clear, even if his criteria for inclusion have some of the limitations outlined by Ezell. In a number of cases, Ballard relies on second-hand evidence for what prove to be rather sketchy examples of literary activity, but Ballard is, after all, celebrating learned ladies and, as his title page indicates, they need not be authors to be seen as learned. So, for example, as well as giving us information about Margaret Roper, Ballard includes Thomas More's other daughters, Elizabeth Dancy and Cecilia Heron, even though he knows little about what they actually produced, to demonstrate the learning he deduces from references to them in Erasmus. This is not to say that Ballard is mistaken in adding them to the roll call of learned women, but a certain frustration must have been a possibility for his readers when they were left so often with tantalizing suggestions about various women's activities which cannot be illustrated with any concrete examples. Ballard's painstakingly compiled information became a vital resource for those who followed him, and many references in various biographical and critical works simply repeated Ballard's material.[77] (It is perhaps worth noting here that the most famous of all eighteenth-century studies of poets, Samuel Johnson's *The Lives of the Poets*, includes no women at all amongst its fifty-two subjects, even though Johnson includes such obscure seventeenth-century poets as Pomfret, George Stepney, and John Phillips.)

I will be discussing references to specific authors in Ballard and those who followed him in more detail in later chapters. At this point, however, I do want to continue to offer a brief overview of the way that early modern women writers

---

[76] Ibid. 87.     [77] On this, see Ezell's careful discussion, ibid. 78–88.

were discussed and reproduced in the course of the eighteenth and nineteenth centuries. Margaret Ezell notes how Theophilus Cibber's *Lives of the Poets* (1753) is dependent upon Ballard, but that Cibber does include a number of the dramatists omitted by the more squeamish antiquarian.[78] Cibber's account of Aphra Behn, for example, is detailed, although mostly biographical. Cibber defends Behn against the slurs that were mounting in the eighteenth century: 'There are marks of fine understanding in the most unfinished piece of Mrs Behn . . . Mrs Behn suffered enough at the hands of supercilious prudes, who had the barbarity to construe her sprightliness into lewdness; and because she had wit and beauty, she must likewise be charged with prostitution and irreligion.'[79] Cibber does provide the kind of critical, literary commentary that Ballard lacks. For example, in his account of Katherine Philips, he notes that her 'poetry has not harmony of versification, or amorous tenderness to recommend it, but it had a force of thinking, which few poets of the other sex can exceed, and if it is without graces, it has yet a great deal of strength.'[80]

    The most significant eighteenth-century publication that actually transmitted women's writing, rather than just information about women writers, was George Colman and Bonnell Thornton's anthology *Poems by Eminent Ladies*, first published in 1755, and then in expanded editions in 1773 and 1780. Colman and Thornton offer a brief but enthusiastic preface, noting that 'There is indeed no good reason to be assigned why the poetical attempts of females should not be well received, unless it can be demonstrated that fancy and judgment are wholly confined to one half of our species; a notion, to which the readers of these volumes will not readily assent' (A2). A culling has occurred, as the editors explain (one in accordance, one might say, with Ballard's principles): 'it was therefore thought better to omit those pieces, which too plainly betrayed the want of learning' (A2v). Colman and Thornton acknowledge that the information they supply about the writers is indebted to Ballard and Cibber. They offer generous selections of poems by Barber, Behn, Carter, Cavendish, Chudleigh, Cockburn, Grierson, Jones, Killigrew, Leapor, Maiden, Masters, Montague, Monk, Philips, Pilkington, Rowe, and Winchelsea—in other words, this is a Restoration and eighteenth-century anthology. Margaret Ezell discusses how the anthology changes its focus as it is reissued and expanded, so that the selection from Behn starts out at forty-nine poems and ends up at only four, clearly reflecting changes in taste in the course of the eighteenth century.[81] As Ezell explains, there is a considerable narrowing of focus in the anthology's increasing

---

[78] Ezell, *Writing Women*, 89–90.

[79] Theophilus Cibber, *The Lives of the Poets of Great Britain and Ireland* (1753), iii. 27.

[80] Ibid., ii. 157.

[81] It is, however, worth noting that separate editions of Behn's works continued to appear in the eighteenth and nineteenth centuries, although with diminishing frequency: notably in collections published in 1718, 1722, 1735, 1741, 1800, 1820, and 1871; see the detailed discussion of this in Ch. 7, below.

emphasis on more 'decorous' styles of poetry, which fed into nineteenth-century demands for female authors of delicate sensibilities.[82]

In the early nineteenth century, the Shakespeare scholar Alexander Dyce produced what remains the most impressive anthology of women's poetry to be published prior to the twentieth century: *Specimens of British Poetesses* (1825). Dyce offers a selection of poems by eighty-nine women arranged chronologically from Juliana Berners through to L. E. Landon, with a brief note on each author. Dyce aims at breadth of coverage, and writers are represented by only a few poems. Dyce's range of early modern women is impressive: Askew, Queen Elizabeth, Melville, Carew, Sidney, Wroth, Anne Arundel, Diana Primrose, Mary Fage, Anna Hume, Anne Bradstreet, Anne Collins, Mary Morpeth, Elizabeth of Bohemia, Philips, Boothby, Cavendish, Killigrew, Anne Wharton, Anne Taylor, Behn, Pix, Chudleigh, Monk, Winchelsea—and a very large range of eighteenth-century poets. Indeed, no one would match Dyce's scholarship and scope until very recently. It is true, as Margaret Ezell once again points out, that Dyce continues the trend towards representation of the 'genteel' image of women's writing, leaving aside, as do the nineteenth-century anthologizers who follow him, disreputable writers and disreputable poems.[83] Dyce expresses, in his preface, a desire to 'exhibit the growth and progress of the genius of our countrywomen in the department of Poetry' (p.iii), and no one approaches him for the range of those he singles out for inclusion. To take one example of Dyce's originality, he prints two of Mary Wroth's songs from *Urania*. The first, 'Who can blame me, if I love?', occurs at the end of Book One of the romance, and, given that it was not reproduced before Dyce, it is clear that he at least read through the poems in *Urania*, if not the whole romance itself, in order to extract the two poems he prints. (The second, 'Love, a child, is ever crying', comes from the appended sonnet sequence.) Dyce's methodical approach is underlined by the fact that, for example, Frederic Rowton's popular *The Female Poets of Great Britain* (1848) simply reprints the same Wroth poems (with some additional commentary), making it fairly clear that Rowton did not look at *Urania* for himself. Dyce's energetic and original research is evident throughout his treatment of a number of writers who were, by the early nineteenth century, extremely obscure, as the list above indicates. Indeed, virtually all of Rowton's early modern women's poems are taken directly from Dyce: the parallel choices could not be coincidental, but are rather a sign of Dyce's impressive selection (and Rowton's laziness).[84]

[82] Ezell, *Writing Women*, 112–17.

[83] Ibid. 119–20; There are exceptions to this in the continuing interest in certain individual authors, such as Margaret Cavendish, and indeed Aphra Behn, who will be discussed in detail in later chapters.

[84] The only exception is Bradstreet, in every other case Rowton's selection is the same as Dyce's. A. H. Bullen, who certainly read his source material with care, in *Poems Chiefly Lyrical from Romances and Prose Tracts of the Elizabethan Age* (London: Nimmo, 1890), says that he 'could not find much

George Bethune's *The British Female Poets* (1848) is rather less appreciative of early modern women poets than Dyce, as evidenced by his low opinion of Katherine Philips's talent: 'how small a portion of talent then made a woman remarkable' (p. vi).[85] Bethune views 'the older female writers of rhyme' as being of antiquarian interest only, and so offers few examples of their work, preferring to reserve 'the bulk of the book for more copious extracts from those whose writings are most rightly appreciated for moral and poetical excellence' (p. vi).

Matilda Betham's *A Biographical Dictionary of the Celebrated Women of Every Age and Country* (1804) includes entries on twenty-five early modern women writers, leaning heavily on Ballard for information and seldom offering very much detail for any of her entries. In Eric Robertson's *English Poetesses* (1886), a cross between a critical study and an anthology, only Philips, Behn, and Cavendish are discussed in any detail, and the reader is told that only two of Behn's poems can be reproduced, and that Philips is 'not very interesting to the modern reader' (4)—Cavendish fares rather better thanks to the usual nineteenth-century interest in her biography of her husband.

While it is certainly the case that, as Ezell so effectively demonstrates, the range of early modern women's writing, and of early modern women writers, dwindled during the course of the nineteenth century, there was still some recognition of this body of work, however attenuated.[86] As will be seen in succeeding chapters, particular authors (notably Behn, Philips, Cavendish, Queen Elizabeth, Lucy Hutchinson) retained a higher profile for specific reasons, and had their work reprinted in a variety of ways. General attitudes towards early modern women did end up restricting approaches to their work by the beginning of the twentieth century. Ezell notes, for example, that Virginia Woolf's impressions of early modern women's writing were coloured by the limitations of its representation in the nineteenth century.[87] Yet Woolf was, in a number of instances, exposed more directly to this writing than simply via anthologies. It is also worth considering, especially in relation to Woolf, the representation of early modern women writers in the *Dictionary of National Biography*, edited by Woolf's father, Leslie Stephen. There are some quite impressive articles on early modern women writers in the *DNB*. For example, Sidney Lee may find Wroth's *Urania* 'tedious . . . long-winded and awkward', but he provides an impressively detailed (and accurate) overview of Wroth's life, and warmer appreciation of her poetry than of her prose.[88] Everard Green

that was satisfactory' (p. xix) amongst Wroth's poems; Bullen prints, like Dyce, 'Who can blame me if I love', but his second choice is original: 'Love, what art thou?', an eclogue from the end of Book One of *Urania*.

85  References to George Bethune, *The British Female Poets* (Philadelphia, 1848).
86  See Ezell, *Writing Women*, 104–30.
87  Ibid. 103.
88  *DNB*, s.v. Wroth, Lady Mary.

offers a notable defence of Aphra Behn at a time when her reputation (prior to Montague Summers's 1915 edition of her writing) was at a low ebb: 'Her genius and vivacity were undoubted; her plays are very coarse, but very lively and humorous, while she possessed an indisputable touch of lyric genius.'[89] Joseph Knight's entry on Margaret Cavendish is very detailed and a judicious mixture of cautious praise and a fair bit of blame: 'Her philosophy is the dead weight which drags her to the ground. In these deliveries an occasional piece of common sense is buried in avalanches of ignorance and extravagance. Her life of the duke is in its way a masterpiece.'[90] Woolf's much quoted comments on Cavendish may well have their seeds in this entry. In the essay on Cavendish which she wrote for *The Common Reader* (1925), Woolf too (if more memorably) offered a mixture of admiration and criticism: 'though her philosophies are futile, and her plays intolerable, and her verse mainly dull, the vast bulk of the Duchess is leavened by a vein of authentic fire'.[91] Woolf believes Cavendish to be 'noble and Quixotic and high-spirited, as well as crack-brained and bird-witted'.[92]

Despite the current tendency to question the limitations of Woolf's approach to early modern women writers, she was part of a genuine resurgence of interest in at least some of them in the early twentieth century.[93] This is, in part, manifested in editorial work, as well as critical commentary. The most notable instance, which will be discussed in more detail in Chapter 7, is Montague Summers's 1915 edition of the works of Aphra Behn, which allowed anyone interested to sample the entire range of Behn's work, very ably edited by Summers, with helpful information about each text, including a fair amount of annotation and an enthusiastic general introduction, praising all her work, but singling out her comedies for special praise.[94]

The details of this overview will be fleshed out in succeeding chapters, as the fortunes of individual writers and groups of writers are discussed, but it should be clear that many early modern women writers did not disappear from view during the eighteenth and nineteenth centuries, and those who did were perhaps not proportionately more numerous than male writers who dropped off the

---

[89] *DNB*, s.v. Behn, Aphra.

[90] *DNB*, s.v. Cavendish, Margaret; of course not all entries on early modern women writers were so appreciative; for example, A. H. Bullen dismisses Elizabeth Cary's *Mariam* as 'tedious'.

[91] Virginia Woolf, 'The Duchess of Newcastle', *Collected Essays*, ed. Andrew McNeillie (London: Hogarth Press, 1994), iv. 87.

[92] Ibid.

[93] For a stimulating account of Woolf's general engagement with the Renaissance (including women writers, though they do not figure as largely as male writers), see Juliet Dusinberre, *Virginia Woolf's Renaissance* (London: Macmillan, 1997); Alice Fox's earlier study, *Virginia Woolf and the Liuterature of the English Renaissance* (Oxford: Clarendon Press, 1990), does not mention women writers at all.

[94] *The Works of Aphra Behn*, ed. Montague Summers (London: Heinemann, 1915).

literary map. Given the enormous range of this writing, as evidenced in this still very limited overview, the fortunes of individual examples or groups of examples point to a more complex history of transmission and reception than has been realized—or at least than has been explored in any detail up until now, despite Margaret Ezell's signposting of the way.

# 2

# Poets High and Low, Visible and Invisible

I want to begin this chapter by discussing a dramatically contrasting pair of writers: one a queen and the other an out-of-work maid. Elizabeth I wrote a considerable amount in every conceivable genre, beginning at a very early age. The obscure Isabella Whitney published two small collections of poetry in 1567 and 1573 and then fell silent. Queen Elizabeth's writing was preserved, commented upon, and transmitted in a dizzying variety of ways; Isabella Whitney remained virtually unnoticed until quite recently.

## QUEEN AS POET

As mentioned in the previous chapter, the 11-year-old Princess Elizabeth translated Marguerite de Navarre's 1532 religious meditation *Le Miroir de l'âme pécheresse* as *The glasse of the synnefull soule* in 1544 for her stepmother, Queen Catherine Parr, most probably using a copy of the 1533 edition of the *Miroir* which Marguerite had sent to Elizabeth's mother Anne Boleyn.[1] The presentation manuscript of this little book is written in Elizabeth's clear, carefully controlled hand. The text was later edited by John Bale and published in Germany in 1548. There were new editions printed in England in 1568 and 1682, as well as the appearance of the text in Bentley's *Monument of Matrons* (1582).[2] Elizabeth went on to translate a number of religious works, most notably Catherine Parr's *Prayers or meditations*, Bernardino Orchino's *De Christo sermo*, and Calvin's *Institution Chrétienne*. When she was Queen, Elizabeth produced a number of notable speeches, and many of her letters are also extant. Her poetry is less plentiful, especially after one discards dubious attributions. However, the poems that Elizabeth did write were frequently reproduced, and attracted a considerable amount of attention. I want here to focus on an example which illustrates, not so much Elizabeth's talents as a poet, but rather what might be termed the affect carried by poems authored by her (or thought to be authored by her).

---

[1] For a detailed account see the elaborate edition, including a facsimile text, of *Elizabeth's Glass*, ed. Marc Shell (Lincoln: University of Nebraska Press, 1993).

[2] For Bentley, see Ch. 1, above.

Elizabeth's most circulated lyric was apparently written in response to Mary Queen of Scots' arrival in England in 1568, and the resulting anxiety over a possible Catholic rebellion. The poem appeared in a number of verse miscellanies in the early 1570s (exactly the same time as the publication of Whitney's first volume). I quote it here from Leicester Bradner's edition: this text is a modernized version of the transcription found in Bodleian MS Rawlinson Poet. 108.

> The doubt of future foes exiles my present joy,
> And wit me warns to shun such snares as threaten mine annoy;
> For falsehood now doth flow, and subjects' faith doth ebb,
> Which should not be if reason ruled or wisdom weaved the web.
> But clouds of joys untried do cloak aspiring minds,
> Which turn to rain of late repent by changed course of winds.
> The top of hope supposed the root upreared shall be,
> And fruitless all their grafted guile, as shortly ye shall see.
> The dazzled eyes with pride, which great ambition blinds,
> Shall be unsealed by worthy wights whose foresight falsehood finds.
> The daughter of debate that discord aye doth sow
> Shall reap no gain where former rule still peace hath taught to know.
> No foreign banished wight shall anchor in this port;
> Our realm brooks not seditious sects, let them elsewhere resort.
> My rusty sword through rest shall first his edge employ
> To poll their tops that seek such change or gape for future joy.[3]

This poem circulated in a number of manuscripts, but its most famous contemporary appearance was in George Puttenham's *Art of English Poesy*, published in 1589, but written about twenty years earlier.[4] Puttenham quotes the entire poem in his chapter 20, in the final section of the treatise, which is concerned with ornament. The ornament in question is the figure Puttenham styles 'The Gorgious', following the Greek 'Exargasia' (247). Puttenham explains that this is a figure of amplification: 'a masse of many figuratiue speaches, applied to the bewtifying of our tale or argument' (ibid.). Puttenham goes on to say:

I finde none example in English meetre, so well maintaining this figure as that dittie of her Maiesties owne making passing sweete and harmonicall, which figure being as his very originall name purporteth the most bewtifull and gorgious of all others, it asketh in reason to be reserued for a last complement, and desciphred by the arte of a Ladies penne, her selfe being the most bewtifull, or rather bewtie of Queenes. And this was the occasion: our soueraigne Lady perceiuing how by the Sc Q. residence within this Realme at so great libertie and ease (as were scarce meete for so great and daungerous a prisoner) bred secret factions among her people, and made many of the nobilitie incline to fauour her partie: some of them desirous of innouation in the state: others aspiring to greater

---

[3] *The Poems of Queen Elizabeth I*, ed. Leicester Bradner (Providence, RI: Brown University Press, 1964).

[4] George Puttenham, *The Arte of English Poesie*, ed. Gladys Willcock and Alice Walker (Cambridge: Cambridge University Press, 1936), pp. xliv–liii, further references in parentheses.

fortunes by her libertie and life. The Queene our soueraigne Lady to declare that she was nothing ignorant of those secret practises, though she had long with great wisdome and pacience dissembled it, writeth this ditty most sweet and sententious, not hiding from all such aspiring minds the daunger of their ambition and disloyaltie: which afterward fell out most truly by th'exemplary chastisement of sundry persons, who in fauour of the sayd Sc. Q. declining from her maiestie, sought to interrupt the quiet of the Realme by many euill and vndutifull practises. (247–8)

In his appreciation, Puttenham manages to fuse the political context of Elizabeth's poem and its rhetorical technique. At first glance, exargia seems a curious figure to characterize the poem, given its clear didactic thrust. But it is undeniable that the poem's rhetoric and its politics are interconnected: the elaborations of Elizabeth's constitutional dilemma spin out into an ingenious series of dichotomies (foes/ioy, falsehood/faith). The poem is directed, not just at those who might be tempted to rally around the figure of Mary, but also against 'aspiring minds' in general. It is in that sense a potent example of Elizabeth asserting her authority. Its transmission points to the effectiveness of that assertion. For Elizabeth, her character as monarch included her confidence in her intellectual abilities. Her poetry formed part of Elizabeth's self-representation, and as such it was eagerly seized upon, as testified to by the transmission of this particular poem. Puttenham's treatise begins with a compliment to Elizabeth, acknowledging her literary skills: 'But you (Madame) my most Honored and Gracious: if I should seeme to offer you this my deuise for a discipline and not a delight, I might well be reputed, of all others the most arrogant and iniurious: your selfe being already, of any that I know in our time, the most excellent Poet' (4).

Indeed, Puttenham's treatise is studded with references to Elizabeth and includes, as well as the Queen's poems, Puttenham's poetry in her praise. All of Elizabeth's speeches and writings were seen as possible revelations of her true feelings, and this poem is no exception. Its apparently personal nature (at least as interpreted by those who transmitted it) is evident in its appearance in the Arundel Harington manuscript. This manuscript collection of Tudor poetry was mostly compiled by two generations of Haringtons: John Harington of Stepney and Kelston and his son, Sir John Harington of Kelston, the son being the translator of *Orlando Furioso* and godson of Queen Elizabeth.[5] This manuscript miscellany famously contains a large number of poems by Wyatt and Surrey, and it offers a wide range of examples of Tudor poetry; John the father compiled verses by himself and his contemporaries, and John the son interleaved poetry of the later sixteenth century. Elizabeth is represented in the manuscript by two poems: the one being discussed here (poem 238 in Hughey), and a translation of Petrarch's 'Trionfo dell'Eternità' (poem 320 in Hughey). As the poem appears in this manuscript, there are significant variants, starting with the first line which,

---

[5] Ruth Hughey, ed., *The Arundel Harington Manuscript of Tudor Poetry*, 2 vols. (Columbus: Ohio State University Press, 1960), 26; further references to this edition.

in Arundel Harington, reads 'The dread of future foes exile my present Ioy' (276). In the late eighteenth century the Harington family papers were plundered by the 14-year-old Henry Harington to compile a miscellany, which was published in 1769 as *Nugae Antiquae*. Elizabeth's poem appears in *Nugae Antiquae*, evidently derived from a different manuscript to Arundel Harington, preceded by a fragment of a letter, apparently from Sir John Harington, explaining the poem's provenance:

Good Madam,
Herewith I commit a precious jewell, not for your ear, but your eye; and doubt not but you will rejoice to wear it even in your heart: it is of her Highness own enditing, and doth witness, how much her wisdom and great learning both outweigh even the peril of state, and how little all worldly dangers do work any change in her mynde. My Lady Wiloughby did covertly get it on her Majesties tablet, and had much hazard in so doing; for the Queen did find out the thief, and chid for spreading evil bruit of her writing such toyes, when other matters did so occupy her employment at this time; and was fearful of being thought too lightly of so doing. But marvel not, good madam, her Highness doth frame herself to all occasions, to all times, and to all things, both in business, and pastime, as may witness this her sonnet.[6]

This letter names the source of the poem as Lady Willoughby. It is possible that this is Lady Elizabeth Willoughby, who was notorious for her acrimonious relationship with her husband, Sir Francis Willoughby.[7] In the late 1560s she was often at court, rather than at home, much to the ire of her husband. Given that Puttenham's source is different, one cannot take seriously the idea that Lady Willoughby's bold and surreptitious copying of the poem represents a unique act that truly roused the Queen's ire. Rather, this is a typically staged account of poetry as a trifle: one echoed by many aristocratic writers who, in the spirit of courtly sprezzatura, saw their poems as mere toys.[8] The 'truth' about the poem is not so much Elizabeth's token protestation that it is a toy, but Harington's characterization of it as the Queen's response to the perils of state, and also his notion of it as an example of her ability to adapt to 'all occasions'.

Jennifer Summit points to 'The Doubt of Future Foes' as a significant marker of the Queen-as-poet: a description of her typified by Puttenham but, Summit notes, often passed over by New Historicist critics who see Elizabeth as 'excluded from literary agency'.[9] In Summit's reading, the poem also exemplifies the Queen's

---

[6]  Henry Harington, *Nugae Antiquae* (London: W. Frederick, 1769), 58.

[7]  See the account of Lady Elizabeth Willoughby in Alice T. Friedman, 'Portrait of a Marriage: The Willoughby Letters of 1585–6', *Signs*, 11 (1986), 542–55; she seems to me to be a more likely candidate than Katherine Willoughby, Duchess of Suffolk, suggested by Jennifer Summit, ' "The Arte of a Ladies Penne": Elizabeth I and the Poetics of Queenship', in Peter C. Herman, ed., *Reading Monarch's Writing* (Tempe, Ariz.: MRTS, 2002), 93.

[8]  The best account of this remains Katherine Duncan-Jones, 'Philip Sidney's Toys', in Dennis Kay, ed., *Sir Philip Sidney* (Oxford: Clarendon Press, 1987), 61–80.

[9]  Summit, 'Arte', 82.

relationship to discourses of secrecy which are central to Puttenham's notion of allegory as the most important poetical figure because it withholds meaning.[10] As Summit points out, this can in turn be associated with Elizabeth's relationship with Mary Queen of Scots: a relationship carried out via 'the circulation of texts', which had to negotiate Mary's political threat through a delicate balance between private surveillance and public restraint.[11] Summit finally reads Elizabeth's poem as part of the exchange between the two queens which ultimately led to Mary's execution; the poem itself contained a veiled threat of such action, which was in turn responded to by Mary in a variety of ways, including her own poetry, and also the emblematic embroidery which she produced during her captivity (in this particular case, Summit argues, the Oxburgh Hanging).[12]

The political implications of this poem are not fixed, and this is evident in the way it circulated in manuscript at different periods of time in Elizabeth's reign, as well as after her death. Leah Marcus and Peter C. Herman both note that there are manuscript versions of the poem transcribed in the early 1570s, around the time of its probable composition, in association with the Northern Rebellion—this rebellion involved a plot which aimed at the Duke of Norfolk marrying Mary and usurping Elizabeth (for which he was executed in 1572).[13] The poem then reappeared in later manuscripts, after the execution of Mary in 1587. According to Peter Herman, the early manuscripts are Arundel Harington, Folger V.b.317 and Bodleian Rawl. Poet. 108; the later manuscripts are Bodleian Digby 138, BM Harleian 6933, and BM Harleian 7392.[14] It is tempting to speculate about some of the variant readings in relation to these tentative datings of the main early manuscripts. The more subtle 'doubt' of future foes (as opposed to 'dread', the reading in Arundel Harington and in *Nugae Antiquae*—which points to connections between the two Harington sources) hints at some uncertainty about the threat posed by Mary, and also by the other political challenges that were evident in the first period of Elizabeth's reign. One cannot choose between 'doubt' and 'dread' on grounds of authenticity; however, the end of the poem offers a clear image, in any version, of the 'polling' process that will cut down the aspiring minds that challenge Elizabeth's authority.

In the seventeenth century the poem seems to have circulated in a relatively limited number of manuscript miscellanies.[15] By the eighteenth century, Elizabeth was being seen as, in some respects, a charismatic figure who speaks but does not write. George Ballard accorded Elizabeth the longest entry in his *Memoirs of Several Ladies of Great Britain* (1752).[16] Ballard stresses Elizabeth's 'learning and

---

[10] Ibid. 92.    [11] Ibid. 96–7.    [12] Ibid. 94–7.

[13] See Leah S. Marcus's discussion of the changing sixteenth-century contexts for the poem in 'Elizabeth I as Public and Private Poet', in Herman, *Monarch's Writing*, 140–2; see also 270 for Herman's own comment.

[14] Ibid. 270; Herman includes transcripts of all these manuscript versions.

[15] See, e.g. Inner Temple Library MS Petyt 538, vol. 10.

[16] See the discussion of Ballard in Ch. 1; references here are to George Ballard, *Memoirs of Several Ladies of Great Britain*, ed. Ruth Perry (Detroit: Wayne State University Press, 1985).

great abilities'(212), noting her translations, but of her poetry he only mentions the evidence in *The Art of English Poesy*, and does not quote or discuss what he finds there (223). But by the end of the eighteenth century, perhaps in part owing to the impetus of *Nugae Antiquae*, Elizabeth's poetry was being seen as an essential part of her identity as learned Queen; this occurred alongside the general elevation of Elizabeth as a charismatic icon of a glorious period of English history. A good example of this is Horace Walpole's *Catalogue of Royal and Noble Authors*, first published in 1758 by Walpole himself at his Strawberry Hill Press, but later reprinted and enlarged with additions by Thomas Park. (In 1804, Park had edited *Nugae Antiquae*.) Walpole quotes Camden's comment that Elizabeth 'either read or wrote something every day' (88), and notes in his entry an impressive list of works by her, including numerous letters.[17] Walpole quotes from Puttenham (91–2), but does not quote 'The Doubt of Future Foes' itself, preferring to quote her translation from Seneca (102–9).

An even tougher stance is taken by Alexander Dyce in *Specimens of British Poetesses* (1825).[18] Dyce reproduces Puttenham's description of 'The Doubt of Future Foes', and the poem itself. He notes its reference to Mary Queen of Scots, and then places Elizabeth by stating: 'The following farewell to France, written by that lovely, unfortunate, but surely not guiltless woman, will shew how much her poetical powers were superior to those of Elizabeth' (18). Dyce does not explain exactly what he means by Mary's superior poetic powers, but expects his readers to agree without question to this ranking of Elizabeth as poet. He emphasizes this in his introduction to the selection, with a scornful account of an entirely imaginary Elizabeth who needed to be assured of her poetic prowess: 'The desire of shining as a poetess was one of the weaknesses of this illustrious queen, and her vanity, no doubt, made her regard as tributes justly paid, the extravagant praises, which the courtiers, and writers of her age, lavished on her royal ditties'(15).

Dyce's dismissal increasingly becomes the norm in the nineteenth century, as Elizabeth's poetry is seen to be worthy of no more than passing interest. George Bethune, in *The British Female Poets* (1848) explains that he includes 'Several specimens of this vain, pedantic, but really accomplished and intellectual woman's poetical efforts' (22). He reproduces 'The Doubt of Future Foes' under the title 'A Ditty', following Puttenham by way of Henry Ellis's *Three Collections of English Poetry of the Latter Part of the Sixteenth Century* (1845). This notion of Puttenham representing a whole claque of flatterers of Elizabeth-as-poet was perhaps set in motion by Thomas Percy in his pioneering and influential *Reliques of Ancient English Poetry* (1765). There he states that Puttenham's book offers 'many sly addresses to the queen's foible of shining as a poetess' (ii. 218). Dyce's unacknowledged echo of Percy's image of the Queen's desire to shine as a poetess

---

[17] Quotations are from Horace Walpole, *A Catalogue of the Royal and Noble Authors of England, Scotland, and Ireland . . . enlarged and continued to the present time by Thomas Park*, 5 vols. (London: John Scott, 1806).

[18] See the discussion of Dyce in Ch. 1, above.

underlines this tradition, which sets up an anachronistic image of the Queen's supposed need for public acknowledgement of her poetry.

Few of the biographies of Elizabeth, up to and including J. E. Neale's famous 1934 volume, mention, let alone discuss, her poetry.[19] Similarly, Elizabeth goes unrepresented in most significant collections of poetry in the nineteenth and twentieth centuries—including, for example, Quiller-Couch's *Oxford Book of English Verse* (1907), and even, more surprisingly, Helen Gardner's New Oxford anthology (1972).[20] Palgrave's *Golden Treasury* (1861), one of the most popular of the Victorian general poetry anthologies, offers a generous selection of Renaissance lyrics by Campion, Carew, Daniel, Dekker, Donne, Drayton, Fletcher, Greene, Herbert, Herrick, Heyward, Jonson, Lodge, Lyly, Marlowe, Marvell, Milton, Nashe, Shakespeare, Sidney, Spenser, Suckling, Wither, and Wyatt, but Elizabeth is unrepresented. This is even the case with collections devoted to Renaissance poetry, such as W. J. Lynton's *Rare Poems of the Sixteenth and Seventeenth Centuries* (1882), Felix Schelling's *A Book of Elizabethan Lyrics* (1895), A. H. Bullen's *Some Shorter Elizabethan Poems* (1903), and Arthur Symonds's *A Sixteenth-Century Anthology* (1905)—indeed, there are no poems by women in any of these collections.

The change in the fortunes of 'The Doubt of Future Foes', which points to the increased interest in both early modern women's writing and political, as opposed to lyric, poetry, may be represented by its inclusion in the fourth edition of *The Norton Anthology of Poetry* (1996)—previous editions represented Elizabeth solely by 'When I Was Fair and Young'. This symbolic inclusion is doubtless due to the editorial endeavours of Margaret Ferguson, who joined the editorial team for the fourth edition and who is a specialist in early modern women's writing. A significant precedent was set in 1972 by Ann Stanford's impressive anthology of women's poetry, *The Women Poets in English*, which included six poems by Elizabeth, including 'The Doubt of Future Foes'.[21] On the more specialized side, David Norbrook and H. R. Woudhuysen's *Penguin Book of Renaissance Verse* (1992), also includes 'The Doubt of Future Foes' along with other examples of women's poetry.

The complex revisioning of Elizabeth in a number of major recent studies has created a context in which the resonances of 'The Doubt of Future Foes' can be

---

[19] J. E. Neale, *Queen Elizabeth* (London: Jonathan Cape, 1934), quotes a stanza of 'The Doubt of Future Foes' simply to illustrate Elizabeth's thoughts about Mary; Neale's biography was frequently reprinted, including a new edition of 1959.

[20] As well as individual searches I have also used the invaluable web-based reference 'Anthologies and Miscellanies' (http://www.english.ucsb.edu/faculty/rraley/research/anthologies/), which provides contents pages and prefaces for dozens of examples.

[21] Ann Stanford, ed., *The Women Poets in English: An Anthology* (New York: McGraw Hill, 1972); Stanford's extensive selection includes poems by Anne Boleyn, Anne Askew, Isabella Whitney, Mary Sidney, Elizabeth Melville, Lucy Harington, Elizabeth Carey, Mary Wroth, Rachel Speght, Diana Primrose, Anne Bradstreet, Anne Collins, Margaret Cavendish, Katherine Philips, Aphra Behn, Ephelia, and Anne Killigrew.

fully appreciated; this new approach to Elizabeth shows no sign of diminishing, and it feeds into the general increase in attention now paid to early modern women's poetry, as attested to by recent collections of poetry, perhaps most notably Jane Stevenson and Peter Davidson's Oxford *Early Modern Women Poets* (2001) and by Jill Seal Millman and Gillian Wright's *Early Modern Women's Manuscript Poetry* (2005).[22]

## MAID AS POET

In 1567 a tiny volume of poetry was published: *The Copy of a Letter, lately written in metre by a young gentlewoman to her unconstant lover. With an admonition to all young gentlewomen, and to all other maids in general, to beware of men's flattery.* The author was Isabella Whitney; she signs herself 'Is W.' on the title page. This book was printed by Richard Jones, who was to publish Whitney's second volume in 1573. Whitney's first publication is certainly modest: two of her poems, 'I.W. To Her Unconstant Lover' and 'The Admonition by the Auctor to all Yong Gentilwomen: And to all other Maids being in Love', are followed by two poems by male writers, replying to Whitney's themes: 'A Loveletter' by W.G. and 'R.W. Against the wilfull Inconstancie of his deare Foe E.T'.

Whitney's accomplished lyrics from this volume have, in recent years, been frequently anthologized, but their initial appearance seems to have caused no stir at all. 'I.W. To Her Unconstant Lover' is a lament in the manner of Ovid's *Heroides*, at times bitter, at times accusatory, at times resigned. As Ann Rosalind Jones notes, 'the newly fashionable mode of Ovid's Heroides' was popular with male poets in the 1560s: in this mode men take on the voice of the abandoned woman.[23] Our knowledge of Whitney's authorship perhaps influences a strong sense of authenticity attributed by many critics to the voice of this poem. The opening two stanzas establish this forceful voice, as Whitney laments her lover's secret marriage, but quickly throws out a sarcastic taunt:

> As close as you your weding kept
> Yet now the trueth I here:
> Which you (yer now) might me have told
> What need you nay to swere?

[22] See e.g. Susan Frye, *Elizabeth I: The Competition for Representation* (Oxford: Oxford University Press, 1993), Philippa Berry, *Of Chastity and Power* (London: Routledge, 1989), Helen Hackett, *Virgin Mother, Maiden Queen* (Basingstoke: Macmillan, 1995), and essay collections such as Julie Walker, ed., *Dissing Elizabeth* (Durham N. C: Duke University Press, 1998) and Carole Levin *et al.*, eds., *Elizabeth I: Always Her Own Free Woman* (Aldershot: Ashgate, 2003).

[23] Ann Rosalind Jones, *The Currency of Eros* (Bloomington: University of Indiana Press, 1990), 43; for an astute reading of Whitney from this perspective, see Danielle Clarke, *The Politics of Early Modern Women's Writing* (Harlow: Pearson, 2001), 192–203.

> You know I always wisht you wel
> So wyll I during lyfe:
> But sith you shal a Husband be
> God send you a good wyfe. (A2)[24]

As the poem unfolds, Whitney compares her lover to a series of classical her-
oes—Aeneas, Theseus, Jason—all of whom, she argues, should be excoriated
for their treatment of women, rather than celebrated for their bravery. In dialogue with the two male-authored poems, Whitney's lyrics are a poised and, for
their time, unique representation of a woman's reaction against the tyranny of the
masculine lyric tradition. In her influential study of the appropriation of the feminine voice of complaint by early modern male poets, Elizabeth Harvey notes that
'The complaint furnishes such a pervasive representation of the female voice that
its querulous tone and exiled condition has come to define a version of woman.'[25]
This certainly seems to be the case when one considers Harvey's examples, most
notably Donne's 'Sappho to Philaenis'. However, Whitney, whose poetry is not
mentioned by Harvey, complicates this notion of 'woman', in part because her
poem is far from simply querulous, in part because the female signature, especially set in the context of the dialogue with male-authored poems in *The Copy of
a Letter*, lends the voice of 'To Her Unconstant Lover' an impressive authority.

This is further developed in Whitney's second published volume: *The Sweet
Nosegay or Pleasant Posy* (1573). This is a much more substantial achievement. It
begins with a dedication by Whitney to George Mainwaring, signed by Whitney
as 'his countriwoman'.[26] Whitney begins with an autobiographical poem outlining her plight in a vivid fashion:

> This Harvest tyme, I harvestlesse,
>     and servicelesse also:
> And subject unto sicknesse, that
>     abrode I could not go (A5v)[27]

She explains how, in order to avoid London's 'stynking streetes, or lothsome
Lanes' she decided to adapt Hugh Plat's 'Flowers of Philosophy' (1572). Her
version of Plat, however, only forms about a quarter of the volume. Whitney then
returns to more autobiographical verse, in a series of 'familier Epistles', mostly

---

[24] Quotations from *The Copy of a Letter* (1567).

[25] Elizabeth Harvey, *Ventriloquized Voices: Feminist Theory and English Renaissance Texts* (London: Routledge, 1992), 141.

[26] R. J. Fehrenbach identifies Mainwaring as ' a member of the prominent Cheshire Mainwaring
family', dedicatee of Whitney's brother Geoffrey's 139th emblem; see 'Isabella Whitney, Sir Hugh
Plat, Geoffrey Whitney, and "Sister Eldershae" ', *ELN* 21 (1983), 10; in this article Fehrenbach
makes what seems to me to be a wholly convincing case for identifying Isabella Whitney as Geoffrey
Whitney's sister.

[27] All references to *A Sweet Nosegay* (1573).

to members of her family. This section opens with a letter to her brother G.W.: that is, Geoffrey Whitney, author of *A Choice of Emblemes* (1586). These epistles are particularly concerned with ideas of service. Isabella Whitney herself was in service to a gentlewoman in London, and her sisters were in the same situation. In a recent essay on this aspect of Whitney's verse, Ann Rosalind Jones notes how service placed women like Whitney in a vulnerable position.[28] Jones outlines how 'Whitney's comments on her life in London emphasize the economic instability of her career as a domestic servant' (23). Jones concentrates on Whitney's poem of advice to her two sisters: 'An order prescribed by Is W. to two of her yonger Sisters servinge in London'. Jones places this poem in the context of the volume as a whole, which details Whitney's disappointment and apparent mistreatment as a servant herself. The poem of advice thus takes on overtones of resentment and unease; as Jones explains: 'What appears at first glance to be a pious rhymed homily advising her sisters on their duties to their employers reveals a darker side of resentment and covert accusation against employers incapable of recognizing the merits—or even the humanity—of their maids' (23).

In the following poem, to another sister, 'Misteris A.B.', Whitney evokes a happier prospect of marriage (as opposed to single service), but ends on an ambivalent note, that on the surface seems to point to marriage as a better career than writing, but might also be read as an indication that domestic 'cares' are equally problematic:

> Good Sister so I you commend,
>    To him that made us all:
> I Know you huswyfery intend,
>    though I to writing fall:
> Wherefore no lenger shall you stay,
> From businesse, that profit may.
>
> Had I a Husband, or a house,
>    and all that longes thereto
> My selfe could frame about to rouse,
>    as other women doo:
> But til some household cares mee tye,
> My bookes and Pen I wyll apply. (D2r)

Whitney continues the influence of *Heroides* in this volume, comparing herself to Dido, and entering into another exchange with male writers over her lot. The volume as a whole concludes with Whitney's most ambitious poem: 'The Will and Testament', couched as a will made when Whitney was forced to leave London. Wendy Wall's incisive discussion of this poem places it in the context of early modern women writers' negotiations with print culture. The lengthy poem

---

[28] Ann Rosalind Jones, 'Maidservants of London', in Susan Frye and Karen Robertson, eds., *Maids and Mistresses, Cousins and Queens: Women's Alliances in Early Modern England* (New York: Oxford University Press, 1999), 21–32.

is a mock will in which Whitney anatomizes London, criticizing its many faults but also memorializing a city which she is forced to leave and which is clearly full of cherished memories. As Wall points out:

> At the end of the text, she takes possession of her circumstances and her body through a staged dispossession, a bestowal of her wealth onto the city of London and her body into the grave. Her spiritually healthy mind reveals itself by articulating its 'will' in the moment of the complete dissolution of the ailing body.[29]

Of course, as Wall goes on to note, Whitney is impersonating an ailing body in order to exploit a genre for what might be called satirical ends. With the 'Will and Testament' poem, Whitney builds upon her previous use of the complaint, and moves into a broad and ambitious mode of social criticism; she creates what Wall calls a 'myth of ownership' as she transforms a position of apparent weakness (rejected, female, unemployed, unmarried) into a position of strength (chronicler of the city, witty, independent, poet). [30] This is not the whole story of the volume, for Whitney is aware of her continuing vulnerability:

> And tell them further, if they wolde,
>    my presence styll have had:
> They should have sought to mend my luck:
>    which ever was too bad. (E8)

*A Pleasant Nosegay* is a quite extraordinary intervention in the almost entirely male world of published Elizabethan poetry. However, while we have no direct evidence for what happened to Whitney after this publication, she virtually fell silent, and certainly published no further volumes under her own name. Some evidence has been presented for her authorship of a poem in an Elizabethan anthology entitled *A Gorgeous Gallery of Gallant Inventions*, edited by Thomas Proctor and printed in 1578 by Richard Jones, who printed Whitney's own volumes.[31] Randall Martin musters a considerable amount of evidence for Whitney's authorship of 'The Lamentation of a gentlewoman upon the death of her late-Deceased Friend, William Gruffith'. Although Martin's evidence for Whitney's authorship is all circumstantial, it is quite compelling. However, while this adds an interesting poem to Whitney's *oeuvre*, it still indicates that she did not have a significant presence after publication of her second volume—from this perspective it is perhaps significant that Whitney did not sign the Gruffith poem, given that poems in her earlier collections are signed over and over again.

While it is not possible to equate book survival rates with popularity, given the ephemeral nature of many volumes (including small quartos like Whitney's), it is worth noting that only one copy survives of each book of poems: *Copy of a Letter*

---

[29] Wendy Wall, 'Isabella Whitney and the Female Legacy', *ELH* 58 (1991), 48–9.
[30] Ibid. 50.
[31] See Randall Martin, 'Isabella Whitney's "Lamentation upon the death of William Gruffith"', *Early Modern Literary Studies*, 3 (1997), 1.

at the Bodleian Library, and *Sweet Nosegay* at the British Library. This underlines Whitney's disappearance from the literary world. As far as I have been able to tell, none of her poems was transmitted in print or manuscript from their publication until the twentieth century, when interest in her was stirred by the feminist revival of attention paid to early women writers. After being anthologized in 1972 in Ann Stanford's *The Women Poets in English*, Whitney's work became accessible in Betty Travitsky's edition of the 'Will and Testament' in 1980 in *English Literary Renaissance*, and the whole of her work appeared in a facsimile edited by Richard Panofsky, published by Scholars' Facsimiles in 1982.[32] From that point on, following early critical work by Betty Travitsky, Panofsky, and Fehrenbach, Whitney assumes some prominence in discussions of early modern women's writing and in anthologies, but her elision from the 1570s to the 1980s neatly illustrates the marginal state of so much early modern women's writing from this period.

## POETRY VISIBLE AND INVISIBLE

Early in the seventeenth century, Aemilia Lanyer offers a parallel example of an ambitious poet who fell silent after a very short time. But in contrast to Whitney's comparative anonymity, enough information about Lanyer exists for Susanne Woods to have written a quite detailed biography. Lanyer's single volume of poetry, *Salve Deus Rex Judaeorum*, was published in 1611. *Salve Deus* can be seen as a bid for patronage by a woman who started out promisingly, but who had fallen on hard times. Lanyer was the daughter of a court musician, Baptista Bassano, and in her youth she moved in court circles, eventually becoming the mistress of Henry Cary, Lord Hunsdon, the Lord Chamberlain of Elizabeth's court.[33] When she became pregnant in 1592 she married Alfonso Lanyer, another court musician. Her hopes for her husband's advancement were disappointed, and after his death in 1613 Lanyer entered into a series of legal disputes over the inheritance of Alfonso's hay and grain patent. Aemilia Lanyer ran a school from 1617 to 1619 and then lived with her son Henry, who continued the family tradition, and was a court flautist. Lanyer published nothing after *Salve Deus*, and died in 1645.

Lanyer's volume of poetry begins with a series of dedications to powerful women: Queen Anne; Princess Elizabeth; Arbella Stuart (King James's cousin,

[32] *ELR* 10 (1980), 76–94; *The Floures of Philosophie by Sir Hugh Plat*, ed. Richard Panofsky (New York: Scholars' Facsimiles, 1982); this contains both *Sweet Nosegay* and *Copy of a Letter*; Whitney is discussed in two Ph.D. dissertations written in the 1930s: Ruth Hughey, 'Cultural Interests of Women in England from 1524 to 1640', Cornell University, 1932; Charlotte Kohler, 'The Elizabethan Woman of Letters', University of Virginia, 1936.

[33] Biographical information is taken from Susanne Woods's excellent study *Lanyer: A Renaissance Woman Poet* (New York: Oxford University Press, 1999).

who had a claim to the throne, but who by 1611 was exiled from the court as punishment for defying James and eloping with William Seymour); Susan Bertie, Countess of Kent (named in this poem as 'Mistris of my youth' (c2), an indication that Lanyer served in the Duchess's household); Mary Sidney, Countess of Pembroke (patron and poet); Lucy Russell, Countess of Bedford (another very powerful patron); Margaret Clifford, Countess of Cumberland; Katherine Howard, Countess of Suffolk; and Anne Clifford, Countess of Dorset. In her dedications, Lanyer appeals to each of these women in a unique fashion, couched to reflect their individual interests and positions in Jacobean society. Indeed, it seems that Lanyer tailored individual presentation copies of *Salve Deus* to suit dynastic and political allegiances, so that, for example, a number of copies do not have the poem to Arbella Stuart. Lanyer makes the most of her personal connections to Susan Bertie and to Margaret and Anne Clifford, who both figure in the country house poem 'To Cookham' which concludes the volume. (Anne Clifford herself will be discussed at length in Chapter 4.) Some of the dedicatory poems, most notably the one to Mary Sidney, are accomplished and original pieces of work.

The religious poem *Salve Deus* itself is an ambitious account of the Passion of Christ, told specifically from a female perspective, and containing the now often extracted and anthologized 'Eve's Apology', which takes men to task for their misogyny, and which specifically offers a defence of women within the Christian religious tradition. The volume concludes with 'The Description of Cookham', a poem celebrating Lanyer's connection with Margaret and Anne Clifford and mourning her exile from their patronage. This country house poem predates Jonson's 'To Penshurst'. It also offers a celebration of Anne Clifford's marriage to Richard Sackville, Earl of Dorset—a marriage that did not fulfil its promise, as Chapter 4 will show.

One can only speculate that *Salve Deus* failed to attract the patronage Lanyer aimed for, and that may well have been why she did not publish anything else. One of the presentation copies found its way from Margaret Clifford to Prince Henry (who was heir to the throne), but there is no record of Lanyer returning to service in the household of either former patron. No references to Lanyer have been traced thus far up until the nineteenth century, when Alexander Dyce wrote to the Oxford scholar and antiquary Philip Bliss, explaining that he owned Prince Henry's copy of *Salve Deus*, and that he 'made up' his imperfect copy by inserting the missing dedications from another incomplete copy.[34] Lanyer, like Whitney, had to wait until the twentieth century for her rediscovery, but that event occurred through a different avenue to the more usual feminist reinvestigation of early women's writing.

On 23 January 1973, the historian A. L. Rowse wrote an article in *The Times* headed: 'Revealed At Last: Shakespeare's Dark Lady', in which he announced

---

[34] Dyce's letter is reproduced in the facsimile of *Salve Deus* introduced by Susanne Woods in The Early Modern Englishwoman facsimile series, Series 1, vol. 10 (Aldershot: Ashgate, 2001).

that the mysterious 'dark lady' of the sonnets was in fact Aemilia Lanyer.[35] Rowse moves from the circumstantial evidence derived from the sonnets and *Love's Labour's Lost* about Shakespeare's 'dark' lover, to fascinating information about Aemilia Lanyer which he discovered in the diary of Simon Forman, an Elizabethan astrologer and medical practitioner. Lanyer first visited Forman in 1597, and Forman's diary provides much of the biographical information we have about her early life, including her affair with Hunsdon, her ambitions for her husband, and her miscarriages.[36] Forman, having cast her horoscope, tried to seduce Lanyer, with only very limited success (she allowed him only to caress and kiss her). Rowse spins from this information a tale he was to elaborate later, with Lanyer as (in his mind) the indisputable candidate for the dark lady he confidently assumes must have been a real person.[37] Rowse reiterated his claim in a revised edition of Shakespeare's sonnets, but then took the significant step of publishing an edition of *Salve Deus* as *The Poems of Shakespeare's Dark Lady* in 1978.[38] While it is understandable that Susanne Woods, in her scholarly edition of Lanyer, complains that 'Rowse's fantasy has tended to obscure Lanyer as a poet',[39] Rowse's decision to edit *Salve Deus* certainly brought Lanyer's poetry from almost total obscurity to the wider attention of scholars and a more general readership. It is true that Rowse uses the edition to reiterate his case for Lanyer's relationship with Shakespeare, but Rowse also describes Lanyer as 'the best woman poet in that age, except for Sidney's sister, the Countess of Pembroke' (p.xii), and compares her favourably to Elizabeth I. The compliments may be somewhat backhanded, but Rowse states that Lanyer 'had natural facility' and was 'exceptional and superior' (ibid.). More importantly, despite all of Rowse's special pleading on behalf of his case for Lanyer as the dark lady, he does allow the reader access to a reasonable text of the entire volume of *Salve Deus*, and that access did bring Lanyer a considerable new readership until it was succeeded by Woods's edition in 1993.

Until the mid-seventeenth century, most women's poetry disappeared after first publication, the exceptions being women of considerable social prominence, such as Queen Elizabeth. A parallel to Lanyer can be traced, following

---

[35] *The Times*, 23 Jan. 1973, 12: the claim was advertised beside the front page title as 'A. L. Rowse Discovers Shakespeare's Dark Lady'; the claim was then expanded in Rowse's revised edition of his biography of Shakespeare: A. L. Rowse, *Shakespeare the Man* (London: Macmillan, 1973), ch. 6. Rowse's claim attracted considerable interest from the academic and non-academic community: Agatha Christie wrote an appreciative letter to *The Times* wondering if Lanyer/the dark lady might not also be the source for Shakespeare's Cleopatra, *The Times*, 3 Feb. 1973, 15.

[36] The visits to Forman were first discussed by Rowse, but see the detailed and more accurate account of them in Woods, *Lanyer*, 19–28.

[37] Rowse's claims are given a typically witty and incisive summing up and dismissal in Samuel Schoenbaum, *Shakespeare and Others* (Washington: Folger Books, 1985), ch. 4.

[38] A. L. Rowse, *Shakespeare's Sonnets: The Problems Solved*, 2nd edn (London: Macmillan, 1973); A. L. Rowse, *The Poems of Shakespeare's Dark Lady* (London: Jonathan Cape, 1978), parenthetical references are to this edition.

[39] *The Poems of Aemilia Lanyer*, ed. Susanne Woods (New York: Oxford University Press, 1993), p. xix.

Rowse's invidious comparison, through the fortunes of Mary Sidney, Countess of Pembroke. Like her niece Mary Wroth, Mary Sidney's literary career was overshadowed by that of her famous brother Philip Sidney. In Mary Sidney's case, not only did she see her task as the preservation and dissemination of her version of her brother's literary legacy (as opposed to that promulgated by a male friend like Fulke Greville), but her own writing (in contrast to Wroth's), was in some ways based upon a series of homages to Philip.[40] This is most evident in Mary Sidney's metrical versions of the Psalms, which literally involved editing and continuing Philip's efforts, which had ended with Psalm 43, so that Mary produced versions of Psalms 44 through to 150. As well as a few original poems, Mary Sidney produced three major translations: of Robert Garnier's 1585 play *Marc Antoine* as *Antonius* (about 1590); of Philippe de Mornay's *Excellent discourse de la vie et de la mort* (1576); and of Petrarch's *Trionfo della morte* (1348). De Mornay's work had a particular connection to Philip Sidney: he was a Huguenot who, like Philip, strongly opposed Elizabeth's proposed marriage to the Catholic duc d'Anjou (Philip's written opposition led to his exile from court).

This is not to say that Mary Sidney's writing should be seen simply in relation to her brother, but her brother's legacy enabled Mary to assume a position as writer/translator that was already imbued with the gravity that increased as Philip became elevated posthumously into the role of martyr for the Protestant cause. This aspect of Mary Sidney's writing has been most vividly conveyed by the title of Margaret P. Hannay's 1990 biography of her: *Philip's Phoenix*.[41] One also needs to see Mary Sidney's writing as political, in so far as she helps to continue the Protestant lobbying of the family as a whole. As Hannay points out, Mary's literary activity was at its height from 1588 until her husband's death in 1601; when she lost her role as Countess of Pembroke (the estate and title being inherited by Mary Talbot, her daughter-in-law), her activities as writer, editor, and patron diminished.[42]

As Mary Sidney's editors note, the decision to publish Philip's works was a significant moment in the shift from a manuscript to a print culture, although recent work on manuscript transmission has emphasized that the two forms of 'publication' existed side by side in the seventeenth century.[43] Mary's publication of her own work illustrates exactly this situation: she put de Mornay's *Discourse*

[40] The most sophisticated examination of the interconnections between the Sidney family remains, in my view, Mary Ellen Lamb, *Gender and Authorship in the Sidney Circle* (Madison: University of Wisconsin Press, 1990), but see also Gary Waller, *The Sidney Family Romance: Mary Wroth, William Herbert, and the Early Modern Construction of Gender* (Detroit: Wayne State University Press, 1993).

[41] Margaret P. Hannay, *Philip's Phoenix: Mary Sidney, Countess of Pembroke* (New York: Oxford University Press, 1990).

[42] Ibid., pp. x–xi.

[43] *The Collected Works of Mary Sidney Herbert*, ed. Margaret P. Hannay *et al.* (Oxford: Clarendon Press, 1998), i. 48; on this topic see esp. Harold Love, *Scribal Publication in Seventeenth-Century England* (Oxford: Clarendon Press, 1993) and Arthur Marotti, *Manuscript, Print and the English Renaissance Lyric* (Ithaca, NY: Cornell University Press, 1995).

and *Antonius* into print in 1592, in a volume published by William Ponsonby, the printer of both Fulke Greville's 1590 edition of *Arcadia*, and of Mary Sidney's radically different 1593 edition of *Arcadia*. *Antonius* was reprinted by Ponsonby on its own in 1595; the *Discourse* on its own in 1600. Taken together with the 1593 *Arcadia*, the 1592 printing of Mary Sidney's two translations shows her clear intention to link her literary endeavours with those of her brother. Mary's own volume is not as elaborate as the 1593 *Arcadia*, but it is substantial and asks to be taken together with Philip's work, especially when one considers that the *Arcadia*'s full title (on the title page of both 1590 and 1593) is *The Countess of Pembroke's Arcadia*. The title page of the *Discourse* and *Antonius* again uses Mary Sidney's aristocratic title: 'done in English by the Countesse of Pembroke'. Mary Sidney emphasizes her rank and status as part of the general claim for the family's position (given that they were not particularly in favour with the Queen in the early 1590s).

While Sidney put her translations of the *Discourse* and *Antonius* into print, her continuing work on metrical versions of the psalms circulated in manuscript.[44] The distinction is perhaps due to the more personal nature of the Sidney Psalter—while the psalms circulated in a variety of manuscript versions, the version now entitled Manuscript J preserves a presentation version (probably for the Queen) with title page and preliminary matter, including Mary's poem in commemoration of her brother 'To the Angell spirit'.[45] Mary offers up her translations as part of the memorializing of her brother, but also in a gesture which implies that she has literally been imbued with his literary spirit, as the ink/blood passes from him to her:

> Immortal Monuments of thy faire fame,
> 　　though not compleat, nor in the reach of thought. . . .
> Yet there will live thy ever praised name.
>
> To which theise dearest offrings of my hart
> 　　dissolv'd to Inke, while penns impressions move
> 　　the bleeding veines of never dying love:
> I render here: these wounding lynes of smart
> 　　sadd Characters indeed of simple love. (i. 112)

Given the status of Mary Sidney, both in her own right, and as keeper of the Philip Sidney flame, it is not surprising that her writing circulated widely from the time of composition. Two powerful interpretations of Mary Sidney's literary

---

[44] The psalm manuscripts are described in detail in *Works*, ii. 308–57, but it is also worth noting H. R. Woudhuysen's magisterial account of the manuscript circulation of Philip Sidney's works, which more peripherally considers Mary Sidney: *Sir Philip Sidney and the Circulation of Manuscripts 1558–1640* (Oxford: Clarendon Press, 1996).

[45] My information on the extremely complex relationship of the manuscripts of the psalms stems from *Collected Works*, ii. 308–36.

activities in the context of early modern women's writing have been advanced by Wendy Wall and by Jonathan Goldberg. Wall, in her influential book *The Imprint of Gender*, sets Sidney against attempts by women writers to legitimate their right to enter the masculine world of letters—a world haunted, when publication was involved, by male authors' fears of 'weakness' associated with femininity.[46] In Wall's terms, Sidney's 'authorizing' strategy involved both the production of religious verse, and the use of her brother's reputation to justify her writing.[47] While this is, as I have been arguing, clearly part of Sidney's self-presentation, Wall underestimates the significance of the combination of print and manuscript publication on Sidney's part, even if the psalms did become the most acclaimed part of her literary output. At the same time, Wall pushes the apparent divide between manuscript and print, original composition and translation, religious and secular writing, into a more rigid dichotomy than actually existed. It is certainly true that many commentators at the time wanted to place women on the 'safe' side of this divide: to see them as modest translators, writers of religious works, which circulated 'privately'. As Wall explains, we need to avoid a modern misinterpretation of this situation: manuscripts (especially in a case like the Sidney psalms) were a form of publication which could circulate widely; as we have already seen, such religious writing was far from 'safe', but had an active political component; and translation needs to be seen as a much more active and engaged form of literary production than it may appear through the distorting lens of Romantic views on authorship. Wall makes these points as part of her overall analysis of how different early modern women negotiated their way into authorship.

Some of these points also form part of Jonathan Goldberg's provocative view of Mary Sidney. As I have already noted in the Introduction to this book, Goldberg, in *Desiring Women Writing*, offers what he sees as a corrective to the restrictive scholarly account of early modern women writers—an account which, in his argument, places them in anachronistic categories that repress in particular their manifestation of desire.[48] Goldberg specifically offers a salutary account of translation in general, and of early modern women as translators, which turns on its head the notion of translation as a 'secondary' activity in the Renaissance. In a typical move, taking Mary Sidney's translation of Petrarch as his example, Goldberg reads a transgressive desire back into this translation that scholars praise for its literalness, emphasizing throughout that Sidney resists the rather repressive notion that conservative modern ideas of translation impose upon her. Goldberg counters these with a Derridean undoing of the hierarchy behind original/translation, just as he undoes the notion of Mary Sidney as derivative, pious, and dutiful.

[46] Wendy Wall, *The Imprint of Gender* (Ithaca, NY: Cornell University Press, 1993), 310–19.
[47] Ibid. 311.
[48] Jonathan Goldberg, *Desiring Women Writing: English Renaissance Examples* (Stanford, Calif.: Stanford University Press, 1997); see the discussion in the Introduction, above.

In the seventeenth century responses to Mary Sidney's writing can be seen to complement these more radical interpretations of her work by Wall and Goldberg. As a patron, she attracted praise from clients and potential clients which often included reference to her own literary output. Aemilia Lanyer's dedicatory poem praises 'Those holy sonnets', annotated as 'The Psalms writen newly by the Countess Dowager of Pembroke'.[49] Most notably, Donne in his poem 'Upon the translation of the Psalmes by Sir Philip Sidney, and the Countesse of Pembroke his Sister', famously characterized brother and sister as 'this *Moses* and this *Miriam*', who 'tell us *why*, and teach us *how* to sing', concluding: 'We thy Sydnean Psalmes shall celebrate'.[50] Mary Sidney's image became inextricably linked with the psalms, both through praise from clients or would-be clients like Donne, Jonson, or Daniel, and also through her own careful construction of her public reception. This is most famously illustrated in the van de Passe engraving, done in 1618, showing Sidney holding a volume clearly labelled 'Davids psalmes'—an engraving that was for public sale.[51]

The seventeen extant manuscripts of the psalms point to their wide dissemination during the seventeenth century. As Sidney's editors point out, apart from early manuscripts registering Mary Sidney's extensive process of revision, later manuscripts record their owners' emendations, and other evidence of their use, including annotations pointing to their use in worship.[52] Sir John Harington owned two manuscripts, and also sent a selection of psalms and Sidney's Petrarch translation to Lucy Harington, Countess of Bedford.[53] In due course, eight of the psalms in Harington's possession were published in *Nugae Antiquae*, but appearances in print were extremely rare until the nineteenth century, so that the psalms remained part of manuscript rather than print culture for the entire seventeenth and much of the eighteenth century.[54]

That Mary Sidney's achievements remained well recognized is attested to by Ballard's account of her. He notes that 'her genius inclined her to poetry', and then offers a careful defence of her learning against those who argued that she had no Hebrew and accordingly required assistance with her translations.[55] Ballard's special pleading reflects his own interest in women of learning; in fact, Sidney relied, not on Hebrew, but on what her editors term 'standard Protestant texts': the Coverdale Psalter, Geneva Bible, and commentaries of Calvin and Beze.[56] Ballard notes the publication of the *Discourse* and *Antonius* but typically says little about the poetry itself.

Walpole includes 'A Dialogue Between Two Shepherds' and a chorus from *Antonius* in his *Catalogue*, affording Sidney less space, but more praise, than Elizabeth's

[49] Lanyer, *Poems*, 27.

[50] John Donne, *Complete English Poems*, ed. C. A. Patrides, rev. Hamilton (London: Everyman, 1996), 368–9.

[51] Reproduced in Hannay, *Philip's Phoenix*, 59; see her account on 193.

[52] See *Works*, 308–56.          [53] Hannay, *Philip's Phoenix*, 107.

[54] For details of the publication of *Nugae Antiquae* see the earlier discussion in this chapter.

[55] Ballard, *Memories* 251–2.          [56] *Works*, ii. 11.

literary endeavours receive.[57] Walpole describes the extract from *Antonius* as a 'specimen of her ladyship's polished elegance in lyrical versification'.[58]

Interest in the psalms increased, although intermittently, after their publication in 1823 in a volume generated by the enthusiasm of Henry Cotton, a fellow of Christ Church, Oxford, and edited by S. W. Singer.[59] This volume is noted by Dyce, who praises the 'elegant specimens' of Mary Sidney's poetry, and prints the pastoral dialogue she wrote for a planned visit of the queen to Wilton in 1599, and a chorus from *Antonius*.[60] In 1877 John Ruskin published a remarkable, idiosyncratic edition of the Sidney psalter as the second volume of his *Bibliotheca Pastorum*. He entitled the edition *Rock Honeycomb*, and in his preface muses about the simple musical pleasures of the Coniston Band, and advances the cause of the musical psalms as a 'folk' counter to 'our luxurious art of the oratorio' (106).[61] Typically, Ruskin claims that 'if ever Old England again becomes Merry England, the first use she will make of her joyful lips, will be to sing psalms' (106–7). Psalm singing forms part of Ruskin's elaborate educational programme. Unfortunately, in this edition Ruskin does not discuss Mary Sidney's hand in the psalter, although he does recognize her contribution.[62]

At the beginning of the twentieth century the revival of interest in Philip Sidney was spurred by the discovery of manuscripts of the original 'Old' *Arcadia*, and the complete edition of his *Works* edited by Albert Feuillerat from 1912 to 1926. Mary Sidney did not enjoy the same revival of interest. William Ringler's scholarly and influential edition of Philip Sidney's poetry prints only the first forty-three psalms in texts which strive to eliminate Mary Sidney's alterations and emendations.[63] On the other hand, the complete psalms were edited by John Rathmell and published a year after Ringler, leading to a gradual rise of interest in the psalms themselves, which fed into work done on Mary Sidney by Gary Waller, who produced a critical biography and an edition of her work in the late 1970s.[64] Mary Sidney demonstrates how what might be called the status of women writers, especially in the period before the 1650s, had a direct impact on just how visible they remained in succeeding centuries. Some of the strength of

[57] Walpole, *Catalogue*, ii. 199–207; see the discussion of his account of Elizabeth above.

[58] Ibid. 206.

[59] *Psalmes of David*, ed. Samuel W. Singer (London: Chiswick Press, 1823); Cotton wrote about the psalms in the *Christian Remembrancer*, 3 (June 1821).

[60] Alexander Dyce, *Specimens of British Poetesses* (1825), 32–9.

[61] References are to *The Works of John Ruskin*, ed. E. T. Cook and Alexander Wedderburn (London: George Allen, 1907), vol. xxxi.

[62] The reference to Mary Sidney comes in *Fors Clavigera*, rather than in *Rock Honeycomb*; ibid., vol. xxv.

[63] *The Poems of Sir Philip Sidney*, ed. W. A. Ringer (Oxford: Clarendon Press, 1962); it was of course perfectly natural that Ringler should exclude Mary Sidney's efforts from an edition of her brother's poetry.

[64] J. Rathmell, ed., *Psalms of Sir Philip Sidney and the Countess of Pembroke* (NY: New York University Press, 1963); Gary Waller, *Mary Sidney, Countess of Pembroke* (Salzburg: Institut für Anglistik & Amerikanistik, 1979); Gary Waller, ed., *The Triumph of Death* (Salzburg: Institut für Anglistik, 1977).

what might be called the Sidneian tradition of the woman writer can be seen in the work of Mary Wroth, who is discussed in detail in the next chapter. While many other women wrote poetry in the first half of the seventeenth century, some of which was printed, and much of which circulated in manuscript, their visibility remained low. However, I want to end this chapter with a brief consideration of Anne Bradstreet, who illustrates how special circumstances can run counter to this general pattern.

## ANNE BRADSTREET: AMERICA'S TENTH MUSE

Bradstreet's unique position in the history of early modern women's writing can be illustrated by my hesitation in deciding just how much information to provide about her. For American readers of this book, Bradstreet, their first published poet, is likely to be seen as a canonical author with considerable exposure to a wide range of readers (including schoolchildren), whereas for my other readers she is unlikely to be particularly well known. Anne Bradstreet and her husband Simon emigrated to America with Anne's family in 1630.[65] Both Anne's father Thomas Dudley and her husband served as governors of the colony of Massachusetts. Anne Bradstreet wrote poetry from at least the late 1630s, poetry which evidently circulated amongst friends and relatives until 1647, when John Woodbridge, her brother-in-law, took a manuscript to England and had it printed as *The Tenth Muse* by Stephen Bowtell in 1650.[66] In a preface to the 'Kind Reader', Woodbridge explains that *The Tenth Muse* was published without Bradstreet's knowledge: 'I have presumed to bring to publick view what she resolved should never in such a manner see the Sun' (526). While this was a common disingenuous avowal by early modern authors, in Bradstreet's case it seems genuine, as in a later poem, 'The Author to Her Book', she laments that her manuscript was 'snatcht from thence by friends, less wise then true | Who thee abroad, expos'd to publick view' (177). But at the same time Bradstreet does claim ownership of her volume, and only regrets that she did not have the chance to polish it further before its appearance—a lack she has now made good (this poem appeared in the posthumous 1678 volume *Several Poems*):

> Thy Visage was so irksome in my sight;
> Yet being mine own, at length affection would
> Thy blemishes amend, if so I could (178)

All the *Tenth Muse* poems that appear in *Several Poems*, which was published in Boston, were substantially revised, although there is no direct evidence to

    [65] Biographical information stems from Elizabeth Wade White, *Anne Bradstreet* (New York: Oxford University Press, 1971).
    [66] Bibliographical information and quotations are from *The Complete Works of Anne Bradstreet*, ed. Joseph McElrath and Allan Robb (Boston: Twayne, 1981).

indicate that Bradstreet herself was responsible for the revisions.[67] While the Bradstreet hailed by authors such as Adrienne Rich or John Berryman is the author of the intimate and personal poems which appeared first in *Several Poems*, the poetry of *The Tenth Muse* is, in contrast, ambitious, public, political poetry.[68] The volume as printed by John Woodbridge begins with a series of commendatory verses from Woodbridge himself, and a number of other friends and relations. (The effect is not unlike that of Margaret Cavendish's 1653 *Poems and Fancies*, discussed below in Chapter 6, although *The Tenth Muse* is a more modest volume, in every way.) Much of *The Tenth Muse* consists of Bradstreet's long, ambitious quarternion series: an account of the four elements, four humours, four ages of man, four seasons, and the four monarchies (the ancient monarchies of Assyria, Persia, Greece, and Rome). While much of this poetry is conventional, it begins with a combative and much-quoted prologue proclaiming Bradstreet's right to insinuate herself into the ranks of poets:

> I am obnoxious to each carping tongue,
> Who says, my hand a needle better fits,
> A Poets Pen, all scorne, I should thus wrong;
> For such despight they cast on female wits:
> If what I doe prove well it wo'nt advance,
> They'l say its stolne, or else, it was by chance. (7)

The quarternions themselves may be conventional in subject matter, but they represent what might be seen as an ambit claim by Bradstreet for an overarching authority: a demonstration of scholarly competence. This is accentuated by the overtly political poetry which follows. Recently, Patricia Pender has stressed the political valencies of 'A Dialogue between Old England and New', the poem which immediately follows the quarternions, as a way of undermining the tendency amongst critics to assert that the poetry of *The Tenth Muse* is sterile, and also unattached to the issues of gender which render the later poems so interesting to modern readers.[69] This poem, dated 1642, is both an analysis of the beginnings of the Civil War (seen very much in religious terms, as one might expect), and an establishment of Bradstreet's interest in the political implications of maternity—a theme that Pender sees as carried on into Bradstreet's homage to Queen Elizabeth. Bradstreet's rather belated elegies for Philip Sidney, Du Bartas,

---

[67] While logic might seem to indicate that, given what Bradstreet says in 'The Author to Her Book', she was responsible for the emendations in *Several Poems*, Joseph McElrath argues strongly that authorial revision cannot be assumed: see his 'The Text of Anne Bradstreet: Biographical and Critical Consequences', *Seventeenth Century News* (Summer 1976).

[68] See Adrienne Rich's preface to Jeannine Hensley's edition, *The Works of Anne Bradstreet* (Cambridge, Mass.: Harvard University Press, 1967); John Berryman, 'Homage to Mistress Bradstreet' (1956).

[69] Patricia Pender, 'Disciplining the Imperial Mother: Anne Bradstreet's "A Dialogue Between Old England and New"', in Jo Wallwork and Paul Salzman, eds., *Women Writing 1550–1750* (Bundoora: Meridian, 2001), 115–31.

and Elizabeth align her with the Protestant celebration of Sidney and Elizabeth in particular. The celebration of Sidney and Elizabeth enables Bradstreet to join with many others in mounting a nostalgic critique of the reign of Charles I, seeing it in particular as demonstrating a decline from a purer religious spirit.

While it is difficult to determine the readership for *The Tenth Muse*, it was evidently a success, particularly with those who admired Bradstreet as an exemplary woman writer.[70] This is most notable in Bathsua Makin's acknowledgement of her in *An Essay to Revive the Antient Education of Gentlewomen* (1673), a justification for the education of women which relies on lists of women who have excelled in a variety of areas of learning. Women poets form an important category for Makin, and there Bradstreet is duly praised: 'How Excellent a poet Mrs. *Bradstreet* is, (now in *America*) her Works do testify' (20). In her account of early responses to Bradstreet, Pattie Cowell notes that *The Tenth Muse* was listed in *London's Catalogue of the Most Vendible Books in England* (1658), and that it was also noted as 'not yet extinct' in Edward Phillips's *Theatrum Poetarum* (1674).[71] But Bradstreet's future, as Makin noted, did indeed lie in America, beginning with the publication of an expanded and revised edition of *The Tenth Muse* in Boston in 1678 as *Several Poems Compiled with Great variety of Wit and Learning, full of delight*. This edition was prefaced by an elegy by John Norton (Bradstreet died in 1672), and a new commendatory poem by John Rogers, Bradstreet's nephew, who became President of Harvard. This volume printed eighteen new poems, most of them the more personal lyrics about her husband and children that have become Bradstreet's most admired form of poetry. From this point on, Bradstreet assumed a position within American literature that no English woman from the same period achieved. Puritan New England celebrated Bradstreet, starting with Cotton Mather, who praised her in his *Magnalia Christi Americana* (1702), noting 'the Fame with which the Poems of one descended from him [i.e. from Bradstreet's father] have been Celebrated in both Englands', and stating that the 'Poems, diverse times Printed, have afforded a grateful Entertainment unto the Ingenious, and a Monument for her Memory beyond the Stateliest Marbles'.[72] *Several Poems* was the only book of poetry recorded as being in Jonathan Edwards's library.[73] Bradstreet's influence has been traced through a number of eighteenth-century American poets and, more significantly, *Several Poems* itself was reprinted in 1758.[74] Bradstreet's reputation remained strong in the nineteenth century, culminating in an impressive edition of her poetry by John Harvard Ellis in 1867 with an appreciative introduction which initiates the long-standing preference

---

[70] For a valuable account of Bradstreet's early reputation see Pattie Cowell, 'The Early Distribution of Anne Bradstreet's Poems', in Pattie Cowell and Ann Stanford, eds., *Critical Essays on Anne Bradstreet* (Boston: G. K. Hall, 1983), 270–9.

[71] Cowell, 'Distribution', 272.

[72] Cotton Mather, *Magnalia Christi Americana* (1702), ed. Kenneth B. Murdock (Cambridge Mass.: Belknap Press, 1977), book 2, 233

[73] Cowell, 'Distribution', 273.          [74] Cowell and Stanford, *Critical Essays*, xx–xxi.

for the later, personal poems over the ambitious quarternions.[75] A modernized edition appeared in 1897, albeit with a fairly negative introduction by Charles Eliot Norton.[76] While interest in Bradstreet accelerated after Adrienne Rich's appreciation, which prefaced Jeannine Hensley's 1967 edition, her reputation was already securely established earlier in the twentieth century. Ellis's edition was reprinted in 1932, and Bradstreet was anthologized extensively, including in Conrad Aiken's *American Poetry* and, perhaps most significantly, in F. O. Mathieson's 1950 *Oxford Book of American Verse*.[77]

While it is clearly wise to avoid making too many generalizations about the transmission of women's poetry written from the 1550s to the 1650s, it is at least possible to distinguish between the interest in the work of women of high rank, like Queen Elizabeth or Mary Sidney, and women like Isabella Whitney or Aemilia Lanyer, whose poetry was evidently seen by their contemporaries as ephemeral. I have, in my consideration of Anne Bradstreet, glanced ahead to the middle of the seventeenth century, when this situation changed, and I will return to this moment in history in a later chapter. But at this point I want to turn to the uneven fortunes of Mary Wroth, whose ambitious literary projects were not spared from criticism by her status as a scion of the Sidney family.

[75] John Harvard Ellis, ed., *The Works of Anne Bradstreet in Prose and Verse* (Charleston, SC: Abram E. Cutter, 1867).

[76] Frank E. Hopkins, ed., *The Poems of Mrs Anne Bradstreet* (New York: Duodecimos, 1897).

[77] Mathieson's anthology begins with six Bradstreet poems, although Mathiesson states that the early poetry is 'unreadable'; *The Oxford Book of American Verse* (Oxford: Oxford University Press, 1950), preface.

# 3

# Mary Wroth: From Obscurity
# to Canonization

## WRITING BACK

The story of Mary Wroth's dramatic increase in visibility over last two decades exemplifies the changes that have taken place in the status of early modern women's writing. At the same time, the attention paid to Wroth does also serve to establish a certain canon of early modern women's writing—a canon which is itself being challenged by many scholars working in the field. Wroth exemplifies aristocratic, literary writing, in distinction to a large number of early modern women who wrote in non-literary forms and who (in increasing numbers in the seventeenth century) came from more humble backgrounds. I will argue in the third part of this chapter that it is also possible to read Wroth's great prose romance, *The Countess of Montgomery's Urania*, as itself enacting a drama of canonization, as well as a fantasy of reinstatement after exile.

Wroth was born into a pre-eminent literary family; as noted in the previous chapter, her uncle, Philip Sidney, was by the early seventeenth century viewed as the archetypal Elizabethan gentleman-poet. Wroth's aunt, Mary Sidney, was a writer and translator and Wroth's father, Robert Sidney, wrote poetry. These members of the Sidney family were engaged in a constant literary dialogue with each other, aptly detailed by Mary Beth Rose as involving a dynamic exchange that crossed generations and that, to at least some degree, empowered the female members of the family in their literary endeavours.[1] Mary Wroth was the eldest daughter of Robert Sidney (Philip's brother) and Barbara Gamage. She was born on 18 October, and although the year of her birth is uncertain, it was probably 1586, in which case she was born the day after Philip died at Zutphen.[2] Given that Wroth incorporated much of her family history into *Urania* and her pastoral play *Love's Victory*, it is worth noting here her large number of brothers and

---

[1] See Mary Ellen Lamb, *Gender and Authorship in the Sidney Circle* (Madison: University of Wisconsin Press, 1990), *passim*.

[2] The best biographical account remains *The Poems of Lady Mary Wroth*, ed. Josephine Roberts (Baton Rouge: Louisiana State University Press, 1983), 3–40; more detailed information about Wroth's relationship with William Herbert is contained in Gary Waller, *The Sidney Family Romance* (Detroit: Wayne State University Press, 1993).

sisters, many of whom appear in *Urania* in suitably disguised form: Katherine, William, Elizabeth, Philip (a girl named after her uncle and sometimes referred to as Philippa by later commentators), Robert, Bridget, Alice, Barbara, and Vere.

During Wroth's childhood, Robert Sidney was governor of Flushing, and she spent some time there with her family, although much of her childhood was spent at the Sidney seat of Penshurst. When he was back in England, Robert Sidney became a noted literary patron, as was his sister Mary Sidney, Countess of Pembroke. Both were also writers, although Mary Sidney's output was considerably greater than Robert's, at least judging by what survives from him (a sequence of poems and songs and an elegy).[3]

In 1604 Mary married Sir Robert Wroth. In contrast to the cultured and literary members of the Sidney family, Wroth seems to have had no cultural inclinations, and was renowned instead for his passion for hunting, which endeared him to King James, who appointed him his Riding Forester. As was so often the case with aristocratic allegiances, Mary was married to Robert Wroth for what we might call pragmatic reasons. It is almost certain that at the time of her marriage she was in love with her first cousin, William Herbert, the son of Mary Sidney, Countess of Pembroke. William, who figures in *Urania* as the womanizing and unsteady hero Amphilanthus, had been embroiled in a sexual scandal in 1600–1 which left Mary Fitton, the object of his attentions, pregnant, and Pembroke, who confessed to being the father, imprisoned. He only escaped further punishment because the baby died at birth. Having quarrelled with his mother at around the same time, William, who had become Earl of Pembroke in 1601 following the death of his father, arranged a marriage for himself with Mary Talbot—a marriage which was generally a very unhappy one. This unhappiness parallels Mary Wroth's, as her marriage was in trouble virtually from the beginning. Perhaps the most famous reference to this is Ben Jonson's aside to Drummond: 'my lady wroth is unworthily married on a Jealous husband'.[4] During the early years of her marriage, Mary Wroth was an active figure in the court, taking the role of Baryte in Jonson's *Masque of Blackness* (masques play a significant role in the court world depicted in *Urania*). Jonson dedicated *The Alchemist* to Mary, and he praised her poetry in a sonnet addressed to her in words which indicate that he transcribed a number of her poems in manuscript ('since I exscribe your Sonnets, [I] am become | A better lover, and much better Poet').[5]

Robert Wroth died in 1614, leaving Mary in debt, and with a son who was born shortly before her husband died (there has been some speculation about the fact that Wroth only became pregnant after she had been married for ten years). The son died at the age of 2, leaving Wroth with further debts and without her

---

[3] For Mary Sidney, see Ch. 2 above, and Ch. 6 below; for Robert's poetry, see *The Poems of Robert Sidney*, ed. P. J.Croft (Oxford: Clarendon Press, 1984).

[4] *Works of Ben Jonson*, ed. C. H. Herford and P. and E. Simpson (Oxford: Clarendon Press, 1925), i. 142.

[5] Ibid., viii. 82.

husband's estate, which passed to his uncle. At some point after this, Wroth had (or perhaps resumed) a relationship with William Herbert which led to the birth of two children, a daughter named Katherine and a son named William; details are unclear, but they were probably born some time between 1618 and 1621. Little is known about Wroth after the publication of *Urania* in 1621; she seems to have remained in straitened financial circumstances, and probably died around 1650.

Wroth's poems circulated in manuscript before eventually being published as part of *Urania*. While they cannot be dated with complete accuracy, it is clear that her poems were circulating early in the century; in 1613 Joshua Sylvester referred to Wroth in a poem which points to her continuation of her uncle Philip's literary legacy: 'In whom, her Uncle's noble Veine renewes'.[6] Wroth's poems exist in a single surviving autograph manuscript that evidently preceded their publication in 1621.[7] Wroth's editor, Josephine Roberts, has pointed out that the many differences between the manuscript poems and the versions appended to *Urania* indicate that the manuscript did not serve as a copy-text for the printed poems. This would also indicate that other manuscripts were in circulation. Given the nature of the surviving manuscript (beautifully written in Wroth's italic hand), it may have been a presentation manuscript.

Much has been written about the circumstances surrounding the publication in 1621 of Wroth's prose romance *The Countess of Montgomery's Urania*. The publication represents a self-conscious positioning of Wroth alongside her uncle Philip Sidney, in contrast to the literary activities of her aunt, which mainly occurred through scribal publication, rather than in print. Given that Wroth's poetry had been in some circulation, however limited, it is possible to see the publication of *Urania* as the next step in her sense of herself as a literary heir. When placed beside Philip Sidney's printed texts, *Urania* seems to have been designed to evoke an immediate comparison. There were editions of Sidney's *Arcadia* in 1590, 1593, 1599, 1605, 1613, and 1621.[8] These folios generally included Sidney's poetry as well as the *Arcadia*. They were, after 1593, prefaced by Sidney's dedication to his sister (though this dedication was actually written to accompany the *Old Arcadia*), and the brief preface of Hugh Sandford, which had been written for the emended 1593 *Arcadia*, explaining how this is the text authorized by Mary Sidney (as opposed to the version of the *New Arcadia* published in 1590 by Sidney's friend Fulke Greville). *Urania* echoes *Arcadia*'s title, and even more pointedly alludes to Mary Wroth's lineage: 'The Countesse of Montgomeries Urania. Written by the right honorable the Lady Mary Wroth. Daughter to the right Noble Robert Earle of Leicester. And Neece to the ever famous, and renowned Sr Philips Sidney knight. And to the most excellent Lady Mary Countess of Pembroke late deceased'. *Urania* begins on signature B1, starting immediately with the narrative of Book

---

[6] Quoted in *Poems*, ed. Roberts, 19.      [7] See ibid. 61–72.

[8] See Bent Juel-Jensen, 'Sir Philip Sidney . . . A Check-List of Early Editions', in Dennis Kay, ed., *Sir Philip Sidney* (Oxford: Clarendon Press, 1987), 290–314.

One, which seems to indicate that some prefatory matter was intended but did not reach the printer. This does not point to unauthorized publication, given that, as we will see shortly, Wroth's placatory letter to Buckingham disingenuously claims that she never intended to have the book published, but at the same time notes that she had presented Buckingham with a copy. I have argued elsewhere that the publication of *Urania* can be seen as Wroth's attempt to reinstate herself at the centre of the court activity from which she had been removed, perhaps because of her liaison with William Herbert, but also because, following the death of Queen Anne in 1619, women were further alienated from court life (Wroth's father had been Anne's Lord Chamberlain). [9]

It is impossible to know if Wroth was surprised that *Urania* caused a scandal. Her disguised depiction of a number of recognizable people and events was far removed from Philip Sidney's mild personal allusions in *Arcadia*. The detail of some of the stories recounted points to a deliberate re-engagement with the court; these stories may not have been intended to be provocative, but they engage directly with events that were fresh in people's memories. Whatever Wroth's intentions, the most detailed literary (and personal) criticism attracted by her work prior to the twentieth century came from the irascible Edward Denny. Denny was a notable figure in King James's court, whose daughter, Honora, married James's favourite James Hay in 1607 in an elaborate ceremony (Hay became renowned for his extravagant entertainments). This was yet another troubled Jacobean marriage, and in *Urania* it is depicted in some detail, under disguised names (Hay is Sirelius). Wroth recounts Honora's adultery and Denny's violent response, in which he sided with his son-in-law and physically attacked his daughter.[10] Wroth provoked a response from Denny, but it was one which pointed either to a more widespread sense that *Urania* was a *roman à clef* packed with such scandals, or perhaps the fierce nature of Denny's response provoked interested bystanders into a sense that this was a controversial literary event. Denny wrote a vitriolic poem which circulated in manuscript entitled 'To Pamphilia from the father-in-law of Seralius [*sic*]' (Pamphilia is the most significant of Wroth's self-depictions within *Urania*). Two other copies of the poem in seventeenth-century commonplace books have an alternative title which cuts straight past the disguised names: 'To the Lady mary Wroth for writeing the Countes of Montgomeryes Urania'.[11] These copies also point to the circulation of Denny's

[9] See Paul Salzman, *Literary Culture in Jacobean England: Reading 1621* (Houndmills: Palgrave/Macmillan, 2002), 65–75; see also Rosalind Smith's extremely illuminating argument that Wroth's sonnet sequence, together with the publication of *Urania*, has to be seen in relation to her political position, especially vis-à-vis the revival of Spenserian poetry (with a political edge): Rosalind Smith, 'Lady Mary Wroth's *Pamphilia to Amphilanthus*: The Politics of Withdrawal', *ELR* 30 (2000).

[10] For the story in *Urania*, see Mary Wroth, *The First Part of the Countess of Montgomery's Urania*, ed. Josephine Roberts (Binghampton: Medieval and Renaissance Texts and Studies, 1995), 515–16.

[11] *Poems*, ed. Roberts, 33; the poems: ibid. 32–5, the correspondence: ibid. 237–41.

poem and Wroth's reply, and they indicate that the response to *Urania* and the controversy surrounding it was, if not exactly widespread, certainly more far-reaching than Denny alone. This is underlined by the remarks made by the newsletter-writer John Chamberlain. He enclosed Denny's poem in one of his letters to Dudley Carleton, writing:

The other paper are certain bitter verses of the Lord Dennies upon the Lady Marie Wroth, for that in her booke of Urania she doth palpablie and grossely play upon him and his late daughter the Lady Hayes, besides many others she makes bold with, and they say takes great libertie or rather licence to traduce whom she please, and thincks she daunces in a net: I have seen an answer of hers to these rimes, but I thought yt not worth the writing out.[12]

It would be helpful to know who 'they' might be, but Chamberlain, with his usual ear to the ground, reports both a general interest in the romance, and enough circulation of Denny's response to provide him with a copy of both poems.

Denny's poem begins by calling Wroth a 'Hermaphrodite in show, in deed a monster'.[13] The alignment of Wroth's unnaturalness as woman and as writer continues throughout the poem, which sees *Urania* as 'a foole which like the damme doth look'. Denny uses a metaphor that suggests sexual licence on Wroth's part ('common oysters such as thine gape wide | And take in pearls or worse at every tide'), but interestingly he does not point to Wroth's own scandalous affair with Herbert, either because he does not know about it, or because, given Herbert's powerful position, he is fearful of raising it. The poem ends with a couplet quoted by Margaret Cavendish later in the century as an example of the way men warn women against writing: 'Work o th'Workes leave idle bookes alone | For wise and worthyer women have writte none'.[14]

Wroth boldly tackled this response to her work head on. She wrote a verse reply to Denny which turns his poem on its head, enclosing it in an aggressive letter which threatens that she could take further action against him. Wroth makes much of Denny's hot-headedness (in keeping with the depiction of him in *Urania*): 'raging makes you hott' (34). She describes *Urania* as 'a harmless booke', and astutely questions Denny's inability to respond with dignity: 'Men truly noble fear no touch of blood' (ibid.). In her accompanying letter, Wroth protests, 'Nor did I ever intend one word of that book to his Lordships person or disgrace' (237). Denny's reply to this letter points out the absurdity of disclaiming the identifications of Sirelius and Pamphilia and says, pointing to the general response to *Urania* (or at least his perception of it): 'the whole world conceves me to be ment in one of the weakest and unworthiest passages of your booke' (239). He goes on to say 'you count your booke innocent, which all the

---

[12] *Letters of John Chamberlain*, ed. Norman McClure (Philadelphia: American Philosophical Society, 1939), ii. 427.

[13] All quotations are from *Poems*, ed. Roberts, 32–3.

[14] See Margaret Cavendish, *Sociable Letters* (1664), b; and the discussion in Ch. 6, below.

world condemns' (ibid.). In another passage often quoted by those who study early modern women's writing, Denny contrasts Wroth's literary activities with those of her aunt:

But lett your Ladyship take what course yt shall please you with me, this shal bee myne with you to ever wish you well and pray that you may repent you of so many ill spent yeares of so vaine a booke and that you may redeeme the tym with writing as large a volume of heavenly layes and holy love as you have of lascivious tales and amorous toyes that at the last you may followe the rare and pious example of your vertuous and learned Aunt, who translated so many godly books and especially the holly psalmes of David, that no doubt now shee sings in the quiet of Heaven those devine meditations which shee so sweetly tuned heere belowe. (239)

Wroth did indeed align herself with her uncle, author of lascivious tales and amorous toys, rather than with her pious aunt. And to make matters worse, it is clear that Wroth deliberately increased the sexual innuendo of the romance form (interestingly, Sidney reduced it in his revisions of the *Arcadia*). Denny professed particular concern that his name would be maligned 'before all the World and especially before a Wise King'. While he remains conscious of Wroth's power-ful friends, Denny's scarcely veiled threat succeeded in alarming Wroth, who says in reply that she heard that Denny 'us'd all ill and curst courses you could (and) to the King against mee' (240). As Rosalind Smith points out, Wroth did indeed write to the King's favourite, Buckingham, stating that 'I have with all care caused the sale of them to be forbidden', but this letter predates the exchange with Denny.[15] Smith argues that this letter is a kind of insurance policy to protect Wroth against potential scandal. It seems to me that the opening sentence points to some actual, rather than potential, responses to *Urania* ('Understanding some of the strang constructions which are made of my booke'), but I agree completely with Smith in interpreting the letter as fundamentally disingenuous, given that Wroth simultaneously offers to 'shut up' her book, while at the same time noting that no one will return copies to her and perhaps Buckingham might set everyone an example by returning the copy she presented to him.[16] Wroth's manoeuv-ring here is part of the very function of *Urania* as simultaneously a transgressive text and a text intended to re-engage with the court. This was ultimately a lost battle for Wroth: she did not publish the lengthy continuation of *Urania*, which remained in manuscript for the following 374 years. But within this apparent story of constraint lies a more complex situation, which should become clearer as I examine Wroth's work in more detail in the remainder of this chapter.

---

[15] Smith, 'Politics of Withdrawal', 408.

[16] Ibid. 408–13; this forms part of Smith's powerful argument for Wroth's publication of *Urania* as a politically engaged act, related to the activities of the Spenserian poets such as George Wither who were taking a strong stance in 1621 in relation to religious conflict in Europe. Wroth was, in this view, continuing the combative Protestant stance characteristic of Philip Sidney and his successors; for more on this issue, see the section on *Love's Victory* in this chapter, below.

## REWRITING LYRIC POETRY

As noted above, Wroth's poetry circulated in manuscript form some time prior to 1613 (when it was referred to by Joshua Sylvester). There are four surviving sources of her poetry: a manuscript of the song and sonnet sequence 'Pamphilia to Amphilanthus'; a version of this sequence appended to *Urania*, and individual poems within the published text of *Urania* (ascribed to Pamphilia and other characters); poems within the manuscript continuation of *Urania*; and poems within the manuscript of the pastoral play *Love's Victory*.

The manuscript sequence of poems entitled 'Pamphilia to Amphilanthus' resembles to some degree Wroth's father Robert's manuscript of songs and sonnets—which itself has echoes of Philip Sidney's 'Astrophil and Stella'. Like her father, Wroth included a crown of sonnets (although his is unfinished). Wroth then rearranged the poems when the bulk of them were reprinted at the end of *Urania*. The pattern there is: an initial sequence of forty-eight sonnets arranged in groups of six, each group divided by a song. This sequence is signed 'Pamphilia'. Then a single sonnet is followed by four songs; then a further ten sonnets are followed by three songs and a crown of sonnets (that is, fourteen sonnets linked by repeated first and last lines); then four songs, and a final sequence of nine sonnets, concluding again with the signature 'Pamphilia'. There are many revisions to words and punctuation in the *Urania* version of the poetry. It is also important to note that, when they are ascribed to Pamphilia at the end of a 550-page narrative in which she is a leading character, the poems have a different resonance to that achieved in manuscript, where the signature 'Pamphilia' signals Mary Wroth in the way that 'Astrophil' signals Philip Sidney.

Critical interpretation of Wroth's poetry has focused to a considerable degree on her rewriting of the male sonnet tradition, and a critical debate over whether to read her work as inherently about a private, female space, or as engaged in some version of a public debate.[17] The most impressive counter to this double bind is Naomi Miller's revisionist (and detailed) study of Wroth as a writer who 'refashions the emphasis of her culture's governing constructions of femininity'.[18] The general terms of the few direct references to Wroth's poetry make it very difficult to determine how it was interpreted by her contemporaries (whereas Edward Denny's response to *Urania* makes it clear, not just that he was personally affronted at Wroth's depiction of his family, but that he certainly, like John

---

[17] On gender and the sonnet, see especially Elaine Beilin, *Redeeming Eve: Women Writers of the English Renaissance* (Princeton: Princeton University Press, 1987), and Ann Rosalind Jones, *The Currency of Eros* (Bloomington: Indiana University Press, 1990); as noted above, I am wholly convinced by Rosalind Smith's interpretation of Wroth's poetry as politically engaged and far from 'private'.

[18] Naomi J. Miller, *Changing the Subject: Mary Wroth and Figurations of Gender in Early Modern England* (Lexington: University Press of Kentucky, 1996), 236 and *passim*.

Chamberlain, saw *Urania* as directly engaged with court affairs). Ben Jonson's glancing reference to Wroth's sonnets making him a better *lover*, as well as poet, indicates an interpretation that stresses Wroth's depiction of the pangs of love, taking the usual Petrarchan images expressed in a male voice, and giving them to the female voice of Pamphilia. Michael Brennan has argued that Jonson's connections with Wroth could be seen as more extensive than this in terms of literary cross-fertilization, particularly in relation to the nexus between the Sidney and Herbert families and patronage.[19] Brennan reiterates an earlier suggestion of Katherine Duncan-Jones, that the Jonson sonnet may well have been intended to form part of some prefatory poetic material to *Urania*.[20] The idea of Wroth as inheritor of the Sidneian poetic tradition is expressed in a glancing tribute by Joshua Sylvester in a 1613 funeral elegy on the death of Mary's eldest brother, William Sidney.[21] In the preface to the elegy Sylvester suggests that Philip Sidney's tradition has few successors, other than Wroth herself:

> Although I know None, but a Sidney's Muse
> Worthy to sing a Sidney's Worthyness:
> None but Your Owne *AL-WORTH Sidneides     Anagram, * La. Wroth
> In whom, her Uncle's noble Veine renewes

Given the connection with memorials to Prince Henry, Sylvester's lament for William Sidney has political overtones, linking, as did so many Spenserian poets at this period, the Sidney family's adherence to militant Protestantism with Henry as an inspiring alternative to his father, King James.

A somewhat later but more detailed response to Wroth's poetry exists, which points to the way that the poems analyse the intersection between desire, the position of the aristocratic woman, and the functioning of the Jacobean court. This is a poem found in the Wyburd manuscript, which contains a number of poems by Thomas Carew (although Carew's editors do not see him as the author of this particular poem). According to Scott Nixon, who is preparing a new edition of Carew, the provenance of the Wyburd manuscript is largely unknown, but it probably dates from the mid-1630s and it 'has the appearance of a professionally compiled collection of verse, rather than a miscellany assembled piecemeal'.[22] The alignment of this anonymous ode addressed to Wroth, and Carew's

---

[19] See the detailed argument in Michael Brennan, 'Creating Female Authorship in the Early Seventeenth Century: Ben Jonson and Lady Mary Wroth', in George Justice and Nathan Tinker, eds., *Women's Writing and the Circulation of Ideas* (Cambridge: Cambridge University Press, 2002), 73–93.

[20] Katherine Duncan-Jones, review of *Poems*, ed. Roberts, *RES* 36 (1985), 565.

[21] The elegy, entitled 'An Elegy-Epistle Consolatory against immoderate sorrow', is appended to *Lachrimae Lachrimarum* (1613), a collection commemorating the death of Prince Henry (in printing this extract Roberts mistakenly suggests that the elegy for William has the title that is in fact the title of the Henry memorial collection, which contains poems by a number of authors as well as Sylvester), see *Poems*, ed. Roberts, 18–19.

[22] Scott Nixon, 'The Manuscript Sources of Thomas Carew's Poetry', *English Manuscript Studies*, 8 (2000), 196.

poetry of the 1630s, makes sense thematically, given the poem's tone of aristocratic insouciance and its pastoral theme. The poem's opening strikes me as being
quite personal, although my response is not shared by Wroth's editor Josephine
Roberts, who reproduces the poem simply as an example of a 'tribute to her patronage'.[23] If this is simply a tribute to a patron, it is cast in terms of a deeply
personal attachment:

> Ladie, when I from you returne
> (Which be donne never by my will)
> Something does from my heart distill
> Soe heavy, it were not to bee borne
> Save that new hopes the place fulfill
> Of being happie in returne.[24]

The poem aligns the possibility of separation from Lady Wroth with a defin-
ite rejection by the court: 'For ease of my unquiett spiritt | (In which the Court
could see noe Meritt)'. The speaker decides to withdraw to the countryside. The
speaker evokes, as part of his exile, the 'deare pledges of the love | Betweene a
virtuous wife and Mee', but still sees Wroth as the epitome of all that is most
desirable in his retirement: 'Of the best things yo'are one of those'.

This rather simple evocation of the limitations of court life can be contrasted
to Wroth's own treatment of this theme, which resists cliché, in part because it
is able to interrogate all the court's assumptions from the perspective of a female
consciousness. I will quote one of the 'Pamphilia to Amphilanthus' sonnets in full
as an example of Wroth at her most impressive as a poet:

> When every one to pleasing pastime hies
>     Some hunt, some hauke, some play, while some delight
>     In sweet discourse, and musique showes joys might
>     Yett I my thoughts doe farr above thyes prise.
>
> The joy which I take, is that free from eyes
>     I sitt, and wunder att this daylike night
>     Soe to dispose them-selves, as voyd of right;
>     And leave true pleasure for poore vanities;
>
> When others hunt, my thoughts I have in chase;
>     If hauke, my minde att wished end doth fly,
>     Discourse, I with my spiritt tauke, and cry
>     While others, musique choose as greatest grace.
>
> O God, say I, can thes fond pleasures move?
> Or musique bee butt in sweet thoughts of love.[25]

---

[23] *Poems*, ed. Roberts, 19.
[24] All quotations are from ibid. 20–2; I have checked Roberts's transcription against the
manuscript and it is, as usual, completely accurate.
[25] Ibid. 99–100.

This sonnet involves a rejection of the court, not because it has rejected the speaker (as depicted in so many poems like the anonymous 'Ode to Wroth'), but because the female speaker has turned her back on court ideology—specifically, she has set herself aside from the eyes that have been watching her constantly, so that she might converse with her spirit. This internal self-consideration does turn towards thoughts of love in the last line of the poem, but before that we have a strong sense of the speaker's self-contained distance from the vanities of the court. These are the thoughts of someone who has clearly had to distance herself from the court in order to gain what we might now think of as personal space (despite the fact that, as so many social historians have been pointing out, early modern concepts of private space were very different to our own). It is, I think, this highly critical account of the court which is picked up in the anonymous 'Ode', which therefore acknowledges that Wroth's sonnets are far more than simply poems that might make someone a better lover.

This is brought out even more clearly, and self-consciously, in a sonnet which re-examines the Petrarchan topos of the lover's eyes. Once again, it is worth quoting the sonnet in full:

> Take heed mine eyes, how you your lookes doe cast
> > Least they beetray my harts most secrett thought;
> > Bee true unto your selves for nothings bought
> > More deere then doubt which brings a lovers fast.
>
> Catch you all watching eyes, ere they bee past,
> > Or take yours fixt wher your best love hath sought
> > The pride of your desires; lett them bee taught
> > Theyr faults for shame, they could noe truer last;
>
> Then looke, and looke with joye for conquest wunn
> > Of those that search'd your hurt in double kinde;
> > Soe you kept safe, lett them themselves looke blinde
> > Watch, gaze, and marke till they to madnes runn,
>
> While you, mine eyes injoye full sight of love
> Contented that such hapinesses move.[26]

Some of the imagery in this sonnet can be compared to Robert and Philip Sidney's sonnets, although, as I noted above, this imagery in general forms part of the repertoire of Petrarchan love poetry. The woman's eyes are, in Wroth's poem, engaged in a contest with the watching eyes of the court and of potential lovers. Gary Waller offers an interesting account of the 'unusually paranoid' tone of this sonnet (in the context of an argument which justifies such paranoia).[27] There is, in Wroth's sonnet, an aggressive fighting back against the burning eyes of the male (Petrarchan)

[26] Ibid. 106.
[27] Waller, *Sidney Family*, 213; on Wroth's poetry essentially shifting Petrarchan conventions through a radical shift in context, see Beilin, *Redeeming Eve*, 232–43.

lover's gaze, evident in, for example, her father's poetry ('O fair eyes, O dear lights, |
O my delights') and her uncle's poetry ('O eyes, where humble lookes most glorious prove').[28] In the third quatrain, Wroth defies the male eyes that have searched
her hurt 'in double kinde'. The implication of this slightly enigmatic line is that
the woman is wounded by the male eyes which both search in the sense of looking
into a wound, and search in the sense of penetrating the vulnerable female subject.
This fragile sexual situation is reversed by the refusal of these particular female eyes
to allow further 'searching', and that resistance drives the male onlookers to madness. Again, the ever-watchful eyes indicate a court milieu of constant surveillance,
which Wroth counters with the possibility of female resistance.[29]

   While I have noted some early responses to Wroth's poems, I want to pause
here and trace in more detail (as far as this can be done) the reception and transmission of the manuscript poetry (as opposed to the transmission of the poems
when they formed part of the published *Urania*). The provenance of the manuscript of 'Pamphilia to Amphilanthus' that is now in the Folger Shakespeare
Library can only be traced back as far as the library of Isaac Reed, an eighteenth-
century editor of Shakespeare and a great collector of books and manuscripts.[30]
It was bought by Richard Heber and then sold on by Sotheby's in 1836 to
Thorpe, and resold to Sir Thomas Phillipps in the same year; it was then bought
by H. C. Folger in 1899.[31] There is no direct evidence for the whereabouts of
the manuscript prior to its acquisition by Reed.[32] There are four likely places
where the manuscript might have been located originally: the Sidney family seat
of Penshurst; the Herbert seat of Wilton; Mary Wroth's house at Loughton; and
Baynard's Castle, William Herbert's London dwelling where Wroth spent a great
deal of her time. It seems that a manscript of *Urania* was certainly at Baynard's
Castle (where much of it may have been written), as indicated by a 1640 letter
to Wroth from her cousin George Manners, Earl of Rutland, asking for a key
to the narrative's characters: 'Callinge to remembrance the favor you once did
me in the sight of a Manuscript you shewed me in your study att Banerds Cas-
tell'.[33] Books (and paintings) at Wilton were sold off by Philip Herbert, the fifth

   [28] Robert Sidney, song 4, ed. Croft (n. 3 above), 171; Philip Sidney, 'Astrophil and Stella',
sonnet 42, *The Poems of Sir Philip Sidney*, ed. William Ringler (Oxford: Clarendon Press, 1962),
185.
   [29] Here I differ from Ann Rosalind Jones's impressive and detailed reading of the sonnets (still,
to my mind, one of the sharpest interpretations), which stresses Pamphilia's 'self-deprecation'; but
Jones also sees the poetry as 'inflected by her position as a female courtier out of favor with her
monarchs'; see Jones, *Currency* 141.
   [30] See *Poems*, ed. Roberts, 62–3; *Bibliotheca Reediana* (1807), item 1807, 'Pamphilia to
Amphilanthus. Songs, Sonnets &c. written in the time of Q. Elizabeth, or James I beautifully
written and bound in morocco', p. 395; annotated (in Bodleian Library copy) as sold to Heber for
£0.6.6.
   [31] *Poems*, ed. Roberts, 62–3.
   [32] On Reed as collector and editor, see Arthur Sherbo, *Isaac Reed, Editorial Factotum* (University
of Victoria: English Literary Studies, 1989).
   [33] *Poems*, ed. Roberts, 244.

Earl of Pembroke, in the 1660s.[34] Sidney papers at Penshurst, particularly literary manuscripts, were sold during the eighteenth century following on from a decline in Sidney family fortunes largely caused by the improvident seventh Earl in the early eighteenth century.[35] This seems the most likely avenue for the transmission of the 'Pamphilia to Amphilanthus' manuscript to Isaac Reed, although this is purely speculation. P. J. Croft has traced Wroth's father Robert's manuscript collection of poems to an 1833 Sotheby's sale of material collected by Thomas Lloyd in the early ninteenth century.[36]

No one has, thus far, unearthed any early reference to the manuscript poetry—and indeed, despite the notoriety surrounding the publication of *Urania*, only one poem from it was reproduced in the seventeenth century in an altered version in a printed verse miscellany entitled *Wit's Recreations* (1645), where it appeared unsigned. Given that this is the only poem of Wroth's that was reprinted in the seventeenth century, it is worth tracing its rather curious history. The poem in question is the second song from the sequence, which begins: 'All night I weepe, all day I cry, Ay mee'. This song is in both the manuscript sequence and, in the same position, at the end of *Urania*. In 1645 a much shorter adaptation of it was reprinted in the anonymous collection *Wit's Recreations*.[37] The nature of the rather clumsy adaptation can be seen from a comparison with Wroth's first stanza. Wroth writes:

> All night I weepe, all day I cry, Ay mee;
> I still doe wish though yett deny, Ay mee;
> I sigh, I mourne, I say that still
> I only ame the store for ill, Ay mee

This is adapted to:

> All night I muse, all day I cry,
>     Ay me.
> Yet still I wish, though still deny.
>     Ay me.
> I sigh, I mourne, and say that still,
> I onely live my joyes to kill.
>     Ay me.[38]

Given that Wroth's sonnets come at the very end of the fashion for that verse form, it is not surprising that a song, rather than a sonnet, was chosen for

[34] *DNB*, s.v. Herbert, Philip.

[35] See *Poems of Robert Sidney*, ed. Croft (n. 3 above), 6; for the decline of Penshurst in the eighteenth century and the sale of the library, see also Mary Sidney, *Penshurst* (Tunbridge Wells: Goulden and Curry, 1931), 69.

[36] *Poems of Robert Sidney*, ed. Croft, 6.

[37] See *Poems*, ed. Roberts, 93–4, where the adaptation is reprinted as a footnote to Wroth's poem.

[38] Ibid.

reproduction. The song is given a title, 'Sighs', and is placed in the context of fairly typical Cavalier love lyrics. Versions of *Wits Recreations* remained popular through to the Restoration, and there were reprintings of the anthology, with variations, and under the new title *Recreations for Ingenious Head-peeces*, in 1650, 1653, 1654, 1663, 1665, 1667, and 1683. All contained the adaptation of Wroth's song. Until recently, the anthology was thought to have been put together by John Mennes and James Smith, but Tim Raylor (who has undertaken extensive research on Mennes and Smith) has shown that they were not responsible for these volumes.[39] It is frustrating to be unable to ascribe this single adaptation in the seventeenth century of a Wroth poem to a specific author; as it stands, this one instance points to the general fading away of any interest in Wroth's work once the scandal of *Urania*'s publication had died down and a few years passed by. It is perhaps significant that this particular poem is easily detached from *Urania*, from the sonnet sequence, and from Pamphilia as a character, and as a representation of some of the elements of Wroth's work which were connected to the world of the court. This is not to say that Wroth disappeared completely from literary references after 1621, but, as will be evident in the context of the discussion of *Urania* below, the references were minimal.

It is perhaps worth noting here Edward Herbert of Cherbury's witty poem 'Sent to Mary Wroth upon the birth of my Lord of Pembroke's Child', published in the posthumous collection of Herbert's poems in 1665, which puns on Wroth as poet and mother:

> Madam, though I am one of those
> That every Spring use to compose,
> That is, add feet unto round Prose:
> Yet you a further art disclose,
> And can, as every body knows,
> Add to those feet fine dainty toes,
> Satyrs add nails, but they are shrews,
> My Muse therefore no further goes,
> But for her feet craves shooes and hose.
> Let a fair season add a Rose,
> While thus attired wee'l oppose
> The tragick buskins of our foes.
> And herewith, Madm, I will close,
> And 'tis no matter how it shews,
> All I care is, if the child grows.[40]

[39] Tim Raylor, ' "Wits Recreations" Not by Sir John Mennes or James Smith', *Notes and Queries*, 230 (1985), 1–2.

[40] *Poems of Edward Lord Herbert of Cherbury*, ed. G. C. Moore Smith (Oxford: Clarendon Press, 1923), 42.

## THE SCANDAL OF *URANIA*

While I have already discussed the circumstances surrounding the publication of *Urania*, in this section I want to examine Wroth's enormous prose romance in more detail. The process of *Urania*'s publication was a calculated gamble on Wroth's part. Despite her straitened circumstances, it is unlikely that Wroth saw the publication of *Urania* as a way of making money. Rather, *Urania* would appear in print, like Philip Sidney's *Arcadia*, as public testimony to Wroth as the inheritor of her uncle's literary mantle, and as a way of re-engaging with court society (and perhaps taking some revenge for various slights to herself and her family along the way). Wroth's direct engagement in the publication of *Urania* is not just testified to by the disingenuous letter to Buckingham discussed above. The elaborate engraved frontispiece by Simon van de Passe, which depicts the Throne of Love enchantment, a key element of the plot of the first part of *Urania*, points to some supervision of publication by someone very familiar with the details of the romance (although this might not necessarily be Wroth herself). Wroth's editor, Josephine Roberts, points to the unusually large number of stop-press corrections, which once again, does not necessarily mean that Wroth herself supervised the printing, but whoever did, carefully collated the printer's work with the author's manuscript.[41]

More convincing evidence of Wroth's engagement with publication is provided by a copy of *Urania* which contains marginal corrections and alterations to the text in Wroth's own hand. Josephine Roberts notes that this volume may have been a presentation copy, or it may have been Wroth's own corrected copy—the latter is a particularly intriguing possibility, given the existence of the lengthy, manuscript continuation of *Urania* which was never printed. It is possible that Wroth's intention was to reissue a corrected and complete *Urania*, but because of the scandal caused by the publication of the incomplete first part, she decided not to go ahead. Josephine Roberts notes that, as well as corrections of errors and changes to individual words, in this annotated copy Wroth rewrites a passage towards the end of the printed text which concerns faithfulness (one of her key themes).[42] This rewriting seems more like a revision for future publication than work done on a presentation copy, though one cannot know for certain what the intention might have been. The fact that there are twenty-nine surviving copies of *Urania* shows that Wroth's folio was carefully preserved by those who bought it (or were presented with it by Wroth).[43]

---

[41] Wroth, *Urania*, 1. cxi.

[42] Ibid., cxv–cxvii; Wroth's annotated *Urania* is available in facsimile with an introduction by Roberts as vol. 10 in The Early Modern Englishwoman series, part 1 (Aldershot: Ashgate, 1996).

[43] The best comparison is Sidney's *Arcadia*; by 1621, as already noted, *Arcadia* had been through six editions; on the estimates of Bent Juel-Jenson, surviving copies range from ten for 1599 to twenty-nine for 1613 (there are thirteen for the 1621 Dublin edition); see Bent Juel-Jenson, 'Sir Philip Sidney', *Book Collector*, 11 (1962), 468–79.

I have already noted the request Wroth received from George Manners for a key to *Urania*. Given the fact that the scandal over *Urania*'s publication centred upon the identification of actual members of the court and their stories, initial interest responded to this kind of identification, beginning with Denny's angry reaction to the depiction of himself and his family, and including John Chamberlain's account of the romance's reception discussed above. Embedded within the romance itself are a series of reflections on the whole question of female authorship and the relationship of women to court politics.

Recent criticism of *Urania* has moved from an understandable emphasis on Wroth as a female author who represents female desire in a variety of ways, to an increasing focus on the political dimension of *Urania*.[44] In the introduction to her edition of Part One of *Urania*, Josephine Roberts offers a detailed analysis of its political contexts, noting how the romance centres on 'one of the most powerful political fantasies of sixteenth and seventeenth-century Europe—the revival of the Holy Roman Empire in the West'.[45] This fantasy is 'realized' in the romance through the character of Amphilanthus, who becomes just such a wish-fulfilment emperor. As Roberts also notes, the publication of *Urania* in 1621 coincides with the crisis surrounding the initial stages of the Thirty Years War. Britain was directly involved through the position of King James's daughter Elizabeth, married to Frederick, Elector Palatine, who helped to precipitate Catholic–Protestant conflict in Europe by accepting the vacant crown of Bohemia, following which Frederick and Elizabeth were driven into exile by the powerful Catholic forces. When *Urania* was in the press late in 1621, pro-Protestant forces in the English parliament had reached an impasse with James, whose policies were all in favour of avoidance of war and conciliation with Spain. The Sidney/Herbert family grouping had traditionally been involved in the Protestant cause from the mid-sixteenth century. Wroth's father Robert Sidney was a strong supporter of the cause of Frederick and Elizabeth, and William Herbert was closely involved with the faction that pressed for English involvement in the European conflict on the Protestant side.[46] *Urania* contains an extraordinarily complex series of intersecting narratives, and Wroth's depiction of political conflict becomes increasingly wide-ranging as the romance proceeds, and the main characters assume roles as leaders of various kinds. Conflict (and the chance of rapport) between East and West becomes a substantial theme in the manuscript continuation of *Urania*; the editors who completed Roberts's edition of Part Two note that 'there is a newly virulent strain of revulsion towards Islam', and that

---

[44] The most powerful and convincing account of Wroth as rewriting a masculine tradition remains Barbara Lewalski's eloquent chapter on Wroth in *Writing Women in Jacobean England* (Cambridge, Mass., Harvard University Press, 1993), ch. 9.

[45] Wroth, *Urania*, i. xxxix.

[46] Roberts notes that the opinion of political historians on the effectiveness of Herbert's Protestant stand has been divided, but recent work has tended to see him as more directly engaged, *Urania*, i. xlvi.

Wroth offers a much more pessimistic view of possible reconciliation between East and West.[47] This political theme also intersects with Wroth's interest in the possibilities of female power, given that a variety of female characters in the romance control the destinies of their countries. Here Wroth may be seen as engaging in the Protestant faction's nostalgia for Elizabeth I as a more militant ruler than James and a symbol (like Philip Sidney himself) of palmier days of English military prowess and triumph over Spain.[48] Wroth's general treatment of geographical, political, and scientific knowledge has been discussed at length by Sheila Cavanagh, who stresses *Urania*'s consideration of a wide range of issues that are testimony to Wroth's acute engagement with early modern systems of belief.[49] This engagement is, I would want to stress, always politically aware.

In a stimulating essay on women readers in *Urania*, Mary Ellen Lamb notes that, from the many scenes of reading embedded within the romance, one can see that Wroth 'pushes the representation of the woman reader as defined by erotic impulses (her own or others) toward a representation of the woman reader as defined by intellectual achievement and perhaps even by worldly power.'[50] Reading and writing are always at least doubled in *Urania*; notably in Wroth's detailed portrait of, not one, but two female writers: the constant and virtuous Pamphilia, and the wayward, untrustworthy, at times mad, but still often endearing, Antissia.

In a notable scene in Part One, Antissia, overwrought by her spurned love for Amphilanthus, writes a passionate poem expressing her love, reads her poem, 'but then whether judgement of seeing them but poore ones, or humble love telling her that she had committed treason to that love, moved her, I cannot justly tell, but some thing there was that so much molested her as she leap'd from her stoole, ranne to the fire, threw in the paper'.[51] After burning her poem, Antissia finds herself still in thrall to her passion, and she (in a scene reminiscent of the satire directed at pastoral lovers carving verses in trees in *As You Like It*), carves verses into a willow tree, 'till she had imbroidered it all over with characters of her sorrow'.[52] She sits in the tree crowned with 'despised love': 'this was the reward for her affection, and which most poore loving women purchase'.[53]

In contrast to Antissia, Pamphilia's writing is, we might say, embedded in private spaces. And yet, in Part Two of *Urania*, Antissia is cured of her madness by the enchantress Melissea, and the whole concept of the two women as contrasts who reinforce certain constrictive patterns for women writers is

[47] Mary Wroth, *The Second Part of The Countess of Montgomery's Urania*, ed. Josephine Roberts with Suzanne Gossett and Janel Mueller (Tempe, Ariz.: RETS, 1999), pp. xxxiii–iv.

[48] Sheila Cavanagh notes that Wroth elides the differences between Catholics and Protestants within the romance, instead classifying characters collectively as Christian, as opposed to those who are 'barbarian', Sheila T. Cavanagh, *Cherished Torment: The Emotional Geography of Lady Mary Wroth's Urania* (Pittsburgh: Duquesne Univesity Press, 2001), 31.

[49] Ibid., *passim*.

[50] Mary Ellen Lamb, 'Women Readers in Mary Wroth's *Urania*', in *Reading Mary Wroth*, ed. Naomi Miller and Gary Waller (Knoxville: University of Tennessee Press, 1991), 221.

[51] *Urania*, i. 327.        [52] Ibid. 328.        [53] Ibid.

overturned. Indeed, as many commentators have pointed out, the whole of the second part of *Urania* interrogates romance assumptions about heroism, about writing, and about political engagement. It is worth asking a few more questions, at this point in my account of Wroth, about exactly how *Urania* can be read. Many modern readers have quailed, not so much at the sheer bulk of *Urania* (though, at 1,081 pages in the modern edition, the bulk is rather frightening), as at the multitudinous stories, which seem to become more ravelled as they go on. In this sense, Wroth is, as Helen Hackett has astutely noted, heir to and adapter of the long medieval tradition of romance, and she also anticipates the complications of the French heroic romance which flourished two decades after *Urania*'s publication.[54] The modern edition of both parts of *Urania* allows the wearied reader to disentangle the stories of the various characters because both volumes provide detailed indexes for individual characters. Not only does this enable the stories to be followed easily, but it also clarifies the dynastic interrelationships between the characters. (And incidentally, indicates how, in the second part, Wroth herself still needed to clear up some interrelationships and dangling or contradictory plot strands.[55]) But it is possible that this modern hesitation before the complexity of Wroth's narrative was not felt by seventeenth-century readers. It seems to have taken Edward Denny (or his informant) only a matter of a few months after *Urania*'s publication to 'interpret' the story of Sirelius.[56] The narrative of Sirelius's marriage comes very late in Book Four of the published *Urania*—that is, the reader needs to get through 435 pages of the folio, reading, one assumes, with great attention, before the fairly brief account that enflamed Denny takes place. It is a short, embedded story, rather than a major plot strand, and so would have demanded close reading, especially as the names of the characters in the narrative do not signal their relationship to the real people involved, unlike, say, the anagrammatic Lindamira (= Lady Mary [Wroth]). If John Chamberlain testifies to a general sense of embedded stories in the romance, then it is possible to see *Urania*'s readers as performing a very different reading 'process' to that performed (or backed away from) by its readers today.

*Urania* was not alone in tempting early modern readers by the promise of a *roman-à-clef*. I have discussed at length elsewhere the significant coincidental publication in 1621 of John Barclay's Latin romance *Argenis*, a political allegory which quickly spawned editions with the 'keys' demanded by readers like Sir George Manners, who asked Wroth to expand his 'key' to the characters in

---

[54] For an excellent account of Wroth in relation to a variety of aspects of the romance, see Helen Hackett, *Women and Romance Fiction in the English Renaissance* (Cambridge: Cambridge University Press, 2000), ch. 10.

[55] See *Urania*, II. xxx.

[56] *Urania* was entered in the Stationers' Register on 13 July 1621, and was probably in print by September; as noted above, Denny's verse circulated some time before his letters to Wroth, which were written in mid-Feb. 1622; see *Urania*, I. xvii.

*Urania.*[57] Manners writes to Wroth in May 1640, at a time when, thanks to *Argenis*, the notion of romance as political *roman-à-clef* was still very much the fashion. The very entangled narrative details that readers today may find daunting could, going on these examples, have had the opposite effect on *Urania*'s contemporary readers, who combed it for references to real people and events. At this level, such a reading moves between personal and political events, reflecting Wroth's ability to connect romance as emotional expression, and romance as vehicle for historical and political commentary. This is particularly the case with *Urania*, which was clearly intended, upon publication, to be an intervention in the unfolding events of 1621. The final work of Wroth's to be discussed, however, before I move on to trace her fortunes through later readings of her work, is, in contrast to *Urania*, balanced rather more delicately between public and private realms.

## SHUTTING UP *LOVE'S VICTORY*

In this section, I want to raise some questions about the textual history of Wroth's pastoral play *Love's Victory*. My suggestions are often quite speculative, but I believe that they cast new light on a play that has recently been attracting some attention. My speculations about *Love's Victory* began through work I undertook on an edition of early modern women's writing for Oxford World's Classics.[58] *Love's Victory* exists in two manuscripts: one at Penshurst, the Sidney family seat, and one (incomplete) at the Huntington Library. As part of my editorial work, I planned to consult the Penshurst manuscript, even though it is available in a facsimile edition prepared by Michael Brennan.[59] Accordingly, I sent an email to Philip Sidney, Viscount de L'Isle, explaining the nature of my edition and asking if I could look at the Penshurst manuscript of *Love's Victory* when I visited England in July 1998. I received an email back which stated that the Viscount held the copyright of the Penshurst *Love's Victory* manuscript, and that he had no intention of allowing it to be used as the basis for a 'popular' edition. He pointed out that his father had authorized the Roxburghe Club facsimile edition, and that that was quite enough for the purposes of scholarly endeavour. My Oxford editor told me that I was on no account to challenge the Viscount, and that my text would need to based on the Huntington manuscript, not the Penshurst manuscript. So not only was the door of the Penshurst library firmly shut against me, but my use of the manuscript was circumscribed.

---

[57] See the quotation from Manners above, and see my discussion of *Argenis* in Salzman, *Literary Culture*, ch. 3.

[58] *Early Modern Women's Writing*, ed. Paul Salzman, World's Classics (Oxford: Oxford University Press, 2000).

[59] *Lady Mary Wroth's Love's Victory: The Penshurst Manuscript*, ed. Michael Brennan (London: Roxburghe Club, 1988).

I recount this tale of the petty tribulations of an editor because it seems to me to be quite relevant to a lot of aspects of *Love's Victory*, especially in relation to key aspects of Wroth's work as a whole that have been the focus of this chapter so far. This is particularly the case in relation to the dichotomy, mentioned above, that has been set up between scholars like Jeff Masten, who have wanted to see Wroth's endeavours as essentially to do with the construction of female subjectivity within a private space, and those who want to see her foray into print with the publication of *Urania* as an attempt to engage in what might be called public discourse.[60] *Love's Victory* is fascinating in relation to these issues because, while it is clearly a more private work than *Urania*, in so far as it had manuscript circulation, as a play that may well have been performed, even if only within a family circle, it has a communal life. It also seems to me that, in terms of its genre, *Love's Victory* is a significant contribution to the political use of pastoral during the reigns of James and Charles.[61]

There is no direct evidence for the date of *Love's Victory*'s composition, but it seems likely that Wroth was writing it in 1621 or 1622, although we will probably never know the exact date.[62] As discussed above, the publication of *Urania* involved Wroth in a major backlash. I have already discussed Wroth's precautionary approach to Buckingham, and want here to quote the opening of her letter to him of 15 December 1621:

My Lord. Understanding some of the strang[e] constructions which are made of my booke contrary to my imagination, and as farre from my meaning as is possible for truth to bee from conjecture, my purpose noe way bent to give the least cause of offence, my thoughts free from soe much as thinking of any such thing as I am censured for; I have with all care caused the sale of them to bee forbidden, and the books left to bee shut up.[63]

---

[60] See Jeff Masten, ' "Shall I turne blabb": Circulation, Gender and Subjectivity in Mary Wroth's Sonnets', in Naomi Miller and Gary Waller, eds., *Reading Mary Wroth* (Knoxville: University of Tennessee Press, 1991), 67–87.

[61] On *Love's Victory* as a specifically female form of pastoral, see esp. Carolyn Ruth Swift, 'Feminine Self-definition in Lady Mary Wroth's *Love's Victorie*', *ELR* 19 (1989), 171–88; Barbara Lewalski, 'Mary Wroth's *Love's Victory* and Pastoral Tragicomedy', in Miller and Waller, *Reading Mary Wroth*, 88–108; for a complex and fascinating reading in terms of the political situation and the verbal and other games played by Queen Anne's female courtiers, see Louise Schleiner, *Tudor and Stuart Women Writers* (Bloomington: Indiana University Press, 1994), ch. 5.

[62] This date has been challenged by Marion Wynne-Davies, in a detailed and important account of the family allusions in the play, ' "Here is a sport will well befit this time and place": Allusion and delusion in Mary Wroth's Love's Victory', *Women's Writing*, 6 (1999), 47–63. Some of Wynne-Davies's most interesting arguments concern Wroth's depiction of her relationship with Herbert, but some of these re-imaginings may have been due to the generic features of *Love's Victory* as pastoral play, rather than to changes in Wroth's relationship. The fact that the manuscript collected by Dering which became the Huntington manuscript was almost certainly acquired by Dering between 1619 and 1624 helps to narrow the possible composition time: see Arthur Freeman, review of the Brennan edition, *Library*, 6th ser. 13 (1991), 168–73; and Arthur Freeman, '*Love's Victory*: A Supplementary Note', *Library*, 19 (1997), 252–4; throughout this essay I am greatly indebted to information supplied in Freeman's two notes.

[63] *Poems*, ed. Roberts, 236.

Wroth was left with a massive continuation of *Urania* that she never published. In this context, *Love's Victory* is important because, at the most obvious level, it too was not published by Wroth. On the other hand, I do not believe that it is possible to see *Love's Victory* as a retreat from the public exposure that got Wroth into trouble with *Urania*; certainly not if we avoid anachronistic distinctions between public and private which do not really obtain in this case. Here I am in complete agreement with Marion Wynne-Davies's suggestive notion of Penshurst as, in some senses, a 'safe house' for Wroth, but in other ways a potentially imprisoning environment.[64] *Love's Victory* seems to me to be a careful negotiation of Wroth's dilemma. In it she continues to use the *roman-à-clef* methods of *Urania* in order to explore her own marital and sexual situation alongside allusions to other members of her family, including Philip Sidney. As I have already noted, for the Sidney/Herbert families, the genres of romance and pastoral had powerful political implications, as did any evocation of Philip Sidney, whose iconic significance always stood, during the reign of James and Charles, as a challenge to soft policies on European Protestantism. And the transmission and circulation of *Love's Victory* points to a reach beyond the immediate family circle.

The two manuscripts, Huntington Library HM 600 and the Penshurst manuscript, were both written by Wroth herself, and of course we do not know if there were other manuscripts in circulation. The Huntington MS points most importantly to the way that Wroth would not allow her work to be shut up as easily as the letter to Buckingham implies. At some stage, almost certainly before 1624, this manuscript of *Love's Victory* ends up with Sir Edward Dering. Dering lived in Surrenden, Kent, and was an antiquary who, between 1619 and 1624, amassed a huge collection of playbooks.[65] He also presided over amateur performances at Surrenden, and it is possible that these included a performance of *Love's Victory*. Dering's second wife gave him a family connection to Buckingham. He himself sat in the 1625 parliament. How would someone like Dering, who was later to have a rather sad career as a naive member of the Long Parliament, who moved the Root and Branch Bill, but who in committee argued for a moderate preservation of episcopacy, have read *Love's Victory*? This is only speculation, but perhaps Dering read it as a pastoral play in which, while the family allusions I mentioned are present, one can also see a potential attack on a lax court beyond the confines of which the affairs of the characters in *Love's Victory* are played out. Indeed, the sense of criticism from the margins is accentuated by Wroth's own placement; if *Urania* is characterized as an attempt to re-enter court society, rather than just as a depiction of it, then its failure to achieve that means that Wroth might well

[64] Marion Wynne-Davies, '"My Seeled Chamber and Dark Parlour Room": The English Country House and Renaissance Women Dramatists', in S. P. Ceresano and Marion Wynne-Davies, eds., *Readings in Renaissance Women's Drama* (London: Routledge, 1998), 60–8.

[65] For Dering see T. N. S. Lennam, 'Sir Edward Dering's Collection of Playbooks, 1619–1624', *SQ* 16 (1965), 145–53; unfortunately no titles are named in Dering's list of his acquisitions.

position *Love's Victory* as a complex negotiation of spaces, including the court and its margins, Penshurst, Loughton (her own house), and Baynard's Castle (Pembroke's London house), particularly in relation to the absence of a female court following the death of Queen Anne in 1619.[66]

The manuscript that Dering possessed is what we now call the Huntington manuscript.[67] Therefore, it is an incomplete version of the play, notably missing the last 500 lines present in the Penshurst manuscript. What, exactly, does that say about Dering as a collector of playbooks who also liked to have them performed? I have more speculations to come about the incompleteness of this manuscript, but at this point I simply want to stress that Wroth provided Dering with a less than satisfactory performance text, unless this manuscript is not the only one he had at that time. It is certainly the only one that was left in Surrenden in 1845, when the Victorian antiquary and biographer of Shakespeare, James Orchard Halliwell, had his wife copy out the manuscript of *Love's Victory* which, at that stage, was still in the possession of the Dering family. Halliwell produced extracts from the play in his edition *A Brief Description of the Ancient & Modern Manuscripts in the Public Library, Plymouth*, published in 1853. (Halliwell has caused some confusion, because *Love's Victory* was never in the Plymouth Public Library; rather, Halliwell seems to have deposited there his wife's transcript of the Dering manuscript.) Halliwell had decided that the play 'was not found to be of sufficient interest for publication', and instead he offered some 'brief extracts'.[68] The Dering manuscript was eventually offered for sale by Quaritch in 1899, bought by William Augustus White, and acquired some time later by the Huntington Library.

So this is the most travelled manuscript of *Love's Victory*, but it is also, in many ways, the most puzzling. Not only has its relationship with Halliwell's extracts been the cause of some confusion and speculation, I think that its exact nature is puzzling too. Josephine Roberts, who first identified the handwriting in this manuscript as Wroth's own, noted that Wroth wrote the manuscript in two distinct hands: a formal italic hand for much of the time, but with corrections in Wroth's cursive hand. This led Roberts to conclude that the Huntington manuscript was a working manuscript incorporating corrections and improvements; she pointed to the

---

[66] Marion Wynne-Davies offers a fascinating reading of the family allusions within *Love's Victory* in her important essay, ' "For *Worth*, Not Weakness, Makes in Use but One": Literary Dialogues in an English Renaissance Family', in Danielle Clarke and Elizabeth Clarke, eds., *'This Double Voice': Gendered Writing in Early Modern England* (Houndmills: Macmillan, 2000), 164–84.

[67] The most complete description of the Huntington Manuscript is Josephine Roberts, 'The Huntington Library Manuscript of Lady Mary Wroth's Play *Loves Victorie*', HLQ 46 (1983), 156–74; see also *Love's Victory*, ed. Brennan (n. 59 above), 20–1.

[68] James Orchard Halliwell, *A Brief Description of the Ancient and Modern Manuscripts Preserved in the Public Library, Plymouth* (London, 1853), 212; Freeman clears up the doubts of Roberts and Brennan about the exact relationship between the Huntington Manuscript, the Dering Manuscript, and whatever it was that Halliwell left at the Plymouth Public Library, see Freeman, 'Supplementary Note', 252–3.

Penshurst manuscript (which she then knew only from a description by P. J. Croft) as the 'finished' version of the play, and this is also Michael Brennan's conclusion.[69] The Penshurst manuscript is certainly finished in so far as it has five complete acts, and is written throughout in Wroth's formal italic hand. But I want to ask, once again, at this point, why would Dering have Wroth's working manuscript, and what kind of performance could be produced from such an incomplete version? It is certainly the case that the Huntington manuscript, given that it was in Dering's possession, is our firmest evidence for *Love's Victory* as a text intended for performance, indeed almost certainly performed. And it is the text that ranges most freely beyond the confines of Penshurst or Loughton.

I turn now to the Penshurst manuscript. Brennan speculated that this manuscript had probably always been at Penshurst.[70] Were that true, it could be seen to be most firmly possessed, even shut up entirely, by the Sidney family. However, as Arthur Freeman pointed out recently, this was not exactly the case.[71] In fact, this manuscript was offered for sale by Puttick and Simpson on 25 September 1850.[72] It was mistakenly described by Puttick and Simpson as 'Love's Victory, a Masque, in the autograph of MARY SIDNEY.'[73] The manuscript was bought by Thomas Thorpe for £3 7s. 6d.[74] Thorpe was a book dealer, and at some stage the manuscript found its way to Penshurst—perhaps immediately, perhaps through some intermediary. This manuscript, as already mentioned, is written in Wroth's formal italic hand. It contains a complete text of the play and often includes character lists before each scene, as well as minimal stage directions (normally to mark exits). A list of actors' names has been added to the end of the manuscript by someone other than Wroth; this might possibly be a cast list written in a seventeenth-century hand, but it is unidentified. The Penshurst manuscript is in its seventeenth-century binding, decorated with the S fermé (S with a stroke through it) that Wroth often used, as did her aunt (it is, perhaps, an indication that these women retain their Sidney identity after marriage, with the stroke indicating its slight dilution).[75] It also has a monogram that Brennan describes as 'the letters PHILMSA and perhaps W and V.'[76] Brennan was puzzled by this monogram, and Freeman points out that it obviously led Puttick and Simpson to ascribe the manuscript to Mary Sidney, and they also announced that the volume contained the monogram of Mary and Philip Sidney.[77] However, Josephine Roberts offers a convincing case for the monogram as a cipher incorporating the letters naming Amphilanthus,

[69] See Roberts, 'Huntington Manuscript', *passim*.     [70] *Love's Victory*, ed. Brennan, 16.
[71] Freeman, 'Supplementary Note', 254.
[72] Ibid.; see Puttick and Simpson Sale catalogue, 25 Sept. 1850, lot 909.
[73] Puttick and Simpson catalogue, 35.     [74] See Freeman, 'Supplementary Note', 254.
[75] See Margaret P. Hannay, *Philip's Phoenix: Mary Sidney, Countess of Pembroke* (New York: Oxford University Press, 1990), 193; Hannay does not comment on the reasons behind Mary Pembroke's use of the S fermé.
[76] *Love's Victory*, ed. Brennan, 16.     [77] Freeman, 'Supplementary Note', 254.

the hero of *Urania*, and representation in the romance of William Herbert.[78] Roberts speculated over the possibility of this indicating that the manuscript may have been a presentation copy for Herbert, because she followed Brennan in assuming that the manuscript had always been at Penshurst. Now that it is clear that it was not, we can perhaps follow her lead and see it as potentially a copy made for Herbert, or at least one alluding to him and to Wroth's relationship with him. From that point of view it is appropriate that this manuscript gives us a play bounded at the beginning and end by Venus, finishing with an S fermé before the last words 'exeunt' and 'finis', including a humbled mother repentant at her attempts to force her daughter to marry against her will—all clear allusions to Wroth's own relationship to marriage and to William Herbert.[79]

Whether this manuscript was or was not once possessed by Herbert, once it found its way to Penshurst it remained shut up even when the Huntington manuscript was being worked on by Josephine Roberts. Brennan explains that P. J. Croft (who edited Robert Sidney's poems), having identified *Love's Victory* at Penshurst, planned an edition of it.[80] Instead, Brennan took on this task; but he produced a very special kind of edition. In 1988 Brennan edited a facsimile of the Penshurst manuscript for the Roxburghe Club. At the time of publication, the Viscount de L'Isle was vice-president of the Roxburghe Club. The Roxburghe Club began in 1812 under the patronage of the second Earl Spencer, whose support had been garnered by an industrious cleric and bibliographer, Thomas Dibdin.[81] The club took its name from the sale of the great book collection of John Ker, third Duke of Roxburghe, many of its first members having gathered at a dinner following the sale on 17 June 1812. Members were essentially book collectors, and included three dukes. Each member was meant to print, for the other members, a scarce volume, one for the club chairman on vellum, as well as one for each member. The first volume produced was Surrey's translation of the *Aeneid*. As its historian drily noted, 'In its early years the Club seems to have taken almost as much interest in its gastronomical as in its literary labours.'[82] Nevertheless, some of the early volumes represent significant nineteenth-century contributions to bibliographical and textual scholarship. Later in the century the club was notable for the way it embraced modern methods of producing facsimile

[78] Josephine Roberts, 'Deciphering Women's Pastoral: Coded Language in Wroth's *Love's Victory*', in Claude Summers and Ted-Larry Pebworth, eds., *Representing Women in Renaissance England* (Columbia: University of Missouri Press, 1997), 163–74.

[79] For the last page of the Penshurst Manuscript see *Love's Victory*, ed. Brennan, 227; Mary Ellen Lamb discusses the cipher in relation to *Urania* in 'The Biopolitics of Romance in Mary Wroth's *The Countess of Montgomery's Urania*', *ELR* 31 (2001), 125–6; she also makes some suggestive comments about *Urania*'s lack of a 'conclusion', 129.

[80] *Love's Victory*, ed. Brennan, p. xiii.

[81] For information I draw on Clive Bingham, *The Roxburghe Club: Its History and its Members, 1812–1927* (Oxford: Oxford University Press, 1928).

[82] Ibid. 3.

editions.[83] In the early part of the twentieth century the club produced some fine works of scholarship, particularly the volumes edited by M. R. James.

Michael Brennan's edition unquestionably continues this tradition of fine scholarship. However, as a Roxburghe Club book, the Penshurst manuscript is not like a scholarly edition produced by a publisher such as Oxford University Press. Presented to the Club by Viscount de L'Isle and, needless to say, beautifully produced, the volume had a much more limited circulation than any commercial edition. And while academics are used to the high cost of the editions upon which they rely, the price of £160 in 1988 means that this volume was acquired by very few academic libraries. Therefore a kind of shutting up has already taken place within the confines of this beautiful edition, later compounded by the restrictions placed by the current Viscount de L'Isle on what we might call the wider transmission of the contents of the Penshurst manuscript to hoi polloi.

This is particularly disturbing if Penshurst is seen as the superior text. Both Josephine Roberts and Michael Brennan assume that the relationship between Huntington and Penshurst is that Huntington is an incomplete, first working draft for a play perfected in the Penshurst text. That would certainly confirm a certain kind of entrapment: Wroth's last thoughts captured (from another point of view some might say preserved and protected) at Penshurst, and then in turn by the Roxburgh Club. But I am not sure about the logic behind this story of the relationship between the two manuscripts. I have already noted that, if Huntington is a first draft, then it seems an odd text to end up with Edward Dering as a playscript. I would also want to maintain that, on a case by case basis, many individual readings in the Huntington manuscript are superior to readings in the Penshurst manuscript.

For example, in Act III Scene ii, Simeana and Climeana have a discussion which turns to Climeana's jealousy caused by the fact that Lissius, the man she loves, is also loved by Simeana. Simeana asks 'Why, what have I to do with whom you love?' In Penshurst, Climeana replies 'Because 'tis hee who doth your passion prove.'[84] In Huntington, this reads 'Because 'tis he who doth your passion move.' This Huntington reading is better because it is clearer and also eliminates an ugly repetition of 'move' two lines later. Indeed, one might conjecture that Wroth changed 'prove' to 'move' to avoid the repetition (though I would not go that far). Ceresano and Wynne-Davies agree with me in adopting the Huntington reading, partly because Wynne-Davies sees Huntington as a later, revised text, with Penshurst as having been written around 1615–18; indeed, they choose Huntington readings over Penshurst readings numerous times.[85]

---

[83] See Nicolas Barker, *The Publications of the Roxburghe Club 1814–1962* (Cambridge: Roxburghe Club, 1964), 40.

[84] *Love's Victory*, ed. Brennan, 118.

[85] See S. P. Cerasano and Marion Wynne-Davies, *Renaissance Drama by Women* (London: Routledge, 1996), 109; further examples from Act IV include: line 127, Huntington 'keep' for

I have to admit that there are also variants which support the idea of Hunt-ington as first draft and Penshurst as final version, but I think that they can be read in more than one way. A good example is the speech by Cupid at the end of Act IV in Huntington. This is not present in Penshurst, where the act just ends with the song of the priests. In Huntington there is a brief speech by Cupid to Venus: 'Now your part coms to play | in this you must somthing sway | soe you shall, and I your child | when you bid can soone bee milde.'[86] This speech is crossed through, perhaps indicating that Wroth decided against including it, and Penshurst therefore represents her final thoughts. However, thematically it fits very well with my sense that in the Huntington manuscript we see a more circumscribed relationship between the mythological characters (who are much reduced in Huntington), and the human characters.

I am not trying to mount a scientific argument based on comparative readings, but rather I am weaving a story about how *Love's Victory* might be seen as less able to be shut up than some people might wish. So, I imagine a scenario in which the Huntington manuscript might represent Wroth's second thoughts on the perfec-tion of the Penshurst manuscript. She therefore might improve some individual readings, but she also decides against a completed text in which the rules of tragicom-edy obtain. In this *Love's Victory*, the action is not framed by Venus and Cupid.[87] The political bite of the pastoral as a Sidneian call to arms is enhanced by an opening in which Philisses is the first character we see, and he is speaking of a kind of exile. This *Love's Victory* ends with Philisses and Musella intent upon suicide, but there is no resolution, and, just as Venus's part is cut, so is the part of Musella's mother. This is a radically and, dare I suggest, *consciously* unfinished text: just like *Urania*, just like *Arcadia*. This is a more improvisatory text, more easily adapted, able to achieve a certain kind of freedom that escapes gatekeepers of all kinds.

## THE FORTUNES OF MARY WROTH

While even *Love's Victory* circulated, albeit in a limited fashion, it is certainly true to say that references to Wroth's work remain slight in number for some 300 years following *Urania*'s publication. I have discussed above some of the verse tributes garnered by Wroth, particularly during the years prior to the pub-lication of *Urania*, when her patronage was being sought by a writer like Ben Jonson.[88] Jonson's friend William Drummond, perhaps prompted by Jonson, wrote both an ode and a sonnet to Wroth, while admitting that he had never met

---

Penshurst 'conceale'; line 144, Huntington 'is That' for Penshurst 'Is it'; line 318, Huntington 'all care' for Penshurst 'dispaire'.

[86] *Love's Victory*, ed. Brennan, 231.

[87] In Huntington, the opening speeches of Venus and Cupid are missing, as are their conversations at the end of Act III and Act V.

[88] The poetic tributes I discuss below were first noted in *Poems*, ed. Roberts, 17–22.

her. In the ode, Drummond praises Wroth's 'spacious thoughts with choice inuentions free', which might indicate some familiarity with her poetry (through Jonson, perhaps).[89] Drummond could be seen as paying a certain amount of homage to Wroth by his very choice of the sonnet as a verse form in which to praise her poetry. Drummond did write quite a number of sonnets; the one addressed to Wroth once again praises her accomplishments (though in very general terms): 'Wher worth accomplisht crownd with glorie shines'.[90]

Chapman singled out Wroth in one of the prefatory sonnets to his translation of Homer. The sonnet is entitled 'To The Happy Starre, Discouered in our Sydneian Asterisme; comfort of learning, Sphere of all the vertues, the Lady Wrothe'.[91] While honouring Wroth as a Sidneian star, Chapman praises her for her adherence to religious truth: 'let true Reason and Religion trie, | If it be Fancie, not iudiciall Right, | In you t'oppose the times Apostasie'.[92] Chapman can be seen, in this instance, as part of the Spenserian poets who saw the Sidney/Herbert family as champions of the Protestant cause and as forming a brake on the policies of King James that they most disliked. When these writers praised Wroth in the period 1610–13, they were, at most, evoking her poetic gifts in relation to her role as patron, but it is worth remembering here the argument detailed above that *Urania* can be seen as part of the tradition of this kind of political intervention. The writer in this group who expressed these ideas most radically was George Wither, who refers to Wroth in his infamous satirical work *Abuses Stript, and Whipt* (1613). Wroth is the recipient of the one of epigrams at the end of Wither's volume, along with her father, William Herbert, Princess Elizabeth, and other influential figures who could be seen grouped together for political purposes.[93] Wither describes Wroth as 'Arts sweet Louer', and the epigram as a whole stresses her function as patron, rather than poet:

> There is no happy Muse this day remaines;
> That doth not for your Worth and bounty owe,
> Euen himselfe, his best and sweetest straines.[94]

As Josephine Roberts explains, this sense of Wroth as patron is reinforced by the fact that she (along with Anne Bacon) was the only female recipient of a reasonably large number of dedications, apart from members of the royal family or the most distinguished aristocratic families.[95] As I have already noted, the

[89] *The Poetical Works of William Drummond of Hawthornden*, ed. L. E. Kastner (Scottish Text Society, Edinburgh: William Blackwood, 1913), ii. 277.

[90] Ibid. 271.

[91] *The Poems of George Chapman*, ed. Phyllis Brooks Bartlett (New York: MLA, 1941), 400.

[92] Ibid.

[93] For this aspect of Wither's work, see Michelle O'Callaghan, *The 'shepheards nation', Jacobean Spenserians and Early Stuart Political Culture* (Oxford: Clarendon Press, 2000), 150–3.

[94] George Wither, *Abuses Stript and Whipt* (1613), X4.

[95] Wroth's aunt, the Countess of Pembroke, received over three times as many dedications as Wroth did; see *Poems*, ed. Roberts, 22.

volume of this kind of dedicatory verse and other tributes diminishes as Wroth loses her position of influence, and even more so after the publication of *Urania*. In 1622 Henry Peacham, in a discussion of heraldry contained in his handbook *The Compleat Gentleman* (1622), illustrates the practice of some women who continued to use a version of their father's coat of arms after their marriage; as part of his commentary on Wroth's use of the Sidney arrowhead, Peacham states that she 'seemeth by her late published Urania an inheritrix of the Diuine wit of her Immortal Vncle'.[96] Josephine Roberts notes the existence of a copy of *Urania* annotated by William Davenporte in the early seventeenth century; these annotations summarize the plot and occasionally praise Wroth's ability as a storyteller.[97]

In 1624 Thomas Heywood refers to Wroth in passing in his wide-ranging book *Gynaikeion*, during a quick round-up of female authorship: 'the ingenious Ladie, the late composer of our extant *Vrania*'.[98] (It is rather puzzling that he doesn't actually name Wroth.) In 1640 Judith Man prefaced her translation of Nicholas Coeffeteau, *An Epitome of the History of Faire Argenis and Poliarchus*, with a brief reference to some predecessors, stating that she 'could produce thee [*sic*] many of my sexe, who have traced me the way, witnesse the translation into French of Sir *Philip Sidney's Arcadia*, the *New Amarantha*, and the *Vrania*, with many others'.[99] From this point in time until the end of the seventeenth century references are sparse (I have noted above Margaret Cavendish's repetition of Denny's admonishment to Wroth, but Cavendish does not actually name Wroth when she quotes Denny).

While there was a considerable increase in the visibilty of women writers after the Restoration, thanks largely to the fame (in various ways) of Cavendish, Aphra Behn and Katherine Philips, there was no real revival of interest in Wroth—which is not so surprising, considering that the literary forms she used were out of fashion. The ever-watchful Gerard Langbaine, in *An Account of the Dramatick Poets* (1691), noted Wroth as a source for James Shirley's play *The Politician* (1655): 'A Story resembling this, I have read in the first Book of the Countess of *Montgomery's Urania*, concerning the King of Romania, the Prince Antissius, and his Mother-in-Law.'[100] Langbaine specialized in combing over likely sources for dramatic plots, but he clearly knew *Urania* well to have picked this one up.

[96] Henry Peacham, *The Compleate Gentleman* (1622), sig. Y–Yv.

[97] Roberts, *Urania*, I includes some of the annotations in her notes to *Urania* I, see e.g. p. 717, n. to p. 15.

[98] Thomas Heywood, *Gynaikeion* (1624), 398.

[99] Sig. B2; *Arcadia's* 1624 French translator was Genevieve Chappelain; the exact identity of the *New Amarantha* is a mystery.

[100] Gerard Langbaine, *An Account of the English Dramatick Poets* (1691), 481; for Wroth's story, see *Urania* I. 33; for a detailed account of the relationship between *The Politician* and its source in *Urania*, see Robert J. Fehrenbach, *A Critical Edition of The Politician by James Shirley* (New York: Garland, 1980), pp. xxx–li.

Wroth is one of a number of English women writers summed up (and largely dismissed) by Edward Phillips in *Theatrum Poetarum* (1675). Phillips provides an account of 'Women Among the Ancients Eminent for Poetry' and then does the same for women among the 'moderns', where he notes: 'the Wife of Sir Robert Wroth, an Emulatress perhaps of Philip Sidney's Arcadia, by her *Vrania*, a Poetical History of the same nature; but much inferiour in Fame' (260).[101] This assessment is repeated in pretty much the same (semi-plagiarized?) words in *The Ladies Dictionary* (1694), where the anonymous author adds a favourite catch phrase: 'a very curious piece' (418).

In the eighteenth and early nineteenth centuries, when, as will be seen in later chapters, some attention was paid to a select group of early modern women writers, Wroth virtually dropped out of sight, not rating a mention by the likes of George Ballard, or even Horace Walpole in his *Catalogue of the Royal and Noble Authors of England* (1758). She does appear in Alexander Dyce's 1825 *Specimens of British Poetesses*, where Wroth is represented by two songs, 'Who can blame me, if I love?' and 'Love, a child, is ever crying'. Dyce notes that Wroth 'in her day . . . enjoyed considerable reputation as authoress of the Urania, a romance interspersed with poetry' (40). Dyce bases the text of the two songs on *Urania*, and judiciously modernizes spelling and punctuation.[102]

Despite a reasonable level of interest in early modern women's poetry during the nineteenth century, Dyce's inclusion of Wroth in his anthology did not spark any interest, and Wroth remained pretty much invisible until interest turned to her romance as part of a general reappraisal of early modern prose fiction. Some attempt to trace the early history of the English novel began in the late nineteenth century, and this, rather than any particular interest in early modern women's writing, sparked an interest in *Urania*. This can be contrasted with the self-conscious tracing back of women's writing by Virginia Woolf, who appears not to have come across Wroth, or at least does not mention her alongside the often quite obscure seventeenth-century writers she discusses.

In 1890 J. J. Jusserand, a French diplomat who eventually became France's ambassador to America, published an ambitious study of Elizabethan fiction entitled *The English Novel in the Time of Shakespeare*. Jusserand discusses *Urania* as part of his detailed chapter on Sidney's *Arcadia*. Disconcertingly for those who have laboured to explain how different Wroth's romance is to Sidney's, Jusserand characterizes *Urania* as 'a complete and pious imitation of Sidney's manner, especially of his defects'.[103] Jusserand's brief account simply picks out a few passages and notes that *Urania* is, like the *Arcadia*, a pastoral romance. *Urania* gets a passing sentence in George Saintsbury's 1913 book on the English novel

---

[101] See my discussion of Phillips in Ch. 1, above.
[102] For more detail on Dyce's selection, see the discussion in Ch. 1, above.
[103] J. J. Jusserand, *The English Novel in the Time of Shakespeare* (1890: repr. London: Ernest Benn, 1966), p. 268.

as a follower of *Arcadia*.[104] In a similar vein, E. A. Baker accords *Urania* a brief paragraph in his wide-ranging *History of the English Novel*, once again disparaging it as an imitation of Sidney: 'copies and outdoes Sidney's utmost extravagances, both in the story and in the mode of telling it'.[105] Wroth is not so much singled out for criticism by these authors, but rather falls victim to their general impatience with the romance form. However, the revival of interest in Sidney's *Arcadia*, which might be dated from C. S. Lewis's glowing account of it in 1954 as a key sixteenth-century text, did not spill over into a concomitant interest in *Urania*. (The terms of Lewis's assessment, even allowing for changes in common English usage, perhaps points towards a split between those who might admire male writing, and those who would ignore writing by women: 'the *Arcadia* is a kind of touchstone. What a man thinks of it . . . tests the depths of his sympathy with the sixteenth century.')[106] As work on Sidney increased in the 1960s, Wroth remained neglected. *Urania* had been treated with imagination and sympathy by an almost invisible post-war critic (compared to Lewis), B. G. MacCarthy, who published a lengthy account of women writers of fiction in 1944. MacCarthy sees *Urania* as a direct product of Wroth's financial problems, and sees this as the reason that *Arcadia* was its model. But in an interesting counter to those who championed *Arcadia* and ignored *Urania*, MacCarthy maintains that Sidney's romance is 'wearying' and 'a digression in the development of the English novel', while *Urania* is saved by the realism of many of its inset stories.[107] MacCarthy singles out the narrative of Perissus and Limena, praising Wroth's use of dialogue and celebrating what she characterizes as Wroth's almost inadvertent anticipation of the strengths of later narrative realism. Ultimately Wroth comes out second best even in MacCarthy's more sympathetic account, this time in a comparison, not with *Arcadia*, but with Barclay's *Argenis*, praised for its greater narrative scope.[108]

Given that *Urania*'s length and complexity are undoubtedly daunting, even for scholars, it is still surprising that Wroth's poetry was as neglected as her prose until the 1980s. The transformation in Wroth's fortunes depended upon a considerable degree of editorial labour, notably that of Josephine Roberts, but also, for the poetry, Gary Waller. Waller began this process with the publication of his edition of 'Pamphilia to Amphilanthus' as a volume in the Salzburg Studies in English Literature series in 1977. Like other scholars working on Wroth at this time, Waller pays tribute to the postgraduate work of Margaret Witten-Hannah, whose doctoral dissertation of 1978 provided extensive information

---

[104] George Saintsbury, *The English Novel* (London: Dent, 1913), 44.

[105] E. A. Baker, *History of The English Novel* (London: H. F. and G. Witherby, 1929), ii. 122.

[106] C. S. Lewis, *English Literature in the Sixteenth Century Excluding Drama* (Oxford: Clarendon Press, 1954), 339.

[107] B. G. MacCarthy, *Women Writers: Their Contribution to the English Novel* (Cork: Cork University Press, 1944), 45 and 46.

[108] Ibid. 50.

about *Urania* and has frequently been drawn on by later criticism.[109] In his intro-duction, Waller cautiously advances the case for Wroth's verse: 'Lady Wroth's poems not only have a minor but interesting place in the development of the early seventeenth century lyric, but also show her to have been a careful and occa-sionally ambitious craftsman.'[110] When Waller's edition was joined by Roberts's complete edition of the poetry in 1983, one could not describe the result as a flood of critical interest, but Wroth became far more visible over the last twenty years, taking her place, as I mentioned at the beginning of this chapter, as the most clearly 'canonical' early modern woman writer before Aphra Behn.

[109] Margaret McLaren/Witten-Hannah, 'Lady Mary Wroth's *Urania*: The Work and the Tra-dition', University of Auckland Ph.D. diss., 1978.

[110] G. F. Waller, ed., *Pamphilia to Amphilanthus, by Lady Mary Wroth* (Salzburg: Salzburg University, 1977), 3; a detailed study of the poetry appeared in the same series in 1982: Mary Nelson Paulissen, *The Love Sonnets of Lady Mary Wroth* (Salzburg: Salzburg University, 1982).

# 4

# Anne Clifford: Writing a Family Identity

## CLIFFORD AS HEIR

Anne Clifford was born in 1590.[1] She was the daughter of George Clifford, third Earl of Cumberland, and Margaret Russell, who was the third daughter of the Earl of Bedford. Soon after Anne's birth, her father became Queen Elizabeth's official 'Champion', and, estranged from his wife, he spent most of his time at court—preceding this, he was a great seafarer, undertaking eleven expeditions to the West Indies. By the time she was just over a year old, Anne was Clifford's only surviving child—two sons who preceded her had died, the second when she was 15 months old. Her mother closely supervised Anne's upbringing, appointing Samuel Daniel as her tutor, and putting her in the care of her Aunt, Anne Russell, Countess of Warwick, who prepared her for a position in the Queen's Household. (Under James, before her marriage, she indeed attained that position, dancing, for example, in Jonson's *Masque of Beauty* and taking the part of Berenice in *The Masque of Queens*, because she, like Berenice, was famous for her beautiful hair.)

George Clifford died in 1605, leaving behind the enormous Clifford estate: a large area of Westmorland and North Yorkshire, including the five castles of Appleby, Brougham, Skipton, Brough, and Pendragon. Technically, Anne should have inherited her father's estates (though not necessarily his titles), because the Clifford inheritance had, during its history, bypassed inheritance through the male in favour of the oldest surviving child, male or female. However, George made a will in 1603 which left Anne £15,000, and the estates to his brother, Francis, who was his successor to the title of Earl.

When the provisions of the will were revealed to Anne and her mother, they promptly moved to Westmorland, where Margaret began to prepare a case for the legitimacy of Anne's inheritance of the Clifford landed estate. At the same time, Francis asserted his rights over the properties, barring Anne and Margaret's attempt to enter Skipton Castle. This contest was to last nearly forty years, until Anne, having outlived her uncle and his sons, finally inherited the Clifford estates

---

[1] The following biographical information is based on the authoritative biography by Richard T. Spence, *Lady Anne Clifford* (Stroud: Sutton, 1997); George C. Williamson, *Lady Anne Clifford* (Kendal: Titus Wilson and Son, 1922), remains a valuable resource, and contains numerous illustrations and some detailed extracts from documents not readily available elsewhere.

and most of the accompanying hereditary administrative titles in 1643. The process of arguing for her inheritance involved both Margaret and Anne in an extraordinarily detailed series of genealogical investigations and the subsequent production of hundreds of pages of copied documents, family trees, and biographical, historical, and autobiographical writing, particularly on Anne's part.

In 1607 Margaret commenced a legal action on behalf of Anne, arguing that Edward II had granted the estates to the nearest heir, male or female, and that accordingly Anne should inherit her father's estates. Margaret also arranged for Anne's marriage in 1609 to Richard Sackville, who became the Earl of Dorset when his father died two days after the wedding. As noted in Chapter 2, it is this wedding that Aemilia Lanyer commemorated in 'The Description of Cookham'. Richard Sackville inherited his family estate of Knole in Kent, and it is there that Anne spent much of her time from 1609 until Richard's death in 1624. Sackville spent much of his time in London, spending large sums of money on gambling while ingratiating himself with the King and leading courtiers—he also had some notoriety as a philanderer, conducting a long affair with Lady Penistone which produced two children. Anne felt herself to be exiled in Knole, far from her mother, who remained in possession of some of the Westmorland estates, which were part of her jointure. Anne was also pressured constantly by her husband to allow her uncle's inheritance to stand, in return for his promise to pay the £15,000, a sum which would have assisted Sackville greatly, given his financial extravagance. Anne resisted all attempts by her husband to persuade her to yield up her claim—these attempts included the removal from her care of Anne's beloved daughter Margaret, who was born in 1614 (after three sons, who died in infancy)—although it is fair to say that Sackville tended to relent quite quickly, and Anne seems to have had a certain amount of affection for him throughout the marriage.

Anne's greatest crisis came, not from her husband's pressure—she had a much stronger character than he—but when her mother died in 1616, leaving her to fight for her rights alone. A series of court judgments had gone against Anne, but she was being asked to accede to the judges' verdict and voluntarily give up her claim, and this idea was totally repugnant to her. This process culminated in an audience with King James in 1617, at which point, according to the account in Anne Clifford's diary:

My Lord and I kneeled by his chair side, when he persuaded us both to Peace, & to put the whole Matter wholly into his hands. Which my Lord consented to, but I beseech'd His Majesty to pardon me for that I would never part with Westmoreland while I lived upon any Condition whatsoever. Sometimes he used faire means & persuasions, & sometimes foul means, but I was resolved before so as nothing would move me (18 Jan. 1617).[2]

[2] Quotations from the early diary are from *The Diary of Anne Clifford 1616–1619: A Critical Edition*, ed. Katherine O. Acheson (New York: Garland, 1995); I have checked all quotations from Acheson against her copy-text, the Portland Papers MS at Longleat House, vol. 23, fos. 80–117.

The stalemate continued until Sackville's death in 1624. For six years after that, Anne lived in her dower estate in Sussex or in her maternal grandfather's house in Buckinghamshire. In 1630 she married Philip Herbert, the Earl of Pembroke, Mary Sidney's younger son. In 1630 Herbert was a powerful figure in King Charles's court—he was Lord Chamberlain, although, unlike his extremely intelligent and literate wife, he was boorish, and entirely uninterested in the life of the mind. He did steer a very cynical and successful path through the early stages of the Civil War, for which Anne seems to have been grateful. While she inherited her estates in 1643 when she became the sole surviving Clifford heir, the Civil War prevented her from moving to them until 1649. Anne made no bones about her Royalist loyalties, and one can only speculate about what conflict this might have caused with Herbert, who switched his loyalty from Charles to Parliament as soon as he recognized which side stood the best chance of winning. Anne's attitude towards her second husband can be seen from her account of her move northwards, when she decided that it was safe to do so: 'The 3rd of June in 1649, I took the last leave of my second husband ye Earle of Pembroke in his lodgings in the Cockpit near Whitehall, which was ye last time he & I ever saw one another' (100).[3] Pembroke died six months later.

Upon her arrival in Westmorland, Anne not only took over her lands, castles, and estates, but also a number of hereditary titles and functions, including that of High Sheriff of Westmorland. She vigorously prosecuted those who had encroached upon her estates, ran a fierce local court, and entered upon an extensive restoration programme, eventually rebuilding all five of her castles. She also embarked upon a memorializing process commemorating her mother, including an almshouse, an elaborate tomb, and even a memorial called the Countess's Pillar, which she placed on the road where she and her mother parted for the last time in April 1616. She continued to refine the elaborate series of manuscript books, called the Great Books, which were in part a record of her claim to the Clifford estates via genealogical and other documentary material, and in part an elaborate record of her day-to-day activities—a record kept up until the day of her death at the age of 86.

Another aspect of this memorializing is the remarkable painting she commissioned when she came into her inheritance. The painting was, for many years, hidden away in the Abbot Hall art gallery in Kendal, with only part of it on display, but was rehoused at Tate Britain during 2003. It is a huge triptych, measuring almost 19 by 9 feet. The left-hand panel shows Anne aged 15—in other words, at the age when she should have inherited the Clifford estates. This is paralleled by the right-hand panel, which shows her in 1643, the year she finally did inherit those estates: her stance and gestures in these panels mirror

---

[3] For ease of reference, I often quote from *The Diaries of Anne Clifford*, ed. D. J. H. Clifford (Stroud: Sutton, 1990), but this edition is extremely unreliable and all quotations from it have been checked against copies of the Great Books held at the Cumbrian Records Office (Kendal WD/Hoth, Hothfield Manuscripts), and emended accordingly.

each other. While in the portrait of Anne at 15, the two inset portraits are of her governess Anne Taylor and her tutor Samuel Daniel, in the right-hand panel the inset portraits are of her two husbands, Richard Sackville, Earl of Dorset, and Philip Herbert, Earl of Pembroke: both agreeably shrunk to a fairly insignificant size, even in the context of the generous size of the painting. The enormous middle panel shows Anne's parents gesturing towards her brothers, depicted as the infants they were when they died (in other words, it is intended to mark Anne's conception in June 1589). The inset portraits in this panel are of her four powerful aunts: Lady Frances Clifford, Lady Margaret Clifford, Lady Anne Russell, and Lady Elizabeth Russell. The central panel is bordered by the coats of arms tracing the complex history of the Clifford/de Veteripont family inheritance. Amongst the many minute details depicted in the painting, for the purposes of this chapter it is worth emphasizing the careful depiction of a number of influential books in Anne's life. In the left-hand panel, the young Anne is surrounded by a library that includes a large number of secular books: Camden's *Britannia* and her tutor Daniel's *Chronicles of England* as well as Daniel's collection of verse; Ortelius's *Theatre of the Whole World*; Gerard's *Herbal*; Castiglione's *Courtier*; Montaigne's *Essays*; *Don Quixote*; Chaucer; Ovid; and Sidney's *Arcadia*.[4] In her early diary Anne often mentions what was being read to her: for, example, on 12 and 13 August 1617 she says, 'I spent most of my time in playing Glecko & hearing Moll Neville reading the Arcadia.' There are also a number of religious works present, including the Bible, and theological works by authors like Bishop Joseph Hall and Downham.

In the right-hand panel, the 56-year-old Anne is surrounded by a larger number of religious works, by authors such as Henry More, John Donne, John King, and George Hakewill. However, literary works are also in evidence, including Jonson's folio *Works*, Herbert's 1633 *Temple*, Donne's *Poems*, Greville's *Works*, and Barclay's political romance *Argenis*. While the painting is extremely impressive, Anne Clifford's greatest achievement lies in her extensive construction of herself as resistant, self-reliant Clifford heir, through her personal diaries and the so-called Great Books.

## WRITING A SELF

In the context of early modern women's diaries and autobiographical writing, Anne Clifford might initially be seen as an example of breadth rather than depth. While there is a religious element to the accounts in the Great Books, there is no real self-searching along the lines of spiritual accounts by women such as

---

[4] For an important discussion of Clifford's books, and of Clifford as reader, see Mary Ellen Lamb, 'The Agency of the Split Subject: Lady Anne Clifford and the Uses of Reading', *ELR* 22 (1992), 347–68; Barbara Lewalski offers a wide-ranging account of Clifford's self-construction in *Writing Women in Jacobean England* (Cambridge Mass.: Harvard University Press, 1993), ch. 5.

Margaret Hoby.[5] While there are moments of intimate personal detail, these are fragmentary and mostly confined to the early diary. Rather, I would argue that the diaries need to be seen in the context of Clifford's sense of herself as heir to the family estates, and in that context they are part of a complex network of writing that has a clear public purpose, even if the 'public' concerned is somewhat different to one envisaged by manuscript publication. Both Mary Ellen Lamb and Mihoko Suzuki have argued that Clifford creates a sense of self (Lamb's telling phrase is 'herself as an heir') through a process of interpretation.[6] For Suzuki this involves Clifford's 'revision of traditional historiography', a process necessary to reinforce female rights, specifically to the Clifford estates, but more generally to a position of power, ultimately achieved when Clifford did return to the north and assumed control of her estates and hereditary privileges.[7] As Suzuki notes, Clifford's lifetime process of defending her claims and then reasserting them when they were finally achieved can be seen as a continuum, with various kinds of 'production', all serving a common purpose, from genealogies to almshouses, diaries to memorial pillars, rebuilt castles to religious precepts.[8] Similarly, Susan Wiseman has offered a convincing account of Clifford as a self-consciously political writer, even in the context of the early diary: 'Clifford sees herself, and invites her reader to see her, in the highly politicized contexts of the law, the contrast between the Elizabethan and Jacobean courts, and by using historical analogy.'[9]

In speaking of Clifford as a writer, it is necessary to widen one's definition along the lines suggested recently by Aaron Kunin, who is at pains to see the various forms of diary/memorial produced by Clifford as part of a single enterprise.[10] Kunin astutely observes that Clifford seldom wrote out her diaries in her own hand; instead, she used a variety of scribes, but she constantly annotated what was written. However, as Kunin argues, this was part of a self-assertive process by Clifford which involved a concerted attempt to dictate how the world should perceive her.[11] Because Clifford's early diaries survive only in a fragmented state, and by way of later transcripts from the eighteenth and nineteenth centuries, it is easy to treat them as if they are virually a separate genre from the Great Books, but I agree with Kunin that this is a misperception, and that all of the writing

<hr/>

[5] Hoby's diary for 1599–1605 makes a fascinating contrast with Clifford's diaries, as does her life. See the discussion in Ch. 1, above.

[6] Lamb, 'Agency', *passim*, and Mihoko Suzuki, 'Anne Clifford and the Gendering of History', *Clio*, 30 (2001), 195–230.

[7] Suzuki, 'Anne Clifford', 211.

[8] Ibid. 213–16.

[9] Susan Wiseman, 'Knowing Her Place: Anne Clifford and the Politics of Retreat', in Philippa Berry and Margaret Trudeau-Clayton, eds., *Textures of Renaissance Knowledge* (Manchester: Manchester University Press, 2003), 205.

[10] Aaron Kunin, 'From the Desk of Anne Clifford', *ELH* 71 (2004), 587–608; while Kunin is to a degree writing against Barbara Lewalski's characterization of the early diary, Lewalski offers an important interpretation of Clifford as an exemplar of female agency in the Jacobean era: see Lewalski, *Writing Women*.

[11] Kunin, 'Desk', esp. 603–5.

which survives is informed by the same aims, although, unlike Kunin, I would not necessarily use the term 'diary' to describe it all.

This sense of continuity is hard to capture because the diary for 1616–19 has received so much attention from literary and historical scholars, and general readers. This is hardly surprising, as it is, after all, both more easily assimilated than the later writings, and far more accessible. Paradoxically, the Great Books, which were designed to speak to posterity, have been largely neglected, up until now, in favour of what would have seemed to Clifford a more ephemeral production.

## THE NATURE OF THE CLIFFORD MANUSCRIPTS

It is worth pausing at this point to outline the different manuscript material which has survived. As noted above, the most visible is the 1616–19 diary, and the summary account of 1603. This diary survives in a transcript by Margaret Bentinck, dating from the mid-eighteenth century, and in a later transcript derived from Bentinck's, in part written out by Elizabeth Sackville, from the 1820s.[12] The earlier transcript was unnoticed in the Portland papers until Katherine Acheson's edition; the Knole manuscript, as will be discussed in detail later in this chapter, was discovered by Vita Sackville-West in the family archives at Knole when she began work on her family history. But Clifford's most ambitious project was the compilation of genealogical information tracing the Veteripont/Clifford line from the twelfth century through to Anne herself. The genealogical material was prepared for Clifford early in the seventeenth century by an antiquary called St Loe Kniveton as part of her case for obtaining her inheritance.[13] Much of the material gathered together during this period was then used to compile, under Clifford's direction, but again using scholarly and scribal assistance, three sets of folio volumes in which the genealogical material was transformed into elaborate illuminated genealogical trees, information was ordered, annotated and re-annotated, and eventually yearly accounts of Clifford's activities after she took possession of her estates were added to a third volume of each set. While there has been some speculation that the three sets were prepared in order for one to be sent to the lawyer Mathew Hale in 1651 to allow him to compile further evidence justifying the inheritance, I believe that Clifford would have had the intention of ensuring that a set was available to pass on to each of her two daughters: Margaret, her eldest surviving child, and therefore the inheritor in turn of the estates, and her second daughter Isabella.[14] From this perspective, while it is clear that a set was required in London for legal and advisory purposes, the multiple sets (like the two copies of the Great Picture), seem to me to confirm Clifford's desire to

---

[12] Acheson offers what seems to me to be clear proof of the identity of both Bentinck and Sackville, and of the reliance of the Knole MS on the Portland MS; see her detailed account, 17–29.

[13] See the discussion in Spence, *Anne Clifford*, 164–8.

[14] See ibid. 177–8.

circulate this material within her family through succeeding generations, most especially via each of her two daughters, thus confirming the continuation of the female line of inheritance.

It is difficult to convey the full impact of the Great Books to someone who has not actually seen them. They are huge folios and they are elaborately illuminated (especially the first two volumes, and especially the first set). The first volume title page points to what might be called the public, social role envisaged for the Great Books; it is worth quoting in full because it conveys some of the weightiness of Clifford's endeavour to have the Great Books serve as a series of monuments to her claims—monuments which would be preserved and read by future generations, just like Great Picture:

> Through the mercies of the holy trinity:
> God the Father, creator of the world
> God the Sonn, Christ Jesus Redeemer of the world
> God the Holie Ghost, sanctifier and preserver of the world
> Doth proceed all blessings, both temporall and eternall.

Under this is an elaborate interwoven rule, followed by (in capitals):

This is the first booke of the recordes concerning the two noble families of the Cliffords. which weare [*sic*] Lords Cliffods [*sic*] of Clifford Castle in Herefordshire, and of the Veteriponts, who were lords Barons and high shreifs [*sic*] of Westmerland Which booke was compiled Anno 1649 by the care & industrie of the Lady Ann Clifford, Countess of Dorsett, Pembroke & Montgomery, Daughter and sole heire of Georg Clifford late Earl of Cumberland, which lady by birthright from her father and his auncestors is Barones Clifford of Westmerland, and Vescy, and High Shreives of that county and Lady of the Honor of Skipton in Craven being lineally descended from both those noble familyes.

This title sums up Anne Clifford's hereditary claims and indicates the nature of the first two volumes of each set of Great Books: genealogical material of various kinds, including the elaborate, illuminated coats of arms and family trees of the Clifford and Veteripont families.[15] The first volume is 200 folios long and it takes a considerable amount of time for a reader to absorb its detail, even in a cursory reading; it brings the family history up to the thirteenth century.[16] The

---

[15] I was able to undertake a limited collation of the two sets of Great Books that were available in the Cumbrian Records Office in Kendal in 2002, and will at times point to some of the significant differences between them. The third set, formerly in private hands, was lodged with the Cumbrian Records Office in 2004. A full collation of the three sets would be an extremely valuable, if time-consuming, exercise.

[16] I have taken as my copy-text the set that has 'And his Auncesters' at the end of the title page, and number it as 1, the second set as 2: No. 1 seems, on the whole, to be more extensively annotated and elaborately illustrated than No. 2; one telling example is in vol. 3, where copy 1 annotates the lozenge containing Anne's details as 1652, when she was Dowager Countess of Pembroke (fo. 200), whereas in copy 2 the lozenge is dated 1648 with Anne described as 'now Countess of Pembroke' (fo. 155). However it seems that the third set may also be elaborately annotated by Clifford, and the exact relationship between the three sets will not be known until they are fully collated.

second volume, which covers the family history from the thirteenth to sixteenth centuries, begins again with an elaborate title page very similar to that of the first volume, though with an added note, indicating the progressive annotation of the volumes, 'But the Sumaries were not written in till the year 1652'.[17] The gene-alogical material is once again beautifully illuminated; but as a work in progress and a retrospective history, these volumes include the sources for material which again supports the contention that the Clifford inheritance could run through the female line. Thus, for example, a deposition on the inheritance is annotated in the margin as:

In the receipt of the Excheq. is this long presidende [i.e. precedent] to be found, which is a speciall Record to prove the title of Anne Countesse of Pembrooke etc.: to her Inher-itance in westmerland & Craven, and was first taken out of that Office, by Margarett C[o]untes Dowager of Cumberland her Religious and Excellent Mother with great In-dustry & difficulty the 28 of November the 6. yeare of K: James of England, & of Scotland the 42 in the yeare of our lord God 1608. (copy 1, vol. ii, fo. 30)

It is characteristic of Clifford that the Great Books contain an amalgama-tion of what Spence describes as 'their scholarly apparatus, worthy of modern researchers' publications', and the intensely personal and idiosyncratic.[18] This is also evident in the earlier 1616–19 diaries, where the two-column format with retrospective commentary interleaves political and social milestones of vari-ous kinds with Clifford's personal details. This process underlines the way that Clifford constantly positioned her struggles to acquire and then maintain her inheritance within a political context, something that is then emphasized in her insistence on maintaining all her customary rights in Westmorland and, even more important for our purposes, in *recording* her activities.

Clifford's assimilation of family history, personal history, and political asser-tion, becomes most evident in the third volume of the Great Books, which moves from the past to the present. Once again, the third volume has the same elab-orate title page as the first two volumes, and it begins with similar transcripts of documents. The genealogical material, in the usual format of an elaborately illustrated family tree, brings us up to the present, with a record of the mar-riages of Anne's daughters Margaret and Isabella and the number of their chil-dren (though not their names). The Clifford narrative then reaches Anne's great grandfather, Henry Clifford, first Earl of Cumberland (fos. 18 ff.), and it is at this point that the style of documentation and narrative changes. The biography of Anne's father George begins with a heading again calling attention to Anne's position as heir. It begins: 'Sumarie of the Recordes concerning George Lord and Baron of Clifford', notes all his titles including 'high sherriffe of Westmorland', and ends: 'Hee married the Ladie Margaret Russell youngest childe to Francis

---

[17] Copy 1 has an elaborate coloured rule under 'Temporall and Eternal'; this is not the case in copy 2.
[18] Spence, *Anne Clifford*, 164.

Russell second Lord of Bedford By whome he had his onlie Daughter & sole heir that lived the ladie Anne Clifford now Countess Dowager of Pembroke, Dorset, and Montgomery' (fo. 124).

Anne emphasizes the glory of her family when she recounts her father's life, stressing his colonial voyages. This aspect of George Clifford's career is further enhanced for the family records by the separate manuscript of Richard Robinson's account of George Clifford's voyages, another account of them, and accounts of his speeches to Queen Elizabeth on her coronation, and in 1592 when George was made champion of the tiltyard.[19] Given that Anne's aim at this point is to underline the family's achievements, with her position as heir firmly established, she is surprisingly charitable towards her uncle and cousin, Francis and Henry Clifford, who had between them displaced her from her inheritance for almost forty years. Anne's account of them is quite bland, but perhaps she is able to be charitable because she has now arrived at her own story, and more particularly, because the Great Books are for the eyes of posterity.

Placed at the end of all this accumulated weight of family history, and genea-logical and legal documentation, Anne's account of her own life, beginning with her birth, has an inevitable triumphalism. Initially, Anne's account of herself out-lines a process which leads inexorably, through all her trials and assertions of her rights, to the successful inheritance. It symbolically gathers up five centuries of family heritage, and it proves that Anne is a worthy heir because of the strength of purpose she has shown. This is also bound up in the fact that the family his-tory underlines the presence of previous female heirs: strong precedents for Anne, such as Idonea and Isabella, the co-heirs of Robert de Veteripont.

After further family trees, Anne begins her autobiographical account as 'A Summary of the Records and a true memoriall of the life of mee the Lady Anne Clifford' (fo. 270). Here she divides her life up into sections according to her marriages, beginning with her birth and childhood, then moving from 'The course of my life while I was wife and widdow to Richard Sackville Earle of Dorsett' to 'The course of my life while I was wife and widdow to Phillip Harbert Earl of Pembrooke and Montgomerye'. When Clifford then reaches the point at which she was able to travel north and take over her estates, she catches up with the process whereby the Great Books began to be created, and so she shifts into a year-by-year summary, beginning in 1650 with the account of Philip Herbert's death.

Because the Great Books are always in process, rather than ever finished, the yearly summaries, like the earlier material, are annotated and reannotated as the years pass. This process occurs from 1650 until December 1675. Even in the last few months of her life, Clifford continued to record her thoughts and experi-ences, preserved in the diary called the 'day book', largely dictated to her sec-retary Edward Hasell and preserved by his family in their home, Dalemain.[20]

---

[19] The manuscripts are Cumbrian Records Office, WD/Hoth/A988/6.
[20] See Spence, *Anne Clifford*, 176, and the transcript in Clifford, *Diaries*, 229–69.

This diary is a day-by-day account, rather than the summarizing process of the yearly accounts for the preceding twenty-five years, so that it is reminiscent of the 1616–19 diary in giving us a more intimate glimpse of Clifford in the last few months of her life. She notably complains about her confinement, stating more than once 'I went not out of the house nor out of my chamber today'.[21] This is a significant statement because, as the yearly summaries make plain, Clifford undertook a series of progresses each year which served to emphasize her possession of all the different parts of her inheritance, proceeding like a monarch from castle to castle accompanied by her household, carefully recording the fact that she slept in various rooms in the properties she had restored so painstakingly.

If the Great Books as a whole are a palimpsest, revealing successive annotations by Clifford, as she relentlessly added to the evidence which would force posterity to acknowledge, over and over again, the rights she assumed on behalf of her descendants, then the year-by-year summaries are palimpsests in miniature. I want to emphasize once again how important it is that these yearly summaries occur, for the reader of the Great Books, at the end of the massive amount of preceding information about Clifford's family, her battle for her inheritance, and the inheritance itself. (This is, of course, an effect which is lost to a modern reader who only encounters the yearly summaries as part of D. J. H. Clifford's useful, but in this sense circumscribed, edition, in which they are detached from their context in the Great Books and presented as part of a compilation beginning with the earlier diaries.) I will take a random example to illustrate how the yearly summaries are layered in this way.

Each yearly summary is headed by the same formula, and here I will discuss 'In the year of ower Lord God 1653'. In 1653 Clifford was at a comparatively early stage of her reassertion of her rights over her estates; in effect, she undertook a campaign to overturn the tenancy arrangements that had been put in place by her uncle and cousin. What we see in the early paragraphs of 1653 is an interweaving of dynastic information, personal information about Clifford herself, information about contests with her tenants, and information about the memorializing process I have described, in this instance the establishment of the almshouse in her mother's memory. As she points out, Clifford turned 63 in 1653. Reaching her climacteric was a considerable achievement, given the life expectancy at the time, and the vigour with which Clifford approached her responsibilities belied her age.

In dynastic terms, in this extract Clifford focuses on John Tufton, her favourite grandchild. Clifford saw all her grandchildren as important to the continuation of the family, as evidenced by the recording of the birth of her younger daughter Isabella's son William, and the later insertion of the details of his death in 1661. It is perhaps worth noting at this point the constant insertion of biblical references in the yearly summaries. These are more prominent in the set of Great

21 For this phrase see, e.g., 2, 6, 8 Jan.; Clifford, *Diaries*, 231–4.

Books I have labelled Copy One, which is another indication that this set was more personal than the second set.[22] So, for example, in Copy One the recording of the birth of William finishes with references to Jeremiah 29: 6 and 30: 19, and to Genesis 1: 28, 26: 22, 26: 12–14—references to fruitfulness that would have rung hollow after his death at the age of 8. It is typical of Clifford that she should include Genesis 26: 14 (referring to Isaac): 'For he had possession of flocks and possessions of herds, and great store of servants: and the Philistines envied him.' Here are the first entries from 1653 (my text is Copy One, fos. 280–1):

In the beginning of this yeare, one thousand six hundred fiftie three (as the yeare begins on New yeares daie) did I cause severall Courtes to be kept in my name in divers of my mannors within this Countie. But the tennants being obstinate and refractory[23] though they appeared would not aunswere as they were called. And also manie Liases of Eiect-mentt[24] did I cause to be sealled in this Countie in order to a Tryall with my Tennants at Common Law. God send them good success, Isa: C: 30: v: 21.[25]

And the thirtieth day of this Jannuarie, (Being my Birthday) Did I pass my clymactericall yeare of sixty three the yeare (amongst phisitians) accounted so remarkable. Psa: 123.

The twentie eight of this March my Grande-childe Mr John Tufton went from Appleby Castle to yorke, from thence to London, and so to Hothfeild howse in Kentt to his Father and Mother, Brothers, and sisters, and within a while after, to Eaten Colledge, there to studdy where hee now remayned, from the 25 of Aprill, for the most part, till the fifte of July in the yeare following: then he went from thence to Skipton and soe to Oxford by the second of August followinge, to be a Student there.

And in the beginning of this yeare was my Almeshouse here at Appleby quite finished, which had bene almost five yeares a building. So as I now putt into it twelve goode women (eleven of them being widdowes) and the twelft a maymed[26] Maid, and a Mother, a Deceased Ministers widdow, some of whom I putt into the said House in December and the rest in Januarie and the begining of March following. Luke C: 7:v:5: Psa: 116: v: 12: 13: 14[27]

The twentie seventh of this May was my youngest daughter the Countesse of Northampton delivered of her second Childe (which was alsoe a Sonne) in her Lords House called Canbury, by Islington neare London. Who was Christened there the next day after by the name of William. I lying then in my Castle here att Appleby in Westmerland. The Birth of which childe I account as an extraordinary greate Blessinge and Seale of Gods Mercies to mee and myne, Jeremy C: 29: v: 6: ye latter part of it & C: 30:v: 19: Gen: C: 1: v: 28: & C: 26: v: 22: Psa: 116: v: 12: 13: 14. But he dyed to my great griefe and sorrow on

---

[22] Because the D. J. H. Clifford edition of the *Diaries* seems based on copy 2, the biblical allusions are less prominent there; he also occasionally omits them even when they are present in copy 2. Their greater prominence in copy 1 is further evidence for this set being more closely attached to Clifford herself.

[23] D. J. H. Clifford, *Diaries*, mis-transcribes 'refractory' as 'no fractor' then adds 'i.e.' (p. 116).

[24] 'Liases of Eiectmentt' in both copies, mis-transcribed as 'causes of Enactment', ibid.

[25] 'send them good success' in both copies, mis-transcribed as 'save them good signs', ibid.

[26] 'a maymed' mistranscribed as 'an injured', ibid.

[27] Biblical verses not in copy 2.

the 18 day of September in 1661 in his father the earle of Northamptons House at Castle Ashby in Northamptonshire.[28]

This extract is about a quarter of the entire entry for 1653. As noted above, it combines the more overt political manoeuvring as Clifford reasserted her control over her estates and, in a more intimate way, a continuation of the painstaking family history that bolstered her claim in the first place, as John Tufton and the unfortunate William Compton are, in their turn, written into the family records. I have been reiterating the idea that all of Clifford's writing is directed towards an implied audience stretching ever forwards in time: a projection that must have seemed surer as time rolled by, and Clifford moved a further twenty-three years past her climacteric.[29] Her writing did indeed find a series of devoted future readers, and her memorializing was extremely effective, as the next section will indicate.

## THE INHERITORS

Anne Clifford originally intended to divide her Clifford estates between her two daughters. (On Clifford's death in 1676, her dower estates from her two marriages reverted to the Dorset and Pembroke heirs: Richard Sackville, fifth Earl of Dorset, and Philip Herbert, seventh Earl of Pembroke.) However, Clifford's younger daughter Isabella died in 1661 and none of Isabella's children had children themselves (Isabella's last surviving child, Alethea, died in 1678). Clifford's elder daughter, Margaret, married John Tufton in 1629 at the age of 15. Margaret had twelve children. Margaret's eldest son, Nicholas, married Elizabeth Boyle, but they had no children, so when Nicholas died in 1679 (only three years after his grandmother), Clifford's favourite grandson John became fourth Earl of Thanet, and inherited his grandmother's estates. In her will, Clifford continues the process of obsessively controlling her inheritance that is so evident in all her writing.[30] She claimed that, as the last sole Clifford heir, she could dispose of her estates as she pleased, and she bequeathed her Westmorland estates to John Tufton, rather than Nicholas, leaving Nicholas to institute legal proceedings to obtain them. While he was successful, his death, as noted above, ensured that John was sole heir. John, who also had no children, was succeeded by his brother Richard in 1680; Richard, unmarried, was succeeded in 1684 by yet another brother, Thomas, who lived until 1729, but also died without children. The estates then passed to Thomas's nephew Sackville, son of the youngest of Clifford's grandsons, who was also named Sackville.

---

[28] As noted above, the biblical verses are not in copy 2; in copy 1 the sentence about William's death has been squeezed in at the end of the paragraph in a different hand.

[29] Here I am following Susan Wiseman's argument for what she terms Clifford's rearticulation of her past 'to proclaim her restoration', Wiseman, 'Knowing Her Place', 207.

[30] For the details of the will, see Williamson, *Anne Clifford*, app. 5.

What we might call the literary inheritance becomes particularly interesting if we turn back to Thomas Tufton, the sixth Earl of Thanet. He married Catherine Cavendish daughter of Henry Cavendish, the Duke of Newcastle (the son of William Cavendish and stepson of Margaret Cavendish).[31] Catherine's sister Margaret's daughter, Henrietta Cavendish Holles, married Edward Harley, second Duke of Oxford, a great collector of manuscripts. Their daughter was Margaret Bentinck, Duchess of Portland, who retained the more personal material from her father's manuscript collection following its sale to the nation in 1753 (now the Harleian manuscript collection housed in the British Library). Margaret's daughter Elizabeth took these papers with her to Longleat House following her marriage to the Marquess of Bath.[32] Partly because of their literary and antiquarian interests, and also one assumes because of their family connection, the Harley family continued the manuscript transmission of Clifford's written inheritance. A copy of a summary account of the family history, and of Anne Clifford's life, essentially a digest derived from the Great Books, was prepared in 1737 by a Henry Fisher and deposited as part of the Harleian Collection.[33] More significantly, Margaret Bentinck wrote out her own copy of the 1616–19 diary, along with other Clifford material.[34] One can only speculate that this particular diary, with its more intimate account of the young Anne Clifford defiantly asserting her rights against the persuasions of a series of powerful men, up to and including King James, and its glimpses of her close relationship with her mother and with her small daughter Margaret, appealed to Clifford's female descendants, however distant they were. This is reinforced by the later manuscript of the 1616–19 diary, almost certainly copied from Bentinck's transcription by Elizabeth Sackville at Knole around 1826.[35]

One can see this process of engagement by Margaret Bentinck and Elizabeth Sackville, continuing, we will see, through to Vita Sackville-West, Elizabeth Sackville's grand-daughter, as a continuation of a specifically female written tradition that goes back to Anne Clifford's mother Margaret Russell. As noted above, Anne drew immense strength from her mother, and established a series of monuments to her memory, including the Appleby almshouses. Margaret Russell was herself a forceful and highly educated woman (like her sisters, who are themselves commemorated by Clifford in the inset portraits in the central panel of the Great Picture). Russell was actively engaged in alchemical experiments, and her receipt

---

[31] For a detailed consideration of Margaret Cavendish, see below, Ch. 6.

[32] The most concise account of this situation is Clifford, *Diary*, ed. Acheson, 22–3.

[33] This is Harleian MS 6177; part of it is available in J. P. Gilson, ed., *Lives of Lady Anne Clifford* (London: Roxburghe Club, 1916).

[34] This includes the 1603 summary, written, as Acheson notes, in a 'professional scribal hand' (22), as opposed to the rest of the material, which is transcribed by Bentinck.

[35] Once again, see *Diary*, ed. Acheson, 18–22.

book is preserved with Anne Clifford's manuscripts, along with a series of letters from Anne to her mother.[36]

One can see this process as part of the ever-widening transmission within Clifford's descendants of her written inheritance, which sometimes was connected to the material inheritance, but was sometimes quite a separate issue. The Great Books and a lot of accompanying manuscript material were passed down through the family until the twentieth and twenty-first centuries. The Great Books were consulted by considerable numbers of people outside the family, for a variety of reasons, until they were made fully public with the deposit of two sets in the Cumbrian Records Office by Anthony Charles Sackville Tufton, Lord Hothfield, in 1986. A more public transmission of Clifford as a historical figure occurred alongside this familial process.

## THE PUBLIC IMAGE

The Anne Clifford legend, as we might call it, had considerable currency in the eighteenth and nineteenth centuries. Clifford herself sets this entire process in motion, through what Susan Wiseman aptly terms her 'textualisation of land, buildings and life'.[37] We can see its continuation immediately after her death in Bishop Edward Rainbowe's funeral sermon, published in 1677. Rainbowe's elaborate eulogy details all of Clifford's charitable and memorializing activities, but most notably he calls our attention to the Great Books in a reference that once again underlines their position as manuscripts that exist in the—not uncommonly for the seventeenth century—liminal space between private and public. Rainbowe states:

From this her great *Diligence*, her Posterity may find contentment in reading these abstracts of *Occurrences* in her own life; being added to her *Heroick Father's, and Pious Mother's* Lives, dictated by her self; so, they may reap greater fruits of her Diligence, in finding the *Honours, Descents*, and *Pedigrees, Estates*, and the *Titles* and *Claims* of their *Progenitors* to them, comprized Historically and Methodically in three Volumes of the larged [*sic*] size, and each of them three (or four) times fairly written over; which although these volumes were said to have been collected and digested in some part, by one or more, Learned Heads, yet were they wholly directed by her self, and attested to in most parts by her own Hand.[38]

---

[36] The receipt book is WD/Hoth/A988/5; the letters are WD HOTH/988/4, the letters are annotated and summarized by Anne; see the insightful account of Anne and her mother in Lewalski, *Writing Women*, 133–6.

[37] Wiseman, 'Knowing Her Place', 217.

[38] Edward Rainbowe, *A Sermon Preached* (1677), 52.

This statement by Rainbowe is reproduced in George Ballard's account of Clifford, although Ballard himself does not appear to have seen any of Clifford's manuscripts.[39] Walpole relies on Ballard and once again does not seem to have seen Clifford's manuscripts, while Thomas Park, in his 1806 additions to Walpole, states that he has been unable to find the Clifford manuscript material in the Harleian collection.[40] Park does note the sustained eighteenth-century interest in Clifford as a legendary figure, known particularly well to local historians.

For example, in 1795 William Seward tells Clifford's story and reproduces the 1603 summary in *Anecdotes of Some Distinguished Persons Chiefly of the Present and the Two Preceding Centuries*, putting her in varied but usually distinguished company, which would undoubtedly have appealed to her.[41] Spence notes the influence of the Great Books and other manuscript material on regional historians in the late eighteenth and early nineteenth centuries, such as Nicholson and Burns's *History and Antiquities of the Counties of Westmorland and Cumberland* and T. D. Whitaker's *History and Antiquities of the Deanery of Craven*.[42]

The idea of Clifford as an unusual and notable figure is then taken up in such works as Hartley Coleridge's *Worthies of Yorkshire and Lancashire* (1839), which draws upon Whitaker, rather than the diaries, and offers a paean to Clifford as an exemplary woman who 'happily combined the graces and charities of the high-born woman with the sterner qualifications of a ruler'.[43] The sense of Clifford as belonging to regional and family history continued into the twentieth century, as the biographical compilation by George Williamson, published in a limited edition in Kendal in 1922, testifies, as do the family connections (however distant) of those who followed, including D. J. H. Clifford, who edited the diaries in 1990, and Hugh Clifford, who published a family history.[44] In terms of Clifford's writing, however, the complex relationship between Vita Sackville-West and Virginia Woolf produced the most fascinating example of her influence.

## REVENANTS

After Vita Sackville-West compiled her family history, *Knole and the Sackvilles*, in 1922, her publishers, Heinemann, were approached by Maurice Hewlett with a

---

[39] See George Ballard, *Memoirs of Several Ladies of Great Britain*, ed. Ruth Perry (Detroit: Wayne State University Press, 1985), 283–9.

[40] Horace Walpole, *A Catalogue of the Royal and Noble Authors of England, Scotland, and Ireland ... enlarged and continued to the present time by Thomas Park* (London: John Scott, 1806), ii. 178–88.

[41] William Seward, *Anecdotes of Some Distinguished Persons* (London: T. Cadell, 1795), iv. 302–17.

[42] Spence, *Anne Clifford*, 250.

[43] Hartley Coleridge, *Lives of Northern Worthies*, ed. Derwent Coleridge (London: Edward Moxon, 1852), ii. 7.

[44] See Williamson, *Anne Clifford*; D. J. H. Clifford, *Diaries of Anne Clifford*; Hugh Clifford, *The House of Clifford* (Chichester: Phillimore, 1987).

suggestion for another project.[45] According to Sackville-West, Hewlett wrote to Heinemann in the following terms:

What I really want of Miss Sackville-West—and what I shall ask you to get out of her—is an edition of Lady Anne Clifford's Diary. This certainly ought to be published. . . . We are awfully behind the French in seventeenth-century memoirs. You will be doing a service to your country. (p.lxiii) [46]

Sackville-West was clearly flattered by this notion that her commemoration of her heritage was in fact a service to her country. In *Knole and the Sackvilles*, Anne Clifford featured as a source of intimate information about Knole in the seventeenth century. Sackville-West wrote *Knole and the Sackvilles* as a tribute to, and memorial of, the house from which she was exiled. While she does not say so explicitly, she was drawn to Anne Clifford as a fellow exile, although, paradoxically, Clifford was exiled from her estates in the north of England, and Sackville-West's beloved Knole was, for Clifford, a prison in which she was confined by her husband, Richard Sackville, Earl of Dorset. The parallel between the two women extends to the fact that Sackville-West was excluded from inheriting Knole because she was female, just as Clifford had to fight to inherit her father's estates.[47] While Vita Sackville-West remained alienated from Knole when it was inherited after her father's death in 1928 by *her* uncle, Charles, Anne Clifford, after a long wait of some forty years, took possession of her estates in Westmorland and assumed all the authority that went with them.[48] It is clear from Sackville-West's description that she takes some vicarious pleasure in Clifford's triumph; she writes:

Anne . . . remained single-hearted throughout: she was the legal heiress of the North and the North she would have; and in the midst of the otherwise sordid and mercenary dispute, in which Dorset used every means of coercion, she remains fixed in her perfectly definite attitude of obstinacy, unswayed by her husband, his relations, her own relations, their friends, the Archbishop of Canterbury, and even the King himself, their remonstrances, their threats, their vindictiveness, and the actual injuries she had to endure over a long stretch of years. In the end she got the better of them all, and the last picture of her left by the 'Lives' is that of a triumphant and imperious old lady. (67)[49]

Admittedly, Sackville-West goes on to call Clifford a 'patriarchal old despot' (ibid.), but this phrase too is rather admiring in tone. Sackville-West concluded

---

[45] Victoria Glendinning, *Vita: The Life of V. Sackville-West* (London: Weidenfeld and Nicolson, 1983).

[46] Parenthetical references to Vita Sackville-West, ed., *The Diary of the Lady Anne Clifford* (London: William Heinemann, 1923).

[47] This parallel is pointed out by Nicky Hallett in Nicky Hallett, 'Anne Clifford as Orlando: Virginia Woolf's Feminist Historiology and Women's Biography', *Women's History Review*, 4/4 (1995).

[48] This point is also made by Suzuki.

[49] Parenthetical references to Vita Sackville-West, *Knole and the Sackvilles* (Tonbridge: Ernest Benn, 1922; rpt. 1984).

later editions of *Knole and the Sackvilles* with an appendix recording 'with sorrow' (215) the relinquishment of Knole to the National Trust in 1947. Admirers of Sissinghurst might say that Vita Sackville-West's exile from Knole had its compensations, but throughout her adult life Sackville-West was in mourning for the loss of Knole, and she was strongly drawn to Anne Clifford as an example of a woman who moved from exile to a triumphant return and mastery of her estates. In 1928 Sackville-West wrote to her husband describing a nocturnal visit to Knole, and stating 'there is some sort of umbilical cord that ties me to Knole'; on another occasion she specifically described herself as being like 'the ghost of Lady Anne Clifford'. [50]

Sackville-West also notes that the older, triumphant Anne Clifford is a less attractive personality than the young woman held captive at Knole. Sackville-West observes that: 'This vigorous mind was not, perhaps, planned on a very broad scale. It was self-centred and self-sufficient; severe but not reckless; no fine carelessness endears her to us, or surprises' (*Knole and the Sackvilles*, 82).

The young Clifford of the early seventeeth-century diary is a different figure, and, as noted above, women like Margaret Bentinck, Elizabeth Sackville, and Vita Sackville-West were drawn to the intimacy of the 1616–19 diary, with its personal details; for example, Clifford writes: 'I used to wear my hair color'd velvet every day & learned to sing & play on the bass Viol of Jack Jenkins my Aunt's Boy' (16). It is this kind of detail that makes the young Clifford in particular an attractive figure, who appears to give the reader occasional intimate glimpses of herself.

In her introduction to the Diary, Sackville-West begins by being rather in thrall to the charms of Anne Clifford's father, who was, for Sackville-West, the archetypal Elizabethan adventurer. For Anne Clifford, her father was a complex figure who ultimately brought about her alienation from her estates; in contrast, for Vita Sackville-West George Clifford is a colourful figure who evokes the Elizabethan age. Anne idolized her mother; Sackville-West, on the other hand, had very ambivalent feelings about *her* mother. Accordingly, she describes Anne Clifford's position in a way that undermines Margaret Russell's character: 'I imagine Anne Clifford, then, in a childhood restrained on the one hand by the severe and virtuous influence of an ever-present mother, and coloured on the other hand by the fable of an adventuorus and almost legendary father' (pp. xxvi–vii). This representation of Clifford's parents is very different to her own perception, which elevated her mother to a guiding model of steadfastness, especially during her time at Knole, when they were separated by such a great distance for such a long period of time.

Sackville-West's projection of her own circumstances on to Anne Clifford becomes strongest when she contemplates Clifford's time at Knole; she writes:

---

[50] Glendinning, *Vita*, 196; Nigel Nicolson, ed., *Vita and Harold: The Letters of Vita Sackville-West and Harold Nicolson* (Stroud: Phoenix, 1992), 196. Sackville-West's love of Knole and sadness at her loss of it form a central theme in Glendinning's biography.

'Knole I have seen as Anne Clifford saw it, quietly magnificent, down there in Kent, with its grey towers and wide lawns and glinting windows, and the flag floating high up in the cool empty blue' (p. xxxiii). Sackville-West's sense of connection to the Elizabethan and Jacobean Knole is evident throughout her account of Clifford, who supplied her with a portrait of a woman into whose situation she could project her own longings. Ultimately, this was intertwined with Virginia Woolf's imaginative revisioning of Vita as the protagonist in *Orlando*, published in 1928, an image which is at its most vivid when it constructs an imaginary Elizabethan gentleman. Nicky Hallett has made a strong case for a connection between Orlando and Anne Clifford, particularly apparent in Woolf's early drafts of *Orlando*.[51] When *Orlando* was first published, it was illustrated with a series of photographs that served to strengthen the homage to Vita Sackville-West (and indirectly the connection with Clifford). The frontispiece showing Orlando as a boy is in fact taken from a portrait of Edward Sackville, son of the fourth Earl of Dorset; the 'Archduchess Harriet' is a portrait of the fourth Earl's wife Mary Curzon; and the photograph of Orlando as ambassador is from a portrait of Lionel Sackville, the seventh Earl. All these portraits were sourced from the Knole collection by Woolf and Sackville-West; three further photographs of Orlando are in fact photographs of Vita Sackville-West.[52] Hallett argues that Clifford was in part a model for Woolf's revisioning of women's history. This is a most suggestive way of looking at Woolf's encounter with Clifford through the medium of Vita Sackville-West.

Indeed, at this time Sackville-West and Woolf's close relationship fed into their interest in a variety of early modern women writers and historical figures. Woolf turned to Sackville-West's edition of the Diary in her essay 'Donne after Three Centuries' when she wanted to conjure up a picture of Donne's relationship to female patrons. Woolf sees, in the diary, a quite different Clifford to the figure identified with in complex ways by Sackville-West. Woolf notes how Clifford combined her materialism with a hearty interest in literature: 'A great heiress, infected with all the passion of her age for lands and houses, busied with all the cares of wealth and property, she still read good English books as naturally as she ate good beef and mutton.'[53] Woolf was particularly taken with the story that Clifford had texts pinned to her bed curtains, and Woolf embroiders this notion into a surreal image linking Clifford with a more famous solipsist; Woolf writes: 'Words from great writers nailed to the walls of the room in which she sat, eternally transacting business, surrounded her as she worked, as they surrounded Montaigne in his tower in Burgundy.'[54] Nicky Hallett notes how

---

[51] See Hallett, 'Clifford as Orlando', *passim*.

[52] For a brief account of the photographs, see Sheila M. Wilkinson and Stuart N. Clarke, 'Illustrations in the First Editions of *Orlando: A Biography*', Virginia Woolf Society of Great Britain, www.orlando.jp.org/VWSGB/dat/illusOr.html (accessed 29/03/05).

[53] Virginia Woolf, *The Common Reader: Second Series* (London: Hogarth Press, 1932).

[54] Ibid.; this image of Clifford has its origins in Rainbowe's funeral sermon.

Woolf returned to Clifford towards the end of her life when she was working on what she conceived as a history of English literature.[55] She made further reading notes on Clifford's Diary in 1940.[56] In a chapter that exists in a series of unpublished drafts, Woolf begins her account of 'The Reader' with the image of Clifford, who is seen here by Woolf as someone who records possessions: 'As if to solidify her possessions she wrote out inventories of them' (427). Woolf also astutely notes how 'The sense of the body permeates her pages' (ibid.). Ultimately, Woolf captures Clifford turning to Chaucer for solace when, in Woolf's words, 'even this carapace of possessions proved too heavy for her' (ibid.). In the end, Woolf sees Clifford as a reader, rather than as a writer; her emphasis is on the early Diary, and obliquely on some of the information recorded in George Williamson's massive 1922 biography of Clifford.[57]

I will be returning to Woolf and Sackville-West's engagement with early modern women's writing in Chapter 7, when I come to consider Aphra Behn, who was a key figure for both women. Indeed, Behn and Clifford became for Sackville-West contrasting figures intimately bound up, in the end, in her attitudes towards Woolf. But I want to end this chapter with a brief account of Clifford's increasing visibility, as she has moved into a prominence that would certainly have delighted her. The fierce memorializing process engaged in by Clifford, both through her writing and through other means, such as paintings, monuments, and buildings, seems more successful than ever. The Great Picture has spent some time away from the comparative obscurity of the Abbot Hall art gallery in Kendal (where it was often not fully on display) to pride of place in Tate Britain. The third set of Great Books has joined the other two in the Cumbrian Records Office. There are editions of the early diary and at least a partial edition of autobiographical material from the Great Books, as well as an authoritative biography. Perhaps most fitting of all, it is now possible to pay homage by undertaking an Anne Clifford pilgrimage: a guided walk along 'Lady Anne Clifford's Way' from Penrith to Skipton, taking in a whole series of Clifford sights and memorials, further confirmation that Clifford succeeded in her quest for secure recognition.[58]

[55] Hallett, 'Clifford as Orlando', *passim*.

[56] See Brenda R. Silver, ' "Anon" and "the Reader": Virginia Woolf's Last Essays,' *Twentieth Century Literature: A Scholarly and Critical Journal*, 25/3–4 (1979).

[57] Woolf wrote to Sackville-West on 26 Dec. 1940 asking if she could bring her 'a life of Lady Clifford', Virginia Woolf, *A Reflection of the Other Person: The Letters of Virginia Woolf*, iv. (London: Hogarth Press, 1978).

[58] A number of companies offer a guided walk along Lady Anne's Way; see the detailed guide by Sheila Gordon, *Lady Anne's Way* (Hillside, 1995).

# 5

# Prophets and Visionaries

Women have always been represented among the ranks of prophets and visionaries, but in the seventeenth century, in Britain, particularly large numbers of women emerged from within the burgeoning radical religious movements that flourished during a period of political upheaval. Some had specific (and often changing) religious associations, some were solitary individuals who emerged into public prominence for a variety of reasons. Because of the inextricable connections between religion and politics in the early modern period, all of these women's prophetic and visionary activities had a political dimension. In the words of Elaine Hobby, who helped pioneer the recognition of the scope of women's prophetic activity during this period, 'Biblical language and allusion are used to produce radical critiques of state structures and the politics of education.'[1] While studies of the English Revolution and of religious nonconformity have long recognized the role of women, who were particularly prominent in movements like Quakerism, only in recent years have we seen more detailed accounts of the considerable body of writing left behind by these women.[2] Although she does not discuss the genres of this chapter in any detail, Mihoko Suzuki's powerful argument relating women and apprentices in the seventeenth century as agents who were able to express a challenge to authority within the early modern state is extremely useful in capturing the way that women could shift the relationship between power and those apparently on the margins of power.[3] Suzuki notes that, while writers earlier in the seventeenth century like Aemilia Lanyer or Rachel Speght challenge misogynistic conceptions of gender, 'a public did not exist in early seventeenth-century England for either author; nor did it exist for the imaginary of political

---

[1] Elaine Hobby, 'The Politics of Women's Prophecy in the English Revolution', in Helen Wilcox et al., eds., *Sacred and Profane: Secular and Devotional Interplay in Early Modern British Literature* (Amsterdam: VU University Press, 1996), 295; see also Hobby's *Virtue of Necessity: English Women's Writing 1649–1688* (London: Virago, 1988).

[2] The significant general studies culminate, from a literary studies perspective, in Nigel Smith's *Perfection Proclaimed: Language and Literature in English Radical Religion 1640–1660* (Oxford: Clarendon Press, 1989); women are the subject of two impressive studies from, respectively, a historical and a literary perspective: Phyllis Mack, *Visionary Women: Ecstatic Prophecy in Seventeenth-Century England* (Berkeley: University of California Press, 1992); Hilary Hinds, *God's Englishwomen: Seventeenth-Century Radical Sectarian Writing and Feminist Literary Criticism* (Manchester: Manchester University Press, 1996).

[3] Mihoko Suzuki, *Subordinate Subjects: Gender, the Political Nation, and Literary Form in England 1588–1688* (Aldershot: Ashgate, 2003).

equality for women'.[4] But, as Suzuki suggests, the upheaval of the Civil War did produce, not simply more women writers prepared to enter the public sphere of print, but more of an audience for them, and although the writers discussed in this chapter are not Suzuki's central focus, they reinforce her claims for this change in the mid-seventeenth century. As will be seen below, prophetic writing by women took a variety of forms, many of which redefined religious possibilities for women, especially within radical religious groups, which accordingly allowed for a political intervention on their part.

In this chapter I want to use four very different women to represent different strands in this phenomenon, and in particular, in keeping with the themes of this book, I want to look at the very different ways in which their writing was received and either abandoned or preserved. The women in question are: Lady Eleanor Davies/Douglas, an aristocratic woman whose visions and prophecies ultimately set her against both King Charles I and Cromwell; the Fifth Monarchist Anna Trapnel, whose visions occurred during a particularly delicate stage in the Interregnum, during the Barebones Parliament (1654); Margaret Fell, the most significant Quaker besides George Fox in the seventeenth century; and Jane Lead, whose writings, in contrast to those of Fell, lapsed into obscurity with the decline of her religious group, the Philadelphian Society.

## ELEANOR DAVIES

In 1625 Eleanor Davies had a vision which involved a prophecy spoken to her by Daniel; she described it (in the third person) in her 1641 *Appeal to the High Court of Parliament* as follows:

so came to Passe in the yeare aforesaid, 1625. Shee awakened by a voyce from Heaevn [*sic*], in the fifth moneth, the 28. of July, early in the Morning, the Heavenly voice uttering these words.
'There is Ninteene yeares and a halfe to the day of Judgement, and you as the meek Virgin. These sealed with Virgins state in the Resurrection, when they not giving in Marriage.' (80–1)[5]

Davies was the daughter of George Touchet, Earl of Castlehaven.[6] She married the poet and lawyer Sir John Davies in 1609. After her 1625 vision, Davies went to visit Parliament (which was meeting in Oxford), and presented Archbishop Abbot with a pamphlet interpreting Daniel's prophecy. From this point

    [4] Suzuki, *Subordinate Subjects*, 131.
    [5] References in parentheses are to *Prophetic Writings of Lady Eleanor Davies*, ed. Esther S. Cope (New York: Oxford University Press, 1995).
    [6] Biographical information is taken from Esther S. Cope's impressive study, *Handmaid of the Holy Spirit: Dame Eleanor Davies: Never Soe mad a Ladie* (Ann Arbor: University of Michigan Press, 1992).

on, Davies entered into her calling, and produced dozens of printed pamphlets from 1625 until her death in 1652. She began by predicting (accurately) the death of her husband and, more significantly, the death of George Villiers, Duke of Buckingham (who was assassinated in 1628). Esther Cope has divided Davies's work into three distinct stages.[7] From 1625 until 1633, Davies concentrated her prophecies on the court, trying to persuade King Charles to harden his stance on Catholicism. After the death of her husband, she married Archibald Douglas. Both husbands opposed Davies's spiritual mission; indeed, both burnt copies of her work. In both cases, she saw prophecies of their doom fulfilled: in Douglas's case, this involved a descent into severe mental illness—amongst other disappointments, this incapacity undermined Douglas's claim to be Charles's elder half-brother and therefore rightfully king! (Davies kept pressing this claim throughout her prophetic career, seeing the results of the Civil War as being in part a punishment for Charles's lack of legitimacy.) From 1633 to 1640, Davies became disaffected with the court's indifference to her warnings, and this was greatly exacerbated by the appointment of William Laud to the Archbishopric of Canterbury. She had her writings published in the Netherlands and, when she returned to England, they were burnt by Laud, and she was imprisoned. Later, following a visit to Lichfield Cathedral in which she sat on the bishop's throne and declared herself primate and metropolitan, after vandalizing the new altar-hanging, Davies was committed to Bedlam. (From Davies's point of view, this was a sensible act of resistance to Laudian moves towards what she would see as Papist ceremony.) After 1640, Davies felt herself vindicated and her prophecies fulfilled, especially following the execution of Laud in 1645 and of King Charles in 1649. During this period, Davies's prophecies became particularly apocalyptic, as was the case with many such writings during this time, including Anna Trapnel's visions, discussed below.

Davies's prophecies are allusive and constantly reintegrate her experiences into a narrative of spiritual import. She returns again and again to key moments (such as her first vision, or the burning of her work), and threads these details through with biblical quotation. While passages are often opaque, her voice is distinctive and powerful. This can be illustrated by one of her shorter tracts which can be quoted here in full. It is an address to Cromwell which, typically, makes much of anagrams and associations of Cromwell's initials and symbols for the sun and moon, and the eyes and horns of the lamb of revelation. At this stage, Davies was looking to Cromwell to vindicate her apocalyptic prophecies:

The Benediction. From The A:lmighty O:mnipotent.
*I have an Errand to thee O: Captain.*
2 Kings 9.5.
Printed in the Year, 1651.
For the Army's General, His Excellency.

---

[7] *Prophetic Writings*, pp.xvi–vii.

My Lord,
Your interest in the nation's unparalleled troublesome times: the flaming sword for
expelling the man in your hand, which crowns with no inferior honour that name of
yours: hereof by her hand a touch presented. Derived from his own, namely A. & O.
Letters of no mean latitude: armed beside with his sword: sun and moon when as stood
in admiration, witness ☉    ☽ their golden characters, styled eyes and horns of the lamb,
&c. Their voice gone out into all lands, Psal. (Rev. 5.) Like theirs here, every one when
the fifty days at an end, heard in his proper language, &c. (Acts. 2). The prophet Joel
as foresaw and others: By whom deciphered his thundering donative of the crown and
bended bow (Rev. 6.). That seal or box of nard opened; as much to say, O: Cromwell,
renowned, be victorious so long as sun moon continues or live ever.
Anagram, Howl Rome: And thus with one voice, come and see, O: C: Conquering and
to Conquer went forth.
My Lord,
Your Humble Servant,
Eleanor.
O C tob. 28
A° 1651.

Here we can see Davies's method of personalizing her prophetic utterances,
so that her readings of public events also relate directly to her private life. By
this stage of her career, Davies's confidence remained undiminished, despite her
multiple imprisonments—her defiance of authority is typical of radical religious
figures of the seventeenth century. Davies differs from the other women discussed
in this chapter both in her social status and in her attitude towards her texts.
Her aristocratic background is evident throughout her impassioned defence of
her family honour, and in the considerable learning she brings to her writing.
She also treated her texts in a similar way to Margaret Cavendish (discussed in
the next chapter), annotating them, and adding material by hand, and therefore
turning printed texts into hybrids that have some of the attributes of manuscripts.
This is not unlike the constant re-annotation of Anne Clifford's Great Books, as
discussed in the previous chapter, although Clifford's texts are, of course, purely
manuscript works. Through this process, which includes handwritten titles and
annotations, similar to Clifford's, which bring details up to date, Davies asserts
a control over her texts as individual pieces of writing, rather than the anonymous, multiple products of the printing press.[8] This marking of individual copies
means not only that each copy may be unique, but also that the writer has literally
made her mark on individual copies—here I would maintain that this process,
as exercised by writers like Clifford or Davies or Cavendish, is different from
the creation of individualized copies by Aemilia Lanyer when she rearranged
dedications to suit individual recipients. Rather, it can be associated with the

---

[8] It is worth pointing out here that, because of printing methods which included continuous
press correction, early modern printed texts are often unique individuals, rather than identical
copies.

process, explored a great deal lately by scholars who have changed our perceptions of manuscript transmission in the period, whereby individual works are taken possession of and often altered by compilers of manuscript miscellanies and anthologies of various kinds.[9] With Davies and Cavendish, the author, rather than the reader, is involved in what might be called continued possession of the individual text, because it has been marked in a unique way. In Davies's case, this is mostly in the form of handwritten titles, and occasional annotations—as we will see in the next chapter, in Margaret Cavendish's case this process was more one of constant revision (as was the case with Clifford's Great Books).

In a provocative account of the relationship between writing, gender, and the state during this period, Megan Matchinske notes how 'Millenial writing proved a particularly useful and surprisingly militant forum for airing political and religious grievances in the years leading up to the English Civil War.'[10] Much of this writing articulated, in Matchinske's terms, a male subject, and she argues that Davies was ultimately unable to shift the grounds of subjectivity, so that her writings were seen as mad and she was confined to Bedlam.[11] A rather more positive assessment of Davies's writing is put forward by Joad Raymond in his wide-ranging and comprehensive study of early modern pamphlets.[12] Raymond notes how Davies exploited the pamphlet form and stresses her increasing radicalism in the 1640s: 'Her prophetic voice seems to have been influenced by the political polarisation and radicalisation that took place in political theory and popular print.'[13]

For all the care with which Davies launched her numerous works (she published over sixty), they had little afterlife. At the time of publication, they clearly had a dramatic effect, and the audience addressed directly by Davies responded, usually with anger and punishment, to her expostulations. Given that Davies was jailed and committed to Bedlam for her works, their impact was significant. But it is important to emphasize that their publication was clearly intended to reach well beyond those directly addressed in Davies's writing (Archbishops Abbot or Laud, King Charles, Oliver Cromwell) to a diverse implied audience. Esther Cope notes that only one of Davies's publications was reprinted between their first appearances and 1978: *Strange and Wonderful Prophecies* (1649).[14] What we might call an identification with writing and the text is quite different from

---

[9] See Harold Love, *Scribal Publication in Seventeenth-Century England* (Oxford: Clarendon Press, 1993), and Arthur F. Marotti, *Manuscript, Print, and the English Renaissance Lyric* (Ithaca, NY: Cornell University Press, 1995).

[10] Megan Matchinske, *Writing, Gender and the State in Early Modern England* (Cambridge: Cambridge University Press, 1998), 129.

[11] Ibid., ch. 4.

[12] Joad Raymond, *Pamphlets and Pamphleteering in Early Modern Britain* (Cambridge: Cambridge University Press, 2003).

[13] Ibid. 296.

[14] *Prophetic Writings*, p.xviii; a facsimile of *Strange and Wonderful Prophecies* was published by Charles Hindley in the third volume of his *Miscellanea Antiqua Anglicana or The Old Book Collector's Miscellany* (1873), a large collection of various pamphlets including work by John Taylor and

the way Anna Trapnel related to *her* prophetic utterances, and she serves as a fascinating contrast to Davies.

## ANNA TRAPNEL: THE PROPHETIC VOICE EMBODIED

In early January 1654, as the Council of State was examining the Fifth Monarchist Vavasour Powell, a woman in the audience who was part of the Fifth Monarchist congregation fell into a trance, and for eleven days after that Anna Trapnel, in the words of her editor Hilary Hinds, 'sang, prayed and prophesied, attracting an increasingly large and high profile crowd'.[15] As I have already mentioned, Trapnel's challenging visions came at a time of political crisis, when the most radical forces in the Civil War had been struggling to gain some ground over the more conservative forces. It was in the early 1650s that political and religious movements like the Levellers and the Fifth Monarchists challenged forms of social authority in a particularly effective way, to the degree that radical change in the political and church systems seemed a real possibility.[16] While the Levellers might be seen as a secular and quasi-democratic movement (with roots in earlier forms of protest, especially rural protest against authority), Fifth Monarchists embraced an apocalyptic religious foundation for their radical political vision. By 1654 England had moved from a monarchy, to government by the 'Rump' parliament, to government by a select Assembly of Saints, known as Barebones Parliament (named after one member, Praise-God Barbon). The Barebones Parliament (not strictly speaking a Parliament, as it was selected by Cromwell and a group of army officers) contained a number of Fifth Monarchists, and it rapidly undertook a series of radical moves, including the abolition of the Court of Chancery and tithes.[17] But by the end of 1653 the radicals gave way, and Cromwell was made Lord Protector and governed alongside a Council of State, which was in part a military body. Thus, Anna Trapnel's intervention represents an example of continued radical resistance to this reining in of Fifth Monarchist ideals. It represented a direct challenge to Cromwell and to the conservative direction in which he was taking the country.

Trapnel epitomizes the way that women from comparatively humble backgrounds emerged as radical voices during the period of political and religious upheaval in the seventeenth century. The daughter of a shipwright, Trapnel lived in Hackney. As Nigel Smith points out, her mother had a powerful influence on

Mother Shipton's prophecies—Hindley later confessed in *Notes and Queries* (1873) that he had invented some of the Shipton prophecies.

[15] Anna Trapnel, *The Cry of a Stone*, ed. Hilary Hinds (Tempe: Arizona Center for Medieval and Renaissance Studies, 2000), p.xvii.

[16] The most influential account of these groups remains Christopher Hill's classic *The World Turned Upside Down* (Harmondsworth: Penguin, 1975); for Fifth Monarchists in particular see Bernard Capp, *The Fifth Monarchy Men* (London: Faber, 1972).

[17] For a detailed account see Austin Woolrych, *Commonwealth to Protectorate* (Oxford: Oxford University Press, 1982).

her attitude towards religion, and on her deathbed she bequeathed her daughter a double blessing from God, and a vocation as a prophet.[18] In contrast to Eleanor Davies, Trapnel was partly empowered by being a member of a radical congregation, just as Quaker women were empowered through their membership of a radical religious group. Another Fifth Monarchist woman, Mary Cary, had published prophecies in 1651, offering a direct precedent for Trapnel's visions of the imminent arrival of King Jesus.[19]

Trapnel's eleven day period of visionary activity at Whitehall could be described as an amalgamation of a number of distinct genres: spiritual autobiography, prophecy, vision, song, poetry, and political advocacy.[20] It produced two different texts, neither of them directly authored by Trapnel herself: *Strange and Wonderful News From Whitehall*, which seems to have been published almost immediately after Trapnel's eleven days of prophecy, probably in March 1654, which is rather like a newsletter, and the later and much fuller *The Cry of a Stone*.[21] In *The Cry of the Stone*, an amanuensis, who calls himself the 'relator', reproduces Trapnel's autobiographical statements, her prophecies, and her songs (printed as poetry), noting the context for these, and occasionally explaining how he was unable to take down all or any of Trapnel's words at particular moments. There was clearly an enormous amount of interest in Trapnel, testified to not just by the visitors who attended her in person, but by the two editions of *The Cry of a Stone* that appeared in 1654, and a third volume, *A Legacy for Saints*, also published in 1654.[22] Trapnel herself wrote *Anna Trapnel's Report and Plea*, but a huge later volume of prophecies, which exists only in a single, incomplete copy at the Bodleian Library, probably published in 1659, once again uses the format of an amanuensis writing down Trapnel's visions and prophecies.

*The Cry of a Stone* exemplifies the mixed modes I noted as being characteristic of Trapnel's visions; the reader of this volume moves from fairly dry, factual autobiographical detail, to apocalyptic visions, to political advice, to songs, and back again. But, as a whole, the volume constantly reinforces Trapnel's Fifth Monarchist attack on Cromwell, and on his representation of the forces pulling back from the radical religious possibilities of the revolution. This often takes the form of a direct rebuke:

If he were not (*speaking of the Lord Cromwell*) backslidden, he would be ashamed of his great pomp, and revenue, whiles the poor are ready to starve, and art thou providing great palaces? Oh this was not Gideon of old, oh why dost thou come to rear up the pillars, the stones which are laid aside? (54)

---

[18] See Smith, *Perfection Proclaimed*, 49, and also the account by Hinds in *The Cry of a Stone*, p.xix.

[19] Mary Cary, *Little Horn's Doom and Downfall* (1651); *A New and More Exact Map or description of New Jerusalems Glory* (1654).

[20] This point is well made by James Holstun, who is at pains to ensure that Trapnel is read politically in *Ehud's Dagger: Class Struggle in the English Revolution* (London: Verso, 2000), ch. 7.

[21] For the dates see *Cry of a Stone*, ed. Hinds, p. xviii.

[22] See ibid., p. l.

Here Trapnel hits out specifically at Cromwell taking up residence at White-hall, but in more general terms this is also a call to arms to resist the encroach-ment of a quasi-monarchical system on what a short time earlier promised to be the rule of the saints and the coming of King Jesus. The army had been the centre of Fifth Monarchist power, but the revoking of the Barebones Parliament saw most of those with power in the army side with Cromwell. Trapnel still asks the members of the army with true faith to return to the Fifth Monarchist cause:

> Poor sergeants that were honest men
> Oh how are you fallen.
> Oh how are you now taken with
> The vanity of men?
> Oh sergeants leave off this your work,
> And get some other thing,
> Your pay'll be sweet to follow him,
> Who is your Lord and King. (20)

As scholars have paid increasing attention to Trapnel, two approaches to her have emerged. One is what might be termed the political interpretation, which I have been pursuing here; the second, in part inspired by aspects of feminist theory interested in the disruptive potential of *écriture féminine*, sees Trapnel as engaged with what Hilary Hinds, in the most sustained example of this form of criticism, terms 'the materiality of language'.[23] This use of feminist theory has certainly offered a fruitful way of making these often opaque texts speak to a modern reader, but at the cost of flattening out Trapnel's political context, and turning an engaged polemic into something considerably more solipsistic.[24] The most impressive political interpretation of Trapnel thus far forms part of James Holstun's provocative book on class struggle and the English revolution.[25] With Trapnel, as with his other examples, Holstun is eager to overturn revisionist historians' tendency to erase conscious, ideological engagement with issues sur-rounding the Civil War, and he sees Trapnel's Fifth Monarchist career as an exemplary instance of the empowerment of previously marginalized positions. Holstun specifically wants to rescue Fifth Monarchist ideas from being tarnished by historians as extreme and irresponsible, and accordingly he reads Trapnel's interventions as examples of highly self-conscious political acts.[26] Holstun spe-cifically sees Trapnell's actions at Whitehall as part of a blurring of boundaries

---

[23] Hinds, *God's Englishwomen*, 125.

[24] A recent impressive approach, which circumvents this dichotomy, is the chapter on Trapnel in Erica Longfellow's *Women and Religious Writing in Early Modern England* (Cambridge: Cambridge University Press, 2004); Longfellow offers a productive reading of Trapnel's balance between self-abnegation and authority (see ch. 5 passim).

[25] Holstun, *Ehud's Dagger*, esp. ch. 7; to Holstun may be added Maria Magro, 'Spiritual Autobiography and Radical Sectarian Women's Discourse: Anna Trapnel and the Bad Girls of the English Revolution', *Journal of Medieval and Early Modern Studies*, 34 (2004), 405–37.

[26] Holstun, *Ehud's Dagger*, 274.

between public and private spheres because, as he puts it, she 'proceeded to turn her prophecy chamber into a hybrid public/private space'.[27] This is also part of Susan Wiseman's analysis of Trapnel, which emphasizes her ability to replace an earthly patriarchal constraint with a heavenly patriarch who is, ultimately, liberating.[28] As will be evident from the tenor of my argument throughout this chapter, I agree with Holstun's emphasis on the political efficacy of Trapnel's actions. However, it is, I think, necessary to make some distinction between a work like *The Cry of a Stone*, which was not written by Trapnel herself, and which contains such a mixture of genres, and a more explicitly polemical and self-authored work like *Anna Trapnel's Report and Plea*.

As I have already discussed, *The Cry of a Stone* is a transcript of some parts of Trapnel's Whitehall prophesying. In contrast to the textual possessiveness I have noted as being characteristic of Eleanor Davies, Trapnel's attitude is, implicitly, that her words, not her writing, are the essence of her testimony. As part of this process, as a number of scholars have pointed out, Trapnel literally embodies her prophetic interventions, as through a process of fasting, as well as producing utterances, prayers, and songs, she is a vessel filled with a divine spirit.[29] But following on from her Whitehall experience, Trapnel, by now notorious, went on something akin to a spiritual progress to Cornwall (home county of a number of radical members of the Barebones Parliament). This trip led to her arrest and examination by the Sessions Court, the text of which forms part of *Anna Trapnel's Report and Plea*. Trapnel was also taken to London and imprisoned in Bridewell, which she turned into an occasion for martyrdom and proselytizing. Trapnel's account of this next stage in her activities moves her texts in a new direction, as the *Report and Plea* is self-authored and much more assertively interventionist; as James Holstun notes:

The very titles of Trapnel's 1654 tracts reveal a striking movement into a public identity and voice, as we move from *The Cry of a Stone*, with its suggestion of an inanimate object forced into a voice against its nature; to *A Legacy for Saints*, whose prematurely posthumous title protects Trapnel from accusations of self-will and forwardness; to *Anna Trapnel's Report and Plea*, with its public, forensic, and combative assertion of her own (and the Fifth Monarchist) case.[30]

Indeed, reading *Anna Trapnel's Report and Plea* is a dramatically different experience, as Trapnel not only writes the text herself, but allows the reader to experience a canny, witty, self-possessed, and defiant political figure, who takes on those in

---

[27] Ibid. 280; see also Magro, 'Spiritual Autobiography', 420–1.

[28] Holstun refers to Susan Wiseman's important essay 'Unsilent Instruments and the Devil's Cushions: Authority in Seventeenth-Century Women's Prophetic Discourse', in Isobel Armstrong, ed., *New Feminist Discourses* (London: Routledge, 1992), 176–96.

[29] On this point, as well as Hinds, *God's Englishwomen*, see Diane Purkiss, 'Producing the Voice, Consuming the Body: Women Prophets of the Seventeenth Century', in Isobel Grundy and Susan Wiseman, eds., *Women, Writing, History: 1640–1740* (London: Batsford, 1992), 139–58.

[30] Holstun, *Ehud's Dagger*, 295.

authority and defeats them. As well as offering a clearly defined narrative with a momentum produced by her journey to Cornwall and her prosecution and imprisonment, Trapnel enlivens the text with dramatized versions of her exchanges with her judges. At this point, Trapnel is able to offer a telling, dramatized version of what is essentially a polemical (and political) triumph, as she trumps her judges every time. To take just one example of her wit, Trapnel is particularly effective in countering the judges' concern over her boldness in travelling to Cornwall, despite having, as they put it, 'no lands, nor livings, nor acquaintances' there. This is a significant political moment, because Trapnel is able to reach for an irreproachable religious justification for what was clearly a political campaign:

> Launse said, *Pray Mistriss tell us, what moved you to come such a journey?*
> A.T. *The Lord gave me leave to come, asking of him leave, witherever I went: I used still to pray for his direction in all I do: and so I suppose ought you,* I said.
> Justice Launse. *But pray tell us, what moved you to come such a journey?*
> A.T. *The Lord moved me, and gave me leave.*
> Launse. *But had you not some extraordinary impulses of Spirit that brought you down? Pray tell us what those were.*
> A.T. *When you are capable of extraordinary impulses of spirit, I will tell you; but I suppose you are not in a capacity now*: for I saw how deridingly he spoke.[31]

In her detailed reading of this text, Hilary Hinds points to a double audience, as Trapnel addresses both sympathizers and antagonists in the course of her narrative, bolstering the morale of the former, and countering any suggestions that she is deluded which might be harboured by the latter.[32] Hinds argues that, during this process, as was the case with her court appearance, Trapnel converts antagonists into sympathizers.[33] Accordingly, this is also a narrative aimed at expanding the Fifth Monarchist ranks.

As the Protectorate tightened its grip, Trapnel's Fifth Monarchist intervention became less and less visible. From 1657 to 1659 Trapnel resumed her visionary activity in association with a splinter group of Fifth Monarchists who remained resolute in their radical perspective. After the publication of a fairly brief collection of Trapnel's songs/sermons/prophecies in 1657 as *A Lively Voice for the King of Saints and Nations*, this activity resulted in the publication of a huge volume that harks back in nature to *The Cry of a Stone*, although Matthew Prineas, in his excellent account of the exact spiritual nature of the poetry, sees it as a new departure for Trapnel.[34] The sheer size of this publication, a massive folio of 990 pages (which incorporates the material from *A Lively Voice*), indicates that Trapnel's small, faithful core of remaining followers were able to get something substantial

---

[31] *Anna Trapnel's Report and Plea* (1654), 16—I have silently corrected some misplaced words in this quotation.

[32] Hinds, *God's Englishwomen*, 164–70.

[33] Ibid. 169.

[34] Matthew Prineas, 'The Discourse of Love and the Rhetoric of Apocalypse in Anna Trapnel's Folio Songs', *Comitatus*, 28 (1997), 90–110.

into print as testimony to Trapnel's continuing vision. This volume survives only in a single copy, missing its title page, held by the Bodleian Library.[35] The fact that there is only one remaining copy may indicate a certain popularity that Trapnel still maintained, given that one could argue that all other copies may have been hoarded and read until they disintegrated. But given the size of the volume, the lack of preservation also points to Trapnel's dimming reputation, and the lack of a continuing readership beyond the seventeenth century.

Trapnel's poetic and prose meditations are arranged in this volume in a series of diary-like entries, starting with 'Eighth Month, 11 day, being the first day of the Week, at nine of the Clock, 1657' (B). (The numbering of months and days is part of the radical religious tradition behind Fifth Monarchism.) The entries chart a lengthy period of prophecy, prayer, and reflection by Trapnel, but in the case of this volume, the overall effect is now of a much more controlled presence and voice addressing a group of the initiated. The poetry of this volume is similar to that in *The Cry of a Stone*: it is simple, song-like and direct:

> O love, thou dost delight my soul,
> Of thee I love to sing:
> It doth revive and chear my soul
> For to extol the King. (B4)[36]

Trapnel explicitly names some of the poems as 'psalms', and Erica Longfellow has put forward a convincing interpretation of the poetry as both within the tradition of psalms, and also an account of Trapnel's spousal relationship with Christ.[37] It is worth noting that, while Trapnel's themes remain constant, the poetry of this volume contains somewhat less direct political comment than her earlier works, and could be seen as continuing a process whereby Trapnel and her followers are distinguishing themselves from other sectarian groups. So, for example, at one point in the midst of a poem, there is a comment: 'Whiles this was uttered, the Quakers being present, spake, but could not interrupt; for with more power and swiftness, the Voice went on as followeth' (47).[38] The commentator later explains that a group of Quakers objected to the position on Election being put forward, but they were quelled by what the commentator again calls 'the Voice'. This indicates that Trapnel was still delivering her poetry as a conduit for divine wisdom, but, as the Quakers themselves noted, she was quite conscious of what was going on around her and, to their evident annoyance, responded directly to their objections (48–9). Trapnel also extols, for example, baptism ('I can sing, that when in water I was, | The Dove on me did sight', 126). Trapnel continues to embrace an apocalyptic vision in accordance with Fifth Monarchist ideals, although for much of this volume the political context

---

[35] The volume is Bodleian Arch. A c.16.
[36] Throughout the volume, the poetry is printed in double columns.
[37] See Longfellow, *Women and Religious Writing*, 172–9.
[38] This encounter with the Quakers forms, perhaps deliberately, the final part of *A Lively Voice*.

has faded into a more generalized background: 'The signs of the time, the signs of the time, | *England,* are upon you | But you will not believe those signs' (224).

In the entry for 1 November 1657 Trapnel reverts briefly to prose and offers an account of how it is fourteen years since the advent of her prophetical visions. The tone here is again quite sober, and the visions themselves are sombre and far from fanciful: 'O King, visit the Countries, greatly break forth unto them, and shew thy power to the Nations abroad' (356). The poetry too is almost bland in its evocation of Christ as imminent saviour:

> O blessed be God, that all my life
> Is so here with the Son,
> That all the Devils in hell cannot
> Break in, or upon me throng. (363)

The implication within the poetry is that, once again, amanuenses are taking down Trapnel's words—if that was indeed the case, these songs/poems are an astonishing example of what might be termed an epic poetic vision which harks back to the oral tradition.[39] At the same time, this was also something like a greatly extended service, with occasional breaks for prayers (for example, 24 November: 'After this was Prayer'; 421). These prayers are essentially pep talks for the faithful: 'Let nothing divide you, or break your one-ness . . . you that are baptized into Jesus, you that have received Christ as King, Priest, and Prophet' (428); they reflect the fact that the group may well have been close to fragmenting during the difficult period of 1657–8. In some fascinating passages of explicit political comment, Trapnel notes, 'It is not enough to be against *Cromwel* | And against Apostasie' (457). Later on, Trapnel again refers to '*Cromwel* and his vile soldiers' (486), suggesting their transience.[40] This then builds up to a fierce denunciation of England and an apocalyptic vision of its imminent destruction that occurs at about the halfway mark in the folio (564–90). At this point Trapnel's denunciation takes fire: 'O wo to *Cromwels* Chaplains all' (598). From this point on, the poetry becomes a fierce attack on Cromwell and the England that has allowed him to rule:

> And it was shewed that the Locusts
> So base and thievish be,
> That so they partake of delicacy
> They care not for Gods glory.
> O many such there are abroad,
> And they to *Cromwel* creep. (647)

---

[39] e.g. passages on pp. 376–7 refer at length to pens writing down these words, and to the 'companions' who are being addressed; the earlier passages about the Quakers also imply that Trapnel was speaking in a 'trance'.

[40] See other comments about Cromwell on pp. 539, 564, 641, 647, 796, 824, 840, 889. Prineas sees the folio as 'relatively pacifistic' ('Discourse of Love', 104), but while this may be true comparatively speaking, I would argue that many of the passages I have cited are still combative and strident in their attack on Cromwell.

Much later, Trapnel offers a more pointed, sarcastic critique: 'The Lord hath set us on our feet, | Not *Cromwels* Pompe to maintain' (790). Trapnel also notes what hope once rested in Cromwell, when he 'shin'd so bright and new' (840)— but he has now become, virtually, the Antichrist. However, the volume concludes, not with these denunciations, but with a calmer and touching evocation of the failure of the rich young man to give away his possessions and follow Christ:

> This did require more grace and strength,
> It beautiful did appear,
> But O the young man went away,
> And could not perform it there. (990)[41]

Trapnel and her followers are seen as true disciples, unlike those profiting under the Protectorate, who clearly can be identified with the young man too attached to his wealth. At the same time, this seems a curiously subdued note to end on, evoking a situation that seems to hint at some sort of failure, rather than ultimate (apocalyptic) success.

However, it is hard to see this astonishing book, vividly described by Erica Longfellow as 'a new Fifth Monarchist Bible',[42] as a failure, although it is in many ways something of a mystery. Trapnel's supporters managed to put into print an enormous folio, and it was printed with considerable care and trouble. There are very few errors, and the typesetting and layout are impressive. No one who had encountered the first six sections in the fairly modest *A Lively Voice* of 1657 could have imagined that this material would grow into such a large book. Virtually all the text of *A Lively Voice* has been completely reset, and all errata listed at the end of that book have been corrected in the folio.[43] No printer is listed for *A Lively Voice*, which, like the folio, lacks a true title page. It is possible that the folio was printed by either Thomas Brewster, who was the printer for Trapnel's *Report and Plea* (1654) and *Legacy* (1654), and who also published the Fifth Monarchist Mary Cary's *The Resurrection of the Witnesses* (1653), or Robert Sele, printer for *News from White Hall* (1654).[44] While the size of the folio makes it seem likely that some months would have been required for what, as I have noted, was a careful printing process, it seems likely that it was published late in 1658 (a few months after the last entry, which is 7 August 1658), and therefore some time around Cromwell's death on 3 September 1658.

---

[41] See Matthew 19: 21–2.

[42] Longfellow, *Women and Religious Writing*, 171.

[43] There are numerous small changes to punctuation, as well the correction of errata. The folio omits the last section of *A Lively Voice* (7 Feb. 1657), including 'An Evening Psalm' and 'A Hymne Comparing Davids Sling-stone and the Stone in Daniel' (L–M4).

[44] I would favour Brewster, who, late in 1657, published James Harrington's *Prerogative of Popular Government*, which has an ornamental border similar to that on the first page of *A Lively Voice*. Such things are far from conclusive, as borders were shared between printers, but the ideological thrust of Harrington makes the comparison tempting, if purely speculative.

Perhaps Trapnel's followers printed only a small number of copies, and that is why only one has survived. It seems to me to be most unlikely that a volume of this size would have been read out of existence, or that all copies but one would have been consigned to other uses and so disappeared—such a volume would have been most likely to have been valued, even after its Fifth Monarchist ideals were long forgotten.[45] It is possible that copies were destroyed after the Restoration, although the attack on Cromwell might have been seen as ameliorating Trapnel's radical religious views. Given the lack of evidence on the fate of however many copies of the folio that were produced, it is impossible to determine just how Trapnel's final prophecies were received.[46]

None of Trapnel's texts were reprinted in the eighteenth or nineteenth centuries; like Eleanor Davies, Trapnel had to wait until the late twentieth century before she received any detailed attention, after the notoriety of the 1650s had long faded away. Both Davies and Trapnel, from this perspective, can be contrasted with Margaret Fell, whose writings had a very different history of transmission, owing to her membership of what was to become the most successful and long-lived of the radical religious movements of the Civil War.

## MARGARET FELL AND THE ENDURANCE OF THE QUAKERS

In her 1993 book on women's literary history, Margaret Ezell uses Quaker women's writing as an example of the neglect of kinds of early modern women's writing that fit into no recognizable 'literary' categories.[47] Ezell noted that, despite the fact that Quaker women produced more printed texts than any other group of women in the Restoration, they were largely ignored, even by scholars of seventeenth-century Quaker thought.[48] Even at the time Ezell wrote, there were exceptions to this neglect, the most notable being the work of Elaine Hobby, who has championed Quaker women's writing since her 1988 study *Virtue of Necessity*, but in recent years there has been a much greater recognition of this significant area of early modern women's writing, stimulated from a historical point of view by the extensive account of Quaker women that forms part of Phyllis Mack's

---

[45] In contrast, eighteen copies of *The Cry of a Stone*, clearly Trapnel's most popular and also one could say her most enduring work, are extant (see ESTC). The binding of the Bodleian folio is modest and without any distinguishing features.

[46] The provenance of the folio is not known, prior to its sale to the Bodleian Library by Bertram Dobell in 1901—see the letter from Dobell, attached to the front of the folio, written to the Library in 1914, after he had determined that Trapnel was the author (see his note in *N&Q*, 21 March 1914).

[47] Margaret Ezell, *Writing Women's Literary History* (Baltimore: Johns Hopkins University Press, 1993), ch. 5.

[48] Ibid. 133.

*Visionary Women.*[49] However, it is also important to recognize that the work of the most prominent female Quaker in the seventeenth century was kept in view, especially within the religion she helped to found.

For those not familiar with the details of radical religious groups in the seventeenth century, it is difficult to prevent modern notions of Quakers (pacifist, unthreatening, socially responsible) from shaping the image of Quakers as they emerged in the late 1640s and early 1650s.[50] This idea has been memorably expressed by Christopher Hill, who noted that 'the whole early Quaker movement was far closer to the Ranters in spirit than its leaders later liked to recall, after they had spent many weary hours differentiating themselves from Ranters and ex-Ranters.'[51] As Barry Reay explains, the Quakers began when a number of individuals, including George Fox (later elevated to the founding father of the movement), held similar views about the irrelevance of churches and organized religion and the vital role of an inner communion with God: 'the birth of the Quaker movement was less a gathering of eager proselytes at the feet of a charismatic prophet, than a linking of advanced Protestant separatists into a loose kind of church fellowship with a coherent ideology and a developing code of ethics.'[52] The movement itself experienced phenomenal success, growing nationally to around 40,000 or more by the end of the 1650s.[53] Quakers from the earliest stages of the movement were extremely active in testifying to their beliefs, travelling to far-flung locations (Malta, New England, Surinam), and facing considerable persecution in England and abroad. Women were prominent in the movement from the earliest stages, and, as Phyllis Mack has explained in her detailed study, Quaker women displayed a 'collective energy and audacity' that impressed their audiences.[54] Indeed, women made up a substantial proportion of Quakers, not just as passive adherents to Quaker ideas, but as active and engaged Quaker prophets, proselytizers, and writers. Quaker ideas of the inner light encouraged women, in the early stages of the movement, to participate as equals in meetings, and their writing found a ready outlet in a gathering which produced an extremely large number of published pamphlets.

[49] See Hobby, *Virtue of Necessity*, and also her essay 'Handmaids of the Lord and Mothers in Israel: Early Vindications of Quaker Women's Prophecy', in Thomas N. Corns and David Loewenstein, eds., *The Emergence of Quaker Writing* (London: Frank Cass, 1995), 88–98; see also Mack, *Visionary Women*, chs. 4–10.

[50] As a corrective, the most helpful account is Barry Reay, *The Quakers and the English Revolution* (London: Temple Smith, 1985); for a thorough social history of the early Quakers, which offers a particularly useful account of their social origins and an anthropological account of their practices, see Adrian Davies, *The Quakers in English Society 1655–1725* (Oxford: Clarendon Press, 2000); see also Hill, *World Turned Upside Down*, ch. 10.

[51] Hill, *World Turned Upside Down*, 232.

[52] Reay, *Quakers*, 9.

[53] Ibid. 11; this is a conservative estimate and Reay feels there may well have been 60,000.

[54] Mack, *Visionary Women*, 130.

In the early years of Quaker activity, women as both prophets and writers participated in the kinds of ecstatic spiritual witnessing that won Quakers their name (because some of them quaked when filled with the inner divine light). In this initial period, Quakers might do far more to challenge social hierarchy than their later established actions, such as not removing their hats, and addressing others with the familiar 'thee' and 'thou'—they might, for example, go naked as a sign. This more provocative behaviour reached its most extreme example when James Naylor dressed himself in imitation of Christ and entered Bristol on a donkey.[55] The more apocalyptic aspects of Quaker thought were also expressed in published work, a considerable amount of it written by women. For example, Hesther Biddle in 1655 published a matched pair of tracts warning the two university cities of Cambridge and Oxford to repent and prepare for judgement.[56] Visionary activity and writing continued into the 1660s, the most dramatic example being the travails of Katherine Evans and Sarah Cheevers, who were imprisoned in Malta by the Inquisition and who published an electrifying account of their resistance to all attempts to persuade them to give up their spiritual beliefs. Both had visions as part of this experience, and both had a clear sense of the direct presence of God:

At length the Voice of the Lord arose in katherine, saying, Ye shall not die. And she believed the Lord; for his Goodness did appear much in their fast: He was very gracious to them, and refresh'd them with his living Presence: in which they did behold his Beauty, to their Great joy and Comfort.[57]

Their visionary resistance defeated the Inquisitors, and their account was published in 1662 and revised in 1663. It was then reprinted in 1715 (the year in which an important collection of Margaret Fell's writing also appeared), and was published as part of a collection of tracts in 1850.[58]

The fact that Evans and Cheevers' narrative was reprinted in the eighteenth century indicates that even during the later, sober period of Quaker development, testimonies that were still visionary and quite apocalyptic could be accommodated. But of all these visionary women, it was Margaret Fell who achieved the greatest recognition during the period when Quakers established themselves as adherents to an increasingly viable religion. This was in part because she was married to George Fox from 1669, having had a close association with him from her conversion to Quakerism after meeting Fox in 1652.[59] Fox had been preaching in the North of England since 1648. In 1652 Margaret Fell was mistress of

---

[55] See Reay, *Quakers*, 54–5 for details.

[56] The tracts are *Woe to Thee City of Oxford* and *Woe to the Town of Cambridge*.

[57] *A Brief History of the Voyage of Katherine Evans and Sarah Cheevers* (1715), 50.

[58] The 1850 edition is taken from William Sewell's *History of the Society of Friends* and was published in Manchester by the Manchester and Stockport Tract Depository.

[59] Biographical information which follows is taken from Isabel Ross, *Margaret Fell: Mother of Quakerism* (London: Longmans, Green and Co., 1949), and Bonnelyn Young Kunze, *Margaret Fell and the Rise of Quakerism* (London: Macmillan, 1994).

Swarthmore Hall in Lancashire; she was married to a judge, and when she first met Fox was mother of six daughters and a son. Fox visited Swarthmore Hall, and Margaret Fell was convinced that what he spoke was the truth the first time she heard him, and was even more moved when Fox stood up in her local church and (with the rector's permission) spoke to the congregation, upon which Fell first stood up in acknowledgement of what Fox was saying, and then 'sat down in my pew again, and cried bitterly'.[60] From this point on, Fell was an absolute adherent to the Quaker cause (her husband was not a Quaker but was tolerant towards his wife's views).

In the 1650s Fell was active in the Quaker cause in a variety of ways. Because of her social status, she was able to intercede with authority figures in a way that Fox, who was of fairly humble origins, could not—notably, she wrote several appeals to Cromwell in an attempt to force him to acknowledge the tolerance he had pledged to Fox when they had met. She was particularly instrumental in organizing Quakers in her local area, setting up a regular Quaker Meeting at Swarthmore Hall itself, and assisting Quakers throughout the North. Given that Fell had a young family at this time, she was able to undertake a significant amount of work that would eventually, by the 1660s, be instrumental in moving the Quakers from a radical spiritual movement towards a more coherently organized religion.

Fell began writing Quaker tracts in the mid-1650s, her first being one of a series of addresses to the Jews, who had been allowed back into England by Cromwell late in 1655. This writing is both polemical and infused with the visionary spirit of early Quakerism. *For Menassah Ben Israel* is directly addressed to a rabbi who was particularly concerned to facilitate the re-entry of the Jews to England. After corresponding with Cromwell on the question of readmission as early as 1651, Ben Israel came from Amsterdam to London first in October 1655, and then moved there with his son in 1656. Fell's tract is a general outline of Quaker doctrine about the inner light of God, but it specifically addresses the Jews, and calls for Ben Israel to assist her in achieving what is essentially part of a vision of a messianic nature, as the Jews now return to 'the English nation . . . which is a land of gathering where the Lord God is fulfilling his promise'.[61] This tract was translated into Dutch within a year, and this version was in turn translated into Hebrew—there has been some speculation that this Hebrew translation was undertaken by Spinoza.[62] Fell wrote five tracts in total addressing the issue of Jewish conversion to Quakerism. The last, *The Daughter of Sion Awakened*, published in 1677, is a good example of how her visionary writing continued into a period of more restrained Quaker activity; in it, Fell offers an apocalyptic sense of change:

Out of *Sion*, the Perfection of Beauty, hath God shined, in the Light of his glorious Son, to recover, and to bring back, and to redeem his whole Body, which is his Church, out of all nations, Kindreds, Peoples, Tongues and Languages.

---

[60] Ross, *Margaret Fell*, 11.     [61] Ibid. 90.     [62] Ibid. 92–3.

Now the universal, divine, glorious, infinite, invisible God is shining in the dark places, in the hearts of men and women.

There is a Day dawning in the heart, and a Day-star arising, which the Night hath been over since *Adam*. Even the everlasting Day is dawning in the hearts of men and women, glorious Praises to the highest forever. (3)

Much of the language of this tract is powerful and evocative, in the plain style that Quakers made their own. As well as calling the world in general (and the Jews in particular) to repentance and acknowledgement of the divine inner light, it touches on one of Fell's (and Quakerism's) most famous themes: the equality of men and women: 'he hath made no difference in this Work between Male and Female, but they are all one in Christ Jesus, whose Faith and Belief stands in his name and Power, who are sanctified and cleansed' (18). Quaker women offered a particularly powerful challenge to the notion of female modesty and silence, as they were actively engaged in preaching. As Richard Bauman has explained, in his insightful study of the tension between speech and silence in early Quaker activity, Quaker thought as a whole had to deal with the potential conflict between an individual's experience of the inner light, and the public representation of that experience.[63] In terms of the development of Quakerism, Bauman outlines how the challenge of individual freedom was eventually controlled by a hierarchy of elders, and the formal institution of meetings (including separate women's meetings).[64] Bauman also relates this tension to the Quaker ideal of an expression of spirituality which cut through language, and the need for some formal means of expression. While Bauman does not consider the situation of women in Quakerism in any detail, he offers a useful starting point for any consideration of how women as preachers and writers in the Quaker movement contended with opposition within the movement itself, and more particularly from those outside it, who attacked Quakers for their temerity in speaking/writing. This issue has been taken up by Hilary Hinds in her detailed analysis of Priscilla Cotton and Mary Cole's 1655 tract *To The Priests and People of England*. Cotton and Cole offer a polemical defence of women's religious speech and, as Hinds notes, they are able to produce an argument which uses paradox and interpretative dexterity to counter traditional Christian (usually Pauline) arguments for women's silence.[65]

Margaret Fell entered this debate with the production of her most famous tract, *Women's Speaking Justified*, in 1666. As can be seen from Cotton and Cole's tract, there was nothing new in Fell's defence of women's speech, but Fell's tract was published at a time when Quakers were enduring considerable persecution. Fell herself was imprisoned in Lancaster Castle for almost four years between 1664 and 1668; during this period she wrote a large number of published tracts and

---

[63] Richard Bauman, *Let Your Words Be Few: Symbolism of Speaking and Silence among Seventeenth-Century Quakers* (Cambridge: Cambridge University Press, 1983).
[64] Ibid., ch. 9.          [65] Hinds, *God's Englishwomen*, ch. 5.

also a considerable number of letters to fellow Quakers encouraging them in their times of trial. What is particularly interesting about *Women's Speaking Justified*, in this context, is its apocalyptic strand, which is similar to that manifested in the tracts concerned with the Jews such as *The Daughter of Sion Awakened* (discussed above). Fell offers what might be called the standard refutations of passages in scripture that seem to command women to keep silent, notably 1 Corinthians, in which Paul commands women to keep silent in church. This refutation is achieved by seeing the statement, not as a universal command, but as a specific admonition addressed to women and men who were speaking out of turn. But Fell's ultimate justification rests upon a conviction that the second coming is at hand. This involves a fascinating shift from the generally very sombre and judicial prose of the tract to visionary statements like the following:

the Darkness is past, and the Night of Apostasy draws to an end, and the true Light now shines, the Morning Light, the bright Morning Star, the Root and Off-spring of *David*, he is risen, he is risen, glory to the highest for evermore, and the joy of the morning is come, and the Bride, the Lambs *Wife*, is making her self ready. (11)

Accordingly, women are free to speak when they are imbued with the divine spirit—which of course specifically allows Quaker women who are so imbued to speak (and write) with impunity: 'And whereas it is said, *I permit not a Woman to speak, as saith the law*: But where Women are led by the Spirit of God, they are not under the Law; for Christ in the Male and in the Female is one: and where he is made manifest in Male and Female, he may speak' (13). Fell was quite capable of moderating this apocalyptic vein when circumstances required, but it remains a constant in her writing, along with her clear, polemical attack on any position which threatened Quaker stability. As Bonnelyn Young Kunze argues, taken as a whole Fell's writings indicate that 'she had an astute understanding of the theological debate', particularly in relation to issues like the nature of Christ and Quaker ideas of inner light.[66]

Fell wrote numerous letters to fellow Quakers, and she played a vital part in holding the movement together after the Restoration when it was both persecuted and riven with internal dissension. Her position as a maternal figure and as wife of George Fox led inevitably to the preservation and transmission of her work as Quakers grew in strength both in England and in America, where William Penn was extremely close to Fell from 1667 when he became a Quaker. Fell was also a significant contributor to the remarkable quantity of Quaker writing, especially by women, which was published in the seventeenth century initially, and then into the eighteenth century. In her study of the relationship of early Quakers to print culture in the 1650s, Kate Peters argues that the Quaker propensity for publishing their tracts played a significant part in 'the emergence of a recognisable Quaker identity and the development of a nascent Quaker

---

[66] Kunze, *Margaret Fell*, 203.

discipline'.[67] As a whole, Peters's study argues against those historians who have, through their suspicion of print as historical 'evidence', downplayed the radical and political nature of early Quaker ideas. Peters notes how Fell played a signifi-cant role in coordinating the early publications of Quakers, as well as keeping up lines of communication between members. This occurred in the context of a significant control exercised by Quakers over publication in general. Peters's study examines only the early years of Quaker publication (up until 1656) but, as I have noted, Fell herself began publishing a significant number of tracts in the 1660s, at a time when the influence of women in the movement was under pres-sure.[68] While I have just argued that Fell's work, even in the 1660s and 1670s, remained millenarian in many respects, she was certainly part of the more con-servative shift of Quakerism after the Restoration. The canonization of George Fox's work, after the publication of his journal in 1694, went hand in hand with the elevation of his widow, and it is therefore not surprising that Fell's work was collected together early in the eighteenth century.

In 1710 this process occurred with the publication of a substantial volume gathering together Fell's major writings. Despite being titled *A Brief Collection*, the book is in fact some 540 pages long. It is presented, as the full title indic-ates, as a volume recording Fell's life and work, as well as preserving her writing: 'A brief collection of remarkable passages and occurrences relating to the birth, education, conversion, travels, services, and deep sufferings of that ancient, emin-ent and faithful servant of the Lord Margaret Fell; but by her second marriage, Margaret Fox, together with sundry of her epistles, books, and Christian testi-monies to friends and others'. This stresses Fell's status, at the beginning of the eighteenth century, as more than simply a Quaker writer, but as an exemplary figure in the development of Quaker thought and action after the Restoration.

This volume was published by the formidable Quaker printer Tace Sowle, who took over her father's business following his death in 1695, assisted by her mother and her husband.[69] Sowle was the major publisher of Quaker material until her death in 1749; the Fell volume ends with a catalogue of Sowle's publications, which include all the significant Quaker authors at the time. Sowle had published George Fox's works, beginning with the *Diary* in 1694, and then going on to the *Epistles* in 1698 and the tracts in 1706. Sowle's business continued as the major Quaker publishing house, even after her death, until the Friends reorganized the publication of Quaker works in 1829.

The tone of hagiography is set by the first piece in the volume, which consists of 'A testimony from Margaret Fox's children'. This is signed by Fell's four

---

[67] Kate Peters, *Print Culture and the Early Quakers* (Cambridge: Cambridge University Press, 2005), 11.

[68] See Patricia Crawford, *Women and Religion in England 1500–1720* (London: Routledge, 1993).

[69] On Sowle's activities, see Paula McDowell, 'Tace and Andrew Sowle', in James K. Bracken and Joel Silver, eds., *The British Literary Book Trade 1474–1700* (Detroit: Gale, 1996), 249–57.

surviving children in 1710: Sarah Meade (and her husband William); Mary Lower (and her husband Thomas); Susan Ingram; and Rachel Abraham (and her husband Daniel). Fell's daughters and their husbands were active Quakers, and their testimony is not just dutiful family praise, but a calculated summary of her religious virtues. A further series of testimonies follows, from a number of Quakers who knew Fell. The biographical section ends with a collection of Fell's dying words and a short autobiographical account (1–14). Fell's spiritual and political credentials are emphasized by the inclusion of her communications with Cromwell and Charles II, all concerned with attempts to gain tolerance for Quakers, while at the same time stressing a refusal to compromise their central religious principles; as the compilers (G.W. and T.L. : presumably George Whitehead and Thomas Lower) of this material note: 'Observe, by the current series of the former Accounts, it is evident how Faithful and Impartial the said M.F. was in her Christian Testimony, in Warning and Counsel to those in Authority' (38). Then there are a series of letters, starting from the very earliest stages of the movement with a 1653 epistle to the MP Colonel William West (not a Quaker, but a sympathizer), followed by a number of the letters of information and support which were instrumental in holding early Quaker groups together. When gathered together in 1710, these epistles act as monuments to early Quaker history, casting Fell even more firmly in the role of early guiding light, especially representative of the later, triumphant wing of Quaker reasonableness: 'I warn you and charge you, in the Presence of the living God, that you beware of Strife amongst you' (55). There are also epistles which are general statements of Quaker principles, and polemical epistles addressed to those who have not yet seen the light. On page 100, Fell's tracts begin, starting with *For Menassah Ben Israel*, and then moving chronologically through her writings: *A Testament for the Touchstone of all Professions* (1656*)*; *A Loving Salutation to the Seed of Abraham* (1657); *This is to the Clergy* (1660*)*; *An Evident Declaration* (1660); *A True Testimony from the People of God* (1660); *To the Magistrates and People of England* (1664); *A Call to the Universal Seed of God* (1665); *Women's Speaking Justified* (1666); *A Touchstone* (1667); *A Call to the Seed of Israel* (1668); and *The Daughter of Sion Awakened* (1677). The tracts are interspersed with further epistles, and the collection as a whole ends with letters to King William, Edmund Waller, and a final epistle to friends written in 1698 when Fell was 84. The eloquence of Fell's letter to King William underlines her indomitable nature, and seals her position as a Quaker leader, just as the volume itself testifies to her status and influence within the movement.

The collected volume of Fell's works certainly increased her visibility in the early eighteenth century, but during this period and into the nineteenth century she was gradually eclipsed by George Fox, whose diary became the iconic text for representations of early Quaker thought. The 1710 volume does mark out the most significant moment for Fell's writing, as it was not reprinted in either the eighteenth century or the nineteenth (though that may in part be because there were a reasonable number of copies on first publication).[70] As her writing became less available, nevertheless, Fell's legacy was nurtured, especially within the Quaker community, and was consolidated in particular through a series of biographies produced from the nineteenth century into the twentieth. A good early example is the fairly brief biography produced in Philadelphia in 1859, which does at least include a selection of her epistles.[71]

## JANE LEAD AND THE DISAPPEARANCE
## OF THE PHILADELPHIAN SOCIETY

The history of Margaret Fell and the Quakers offers a salutary example of how some forms of early modern women's writing, however provocative, were nurtured and preserved by a supportive religious group. My final example of prophetic writing is a more complex version of such a process. The mystical writings of Jacob Boehme were influential in England from the 1630s, when his work was extensively translated into English.[72] Boehme offered a mystical system that had some affinity with Kabbalistic thought, and also drew on alchemy. Boehme's followers in England were quite diverse and, during the 1650s, included some Quakers and Ranters, although as a whole followers of Boehme were not politically radical, and did not actively challenge established church practices. This became even more apparent after the Restoration, when followers of John Pordage, a clergyman who, from 1649, followed a spiritualist path influenced by Boehme's thought, but fuelled by his own visions, gathered together in London.[73] By 1663, Pordage's circle included Anne Bathurst, whose visionary diary has been discussed in Chapter 1, and Jane Lead, who in 1670, at the age of 46, had a series of visions. Lead began publishing in 1681, the year of Pordage's death, and she began to attract a considerable following in Germany from the 1690s.[74] While Lead edited and introduced a volume of Pordage's work, *Theologica mystica* (1683), her own writing increased until, by the publication of the first volume of her enormous spiritual diary, *A Fountain of Gardens*, in 1696, she had become, in Paula McDowell's words, 'one of the most prolific English women writers of the late seventeenth and early eighteenth centuries'.[75]

McDowell considers Lead's career as part of the general involvement of women in both writing and the book trade in the late seventeenth and early eighteenth

[70] There are, for example, three copies of the 1710 volume in the Friends' Library, London.
[71] *The Life of Margaret Fox* (Philadelphia: Association of Friends for the Diffusion of Religious and Useful Knowledge, 1859); epistles are on pp. 77–109.
[72] The most reliable general account of Boehme in seventeenth-century England is in Smith, *Perfection Proclaimed*, ch. 5.
[73] See B. J. Gibbons, *Gender in Mystical and Occult Thought: Behmenism and its Development in England* (Cambridge: Cambridge University Press, 1996).
[74] Ibid. 143–5.
[75] Paula McDowell, 'Enlightenment Enthusiasms and the Spectacular Failure of the Philadelphian Society', *Eighteenth-Century Studies*, 35 (2002), 516.

centuries.[76] In particular, McDowell stresses the connections non-aristocratic women writers had at this time with a still flourishing oral culture—an idea that, in the context of this chapter, can be seen earlier in the century in Trapnel, whose texts, as I have noted above, have many of the oral characteristics outlined by McDowell.[77] McDowell explains how Lead's remarkable ascent to head the Philadelphian Society shifted her from poverty to a position of considerable influence. Lead was actually in an almshouse in the early 1690s, when the translation of her works into German by a disciple of Boehme created an instant following for her amongst those on the Continent who adhered to theosophical ideas.[78] Eventually Lead's supporters included two significant scholars, Francis Lee and Richard Roach, who helped promulgate her visions, Lee also becoming Lead's son-in-law (the marriage being suggested to Lead in one of her visions).

Lead and her associates decided to reach out to the general public in 1697 by declaring the existence of the Philadelphian Society. Paula McDowell's account of the Society emphasizes how the leaders of the Society were engaged in the conscious cultivation 'of what we might call multiple media publics'.[79] This was partly achieved by the publication of a journal, *Theosophical Transactions*, which began in 1697, and created a strong sense of community amongst its readers, while at the same time heavily promoting Lead's steady stream of books.[80] The major publication effort for the society was the production of Lead's *A Fountain of Gardens* in three volumes over the space of five years (1696–1701).

One can see Lead's writing and her visions as being far less politically challenging than the work of Davies, Trapnel, or even Fell. This is in part simply a matter of how visionary writing positioned itself well after the Restoration, and indeed the Glorious Revolution, in a period when the revolutionary possibilities of the 1650s were long past. (Lead of course was old enough to remember the revolutionary period.) Throughout Lead's writing, the mystical traditional is harnessed for an enlightenment that is fundamentally internal, and disengaged from overt political culture. Lead's message was, as Paula McDowell aptly states, 'a call to psychic action', couched in mystical and figurative terms.[81] Lead specifically follows Boehme in placing great emphasis on the part played in her visions by Sophia, a feminine figure of infinite wisdom, and accordingly a figure who breaks down the masculine characteristics of the Trinity.[82] From this perspective, Lead was claimed as a precursor of modern feminism by Catherine Smith in a series of pioneering essays written in the late 1970s/early 1980s.[83] These may seem slightly dated now in their effort to make Lead seen relevant, but they

---

[76] Paula McDowell, *The Women of Grub Street* (Oxford: Oxford University Press, 1998).
[77] See ibid., ch. 3.
[78] Ibid. 170; see also Nils Thune, *The Behmenists and the Philadelphians* (Uppsala, 1943).
[79] McDowell, *Women*, 172.     [80] Ibid. 173.     [81] Ibid. 197.
[82] On this point, see Gibbons, *Gender*, ch. 7.
[83] See esp. Catherine F. Smith, 'Jane Lead: The Feminist Mind and Art of a Seventeenth-Century Protestant Mystic', in Rosemary Ruether and Eleanor McLaughlin, eds., *Women of Spirit* (New York: Simon and Schuster, 1979), 183–203; and 'Jane Lead: Mysticism and the Woman Cloathed

serve usefully to underline how provocative Lead's version of the feminization of spiritual truth could be.

*A Fountain of Gardens* is a spiritual diary similar in scope to Ann Bathurst's Diary (discussed in Chapter 1), but it contains rather more personal, autobiographical material, much of it in keeping with Lead's position as spiritual leader. For the uninitiated, like so much of this kind of writing, Lead's visions seem monotonous, but for followers able to discern the significance of the recurring symbols of wheels, fountains, fires, seraphim, and so on, each vision is a further insight into theosophical truth. Lead also has a more subdued prose style than Bathurst, and this does add something to her verisimilitude. So, to take a random example, she writes:

November the 4th. 1676
This Day going out, I suffer'd loss, meeting with some scatterings, which for that space stopped the Wheel-work; which being sensible of, I had no quiet, till the holy Watcher came down, and moved it forward again, clearing all that did clog, and made it move heavily. This Word with an Emphatical Power to me came, saying, Oh wherewithal shall a Young Man cleanse his Way. (i. 425)

Lead is also prepared to insert and answer questions raised by doubters, such as 'Query. How are Spirits to be Discerned' (i. 503). Overall, the tone of her writing is an interesting amalgam of the visionary and the conversational—which makes it ideal to communicate with what was an increasing band of followers between 1696 and 1703, the year of Lead's death. Works like *The Messenger of An Universal Peace* (1696) contain a quite disconcerting mixture of visionary material with blandly didactic statements in a section called 'The Marks of a True Philadelphian' at the end of the tract, including, for example, 'A Philadelphian is Kind' (with illustrations).

Following Lead's death, the Philadelphian Society seemed to lose its way, withdrawing from public life and apparently smarting from various satirical attacks on it. Indeed, Paula McDowell has offered a cogent argument for seeing the retreat of the Society as representative of the growing Enlightenment attack upon enthusiasm.[84] This is not to say that the Society's legacy disappeared in the course of the eighteenth century, as its influence, along with Boehme's more powerful influence, can be traced at various points. One of the more interesting is the way in which the Society and Lead's writings influenced William Law in the mid-eighteenth century. Law, famous for his *Serious Call to a Devout Life* (1726), which influenced Wesley (and Samuel Johnson), came under the spell of Philadelphian Society ideas (along with those of Boehme) later in his life, to the degree that he was charged with reading them with the same veneration 'that

with the Sun', in Sandra Gilbert and Susan Gubar, eds., *Shakespeare's Sisters* (Bloomington: Indiana University Press, 1979), 3–18.

[84] See McDowell, 'Enlightenment Enthusiasms', *passim*.

other People read the Scriptures'.[85] This mystical tradition flows through into the later eighteenth century and can be seen most powerfully in William Blake. It must be said that Boehme, rather than Lead, is the predominant influence here, but Lead's writings did not disappear from sight in England or in Germany. Two German translations were published in Stuttgart in 1862, and a French translation in 1894.[86]

Later in the nineteenth century in England, as a reflection of the growing interest in theosophical ideas, Lead's books were again republished, in a fascinating act of homage by the Glasgow publisher John Thomson, who, between 1884 and 1903, appears to have written out six of Lead's books and then reproduced the handwritten copies, probably using the anastatic printing process, and offered them for sale in Glasgow and London, including a selection of extracts from *A Fountain of Gardens*.[87] The interest in theosophy and mysticism in general continued to expand in the early twentieth century. Today, ironically, while Lead's writings are known only to a handful of scholars, even amongst those particularly interested in early modern women's writing, they have flourished on the Web for a variety of reasons. All of Lead's texts, including *A Fountain of Gardens*, can be accessed in what seem to be fairly accurate transcripts from www.passtheword.org—a site dedicated to 'the Spirit of Truth', containing material relating to Boehme as well as to Shakers. Web interest in Lead even includes a site claiming her as an example of alien abduction![88]

## CONCLUSION: WOMEN AND RELIGIOUS EXPERIENCE

As I noted at the beginning of this chapter, during the seventeenth century women visionaries and prophets produced a significant body of writing, much of it interventionist in nature. My four case studies have to represent a very large and diverse group, from the significant numbers of Quaker women through to charismatic individuals like Eleanor Davies. In her historical study of women and religion in the sixteenth and seventeenth centuries, Patricia Crawford concludes that women's engagement with religion during this period had a significant

---

[85] Quoted ibid. 517.

[86] *Der Aufgang zum Berge des Schauens* (Stuttgart, 1862); *Der Himmlische Botschafter* (Stuttgart 1862); *Le messager Céleste de la paix universelle* (Paris: Chamuel, 1894).

[87] Thomson's publications are: *The Revelation of Revelations* (1884), *A Heavenly Cloud Now Breaking* (1885), *The Wars of David and A Peaceable Reign of Solomon* (1886), *The Wonders of God's Creation Manifested* (1887), *The Enochian Walks With God* (1891), *Signs of the Times* (1891), and *The Laws of Paradise* (1903); that Thomson undertook the transcriptions himself is indicated by a note on orthography at the end of *The Revelation of Revelations* (150); the 'handwritten' typeface, that looks like an average nineteenth-century hand, very carefully written, has the flat appearance of anastatic printing as described by Philip Gaskell: *A New Introduction to Bibliography* (Oxford: Clarendon Press, 1973), 269.

[88] www.rense.com/ufo5/lead/htm (accessed 15/5/05).

effect on 'the bounds which had limited them'.[89] Crawford goes on to stress how 'Women's spirituality, which differed from men's, led to them challenging conventional gender roles in the spiritual sphere', and that 'Radical women could also be led by their beliefs to challenge conventional expectations of the sexes in the secular sphere as well.'[90] As we have seen, this is certainly true of Davies, Trapnel, Fell, and Lead, despite the significant differences in context for their activities. From Davies's first prophecies in the 1620s through to Lead's final publications at the beginning of the eighteenth century, England had passed through a period of astonishing political shifts, and these shifts are reflected in the spiritual writing of these women. Women's writing increased in quantity during this period, and also in range. In the next chapter, I will consider Margaret Cavendish, who attempted pretty much every genre available during the seventeenth century, and who had a clear image of herself as an author, alongside Lucy Hutchinson, a figure from the other side of the political fence to Cavendish.

[89] Crawford, *Women and Religion, passim.*       [90] Ibid. 210–11.

# 6

# Margaret Cavendish and Lucy Hutchinson: Authorship and Ownership

## MARGARET CAVENDISH IN THE 1650S: REPRESENTING AUTHORSHIP

When Margaret Cavendish's two handsome folio volumes, *Poems and Fancies* and *Philosophical Opinions*, were published in 1653, depending on the context, one can see them as the culmination of a series of touchstones in early modern women's writing, or as a new challenge to traditions of male writing. Cavendish herself, as we shall see, tended to veer between self-deprecation and self-assertion in a manner calculated to undermine any sweeping generalization one might make about her own sense of her image as female author. As we have seen in the previous chapter, the 1650s saw the production of an impressive range of radical, sectarian women's writing in a variety of genres. Much of this writing was extremely ambitious, but it did not provide a model for the kind of literary and philosophical writing to which Cavendish aspired. One model for Cavendish's literary ambitions may well have been Mary Wroth, and Cavendish seems to have taken Edward Denny's vituperative response to Wroth as a paradigm for masculine disapproval of women's secular writing. Cavendish quoted a version of lines from Denny's poem condemning Wroth in a preface to *Poems and Fancies* (1653), and again in her dedication to her husband William of *Sociable Letters* (1664), her seventh published volume. In the preface 'To All Noble and Worthy Ladies', from *Poems and Fancies*, she imagines how men will censure her:

> And very like they will say to me, as to the Lady that wrote the Romancy,
> Work Lady, work, let writing Books alone,
> For surely wiser Women nere wrote one. (A3v)[1]

When Cavendish looked back at Wroth's ambitious folio of *Urania*, it seems that she saw Denny's reaction inextricably bound up with it, even if her husband stood as a counter-example of masculine encouragement of her literary efforts.

---

[1] References to Margaret Cavendish, *Poems and Fancies* (1653); the dedication to William includes this version: 'My Lord, it may be said to me, as one said to a lady, Work Lady Work, let Writing Books alone, for surely Wiser Women ne'r writ one. But your Lordship never bid me to Work, nor leave Writing', *Sociable Letters*, ed. James Fitzmaurice (Toronto: Broadview, 2004), 38; for Denny and Wroth, see Ch. 3 above.

While Wroth was a local example of a truncated public literary career (even though, as we have seen, her impressive oeuvre had considerable circulation in a variety of spheres), Cavendish had a European context for *her* career, created by her exile from England as a member of Queen Henrietta Maria's court, which retreated to Paris in 1644. After Margaret married William Cavendish in 1645, she lived in exile with him in Rotterdam and Antwerp. (William Cavendish had left England after his defeat at the battle of Marston Moor in 1644.) Recent scholarship on Cavendish has explored the intellectual advantages that accrued from Cavendish's enforced stay in Europe; a stay which included access to figures such as Descartes, Huygens, and Hobbes.[2] In her detailed study of Cavendish's writings from the 1650s, Emma Rees has suggested that Cavendish 'utilised genre in a deliberate and subversive way to articulate and ameliorate her exile'.[3] In Rees's view, Cavendish engages in a highly self-conscious presentation of her self and her ideas. Mihoko Suzuki has also placed Cavendish firmly in a political context, noting especially how in *Orations* (1662) Cavendish addresses a series of political issues connected with more radical Civil War controversies over gender and class.[4] Similarly, in a particularly suggestive article, David Norbrook has analysed Cavendish's situation in terms of 'the complex and often contradictory development of the public sphere in different parts of Europe in the mid-seventeenth century'.[5] From a political perspective, Norbrook's article refines an earlier approach to Cavendish, pioneered in a very influential essay by Catherine Gallagher, which stressed the way that Cavendish's 'Tory' Royalism empowered her as a singular and autonomous female writer.[6] Much of the work on Cavendish that has followed Gallagher has tended to see Cavendish as less singular, both as an individual writer, and in terms of her often conflicting social and political opinions as expressed in her writing. Norbrook argues that it is important to take into account Cavendish's deliberate avoidance of incorporating into her work any direct reference to women who were part of the world of European intellectuals, most notably the scholarly and combative Anna Maria von Schurman. Norbrook is able to argue for a much more nuanced approach

  [2] See esp. Anna Battigelli, *Margaret Cavendish and the Exiles of the Mind* (Lexington: University of Kentucky Press, 1998).

  [3] Emma Rees, *Margaret Cavendish: Gender, Genre, Exile* (Manchester: Manchester University Press, 2003), 186; similarly, Hero Chalmers's account of Cavendish re-emphasizes her Royalist context, in part by aligning her with Katherine Philips and Aphra Behn, which allows for a much more subtle and productive approach and overcomes some of the limitations of Gallagher's account (see n. 6): Hero Chalmers, *Royalist Women Writers 1650–1689* (Oxford: Clarendon Press, 2004), esp. ch. 1.

  [4] Mihoko Suzuki, *Subordinate Subjects: Gender, the Political Nation, and Literary Form in England, 1558–1688* (Aldershot: Ashgate, 2003), 182–202; Suzuki also discusses Cavendish's play *Bell in Campo* from this perspective.

  [5] David Norbrook, 'Women, the Republic of Letters, and the Public Sphere in the Mid-Seventeenth Century', *Criticism*, 46 (2004), 226.

  [6] See Catherine Gallagher, 'Embracing the Absolute: The Politics of the Female Subject in Seventeenth Century England', *Genders*, 1 (1988), 24–39.

to Cavendish's writing by stressing how female intervention in the masculinized public sphere has to be seen on a case-by-case basis.[7]

From this perspective, to return to Cavendish's first publications in 1653, we can see the dual appearance of a volume of literary work and a volume of philosophical speculation as a sign of just how far-reaching Cavendish expected her writing to be. The volumes themselves were presented to their readers with an array of prefatory material, much of it producing a characteristically ambiguous mix of demurral and assertiveness. I will take *Poems and Fancies* as an example, and offer here a detailed analysis of its physical properties on its first appearance, and in its revisions and circulations.

Cavendish wrote the contents of her two first published volumes when she was in England, accompanied by her brother-in-law, Charles Cavendish, in an unsuccessful attempt to convince the Committee for Compounding to release her husband's estates to her.[8] She stayed for eighteen months from 1651 to early 1653, returning to Antwerp without any real financial gain, but with two completed volumes, as she explains in her autobiographical 'True Relation of My Birth, Breeding and Life': 'I writ a Book of Poems and a little Book called my Phylosophical Fancyes'.[9] Cavendish notes that these were not her first writings, as she had composed most of *The World's Olio* (not published until 1655) in Antwerp. Both *Poems and Fancies* and *Philosophical Fancies* were published in London by John Martin and James Allestry, who were to be Cavendish's publishers until the 1660s, when her books began to be published by Anne Maxwell.[10] Martin and Allestry published a selection of scientific and literary works, including the romances of Madeleine de Scudéry and the poetry of Cowley. Their printing is of a high quality and, given that they had no trouble handling Scudéry's immense romances, they were more than capable of producing Cavendish's large folios.

*Poems and Fancies*, like all of Cavendish's works, begins with an elaborate series of prefaces. In her discussion of this aspect of Cavendish's writing, Emma Rees, drawing on some of the theoretical work of Gerard Genette, notes how these prefaces mark a shift from addresses to potential patrons to 'a greater awareness of an active readership'.[11] There are, however, quite different audiences and voices constructed by the different prefaces, which collectively mark what Randall Ingram has characterized as a development in the history of the way in which the book, as object, is conceived by an author who is attempting to control the way in which it

---

[7] Norbrook, 'Women, the Republic of Letters', *passim*.

[8] For biographical information on Cavendish during this period, see Katie Whitaker, *Mad Madge: Margaret Cavendish, Duchess of Newcastle* (London: Chatto and Windus, 2003), ch. 8.

[9] 'True Relation' is part of *Nature's Pictures* (1656), 382.

[10] Cavendish explains in a preface to *Philosophical Fancies* that it was originally intended to form part of *Poems and Fancies*, but was completed too late for inclusion, and so was published as a separate volume.

[11] Rees, *Margaret Cavendish*, 29.

might be read.[12] Indeed, some of the most interesting scholarship on Cavendish has addressed what might be called the physical manifestations of her publication, and the interplay between potential or implied readers and an author who could be almost simultaneously anxious and aggressive about her reputation. In a recent article responding to the pasted slips found in Cavendish's *Plays* (1668), Jeffrey Masten pays particular attention to what he felicitously calls 'her writing practices and the lavish and conflicted performances of her printed texts'.[13]

*Poems and Fancies* has nine prefatory pieces: a dedication to Charles Cavendish; the address to 'all noble and worthy ladies' which includes the reference to Edward Denny's denigration of Wroth's literary activities referred to above; an address to Cavendish's friend and companion Elizabeth Topp, and a reply from Topp; a preface 'To Natural Philosophers'; a preface to the reader; and finally three poems. The tone and implied audience varies greatly between these prefaces, from the warm, familial friendliness of the exchange with Topp, to the apparent self-abasement of the address to natural philosophers, which begins with a confession that Cavendish knows no language other than English, and moves on to the disconcerting statement 'Neither do I understand my owne native Language very well; for there are many words I know not what they signifie' (A6). In her address to the reader, Cavendish also offers an anxious plea for indulgence, dwelling particularly on the image of her book as a child, which she repeats in the poem which is the last prefatory item: 'Condemne me not for making such a coyle | About my Book, alas it is my Childe' (A8v). As a first publication, *Poems and Fancies* bears many such traces of Cavendish's anxiety about venturing into print. At the same time, it also indicates Cavendish's boldness in publishing in such an ambitious manner, and this boldness was to increase over time as Cavendish's books increased in number. One aspect of this is the engraved frontispiece, which first appeared in some copies of *Poems and Fancies*; this shows Cavendish in a classical niche flanked by Athena and Apollo, the caption underneath her extolling both her beauty and her wit.[14] Cavendish used this frontispiece in other volumes, such as *The World's Olio* (1655), and its striking image of self-confident beauty and intelligence is manifested in Cavendish's more assertive modes of writing about her public image.

---

[12] Randall Ingram, 'First Words and Second Thoughts: Margaret Cavendish, Humphrey Moseley, and "the Book"', *Journal of Medieval and Early Modern Studies*, 30 (2000), 101–24.

[13] Jeffrey Masten, 'Margaret Cavendish: Paper, Performance, "Sociable Virginity"', *MLQ* 65 (2004), 54 ; Masten calls attention to Sophie Tomlinson's pioneering essay on Cavendish and performativity: ' "My brain the stage": Margaret Cavendish and the Fantasy of Female Performance', in Clare Brant and Diane Purkiss, eds., *Women, Texts and Histories, 1575–1760* (London: Routledge, 1992); and on more technical aspects of this see James Fitzmaurice, 'Front Matter and the Physical Make-up of *Nature's Pictures*', *Women's Writing*, 4 (1997), 353–67, and 'Margaret Cavendish on her Own Writing: Evidence from Revision and Handmade Correction', *PBSA* 85 (1991), 297–307.

[14] This frontispiece does not, for example, appear in Bodleian Library's Harding 3737 copy, nor in Bodleian P1.22 Jur. Seld., but it does in Huntington Library 12941; it is discussed in Fitzmaurice, 'Front Matter', 354.

Here on this Figure Cast a Glance,
But so as if it were by Chance,
Your eyes not fixt, they must not stay,
Since this like Shadowes to the Day
It only represent's; for Still,
Her Beuty's found beyond the Skill
Of the best Paynter, to Imbrace,
These louely Lines within her face,
View her Soul's Picture, Judgment, witt,
Then read those Lines which Shee hath writt,
By Phancy's Pencill drawne alone
Which Peece but Shee, Can justely owne.

1 Frontispiece to Margaret Cavendish, *Poems and Fancies* (1653); also used for *The World's Olio* (1655). Cavendish is flanked by Athena and Apollo, and is praised in the caption for her beauty and wit.

Huntingdon Library, San Marino, California.

More specifically, the way in which *Poems and Fancies* was put into circulation by Cavendish illustrates another important aspect of her possessive and protective attitude towards her writing.[15] As James Fitzmaurice has explained, a number of Cavendish's texts were hand-corrected in various ways.[16] This includes correcting errata in copies of *Sociable Letters* (1664), and making some alterations to her biography of her husband (1667). Fitzmaurice speculates that this process seems to indicate which volumes were particularly dear to Cavendish—he notes that she hand-corrects *Sociable Letters*, but not *Philosophical Letters*.[17] This may or may not be so, but the process certainly involves a close relationship to individual copies of certain volumes, which might be seen as being treated like children, in so far as the slightly fussy corrections ensure that they go out into the world in as perfect a state as possible. In the case of *Poems and Fancies*, which is not discussed by Fitzmaurice, this first book of Cavendish was subject to a series of revisions as well as corrections, all of which, in Fitzmaurice's terms, show how careful she was about much of her work, despite her frequent protestations of incompetence or lack of skill.

Cavendish hand-corrected some copies of the 1653 *Poems and Fancies* as part of an ongoing revision process which was to see revised editions published in 1664 and 1668.[18] The handwritten alterations are relatively minor, but they mark the beginning of a process of quite substantial revision. To take as an example one of Cavendish's most appealing poems, 'The Hunting of the Hare', one finds that a complete rewriting of the poem takes place between the 1653 and 1664 editions, with some further minor revisions for the 1668 edition. This can be illustrated by the changes to the opening four lines:

> Betwixt two *Ridges* of *Plowd-land*, lay *Wat*
> *Pressing* his *Body* close to *Earth* lay squat,
> His *Nose* upon his two *Fore-feet* close lies,
> Glaring obliquely with his *great gray Eyes*. (1653)

> Betwixt two *Ridges* of *Plowd-land*, sat *Wat*
> Whose Body press'd to th'Earth, lay close and squat
> His *Nose* upon his two *Fore-feet* did lie
> With his gray Eyes he glares Obliquely. (1664)

In 1668 'glares', hand-corrected to 'glared' in Merton College's copy of 1664.

My interest here is not so much in the efficacy of these revisions (in some ways Cavendish's tinkering was counter-productive, as instanced by the change

---

[15] I have explored some of these ideas in relation to Cavendish and Anne Clifford in my essay 'Early Modern (Aristocratic) Women and Textual Property', in Nancy E. Wright *et al.*, *Women, Property and the Letters of the Law in Early Modern England* (Toronto: University of Toronto Press, 2004).

[16] Fitzmaurice, 'Margaret Cavendish on her Own Writing', *passim*.

[17] Ibid. 299.

[18] Of copies I have examined, there are hand-corrections in, for example, Bodleian P1.22. Jur. Seld., and Merton College, Oxford.

above which, in the 1664 version, lost the powerful image of the hare's 'great gray eyes'), as it is in the way that a volume like *Poems and Fancies* was constantly returned to by Cavendish over a period of almost twenty years, so that even when, by the Restoration, she was a far more confident and much published author, she still wanted to keep possession of her texts, and refine them over and over again.[19]

In her detailed reading of *Poems and Fancies*, Emma Rees stresses the political implications of Cavendish's exploration of Atomism, and the relationship of this to Lucretius, whose *De Rerum Natura* was being translated by Lucy Hutchinson just before Cavendish began writing, though there is no evidence that Cavendish knew of this translation.[20] The poems and tales within *Poems and Fancies* seem, at first glance, as heterogeneous as Cavendish's multiple prefaces, but they are indeed linked by a number of ambitious themes. The volume begins with a series of poems exploring Cavendish's interest in a materialist approach to matter. Poems centred on atoms form a series of meditations on a subject that Cavendish had clearly spent a great deal of time considering. Cavendish might well, as Emma Rees argues, have been protecting herself from potential criticism by couching her scientific arguments as poetry, but, given the simultaneous production of *Philosophical Fancies*, it might be truer to argue that Cavendish was inspired by Atomism to the degree that her scientific ideas permeate her creative and scientific writing.[21] The liveliness of the atom poems reflects the vigour with which Cavendish pursued her ideas, as one of her more frequently anthologized poems, 'A World Made by Atoms', illustrates:

> Small *Atomes* of themselves a *World* may make,
> As Being subtle, and of every shape:
> And as they dance about, fit places finde,
> Such *Formes* as best agree, make every kinde.
> For when we build a house of Bricke, and Stone
> We lay them even, every one by one:
> And when we finde a gap that's big, or small,
> We seek out Stones, to fit that place withall.
> For when not fit, too big, or little be,

---

[19] It is perhaps worth noting that Cavendish kept the multiple prefaces to *Poems and Fancies*, but in the 1664 edition added a commendatory poem by William, which begins 'I saw your poems, and then wished them mine'; the arrangement of prefaces remains the same in the 1668 edition, although there are, as noted above, further alterations to the poems themselves.

[20] Rees, *Margaret Cavendish*, ch. 2 and app.; on Hutchinson see below; on Cavendish's relationship to Atomism, see esp. Stephen Clucas, 'The Atomism of the Cavendish Circle: A Reappraisal', *Seventeenth Century*, 9 (1994), 247–73. David Norbrook has speculated that Hutchinson's translation may have been a response to Cavendish's interest in Epicurean ideas, conveyed in the Cavendish circle by Pierre Gassendi in particular; see Norbrook, 'Women, the Republic of Letters', 229.

[21] See Rees, *Margaret Cavendish*, 60; and on the intersection between Cavendish's 'fancy' and her philosophy, see the excellent article by Jay Stevenson, which suggests that Cavendish was well in control of her potentially inflammatory view of the workings of atoms and the materialist universe: 'The Mechanist-Vitalist Soul of Margaret Cavendish', *SEL* 36 (1996), 527–43.

They fall away, and cannot stay, we see.
So *Atomes*, as they dance, finde places fit
They there remaine, lye close, and faste will sticke.
Those that unfit, the rest that rove about,
Do never leave, untill they thrust them out.
Thus by their severall *Motions*, and their *Formes*
As severall work-men serve each others turnes.
And thus, by chance, may a *New World* create:
Or else predestinated to worke my *Fate*. (5)

This poem is only one of dozens of atom poems and poems about the nature of matter that make up the first part of *Poems and Fancies*. Cavendish then moves on to the nature poems, like 'The Hunting of the Hare', which are more immediately appealing to the modern reader, although they are entirely consistent with her over-all concern to enter into an empathic relationship with the world around her. The volume also contains a series of poetic moral discourses, so that, taken as a whole, the poetry offers a complete (and extremely ambitious) philosophical world-view.

Three-quarters of the way through *Poems and Fancies*, Cavendish inserts anoth-er preface addressed 'To Poets', in which she again offers a justification for her writing, noting that 'Women writing seldome, makes it seem strange' (121), but bravely declaring that close scrutiny will show the reader that what Cavendish has produced is 'useful, graceful, easie, comely, and modest' (ibid.). But then Cavendish produces a preface 'To All Writing Ladies', rather more boldly assert-ing 'But this age has produced many effeminate Writers, as well as Preachers, and many effeminate Rulers, as well as Actors' (Aav)—an interesting indication that Cavendish was conscious of the sectarian women discussed in the previous chapter. However, Cavendish's caution was justified if we consider the response of Dorothy Osborne to the publication of *Poems and Fancies*. Writing about what seems already to have been a talking point, Osborne, in a letter to William Temple dated 14 April 1653, declared:

And first let me ask you if you have seen a book of poems newly come out, made by my Lady Newcastle. For God sake if you meet with it send it me, they say 'tis ten times more extravagant than her dress. Sure the poor woman is a little distracted, she could never be so ridiculous else as to venture at writing books, and in verse too.[22]

Cavendish's notoriety may have reached its height after the Restoration, when her famous visit to the Royal Society in 1667 drew crowds, and when Pepys offered a series of fascinated and scornful comments on her appearance and ideas, but Osborne's remark shows how Cavendish's protective instincts about the public-ation of *Poems and Fancies* were justified.[23] And yet, unlike Mary Wroth, Cav-endish did not cease publishing her work after the mockery began, but instead

---

[22] Dorothy Osborne, *Letters to William Temple, 1652–54*, ed. Kenneth Parker (Aldershot: Ashgate, 2002).

[23] For Cavendish's notoriety, see Whitaker, *Mad Madge*, 159.

increased her output for the press, and at the same time increased the range of what she published. In 1655 Cavendish published *The World's Olio* (which, as noted above, had been written before her two 1653 volumes), and *Philosophical and Physical Opinions*, a combination of volumes which, like the 1653 combination of *Poems and Fancies* and *Philosophial Fancies*, underlines the range of genres and ideas Cavendish was prepared to tackle, even this early in her publishing career.

The shift in titles from 'Fancies' to 'Opinions' may be read as a marker of Cavendish's increased confidence in her writing, even over the short space of two years. *Philosophical Fancies* is a fairly brief volume (and, unusually for Cavendish, it is an octavo, rather than a folio), and, in contrast to *Poems and Fancies*, it is simultaneously more modest in appearance yet less self-deprecatory in presentation. Rather than a preface addressed to relatives, friends, or general readers, *Philosophical Fancies* begins with a poetic 'Dedication to Fame', signalling Cavendish's early desire to attain recognition as a thinker and writer. Poems that follow are introspective, as Cavendish addresses her own thoughts and brain. Cavendish does then add a preface to Charles Cavendish, who is thanked profusely for his support and assistance. (Charles died in England in 1653, and while William was clearly a great supporter of his wife's writing, the loss of Charles seems to have been a major blow to her confidence.) The volume itself contains a series of very brief accounts of Cavendish's philosophical views, some in verse, some in prose—the poems are clearly associated with those in *Poems and Fancies*, but the prose pieces are similar to some of the material in *The World's Olio*.

*Philosophical and Physical Opinions* is a much more substantial volume than *Philosophical Fancies*, and its presentation once again reinforces Cavendish's increasing confidence and ambition. It was reprinted in 1663, and then more extensively revised as *Grounds of Natural Philosophy* in 1668. As well as a defensive preface from William, defending Margaret against the charge that she was not the author of her work, *Philosophical and Physical Opinions* has a preface addressed to 'The Two Universities', which begins Cavendish's long campaign for recognition from those who authorized knowledge, a process which included sending copies of her work to various colleges, as we will see in more detail below. There are also numerous epistles to readers.

Despite the expansion of *Philosophical and Physical Opinions* and the greatly increased ambition evident in its overall structure, Cavendish still included in it all the material from *Philosophical Fancies*.[24] She then adds a greatly expanded set of opinions (about another two-thirds more than the first book) before finishing with the same poem, beginning 'Great God, from thee all Infinites do flow'. Further expansion occurred when Cavendish published a new edition in 1668 as *Grounds of Natural Philosophy*; by this stage, the poetry of *Philosophical Fancies* has disappeared and been replaced by a series of prose chapters summing up Cavendish's mature and final thoughts on matter and the natural world.

---

[24] *Opinions* essentially reproduces *Fancies* up until 'The Motion of the Sea' (71).

After *The World's Olio*, the last work that Cavendish published in the 1650s was *Nature's Pictures Drawn by Fancy's Pencil To The Life*, in 1656. This is an ambitious series of narratives in verse and prose, and once again the volume was revised and published in a new edition in 1671. As James Fitzmaurice explains, *Nature's Pictures* offers the reader a quite different engraved frontispiece to the triumphant classical figure in the frontispiece to *Poems and Fancies* (and other volumes) discussed above.[25] Instead, Cavendish offers a domestic image of her husband and her two stepdaughters gathered around a table, listening to her telling them stories. As noted above in Chapter 1, Cavendish's stepdaughters were also writers, although they did not publish their work, and most evidence points to a fairly tense relationship between them and their stepmother, who was virtually the same age as them and who cut a figure in society which they could hardly have appreciated. It is therefore possible to see this domestic frontispiece as a bit of wishful thinking on Cavendish's part. It is in this context also worth noting that the stories in *Nature's Pictures* are often concerned with adventurous young women and their complicated relationship with marriage as an institution. This is most notably the case with 'The Contract', the subject of a subtle interpretation by Victoria Kahn, who analyses it as part of a process by which mid-seventeenth-century romance plots engaged with the issue of a 'political subject who consents to be contractually bound'.[26]

Cavendish published nothing between 1656 and 1662, but after the Cavendishes returned from exile with the Restoration of Charles II, she not only published a new series of books in the 1660s and 1670s, but also revised and reissued all of her 1650s work.[27] Cavendish's ambitions, though not made explicit, were to distinguish herself in every conceivable genre of writing, and, having covered philosophy, metaphysics, science, poetry, essays, and narrative in her 1650s publications, she remedied the obvious lacuna in 1662 with the publication of a collection of her plays. I want to look in some detail at the context for Cavendish's plays, before I then go on to consider the rest of her oeuvre and its ongoing reception.

## WOMEN AND DRAMA FROM 1553 TO 1650

While there is no evidence of the extent to which Cavendish had knowledge of the earliest plays translated and written by women in the sixteenth and early seventeenth centuries, it is worth considering them here in some detail in order to emphasize, as has been the case so often in this book, that there were traditions of women working even in this genre, where they were least evident up until the

---

[25] Fitzmaurice, 'Front Matter', *passim*.

[26] Victoria Kahn, 'Margaret Cavendish and the Romance of Contract', *RQ* 50 (1997), 528.

[27] *Poems and Fancies* was republished in revised editions in 1664 and 1668; *Philosophical Fancies*, as noted above, in 1663 as *Grounds*; *World's Olio* in 1671; and *Nature's Pictures* in 1671.

reopening of the theatres in the Restoration, and the triumph of Aphra Behn on the professional stage.[28] As we have already seen with Mary Wroth's *Love's Victory*, and as the pioneering work by Marion Wynne-Davies and S. P. Cerasano has shown, women, in Wynne-Davies and Cerasano's words, 'did participate in the theatrical culture of the English Renaissance—as authors, translators, performers, spectators and even as part owners of public playhouses'.[29]

This process begins as early as the 1550s, when the young Jane (or Joanna) Lumley, daughter of the Earl of Arundel, translated Euripides' *Iphigenia at Aulis*.[30] There has been some speculation about the date of Lumley's translation, which may have been done as early as 1553, but could have been somewhat later.[31] Briefly mentioned by George Ballard, the translation has been seen by some scholars as intentionally evocative of the execution of Lumley's cousin, Jane Grey—especially as Arundel was directly responsible for Grey's downfall.[32] While earlier scholars criticized the accuracy of Lumley's translation, it is now seen as a conscious shaping of the original text, designed in particular to bring out some possible allusions to contemporary politics, as well as what Jocelyn Catty characterizes as 'on overriding concern with questions of female autonomy and the ideological constraints circumscribing that autonomy'.[33] At the same time, Lumley's rather spare prose translation has a dignified power, made evident in Stephanie Hodgson-Wright's staging of the play in 1997.[34] Lumley's translation was edited in 1909 for the Malone Society by Harold Child, but despite the reasonably widespread availability of that edition, it was virtually invisible until the late 1990s, when it began to receive some attention, doubtless spurred by Diane Purkiss's Penguin edition of it, together with Mary Sidney's *Antonius* and Elizabeth Cary's *Mariam*.[35]

Both *Antonius* and *Mariam* have been far more widely known than Lumley's translation, and Mary Sidney's translation in particular achieved some recognition during the seventeenth and eighteenth centuries, albeit not as much as her poetry did.[36] As I have noted in Chapter 2, Sidney published her translation of

---

[28] See the detailed discussion of Behn in the next chapter.

[29] S. P. Cerasano and Marion Wynne-Davies, eds., *Renaissance Drama by Women: Texts and Documents* (London: Routledge, 1996), p. x. See also Danielle Clarke's chapter on 'Drama and the Gendered Political Subject', in her *The Politics of Early Modern Women's Writing* (Harlow: Pearson, 2001), which stresses the exploration of 'the grounds and conditions of women's speech' (81) in the plays by Lumley, Sidney, and Cary.

[30] The translation is part of a manuscript commonplace book: British Library MS Royal 15A ix.

[31] See the account in Diane Purkiss's edition in *Three Tragedies by Renaissance Women* (Harmondsworth: Penguin, 1998); Stephanie Hodgson-Wright argues for 1553 on political grounds in her essay 'Jane Lumley's Iphigenia at Aulis', in S. P. Cerasano and Marion Wynne-Davies, eds., *Readings in Renaissance Women's Drama* (London: Routledge, 1998), 129–41; while Jocelyn Catty argues for a later date on thematic grounds (based on the maturity of Lumley's treatment of the theme of rape) in *Writing Rape, Writing Women in Early Modern England* (Houndmills: Macmillan, 1999), 136.

[32] George Ballard, *Memoirs of Several Ladies of Great Britain*, ed. Ruth Perry (Detroit: Wayne State University Press, 1985), 144–5; see Hodgson-Wright, 'Lumley's Iphigenia', *passim*.

[33] Catty, *Writing Rape*, 136.        [34] Ibid. 139.        [35] See Purkiss, *Three Tragedies*.

[36] See the discussion in Ch. 2.

Garnier's *Marc Antoine*, together with Philippe de Mornay's *Excellent discours de la vie et de la mort*, in 1592. Sidney notes a date for her translation at the end of *Antonius*: 'At Ramsburie 26 of Nouember 1590' (O2v). Garnier's version of the Antony and Cleopatra story was published in 1578, and it formed a significant part in the Continental humanist interest in Senecan drama. As Mary Sidney's editors point out, Garnier's drama was part of a French dramatic avant-garde.[37] Margaret Hannay has argued that Sidney's translation models a future direction for a politically engaged drama: 'Her work was . . . near the outset of the dramatic movement to comment on contemporary affairs by means of Roman historic allusions.'[38] Like all the literary endeavours of the Sidney family, as we have already seen both with Mary Sidney's poetry, and with Mary Wroth's writing, *Antonius* is engaged with a politics aligned with European Protestantism and its cause.[39] At the same time, critics have also underlined how the play paints a particularly sympathetic picture of Cleopatra, although the play involves, in Mary Beth Rose's incisive interpretation, the 'suppression of Cleopatra's sexual nature', except when she speaks to Antony's dead body.[40]

While *Antonius* was not intended for performance in the public theatre, Sidney's use of a considerable amount of blank verse, and her subtle approach to characterization, need to be emphasized, given that modern readers tend to believe that the term 'closet drama' means 'unactable'.[41] *Antonius* was certainly intended to be given what we would now call a staged reading within Sidney's Wilton circle.[42] When seen in the context of later Senecan drama, including that of public theatre playwrights like Ben Jonson, *Antonius* can be viewed as a significant exemplar of a serious approach to the idea of drama as a complex intellectual entertainment, as well as an emotional one. Sidney might well be seen as answering her brother Philip's famous fulmination, in his *Apology for Poetry* (c.1580), against what he saw as ridiculous stage plays, that were 'neither

[37] *The Collected Works of Mary Sidney Herbert*, ed. Margaret P. Hannay *et al.* (Oxford: Clarendon Press, 1998), i; references are to this edition.

[38] Margaret Patterson Hannay, *Philip's Phoenix: Mary Sidney, Countess of Pembroke* (New York: Oxford University Press, 1990), 127.

[39] See the discussions in Chs. 2 and 3. Although he mentions neither Wroth nor Mary Sidney, Blair Worden's extended consideration of the politics of Philip Sidney's *Arcadia* is relevant to this view of the Sidney family: *The Sound of Virtue: Philip Sidney's Arcadia and Elizabethan Politics* (New Haven: Yale University Press, 1996); see also Clarke, *Politics*, 88–95.

[40] Mary Beth Rose, *Gender and Authorship in the Sidney Circle* (Madison: University of Wisconsin Press, 1990), 132; for this kind of interpretation, see also Tina Krontiris, *Oppositional Voices* (London: Routledge, 1993), ch. 3.

[41] This point is emphasized in Marta Straznicky's important article, which also connects Cavendish's drama to the first flowering of closet drama discussed here: 'Reading the Stage: Margaret Cavendish and Commonwealth Closet Drama', *Criticism*, 37 (1995), 355–90.

[42] This aspect of *Antonius* and the other plays discussed here is stressed by Gweno Williams in her essay 'Translating the Text, Performing the Self', in Alison Findlay and Stephanie Hodgson-Wright, eds., *Women and Dramatic Production 1550–1700* (Harlow: Longman, 2000), 15–41.

right tragedies, nor right comedies'.[43] As a 'right tragedy', *Antonius* remains a sustained and powerful play, if one that might seem circumscribed and a bit stilted to readers brought up on Shakespeare's treatment of the story. Cleopatra's final speech in particular is a fine example of the play's emotional but controlled language:

> The sharpest torment in my heart I feele
> Is that I staie from thee, my heart, this while.
> Die will I straight now, now straight will I die,
> And straight with thee a wandring shade will be,
> Under the Cypres trees thou haunt'st alone,
> Where brookes of hell do falling seeme to mone. (206)

Just as Sidney's psalms achieved a high degree of transmission in manuscript, so the published *Antonius* was much admired and reprinted. It had editions, following the first of 1592, in 1595, 1600, 1606, and 1608. As well as the general tributes to Mary Sidney which flowed from those who genuinely admired her, and from those who sought her patronage, Samuel Daniel wrote a continuation of *Antonius*, titled *The Tragedy of Cleopatra* (1594), which includes a lengthy dedicatory poem to Sidney. The cluster of editions of *Antonius* early in the seventeenth century reflects Sidney's position as patron as well as her role in perpetuating Philip's work and reputation (as we have seen in Chapter 2). While the psalm translations had a significant circulation in manuscript throughout the seventeenth century, that does not seem to have been the case with Mary Sidney's other work, including *Antonius*.[44] Sidney's achievement in *Antonius* was celebrated in Alice Luce's 1897 edition of the translation, published in Weimar. Luce notes positively in her introduction Sidney's contribution to a unique moment in the adaptation of Senecan drama in England.[45] However, as S. P. Cerasano and Marion Wynne-Davies argue, Sidney's play and the mode in general were placed in a less positive light by T. S. Eliot in an influential essay of 1927, 'Seneca in Elizabethan Translation'.[46] In this essay, Eliot does offer a thoughtful defence of Seneca against the general distaste for his kind of tragic drama, and he has some

---

[43] Philip Sidney, *An Apology for Poetry*, ed. Shepherd, rev. Maslen (Manchester: Manchester University Press, 1992), 112.

[44] See the discussion of the psalms in Ch. 2; the widespread manuscript dissemination of Philip's work is discussed in H. R. Woudhuysen's *Sir Philip Sidney and the Circulation of Manuscripts, 1558–1640* (Clarendon Press: Oxford, 1996). The situation continued into the eighteenth century: George Ballard's fairly brief account of Sidney simply notes the publication of *Antonius*, 251. Horace Walpole prints a chorus from *Antonius* in his *Catalogue of Royal and Noble Authors* (London, 1806), ii. 197–8; as does Alexander Dyce in *Specimens of British Poetesses* (London: T. Rodd, 1825), 37.

[45] Alice Luce, ed., *The Countess of Pembroke's Antonie* (Weimar, 1897).

[46] S. P. Cerasano and Marion Wynne-Davies, *Readings in Renaissance Women's Drama* (London: Routledge, 1998), 18.

positive things to say about Daniel's *Cleopatra* (he does not mention *Antonius*), but ultimately concludes that this mode of drama was a dead end.[47]

The third of these 'closet dramas' has now become the most visible: Elizabeth Cary's *The Tragedy of Mariam: The Fair Queen of Jewry* (1613). Cary's play was the first original play by a woman to be published in England, and indeed it remained the only one until Cavendish's 1662 volume. In the 1914 Malone Society edition of the play, Dunstan and Greg established that the 'learned, virtuous, and truly noble Lady E.C.' of the title page of *Mariam* was Elizabeth Cary, wife of Henry Cary, Viscount Falkland.[48] A considerable amount of information about Cary is provided in the biography of her, which was written by one of her daughters some time in the 1640s.[49] Cary, according to this biography, was a precocious autodidact, who taught herself French, Spanish, Italian, Latin, and Hebrew (186).[50] She married Henry Cary in 1602, aged about 17. She was apparently interested in Catholicism from an early stage of the marriage. She was eventually to have eleven children, and at the same time she began to write a series of works, including some now lost, producing *Mariam* some time before 1612, when it was praised by Sir John Davies (along with Mary Sidney's work) in the dedication to his *The Muses Sacrifice* (1612): 'With feet of state, thou dost make thy Muse to meet | the scenes of Syracuse and Palestine'. The reference to Syracuse points to another, now lost, play by Cary, who notes in the dedication of *Mariam* to her sister Elizabeth: 'My first was consecrated to Apollo' (66).[51] Cary went to Ireland with her husband when he was made Viceroy in 1622. When Falkland sent her back to England in 1625, Cary's conversion to Catholicism became public knowledge, and Falkland renounced her, although she was apparently present at his deathbed in 1633. During this period, Cary contrived to send six of her children to the Continent to be educated as Catholics—a process which included having her two youngest sons kidnapped while they were living with their older brother, Lucius.[52] In 1630 Cary translated the inflammatory reply of Cardinal Perron to James I's attack on his work, dedicating the translation to Henrietta Maria at a time when the Catholicism of Charles I's queen

[47] See T. S. Eliot, 'Seneca in Elizabethan Translation', in *Selected Essays* (London: Faber, 1972), 65–105.

[48] See *The Tragedy of Mariam*, ed. A. C. Dunstan and W. W. Greg (London: Malone Society, 1914), pp. vi–viii; the identification was made by Gerard Langbaine and Edward Phillips, see below; see also the authoritative modern edition, ed. Barry Weller and Margaret W. Ferguson (Berkeley: University of California Press, 1994).

[49] The biography forms part of Weller and Ferguson's edition of *Mariam*; see their discussion of its authorship, 1–2.

[50] All references are to Weller and Ferguson, unless otherwise noted; I have taken biographical information from this source and also from the excellent *Oxford DNB* article by Stephanie Hodgson-Wright.

[51] The dedication was cancelled and only exists in two extant copies (Huntington and Houghton libraries); Weller and Ferguson suggest that it represents a first issue and was not included with copies presented for sale (44).

[52] Four daughters became nuns.

was a contentious political issue—the work was, needless to say, ordered to be suppressed by Archbishop Abbot. Cary died in 1639, and a number of scholars have suggested that she is the author of a history of Edward II, published in two different versions in 1680 but said to have been written by an 'E.F.' in 1627.[53]

Regardless of how much else Cary wrote, *Mariam* is a substantial achievement, and in recent years has been seen as a much more significant dramatic achievement than *Antonius*.[54] The dialogue between the characters in *Mariam* is far brisker than it is in the more stately *Antonius*, and Cary often uses a more down to earth language that brings, for example, Salome to life:

> Now stirs the tongue that is so quickly mov'd,
> But more than once your choler have I borne:
> Your fumish words are sooner said than prov'd,
> And Salome's reply is only scorn. (77)

As more criticism has focused on the play, a considerable complexity of characterization has become apparent, exemplified, for example, in Alexandra Bennett's examination of 'female performativity', particularly through an approach which eschews any easy and singular identification of Cary herself with a simple set of principles expressed in the play.[55]

Davies's praise of Cary's drama is a rare seventeenth-century example. While there are dedications to her in the 1614 edition of *England's Helicon*, and in Richard Beling's 1624 continuation of Sidney's *Arcadia*, neither mentions her writing.[56] In Edward Phillips's *Theatrum Poetarum, or A Compleat Collection of the Poets* (1675), Lady Elizabeth 'Carew' is simply mentioned in the catalogue of 'modern poetesses' as one who 'wrote the Tragedy of Mariam' (257).[57] Similarly, Gerard Langbaine, in *Lives and Characters of the English Dramatic Poets* (1699), notes Cary (again spelled as Carew) as *Mariam*'s author, and identifies its source in Josephus (14). George Ballard disarmingly confesses that he had written an entry on Elizabeth Cary for his *Memoirs*, but that it was mislaid, and did not reach the printer.[58]

---

[53] See the discussion of authorship in Weller and Ferguson edn, 12–17.

[54] This is particularly stressed in Stephanie Wright's edition of the play, in which she discusses her 1994 production of it, and notes its theatrical qualities (Keele: Keele University Press, 1996), esp. 20–4.

[55] See Alexandra G. Bennett, 'Female Performativity in *The Tragedy of Mariam*', *SEL* 40 (2000), 293–309; see also the extremely sophisticated reading that forms part of Margaret W. Ferguson's *Dido's Daughters: Literacy, Gender and Empire in Early Modern Europe and France* (Chicago: University of Chicago Press, 2003), discussed below.

[56] The *England's Helicon* sonnet does address her as 'learned' (A2); Richard Beling's *A Sixth Book to the Countess of Pembroke's Arcadia* was first published as a separate volume in Dublin in 1624 (not in London, *pace* Weller and Ferguson, 319, though it did become part of the 1627 London *Arcadia*), and Beling thanks the Viscountess of Falkland for her favours, either acknowledging or angling for her patronage while she was in Ireland, but not mentioning her writing.

[57] In the same way Phillips mentions Mary Sidney as the author of *Antonius* (260).

[58] Ballard, *Memoirs*, 54; I can find no trace of Ballard's entry on Cary in the manuscript of the *Memoirs*, nor is she listed in the manuscript index (Bodleian Library, Ballard MS 74).

Interest in Cary re-emerged in the nineteenth century, however. With his characteristic thoroughness, Alexander Dyce, in *Specimens of British Poetesses* (1825), notes Cary as the author of *Mariam* (following Langbaine), and prints the choruses from Act II and Act IV (28–31). The seventeenth-century biography of Cary was edited by Richard Simpson in 1861 and published by the Catholic Publishing and Bookselling Company.[59] This contains a transcript of the seventeenth-century text, but also a lengthy biographical appendix—which includes a number of key family letters, especially those surrounding Cary's public announcement of her conversion—the only composition discussed in this book is the translation of Perron, which is briefly mentioned. This edition was followed in 1883 by Georgiana Fullerton's biography of Cary.[60] Once again, the motivation behind this biography is admiration for Cary as a model of the persecuted convert: 'many a wife and mother will find in the history of this convert of the seventeenth century, a resemblance with her own' (p. vii). Fullerton herself was a notable convert, following the death of her father Lord Granville, who had been English ambassador to Paris, and she wrote a successful series of novels highlighting conversion and other Catholic issues between 1844 and 1881. Fullerton used Simpson's edition of the seventeenth-century biography as the main source for her biography, but her novelistic skills are evident in the smooth and dramatic narrative which she produces. Once again, despite some brief mention of Cary's literary accomplishments, no mention is made of *Mariam*—Fullerton sees Cary as highly intelligent and a good controversialist, but fundamentally as an exemplary figure, rather than a writer. This simply repeats the pattern set by the seventeenth-century biography, which similarly mentions Cary's writing only in passing, and does not name *Mariam*.

Despite the Malone Society edition of *Mariam* in 1914, Cary's play escaped critical attention almost entirely until Elaine Beilin's pioneering (and still influential) account in *Redeeming Eve* (1987).[61] Since then, Cary has moved from the periphery to the centre of considerable critical and editorial attention, as *Mariam* has, in a sense, had to shoulder the burden of being 'the' Jacobean play by a woman to set against the professional output of Shakespeare, Jonson, and all the rest of the male playwrights. Perhaps for that reason, considerable debate centred for some time on how the play might be read as in some sense proto-feminist.[62] At the present critical moment, however, the debate has moved on and the play is seen in a variety of social and political contexts, now coloured

[59] (London and Dublin: 1861).

[60] Lady Georgiana Fullerton, *The Life of Elisabeth Lady Falkland 1585–1639* (London: Burns and Oates, 1883).

[61] Cary is mentioned briefly in, for example, Myra Reynolds, *The Learned Lady in England* (Boston: Houghton Mifflin, 1920).

[62] See esp. the article by Bennett cited in n. 54; on some of these issues, see Cristina Malcomson and Mihoko Suzuki, eds., *Debating Gender in Early Modern England* (Houndmills: Palgrave, 2002), and, as a useful compendium of source texts, N. H. Keeble, *The Cultural Identity of Seventeenth Century Woman* (London: Routledge, 1994).

by the increasingly sophisticated view of the nature and variety of early modern debates on gender. This is most evident in Margaret W. Ferguson's sustained reading of the play in relation to issues surrounding the position of Catholics in the early seventeenth century, especially after the enactment of the Oath of Allegiance in 1606.[63] To some degree this reading follows on from Barbara Lewalski's sense of the intertwining of Cary's personal circumstances with general political and religious issues.[64] Ferguson offers an account of the character Mariam as, in some ways, analogous to Cary; in Ferguson's memorable phrase, 'she may be read as an ancient Jew equivocally like a modern Catholic wife' (271). Ferguson sees this view of the play as complementing an earlier critical emphasis on its exploration of 'the legitimacy of women's public voice' (283), and its treatment of the issue of women rulers.[65] In the same way, Ferguson explores ideas of race and its connection with gender, and what she classifies in her extended study as 'empire'.

The play's treatment of gender has also been the subject of particularly subtle readings, most notably Jonathan Goldberg's complex and provocative interpretation of the enigmatic character Graphina, who appears in only one scene, but who seems to encapsulate (or at least, seems to after one has read Goldberg's interpretation) a suggestive nexus of ideas about female silence, speech, and writing.[66] In Goldberg's view, Graphina is, in a sense, 'a kind of generic signature making claims for women's writing' (166).

There is no evidence that this recent critical interest in Cary's play has any parallel in the seventeenth century. When Margaret Cavendish wrote her plays in the 1650s, she was inspired by those of her husband, and of other male playwrights. It is also worth noting *The Concealed Fancies* produced by Cavendish's stepdaughters, Elizabeth Brackley and Jane Cavendish, probably in the mid-1640s (see my brief discussion in Chapter 1). As Margaret Ezell pointed out in a pioneering essay on the sisters' manuscript volume of poems, pastoral, and play, the poised and confident nature of *Concealed Fancies*, and its witty take on the common theme of courtship and marriage, is bound up in the professed admiration of the daughters for their father.[67] In a sense, *Concealed Fancies* might be seen as slipping in a dramatic homage to William Cavendish in advance of his

---

[63] Ferguson, *Dido's Daughters*, ch. 6; further references in parentheses; see also Laurie J. Shannon, '*The Tragedy of Mariam*: Cary's Critique of the Terms of Founding Discourses', *ELR* 24 (1994), 135–53, Barbara K. Lewalski, *Writing Women in Jacobean England* (Cambridge, Mass.: Harvard University Press, 1993), 191–4, and, for a different political reading, Clarke, *Politics*, 95–106.

[64] See Lewalski, *Writing Women*, ch. 7.

[65] See Ferguson's own article, 'Running On with Almost Public Voice: The Case of E.C., in Florence Howe, ed., *Tradition and the Talents of Women* (Urbana: University of Illinois Press, 1991), 37–67, and Maureen Quilligan, 'Staging Gender', in James Grantham Turner, ed., *Sexuality and Gender in Early Modern Europe* (Cambridge: Cambridge University Press, 1993), 208–32.

[66] Jonathan Goldberg, *Desiring Women Writing* (Stanford, Calif.: Stanford University Press, 1997), 164–90; further references in parentheses.

[67] Margaret Ezell, ' "To Be Your Daughter in Your Pen": The Social Functions of Literature in the Writings of Lady Elizabeth Brackley and Lady Jane Cavendish', *HLQ* 51 (1988), 281–96.

second wife's similar (and perhaps competing) admiration. At the same time, as Sophie Tomlinson has pointed out, in a discussion which places the play in the context of earlier Caroline depictions of women, there is a certain '*savoir faire*' achieved by the sisters in their construction of female subjectivity, which marks out a significant moment in seventeenth-century theatrical history.[68] This history, in Tomlinson's view, builds upon the increasing visibility of women, seen, for example, in Henrietta Maria's engagement with acting and court drama.[69] As Susan Wiseman points out, in her study of drama during the Civil War period, the closure of the public theatres produced what might be called a level playing field for male and female writers: 'we could . . . see the Civil War bans on drama as in some ways inaugurating a new and temporary equality in the status of plays by men and women since neither sex was likely to have plays staged.'[70] The imagined theatre of the 1650s, which, Wiseman notes, might connect women with a world of power and martial prowess at the time of the plays' composition, was transformed by the time of their publication into a public theatre which allowed women on the stage, and produced a professional woman playwright like Aphra Behn, but which had no place in it for Cavendish's productions.[71]

## CAVENDISH'S PLAYS: 'NATURAL DISPOSITIONS AND PRACTICES'

As I have already noted, the publication of Cavendish's plays forms part of what we might call her second wave of production, when as an individual she was determined to play a prominent role in Restoration literary and scientific culture. This resulted in such actions as her visit to the Royal Society, but it also saw her reissue her works from the 1650s in revised and expanded form, and move on to new genres: not only plays, but also familiar letters (in *Sociable Letters* of 1664), imaginary speeches (*Orations*, 1662), a utopia attached to further scientific work (*The Blazing World*, which formed part of *Observations Upon Experimental Philosophy*, 1666, which was her attack on Robert Hooke's *Micrographia* of 1665), and the biography of her husband (*Life of William Cavendish*, 1667).[72]

In the preface she addressed to William Cavendish in *Plays* (1662), Margaret explains that her inspiration, far from being any of the plays by women examined

---

[68] Sophie Tomlinson, 'Too Theatrical? Female Subjectivity in Caroline and Interregnum Drama', *Women's Writing*, 6 (1999), 67.

[69] See Tomlinson's pioneering book on women and drama in the seventeenth century, *Women on Stage in Stuart Drama* (Cambridge: Cambridge University Press, 2005).

[70] Susan Wiseman, *Drama and Politics in the English Civil War* (Cambridge: Cambridge University Press, 1998), 92.

[71] Ibid. 104; see also Alison Findlay, '"Upon the World's Stage": The Civil War and Interregnum', in Findlay and Hodgson-Wright, *Women and Dramatic Production*, 68–94.

[72] For an account of Cavendish's public activities and the notoriety she achieved in the Restoration, see Whitaker, *Mad Madge*, ch. 13.

in the previous section, was William's own plays, although she sees hers as 'statues' that will not gain the life of the stage:

> my Playes are very unlike those you have writ, for your Lordships Playes have as it were a natural life, and a quick spirit in them, whereas mine are like dull dead statues, which is the reason I send them forth to be printed, rather than keep them concealed in hopes to have them first Acted; and this advantage I have, that is, I am out of the fear of having them hissed off from the Stage, for they are not like to come thereon. (A3)

Similarly, Cavendish explains in the preface to the readers that she fears her plays will not be acted because they are too long, although she initially suggests that they might not be staged because no acting company exists as yet (suggesting that this preface was written before performances started up again in earnest, which happened by mid-1660).[73] In another preface, Cavendish nervously justifies her avoidance of the unities, using Jonson as something of a touchstone, and noting *Volpone* and *The Alchemist* as examples (Jonson spent had spent time at Welbeck and regarded William Cavendish as a major patron—this was, of course, well before he married Margaret Lucas, but Jonson clearly remained an admired figure in the Cavendish household). Margaret Cavendish's frequently expressed admiration for the public theatre as an ennobling experience lends a certain poignancy to her professed insouciance about the lack of performance of her plays. Indeed, by the time she came to write *The Blazing World* (1666), a text which offers a picture of a world in which Cavendish's alter-ego, the Empress, creates a kind of parallel Royal Society in which Cavendish's own scientific ideas are vindicated, Cavendish constructed a similar fantasy about her theatrical vindication, when the Empress asks her to create a theatre which will exist solely to perform Cavendish's plays.[74] On a more practical level, Cavendish finally offers her readers the possibility of bringing her plays to life by reading them aloud—a practice which was common, not just while the theatres were closed, but in private 'performances' before that time: 'when as a Play is well and skillfully read, the very sound of the Voice that enters through the Ears, doth present the Actions to the Eyes of the Fancy as lively as if it were really Acted' (A6v). Marta Straznicky, in her suggestive account of Cavendish's plays in relation to the traditions of closet drama discussed above, argues that Cavendish situates the reader 'on the divide between public and private', making, in Straznicky's view, productive use of some of the tensions between a desire for performance, and an anxiety over the nature of the theatre, in order to create writing with a 'social purpose'.[75]

The 1662 volume of plays indicates yet again how ambitious Cavendish was; it contains no fewer than fourteen plays, seven of them in two parts (of five acts

---

[73] See *The London Stage 1660–1800*, ed. William Van Lennep (Carbondale: Northern Illinois University Press, 1965), i. 21.

[74] *Blazing World*, appended to *Observations Upon Experimental Philosophy* (1666), H1v.

[75] Straznicky, 'Reading the Stage', 360.

each). Virtually all comedies, the plays contain a number of female characters who may be seen as, in part, alter-egos for the author: characters like Lady Contemplation from *Youth's Glory and Death's Banquet*, or Lady Victoria from *Bell in Campo*, or Lady Perfection from *The Religious*, or Lady Solitary from *The Comical Hash*. In terms of the plays' structure, while Cavendish explains that, unlike Jonson, she does not follow the dramatic unities, I think that some of Jonson's influence can be seen in her use of characters somewhat like his 'humours' (including the use of names evoking character traits), and also the use of numerous often quite short scenes (although these are not constructed in exactly the same way as Jonson's classically influenced scenes).[76] In her second collection of plays, which she published in 1668, Cavendish seems resigned to the fact that her only performances would take place in the Blazing World, and she consigns their reputation to posterity in a volume uncharacteristically guarded by only a single preface: 'I will venture, in spight of the Criticks, to call them Plays; and if you like them so, well and good; if not, there is no harm done.'[77]

In contrast to Margaret's situation, William had some success in the public theatre, and one can only speculate if Pepys's misconception that *The Humorous Lovers*, which was staged in April 1667, was written by Margaret rather than William, would have rubbed salt into her wounds.[78] It may have taken 350 years, but posterity has finally rewarded Cavendish, and her plays have not only received a fair amount of critical attention in recent years, but have been performed with some success.[79] It is easy to see why modern readers and critics have been drawn to, for example, *Bell in Campo*, with its female army led by Lady Victoria, and its allusions to the Civil War and its devastating effect on women in particular.[80]

---

[76] Here I disagree slightly with Alexandra Bennett's view of Jonson's influence in her helpful account of Cavendish's dramatic structure and tone, with specific reference to *Bell in Campo* and *The Sociable Companions*, 'Fantastic Realism: Margaret Cavendish and the Possibilities of Drama', in Line Cottegnies and Nancy Weitz, eds., *Authorial Conquests: Essays on Genre in the Writings of Margaret Cavendish* (Madison: Associated University Presses, 2003), 179–94; for a more detailed account of Cavendish's relationship to Jonson, see Julie Sanders, ' "A Woman Write a Play?": Jonsonian Strategies and the Dramatic Writings of Margaret Cavendish', in Cerasano and Wynne-Davies, *Readings*, 293–305.

[77] *Plays Never Before Printed* (1668), A3v.

[78] Pepys did think it 'the most silly thing that ever come upon a stage'; see *The London Stage*, 205; a pre-Interregnum play of William's, *The Country Captain*, had been staged in 1661; William also had some success in collaboration with Shadwell on *The Triumphant Widow* (1674), and provided Dryden with a translated version of Molière as the basis for *Sir Martin Marall* (performed Aug. 1667), see ibid. 111.

[79] Gweno Williams has championed the plays as performable, and as well as a number of theatrical productions, she has produced a DVD of *The Convent of Pleasure* and a teaching DVD which includes a number of performed extracts from a variety of Cavendish's plays: *Margaret Cavendish: Plays and Performance*; for an overview of Cavendish's drama which stresses its theatrical viability see Williams's essay, ' "No Silent Woman": The Plays of Margaret Cavendish, Duchess of Newcastle', in Findlay and Hodgson-Wright, *Women and Dramatic Production*, 95–122.

[80] It comes as no surprise that *Bell in Campo* is available in three modern editions: Anne Shaver, ed., Margaret Cavendish, *The Convent of Pleasure and Other Plays* (Baltimore: Johns Hopkins University Press, 1999), this also includes *Love's Adventures* and *The Bridals*; Alexandra G. Bennett,

The *Convent of Pleasure* has also received some critical attention, particularly because of its interest in cross-dressing, disguise, and issues relating to female independence and education.

Throughout the 1660s, Cavendish continued to work in new genres while at the same time revising and reissuing previous works. In 1664 she published both *Sociable Letters* and *Philosophical Letters*. The appealing *Sociable Letters* covers an enormous range of topics, allowing Cavendish to explore her ideas in a more playful tone—this volume produced a now often-quoted defence of Shakespeare which praises his heterogeneous characters.[81] I have already noted the combined volume of *Observations Upon Experimental Philosophy* and *The Blazing World* (1666); while there is a certain distortion caused by removing *The Blazing World* from its context in the larger scientific work (although it does have a separate title page), it can be read as an independent work and it has become Cavendish's most popular work in recent years, in part because of its narrative verve, and increasingly because of its almost postmodern representation of Cavendish as simultaneously 'herself' and the Empress.[82] Cavendish's 1667 life of her husband was, as we will see below, to become her most enduring work in the eighteenth and nineteenth centuries. From the 1668 *Plays* until her sudden death late in 1673, Cavendish published no new works, although she did produce revised volumes. Indeed, while her death was unexpected, one might see this final stage of Cavendish's publication history as an attempt to consolidate her achievements. Her career had, in the end, intersected with two other women who rose to considerable prominence, and who will be discussed in detail in the next chapter: Katherine Philips and Aphra Behn. In terms of monumentalizing publication, Philips's folio collections (even if unauthorized) were testimony to her influential position as Royalist poet, initially consolidated within a manuscript coterie.[83] Looking back from this period, one can note women writers growing in visibility, but also entering into a series of literary systems which acknowledged their presence. This might be within manuscript publication, as was the case initially for Philips, but was also the case in print from the 1650s to the 1670s and beyond (I am here thinking, not just of obvious cases like Cavendish and Philips, but of volumes like Trapnel's massive 1658 folio, discussed in the last chapter). Because

---

ed., *Bell in Campo and The Sociable Companions* (Peterborough: Broadview Press, 2002); Paul Salzman, ed., *Early Modern Women's Writing: An Anthology 1560–1700* (World's Classics, Oxford: Oxford University Press, 2000); for an account of its relationship both to a play by Jasper Mayne and to Oxford University poets' praise of Henrietta Maria, see Chalmers, *Royalist Women*, 48–51.

[81] See letter 123; *Sociable Letters* has been edited by James Fitzmaurice (New York: Garland, 1997); new edition (Peterborough: Broadview Press, 2004).

[82] Once again, modern editions of *The Blazing World* have fostered this interest; see Kate Lilley, ed., *The Blazing World and Other Writings* (London: Pickering, 1992); Paul Salzman, ed., *An Anthology of Seventeenth-Century Fiction* (World's Classics, Oxford: Oxford University Press, 1991).

[83] This comparison between Cavendish and Philips is pursued most suggestively by Chalmers, *Royalist Women*, chs. 1–3, who is interested in the way both writers can be placed in the context of Royalist ideology.

of her wealth and social position, Cavendish was best placed to publish her work in the style which she felt it merited, but after her death, William continued the process by arranging for the publication of the kind of memorial volume previously reserved for male writers or statesmen.

## ORDERING A REPUTATION

William Cavendish arranged for the publication of a commemorative volume entitled *Letters and Poems in Honour of the Incomparable Princess, Margaret, Duchess of Newcastle*, which was first published in 1676.[84] There is a temptation to view this volume as sycophantic—in contrast to our more studied appreciation of Cavendish's work. But the volume bears close examination as an indication of what we might call the 'value' of the Duchess of Newcastle immediately after her death in 1673. The volume begins with a series of letters from universities and colleges to which Margaret presented copies of her work. William Cavendish died in the year of the volume's publication, and it was then reprinted in 1678, with the new title *A Collection of Letters and Poems: Written by several persons of Honour and Learning, Upon divers Important Subjects, to the Late Duke and Duchess of Newcastle*. The volume begins with a 1658 letter from the rector of the University of Leiden (reflecting the time that the Cavendishes spent in exile in Antwerp). Symbolically, as the initial citation, this letter indicates how significant Cavendish's sense of permanent exile was: as we have seen, both Margaret and William moved, in a sense, from exile in Europe during the interregnum to exile in England when, at the Restoration, William's attempt to position himself close to Charles II came to nothing, just as Margaret's attempts to assume a public role as playwright or philosopher were largely ignored. The rector's brief Latin letter praises Cavendish as 'Illustrissima Domina', but, like the letters from English universities which follow, the rector offers a polite acknowledgement of a gift, rather than an analysis of, or response to, what Cavendish has actually written. A letter from the Senate of Cambridge University addressed to William follows, and while it is much longer, it is still characteristically unspecific, although it havers about whether material is emanating from William or Margaret.

The third letter is addressed to Margaret by the Master and Fellows of St John's College, Cambridge, and it acknowledges two volumes: *Poems and Fancies* and 'Epistles'—presumably *Philosophical Letters* (1664). St John's was William Cavendish's college when he attended Cambridge, and the volume as a whole contains seven commendatory letters from St John's addressed to William, and five addressed to Margaret.[85] Trinity College, Cambridge, addressed three letters

---

[84] *Letters and Poems in Honour of the Incomparable Princess, Margaret, Duchess of Newcastle*, (London, 1676).

[85] Margaret notes that William was far from a model scholar at Cambridge: '[he] was a Student of St. John's Colledg in Cambridg, and had his Tutors to instruct him; yet they could not perswade

each to William and Margaret. The Master of Trinity, John Pearson, a notable theologian, had been a staunch Royalist during the Civil War, and he became a member of the Royal Society (although he was not an active participant).[86] Pearson's membership of the Royal Society may have attracted Margaret's attention, but it seems more likely that Trinity saw the connection with the Duke and Duchess of Newcastle as politically important. Letters were also sent from Queen's College, Christ Church, and St Edmund Hall, Oxford. Not all colleges bothered to acknowledge Cavendish's presentation volumes. Merton College, Oxford, for example, was familiar to Margaret as the place where Queen Henrietta Maria's court was relocated during the Civil War, when Margaret served as a maid of honour to the Queen. Merton received a number of Margaret's volumes, but no letters from the college to her appear in print (though there may be some in manuscript as yet unlocated).

Some patterns in the college letters may be adduced at this point, in order to understand how they function as, essentially, rhetorical exercises in gratitude. The first St John's letter offers some general comments on Cavendish's poetry and philosophy. In both cases, the writers stress a link between Cavendish and nature: 'In your Poems we admire that Life and Spirit, as also that Native, and Even fancie, which, every where, is Conspicuous . . . In your Philosophy there appears, every where, a clear and searching acuteness of Judgement, nothing forced, or Mysterious: All is plain and genuine, meer and natural Nature' (19). While it is true that Cavendish did indeed have a philosophical interest in Nature, the fellows of St John's rely on a traditional association of femininity and the natural world to create an image of artlessness: 'We men find Nature and Truth very coy and sullen . . . But she willingly shews herself all bare and naked to your Grace' (19). In a later letter, the fellows of St John's assure Cavendish that they have set aside a special place in their library for her books, 'according to our slender provision' (27)—the letters from St John's are quick to seize upon any opportunity to solicit a possible endowment.

Cavendish's biography of her husband produced a more nuanced response from the Cambridge Senate and Vice Chancellor (or whoever wrote on their behalf). This is a portent of things to come, as the biography of William Cavendish was to become Margaret's most frequently republished and, one might venture to say, respected work. This letter claims that the biography attracted a close and sympathetic reading: 'in reading it we must acknowledge that we stop'd often, because we could not but admire, every where, both the loftiness of the

---

him to read or study much, he taking more delight in sports, then in learning; so that his Father being a wise man, and seeing that his Son had a good natural Wit, and was of a very good Disposition, suffer'd him to follow his own Genius; whereas his other Son Charles, in whom he found a greater love and inclination to Learning, he encouraged as much that way, as possibly he could', *Life*, Oo1. St John's benefited greatly from the patronage of William's aunt Mary Cavendish, Countess of Shrewsbury,

[86] See *DNB*, s.v. Pearson, John.

argument, and elegancy, and spruceness of the Stile' (23–4). The letter is admirably poised between the usual compliments for all of Cavendish's endeavours, and the perhaps inadvertent admission that this particular work, because of its subject, is truly welcome:

although your Grace can neither dictate nor publish any Work which the University of Cambridge will not own, and esteem, yet for this last Essay of your Graces we retain a most singular affection, and, in testimony thereof, lodge it in the richest Cabinet that we have, our publick Liberary; for the perusal of the present, and succeeding generation, long therefore shall the most valiant, and renowned General live, and your Grace too with him, seeing you have written his enterprises with as great a spirit as he himself perform'd them; hereafter if generous and high born men; if men of War search our Library for a Model of a most accomplished General, they shall find it expressed to the life, not in *Xenophon's Cyrus*, but in the Dutchess of *Newcastle's William*. (24)

Here Cavendish is accorded a certain martial strength derived from the exploits of her husband. But there are potential layers of irony as well: Cavendish's biography has to counter views of her husband which saw him as a coward for leaving England after the Battle of Marston Moor in 1644. Despite the fact that Margaret Cavendish offers an extremely detailed account of her husband's exploits in the Civil War, in the end, the biography offers a very pessimistic view of martial prowess. The very last words of the biography (passed over in silence by the academic admirers of Cambridge) are:

I have observed, That those that meddle least in Wars, whether Civil or Foreign, are not onely most safe and free from danger, but most secure from Losses; and though Heroick Persons esteem Fame before Life; yet many there are, that think the wisest way is to be a Spectator, rather then an Actor, unless they be necessitated to it; for it is better, say they, to sit on the Stool of Quiet, then in the Chair of Troublesome Business. (Eee2)[87]

Margaret Cavendish also implicitly countered her portrait of William with a series of depictions, elsewhere in her writing, of heroic women, notably in the creation of the valiant Lady Victoria in her play *Bell in Campo*: a woman who leads a female army in triumph. When *Bell in Campo* and the *Life of William* are placed side by side, they provide a good example of what some have called Margaret Cavendish's inconsistent nature, and others have praised as her imaginative range and heterogeneous approach to a number of issues. At one and the same time, it is possible to garner quotations and examples of Cavendish as proto-feminist demolisher of male heroic pretension, *and* as slavish admirer of machismo and husbandly virtue. (By the Restoration, William Cavendish's claim to masculine prowess rested upon his skill as a horseman, and letters acknowledging the presentation of his book on horsemanship form a significant part of the collection.)

---

[87]  References to Margaret Cavendish, *The Life of . . . William Cavendish* (1667).

Individual, rather than institutional, letters to Margaret provide more complex evidence of active engagement with her ideas. The first in the volume is a brief note from Kenelm Digby, written from Paris in 1657. Digby, an old friend of William Cavendish, was part of the Cavendishes' Paris circle, debating the merits of Descartes with Hobbes.[88] Digby seems to have remained on cordial terms with the Cavendishes, despite being a Catholic who negotiated with Cromwell in the mid-1650s over religious toleration. It is unclear which volume Digby is acknowledging in this letter; he simply says that it 'affordeth abundant matter' (65), which might point to *Philosophical and Physical Opinions*. Thomas Barlow, Bodleian Librarian, seems to have been a conduit for the delivery of Cavendish's books to a variety of Oxford colleges; he writes on 24 March 1655: 'Your Books were received (as indeed they ought,) with very much respect, and gratitude, and I am commanded by the several Colledges to returne their humblest Thanks to Your Honour' (66). In a 1656 letter, Barlow offers more specific praise of Cavendish's work:

I have as yet only read one Story in your Book, and the Language, and Ingenuity of it, to me seems such, that I am perswaded the famous Monsieur Scudery would wish himself the Author of it. If I mistake not I think I told you in my last, that I had a Manuscript Book in my keeping (for it was never yet printed) which the Author intitles thus—Womens Worth, or a Treatise proving by sundry reasons that Women excell Men, Many of my Sex will hardly believe it, yet I believe your Honour may prove the best Argument in the World to convince them of their infidelity. (70–1).[89]

Cavendish may not have appreciated the Scudéry comparison, given her scorn for the romance genre, but she must have been pleased by praise from Barlow, who became an opponent of the Royal Society and Master of Queen's College—as well as a notable trimmer.[90]

On the side of serious philosophy, there has been some speculation about the one letter from Thomas Hobbes printed in the volume. Anna Battigelli has noted how, despite Hobbes's close relationship with William Cavendish, he kept Margaret 'at a comfortable distance'.[91] Hobbes's letter expresses surprise that she should send him her book: 'For tokens of this kind are not ordinarily sent but to such as pretend to the title as well as to the mind of Friends' (67). Hobbes does note that Cavendish portrays 'truer Idea's of Virtue and Honour than any Book of morality I have read' (68), but sets up a comparison with successful plays, liked by the 'rabble', which may well have served to remind Cavendish of her lack of any popular success.

---

[88] See Whitaker, *Mad Madge*, 92–4.

[89] This letter is mentioned in Whitaker, ibid. 314; Barlow refers to the manuscript treatise in a letter dated 1663, which is either a mistake, or the 1656 letter is misdated (69).

[90] See *DNB*; another layer of irony is present when one considers that the romances were written by Madeleine de Scudéry, but commonly attributed to her brother George.

[91] Battigelli, *Margaret Cavendish*, 65.

Far more substantial commentary is provided by a miscellaneous group of men who had some pretension to learning and letters: Jasper Mayne, Walter Charleton, Joseph Glanville, Constantine Huygens, and Thomas Shadwell. Jasper Mayne, who had been William Cavendish's chaplain at Welbeck, and was, in the Restoration, a canon at Christ Church, Oxford, was approached by Margaret to find someone to translate her work into Latin. Mayne had written plays and poetry in the 1630s, and had also translated Lucian.[92] In the early 1660s, Cavendish had clearly decided that a series of Latin translations would ensure the respectability of her oeuvre. As well as commissioning Mayne, she asked Thomas Tully, principal of St Edmund Hall, to look out for likely translators, and he noted a series of possible candidates on the flyleaf of his copy of *Philosophical Opinions*.[93] Mayne's letter announcing that he has found a translator for Cavendish notes, at the same time, the difficulty in categorizing her work: 'it would pose me something to find a proper place in any Library for your Works to stand in, whether among the Orators, Poets, Philosophers, States-men, or Politicians, since every one of these may be ambitious to stand next you' (94). In a succeeding letter, Mayne announces that he is having her poetry translated by 'a young Scholar', who has been instructed to read Lucretius in preparation for the task (96). In the end, Mayne's young scholar seems to have produced nothing. Anthony à Wood notes in *Fasti Oxonienses* that one James Bristow of Christ Church 'had begun to translate into Latin some of the philosophy of Margaret dutchess of Newcastle, upon the desire of those whom she had appointed to enquire out a fit person for such a matter; but he finding great difficulties therein, through the confusedness of the subject, gave over, as being a matter not to be performed by any'.[94] Thomas Tully's nomination, John Harmar, described by Anthony à Wood as 'mostly in a poor and shabbed condition, whether in his way of living, or habit, he flatter'd all men and powers that were uppermost', translated one or more of Cavendish's plays, 'for which he was well rewarded', Wood remarks, but the translation remained unpublished.[95]

Joseph Glanville offers a more direct and serious engagement with Cavendish's writing. Glanville was a follower of Henry More; his interest in Cavendish's philosophy seems to be genuine engagement, with no thought of currying favour or advancement. Cavendish had attacked More's belief in witches in *Philosophical Letters*.[96] Sarah Hutton has recently discussed Cavendish's engagement with More's thought. including a fascinating account of the way that Cavendish attacked More in *The Blazing World*.[97] Glanville had defended More in his 1666 book *Philosophical Considerations Touching Witches and Witchcraft*. His first letter

---

[92] For a good account of Mayne, see Chalmers, *Royalist Women Writers*, 46–7.
[93] See the discussion in Whitaker, *Mad Madge*, 255–6.
[94] Anthony à Wood, *Athenae Oxonienses* (New York: Burt Franklin, 1817; repr. 1967).
[95] Ibid., iii. 919 and see Whitaker, *Mad Madge*, 255.      [96] Whitaker, *Mad Madge*, 318.
[97] See Sarah Hutton, 'Margaret Cavendish and Henry More', in Stephen Clucas, ed., *Princely Brave Woman* (Aldershot: Ashgate, 2003), 185–98.

printed in *Letters and Poems* asks for Cavendish's opinion on his book (85). It is worth noting that More himself politely acknowledged the volumes sent to him by Cavendish, but was too discreet to pass any comment upon their contents, other than acknowledging them to be 'elegant and ingenious' (91). In a second, more substantial letter, Glanville defends experimentation and argues, against Cavendish, that 'we may arise according to the order of nature by degrees from the exercise of our Senses, to that of our Reasons' (99). Cavendish's debate with Glanville proceeded across several years and, as Katie Whitaker points out, it led to an elaboration of her arguments about 'animist materialism and her belief in nature's free will' in *Grounds of Natural Philosophy*, which she published in 1668.[98] Glanville continues, in a series of letters, to oppose what he saw as Cavendish's materialism. The exchange as it appears in *Letters and Poems* is, of course, one-sided, as we do not have the opportunity to read Cavendish's letters to Glanville, but he certainly provided the kind of engagement with her ideas which she was seeking.

A similarly detailed, though less philosophical, exchange occurred with Walter Charleton. Charleton was another connection to Cavendish via Thomas Hobbes, and an engagement with Atomist theory. In her important article exploring the relationship of Cavendish's philosophy to that of Hobbes, Sarah Hutton notes how Hobbes, Charleton, Digby, and Descartes were an essential part of the 'particular Parisian milieu she inhabited during her exile'.[99] Hutton also notes how, with Charleton as with Hobbes (and, we might add, Glanville), Cavendish was eager to separate out her philosophical position, to ensure that she was not regarded as a mere echo of these male intellectuals.[100] Charleton wrote a long letter to Cavendish in January 1655, acknowledging receipt of *The World's Olio*. Charleton begins with the effusive compliments largely absent from Glanville's letters, but he then goes on to report that he has met those who criticize Cavendish's writings because her language is tainted by 'many Terms of the Schools' (146). Indirectly, this hints at suspicions of plagiarism, or at least the accusation that Cavendish's work was unoriginal. As Whitaker notes, this led to a series of prefaces to *Philosophical Opinions* in which Cavendish angrily refutes the idea that she had much acquaintance with philosophers and formal philosophy.[101] In a later letter, Charleton offers a more detailed and hesitantly critical account of his response to Cavendish's work, disingenuously stating: 'For your Natural Philosophy; it is ingenious and free, and may be, for ought I know, Excellent; but give me leave Madam, to confess, I have not yet been so happy, as to discover much therein that Apodictical, or wherein I think my self much obliged to acquiesce. But, that may be the fault of my own dull Brain'

---

[98] Whitaker, *Mad Madge*, 319.
[99] Sarah Hutton, 'In Dialogue with Thomas Hobbes: Margaret Cavendish's Natural Philosophy,' *Women's Writing*, 4 (1997), 421–32.
[100] Ibid.        [101] Whitaker, *Mad Madge*, 184.

(111). Charleton assures Cavendish that she really loses nothing by the limited response to her philosophical works, given the sad state of learning. Charleton is more reassuring about Cavendish's literary endeavours, but he offers the sort of backhanded compliment that implied, yet again, that Cavendish's artlessness was her main attribute:

Your Invention is too nimble to be fettered, hence it is, that you do not always confine your Sense to verse, nor your Verses to Rhythme; nor your Rhythme to the quantity and sounds of Sillables. Your Descriptions, Expressions, Similies, Allegories, Metaphors, Epithets, Numbers, all flow in upon you of their own accord, and in full Tides: and Verses stand ready minted in the Treasury of your Brain, as Tears in some Women's Eyes, waiting to be called forth. (115)

In the year following this letter, Charleton published a Latin translation of Margaret's *Life of William Cavendish*.[102] It is rather ironic that, of all her works, this was the one that achieved a Latin translation as well as wide and continuing circulation (as discussed below.)

Letters from Thomas Shadwell point to what Whitaker, perhaps with slight exaggeration, calls Cavendish's 'celebrity as an aristocratic patron of letters'.[103] Shadwell acknowledges what he calls the many 'Favours I have received from Welbeck' (130), and he at least nods towards Margaret's dramatic interests. Shadwell also contributed an elegy and a commemorative poem to the small series of poems which end the volume. He claims that 'In Wit and Sense She did excell all Men', but he alludes to Margaret's infertility in a way that might well have angered her if she was not conveniently dead, given the fact that she and William had agonized over their lack of children and had tried numerous remedies in the 1640s.[104] Shadwell writes:

> Though we no Issue of her Body find
>       Yet she hath left behind
> The Nobler Issue of her mighty *Mind*. (167)

In his other poem, Shadwell opens with a stronger compliment: 'Whilst others study Books, I study you', and goes on to praise the depth of Cavendish's philosophical knowledge. The only other poem of note is George Etheredge's smooth tribute, which largely underplays Margaret's writing and concentrates on William's dedication to her.

---

[102] Margaret Cavendish, *De Vita et Rebus Gestis Nobilissimi Illustrissimique Principis Guilielmi Ducis*, trans. Walter Charleton (1668).

[103] Whitaker, *Mad Madge*, 320; Whitaker implies that Margaret had taken over from William as patron, but in fact, when looking in detail at her examples, it is evident that Dryden dedicated *An Evening's Love* to William, not Margaret, and praises her for her *Life of William*, and Shadwell dedicated four plays to William (*The Sullen Lovers, Epsom Wells, The Libertine, The Virtuoso*), and only one, *The Humorists*, to Margaret.

[104] See Whitaker, *Mad Madge*, 110.

As I noted at the beginning of this discussion, the commemorative volume is an impressive tribute to Margaret Cavendish's currency in the 1670s. This could be seen to continue through to comments like Gerard Langbaine's 1691 *An Account of the English Dramatick Poets*, in which he offers judicious praise for Cavendish's plays:

I know there are some that have but a mean Opinion of her Plays; but if it be considered that both the Language and the Plots of them are all her own: I think she ought with Justice to be preferr'd to others of her Sex, which have built their Fame on other People's Foundations: sure I am, that whoever will consider well the several Epistles before her Books, and the General Prologue to all her Plays, if he have any spark of Generosity or Good Breeding, will be favourable in his censure.[105]

Langbaine is implicitly contrasting Cavendish with Aphra Behn, praised earlier in his book for her dramatic achievements, but taken to task for her excessive borrowing, although Langbaine throws in the ameliorating comment that 'whatever she borrows she improves for the better' (17). Given Behn's prominence in the 1670s, and the visibility of a number of other women writers during the decade, the issuing of two memorial volumes is more than simply a tribute to Cavendish's status: they offer an implicit register of her work in relation to other women writers. Cavendish herself, of course, valued her singularity, and the volumes testify to the conflict between her interest in some direct engagement with the masculine world of philosophy and letters, and her fierce protection of what she saw as her unique activity. Ironically, writers like Aphra Behn and Katherine Philips eclipsed Cavendish's visibility, and from the 1690s onwards, Cavendish's literary reputation rested on her biography of William, and the critical comments about her eccentricities and lack of discipline soon outnumbered comments that offered any real engagement with her work.

## FURTHER REPUTATION

In the course of the eighteenth century, there was some acknowledgement of Cavendish's drama, following on from Langbaine's example. So, for example, G. Jacob, in *An Historical Account of the Lives and Writings of Our Most Considerable English Poets* (1719), lists Cavendish's plays and writes:

This Lady (the most voluminous Dramatick Writer of our Female Poets) was Consort to the foremention'd Duke. She had a great deal of Wit, and a more than ordinary Propensity to Dramatick Poetry. All the Language and Plots of her Plays, Mr. Langbain tells us, were her own, which is a Commendation preferable to Fame built on other People's Foundation, and will very well atone for inconsiderable Faults in her numerous Productions. (190–1)

---

[105] Gerard Langbaine, *An Account of the English Dramatick Poets* (1691), 391.

In his *Lives of the Poets* (1753), Theophilus Cibber offers a quite judicious account of Cavendish's upbringing, noting her 'inclination to learning' (ii. 162), and stating that a more formal education would have 'corrected the exuberance of her genius' (ii. 163). This is an idea that was to be repeated right through the nineteenth century. Once again drawing on Langbaine (and Jacob) for an account of her plays, Cibber offers a quite detailed list of her works. Ballard offers a similarly respectful account, but it is quite truncated in relation to Cavendish's books, which, Ballard explains, he is unable to afford to buy—thus emphasizing how her handsome folios had perhaps become collectors' items, but the contents were not reprinted or read.

Indeed, in terms of her actual work, Cavendish's representation was almost entirely limited to a small canon of poems that were reproduced in anthologies during both the eighteenth and nineteenth centuries.[106] The most popular poem in this vein was 'The Pastime and Recreation of the Queen of the Fairies', but, as Katie Whitaker has noted in her summation of changes in Cavendish's reputation, most editors bowdlerized this poem, eliminating 'earthy or physical' moments.[107] A good example is Colman and Thornton's 1755 *Poems by the Most Eminent Ladies of Great Britain and Ireland*, a very popular eighteenth-century anthology (see the discussion in Chapter 1), which prints only two edited sections from 'The Queen of the Fairies'.[108] Cavendish's other popular poem was 'A Dialogue Between Melancholy and Mirth', which again appealed to editors because it was fanciful and, in its own way, picturesque.

In the eighteenth century, while much of Cavendish's actual writing was ignored, she was treated with reasonable deference as a historical figure. The exception, as Whitaker again notes, was Horace Walpole, who was extremely critical of both William and Margaret, although he too prints a truncated version of the 'Queen of Fairies' poem. Walpole is particularly scathing about William and Margaret's mutual admiration: 'What a picture of foolish nobility was this stately couple, retired to their own little domain, and intoxicating one another with circumstantial flattery on what was of consequence to no mortal but themselves.'[109] Mary Hays's 1803 *Female Biography* returns to the more measured views of the earlier eighteenth century: 'she added to acuteness of mind considerable powers of imagination and invention . . . The language and plots of her plays are all original; but her fancy wanted the rein of judgement, her taste correctness, and her mind cultivation' (v. 519).

---

[106] The one exception to this is Alexander Nicol's eccentric volume, *Poems on Several Subjects Both Comical and Serious* (Edinburgh, 1766), which, for reasons which are unclear, appends *The Experienced Traveller* and *The She Anchoret* (both prose pieces from *Nature's Pictures*) to Nicol's poems.

[107] See Whitaker's excellent account, *Mad Madge*, 358–9; Dyce was an exception to this 'cleaning up' process, in *Specimens of British Poetesses* (1825).

[108] G. Colman and B. Thornton, *Poems by the Most Eminent Ladies of Great Britain and Ireland* (London 1755), ii. 56–60; there were four editions of this anthology in the eighteenth century.

[109] *Catalogue of Royal and Noble Authors*, iii. 176–7.

However, some homage was paid to Cavendish at the beginning of the nineteenth century by the bibliophile Egerton Brydges. Brydges apparently could
trace his ancestry back (through his mother) to Henry Cavendish, William's
son.[110] As well as being a founder member of the Roxburghe Club, Brydges
set up his own press, and produced a series of editions of early modern works,
including, for example, Greville's *Life of Sidney* (1816), and *England's Helicon*
(1812). In 1813 Brydges produced an anthology of Cavendish's poetry. In his
brief preface, Brydges offers a mixed account of Cavendish's writing, noting that:

considerable as is the alloy of absurd passages in many of her Grace's compositions, there
are few of them in which there are not proofs of an active, thinking, and original mind.
Her imagination was quick, copious, and sometimes even beautiful. Yet her taste appears
to have been not only uncultivated, but perhaps originally defective. Nothing that I have
yet read of hers, is touched by pathos; which, indeed, does not seem to have been an
ingredient of her mind. On the contrary, we are too frequently shocked by expressions
and images of extraordinary coarseness.[111]

Brydges prints eight poems and an extract from *The Convent of Pleasure*. In
1814 Brydges produced a small volume which extracted the 'True Relation of
my Birth Breeding and Life' from *Nature's Pictures*. Brydges praises this piece of
autobiography, seeing it as free from Cavendish's defects as a writer:

Her Grace wanted taste; she knew not what to obtrude, and what to leave out. She pours
forth everything with an undistinguishing hand, and mixes the serious, the colloquial,
and even the vulgar, in a manner which cannot be defended. In the Life, however, now
reprinted, this great fault is less apparent than in any other of her compositions.[112]

Brydges's two limited editions form the only substantial representation of
Cavendish's writing, apart from the *Life of William*, until Edward Jenkins's 1872
selection, which will be discussed below. Dyce, for example, in terms that were
to be repeated throughout the nineteenth century, says that she 'possessed a
mind of considerable power and activity, with much imagination, but not one
particle of judgement or taste' (88). Dyce does print an unexpurgated text of
'The Pastime and Recreation of the Queen of Fairies', noting that 'it would
be difficult to point out a composition, which contains a more extraordinary
mixture of imagination and coarse absurdity' (89).[113] The professed admiration
of Charles Lamb seems only to have confirmed Cavendish's role as eccentric
and self-deluded. In 1823 Lamb famously called her 'the thrice noble, chaste,
and virtuous,—but again somewhat fantastical, and original-brain'd, generous
Margaret Newcastle'.[114] Lamb particularly admired the *Life of William*: 'no

---

[110] Much of Brydges' genealogical efforts were spent pursuing a dubious claim to the Chandos
title, see *Oxford DNB*, s.v. Brydges, Egerton.

[111] *Selected Poems of Margaret Cavendish Duchess of Newcastle* (Lee Priory, 1813), preface.

[112] *A True Relation* (Lee Priory, 1814), 9.

[113] Dyce also includes 'Of the Throne of Love', 'The Funeral of Calamity', and 'Mirth and
Melancholy'.

[114] Charles Lamb, 'Mackery End, in Hertfordshire', *Elia* (1823).

casket is rich enough, no casing sufficiently durable, to honour and keep safe such a jewel.'[115] But by the time Louisa Costello wrote about Cavendish in *Memoirs of Eminent Englishwomen* (1844), the patronizing tone later made famous by Virginia Woolf had set fast: 'The innumerable books of this persevering authoress were the nuisance of the time in which she lived; and although she reaped little but ridicule by her industry, yet her vanity was such that she never perceived she was being laughed at.'[116] Costello quotes from *The Blazing World*, and offers the usual extracts from 'Queen of Fairies' and 'Mirth and Melancholy'.

There is a lone, dissenting late nineteenth-century voice: Edward Jenkins, who put together a Macmillan Golden Treasury anthology of a selection of poetry, including as well some poems by William, the 'True Relation', some essays, and some examples from *Sociable Letters*.[117] Jenkins defends Cavendish's writings, but disarmingly says: 'amongst sad heaps of rubbish it has seemed to me that there are a few treasures well worth the disinterment'(5). Jenkins subscribes to the notion of Cavendish as fertile but undisciplined:

a genius strong-willed and swift, fertile and comprehensive; but ruined by deficient culture, by literary dissipation and the absence of two powers without which thoughts are only stray morsels of strength, I mean Concatenation and Sense of Proportion. She thought without system and set down everything she thought. Her fancy turning round like a kaleidoscope changed its patterns and hues with a most whimsical variety and rapidity. Nevertheless I believe had the mind of this woman been disciplined and exercised by early culture and study it would have stood out remarkably among the feminine intellects of our history. (8–9)

Jenkins modernizes his texts, but does at least offer a substantial amount of Cavendish's work for what one presumes to have been a general readership.

However, when Eric Robertson in 1883 describes Cavendish as 'a kind of overgrown, spoilt girl', we are, as Katie Whitaker has noted, very close to Woolf's account of her: 'What a vision of loneliness and riot the thought of Margaret Cavendish brings to mind! As if some giant cucumber had spread itself over all the roses and carnations in the garden and choked them to death.'[118] Woolf's characterization of Cavendish has been particularly hard to shift, and for much of the twentieth century, even as other early modern women writers were being treated with reasonable scholarly attention, Cavendish's work was seen as eccentric and undisciplined.[119] There has been a remarkable turn around that might be signposted by the establishment of the Margaret Cavendish Society in 1997, a

[115] 'Detached Thoughts on Books', *Last Essays of Elia* (1833).

[116] Louisa Stuart Costello, *Memoirs of Eminent Englishwomen* (London: Richard Bentley, 1844), iii. 211.

[117] Edward Jenkins, ed., *The Cavalier and his Lady* (London: Macmillan, 1872).

[118] Virginia Woolf, *A Room of One's Own* (Harmondsworth: Penguin, 1974), 62; see Whitaker, *Mad Madge*, 364.

[119] Again there is a good summary of this in Whitaker, *Mad Madge*, 364–6; I have contrasted Clifford and Cavendish in relation to these issues in 'Early Modern (Aristocratic) Women', in Wright *et al.*, *Women, Property*.

body of scholars whose work seems, at last, to fulfil Cavendish's desires for lasting fame. But until that point, even Cavendish's most enduring book, her biography of her husband, received increasingly invidious comparisons with the work of a woman whose star rose as Cavendish's fell.

## THE CAVENDISHES AND THE HUTCHINSONS

In a suggestive article, David Norbrook has shown just how fruitful a comparison between both the writing and the reputations of Margaret Cavendish and Lucy Hutchinson can be.[120] In order to trace this comparison through to the present, it is necessary to return to Cavendish's biography of William, which was first published in 1667. Cavendish's title page names William as a 'Thrice noble, high and puissant Prince', and the biography is intended in particular to vindicate his actions in the Civil War, and to establish the crown's indebtedness to him (and to complain about the neglect he has suffered since the Restoration of Charles II). This seems innocent enough, but in the mid-1660s, dealing with actions during the Civil War was still playing with fire. Cavendish states in her preface 'that your Grace commanded me not to mention any thing or passage to the prejudice or disgrace of any Family or particular person (although they might be of great truth, and would illustrate much the actions of your Life) which I have dutifully performed to satisfie your Lordship'.[121] While Margaret does cover William's early life, for the most part the book is concerned with William's experience in the Civil War and its aftermath. As well as enumerating all the financial details of missed rents during the interregnum, Margaret offers an anthology of William's views on a wide variety of subjects.

I have already noted how Cavendish's desire to see her scientific works translated into Latin was frustrated. Only the *Life* was accorded that dignity, in a faithful translation by Walter Charleton, which was published in 1668. After Cavendish's death in 1673, the English *Life* had a second edition in 1675. The biography received its most scathing attack from Pepys, who memorably wrote in his diary on 18 March 1668: 'stayed at home reading the ridiculous history of my Lord Newcastle wrote by his wife, which shows her to be a mad, conceited, ridiculous woman, and he an asse to suffer [her] to write what she writes to him and of him'.[122] More serious attention began to be paid to the *Life* in the nineteenth century, especially after Julius Hutchinson published an edition of Lucy

---

[120] David Norbrook, 'Margaret Cavendish and Lucy Hutchinson: Identity, Ideology and Politics', *In-Between*, 9 (2000), 179–203.

[121] James Fitzmaurice discusses how two passages in the *Life*, one critical of Charles I for failing to pay William's troops, one accusing Goring and Mackworth of carelessness, were inked out in most copies, and were, in turn, often written back in by readers, see 'Margaret Cavendish on her Own Writing: Evidence from Revision and Handmade Correction', *PBSA* 85 (1991), 302–5; Fitzmaurice also discusses the cancelled and revised preface, which stresses Cavendish's seriousness as a historian.

[122] Pepys, *Diary*, ed. Robert Latham and William Matthews (London: Bell, 1983), ix. 123.

Hutchinson's biography of *her* husband in 1806. In 1856 Mark Lower published an edition of the *Life* together with the 'True Relation', defending Cavendish from Dyce's strictures, criticizing the accuracy of Brydges' edition, and proclaiming 'Among the biographical and autobiographical literature of the seventeenth century, there are but few which exceed in interest the two mentioned in the title-page of this book.'[123] This edition was republished in 1872 in John Russell Smith's Library of Old Authors series. However, by the time the noted historian C. H. Firth edited Cavendish's *Life* in 1886, following on from his edition of Hutchinson's *Memoirs of the Life of Colonel Hutchinson* in 1885, Julius Hutchinson's 1806 edition of the *Memoirs* had been reprinted a number of times and translated into French, while Cavendish's *Life* was seen more as an eccentric rarity. Firth's deliberate act of comparison did mean that, early in the twentieth century, both biographies were republished almost side by side. In his introduction to his edition of Cavendish's *Life*, Firth offers a fairly balanced account of Cavendish's work, noting that 'She has been unduly praised and unjustly depreciated', and falling back upon the usual line that her faults were largely due to her lack of education.[124]

David Norbrook offers a fascinating account of what can be seen as the shadowing of the Royalist Margaret Cavendish by the staunchly Republican and Puritan Lucy Hutchinson. The Hutchinsons led what might be called parallel lives to the Cavendishes'; for example, Colonel John Hutchinson was Governor of Nottingham Castle—the castle which William Cavendish acquired and had restored after the Restoration. As Hutchinson, one of the signatories to Charles I's death warrant, saw his fortunes rise in the more radical stages of the Civil War, so the Cavendishes saw theirs fall, and went into exile. Conversely, William Cavendish interceded on Hutchinson's behalf in 1663, apparently out of respect for his father and his family. As Norbrook explains, after 1648 the Hutchinsons, now perhaps the leading family in the county, set up their estate at Owthorpe in a manner not unlike the Newcastles', including the purchase of paintings by Titian, and the commissioning of a portrait of Lucy Hutchinson that sees her crowned with a laurel wreath, in an image that was to be echoed (with differences) by Margaret Cavendish in the portraits that stressed her image as a writer.[125]

Lucy Hutchinson and Margaret Cavendish had very different upbringings. While perhaps not quite as unschooled as her somewhat disingenuous claims make out, Cavendish, when she decided to join Henrietta Maria's court at Oxford in 1643 at the age of 20, was a cosseted youngest daughter from a wealthy

[123] Mark Anthony Lower, ed., *The Lives of William Cavendish . . . and of his Wife Margaret* (London: John Russell Smith, 1872), p. v; Lower offers a corrected text of Brydges for 'A True Relation' and includes Brydges' preface.

[124] *The Life of William Cavendish*, ed. C. H. Firth (1886: 2nd edn. London: Routledge, 1916), p. xxx.

[125] Norbrook, 'Margaret Cavendish and Lucy Hutchinson', 186–7.

gentry family (who were to lose virtually everything in the Civil War), with the mixture of shyness and boldness that was to last all her life. Cavendish wanted to participate at first hand in the glamour of the court; her intellectual aspirations were fostered after her marriage, particularly by her brother-in-law Charles, and by her experience of the philosophical circle that surrounded William, thus exposing her, as David Norbrook notes, to the 'Moderns' in contemporary thought.[126] Lucy Hutchinson was the daughter of Sir Allen Apsley, Lieutenant of the Tower of London, and, partly owing to her mother's encouragement, she was brought up with excellent Latin, and support for her literary facility—these skills, she explains in her life of her husband, helped to attract him to her.

Lucy married John Hutchinson in 1638 and, during the period of John's military activity, she kept a detailed manuscript account of the events surrounding him (partly, it seems, in response to opposition he faced from local authorities during his time as governor), which she drew on for her later biography.[127] Her first major literary activity seems to have taken place some time in the early 1650s, when, as noted above, the Hutchinsons were in a more settled situation at Owthorpe. As Norbrook explains, in the first of a series of echoes of Cavendish's literary career, Hutchinson translated Lucretius's *De rerum natura*. It remains slightly puzzling as to why the deeply religious Hutchinson was attracted to Lucretius's notorious epic, which represented a materialist, indeed atheist, view of the universe. Norbrook suggests that, as well as the challenge of showing what an accomplished Latinist she was by translating the famously difficult Lucretius, who remained the last major Latin author who had not been translated into English, this task offered Hutchinson the chance to challenge Cavendish, whose Atomist poems and ideas about a (potentially) materialist universe appeared in *Poems and Fancies* in 1653.[128] In this early stage of her ideas about atoms, as Stephen Clucas explains, Cavendish offered 'a thoroughgoing Epicurean atomism', although Clucas cautions that this view was to change quite radically by the time she published *Philosophical and Physical Opinions* in 1655, when, in Clucas's words again, her Atomism became 'a synthesis of materialism and vitalism'.[129] There is no direct evidence to indicate that Hutchinson knew of Cavendish's Atomist poetry and philosophy, but it is at least possible that her Lucretius translation was, in part, a response to Cavendish's bold literary debut.

The surviving manuscript of Hutchinson's Lucretius translation was presented to the Earl of Anglesey in 1675, long after it was written. Hutchinson claims, in the dedication to Anglesey, that she has presented the manuscript to him only because he has asked for it and because she is aware that her version had 'bene

---

[126] Ibid. 183–4; see also Whitaker, *Mad Madge*, 96–7.
[127] Biographical information is drawn from Norbrook, 'Margaret Cavendish and Lucy Hutchinson', and also Norbrook's *Oxford DNB* entry, s.v. Hutchinson, Lucy.
[128] Norbrook, 'Margaret Cavendish and Lucy Hutchinson', 187–8.
[129] Clucas, 'Atomism of the Cavendish Circle', 260, 261.

gone out of my hands in one lost copy' (23).[130] There is, however, a fascinating ambivalence in the tone of the dedication. Hutchinson offers the usual apologies for her work, and seems specifically worried about how the translation of such an irreligious work will affect attitudes towards her (especially given the piety she demonstrates in her life and other writings), and yet she is also clearly proud of the successful completion of such a difficult task: 'I abhhorre all the Atheismes and impieties in it, and translated it only out of youthful curiositie, to understand things I heard so much discourse of at second hand' (23). She claims that she undertook the translation 'in a roome where my children practized the severall qualities they were taught with their Tutors, and I numbered the syllables of my translation by the threds of the canvas that I wrought in' (23–4). This is a calculated statement of feminine modesty, reminiscent of the aristocratic *sprezzatura* expressed by Elizabethan writers like Sidney, who claimed that their works were mere trifles. But it is clear from Hutchinson's meticulous presentation of the poem (the manuscript contains numerous careful corrections) that she still recognized its accomplishment some twenty years after its composition.

Hutchinson's translation is now being seen as a major contribution to a genre which flourished in the seventeenth century. However, her Lucretius remained in manuscript until Hugh de Quehen's 1996 edition. It had apparently never left the Angelsey family until it was bought by the British Museum in 1853 at auction. At this point, it was read by the Classical scholar Hugh Munro as part of his preparation for his 1864 edition of Lucretius. Munro valued Hutchinson's achievement, while at the same time expressing reservations about the accuracy of the translation and its efficacy for a modern audience.[131] In particular, Munro compared Hutchinson favourably with Thomas Creech (who published his translation in 1682 to considerable acclaim).[132] In his fascinating comparison of Hutchinson's translation with later versions of Lucretius by Creech, Evelyn, Beattie, and Dryden, Hugh de Quehen notes how Hutchinson's compressed, flexible verse is more suited to the complexities of Lucretius than later versions, however much more polished they might seem.[133]

It is worth emphasizing that Hutchinson published only one of her works, and it was published anonymously, so in that respect she did not emulate Margaret Cavendish's method of searching for fame, but rather adhered to the more respectable medium of manuscript circulation. The success of the publication of the manuscript of the *Memoirs* in 1806 led to the publication of two further manuscripts, as we will see below, but, despite Munro's interest, the Lucretius translation, along with a body of poetry, remained essentially hidden until very recently.

---

[130] References are to Hugh de Quehen, ed., *Lucy Hutchinson's Translation of Lucretius: De rerum natura* (London: Duckworth, 1996).

[131] See Hugh de Quehen, 'Ease and Flow in Lucy Hutchinson's Lucretius', *SP* 93 (1996), 289.

[132] Ibid. 290–1.        [133] Ibid., *passim*.

## *MEMOIRS*: REINTERPRETING THE NOBLE REGICIDE

After the Restoration, John Hutchinson was viewed with considerable suspicion by Royalists who were angry at his escape from prosecution. Owing in part to the influence of Lucy Hutchinson's powerful Royalist relatives, in part to Lucy Hutchinson's forged letter of repentance supposedly written by her husband, John Hutchinson was not excluded from the Act of Oblivion. But while he led a quiet and private life at Owthorpe, he was a marked man, and was eventually arrested on suspicion of involvement with the so-called Northern plot, and died whilst still a prisoner on 11 September 1664. Some time after that, probably in the mid- to later 1660s, Lucy Hutchinson wrote the manuscript biography of her husband known as the *Memoirs*. While it is impossible to know if the news that Margaret Cavendish was writing the life of her husband, which was published in 1667, inspired Hutchinson to do likewise, it is certainly true that Hutchinson's biography, like Cavendish's, was a pointed justification of the affairs of a man who had, in his wife's eyes, been maligned and misunderstood. Once again, Hutchinson did not publish her work, but clearly intended the manuscript to justify her husband's life to his children, and succeeding generations. Ironically, his immediate descendants were of a quite different political persuasion, and the manuscript was kept secreted within the family until the beginning of the nineteenth century, as will be discussed below.

Compared to Cavendish's typically idiosyncratic narrative of her husband's life and opinions, Hutchinson's text is an ordered and disciplined account, motivated by her ongoing commitment to the same political and religious principles as those held by her husband. While Hutchinson writes in the third person, and seems, on the surface, to be far less 'present' in her narrative than Cavendish is in the *Life of William Cavendish*, this impression is deceptive, for Hutchinson offers the perceptive reader an engaged and ideologically controlled account of events from 1639 through to 1664. Her history of the Civil War and its aftermath is filtered through her account of John Hutchinson's actions, and she does offer a very detailed account of his affairs as Governor of Nottingham Castle. But she is also able to offer a sophisticated and detailed overview of this whole period, including a harsh assessment of Cromwell, and of the general hypocrisy and backsliding of most participants in the war, on both sides. When her account reaches the Restoration, Hutchinson's narrative becomes more a piece of religious testimony, as her husband's martyrdom and exemplary Puritan death are described (again, one assumes, for the edification of his children and descendants).

Far from being edified, the immediate Hutchinson descendants were unwilling to lay claim to their radical forebears, a situation which continued until the *Memoirs* were edited by Julius Hutchinson and published in 1806. Julius explains how Thomas Hutchinson, who was John Hutchinson's half-brother's grandson, refused to allow Lucy Hutchinson's manuscript to be printed despite being solicited to do so by a number of people, including the eighteenth-century Republican historian Catherine Macauley, who knew of its existence (p. ix).[134] In publishing the manuscript, even Julius Hutchinson is at pains to underplay John Hutchinson's more radical opinions, and concludes that, had he lived to see the settled society of 1806, he would certainly have accepted the constitutional monarch and also 'would either have been a conforming member of the Church of England, or at most have only dissented from it in few things, and that with modesty and moderation' (p. xv)!

In his careful account of the editing of Lucy Hutchinson's manuscript, David Norbrook has explained how the received view of Hutchinson as, in some senses, 'conservative and patriarchal', was fostered by editorial changes to her manuscript which subtly shifted her style to confirm her as 'a specifically "masculine" woman writer'.[135] As an example, Norbrook notes the way Julius Hutchinson changes Lucy Hutchinson's feminine personification of 'reason' to a masculine one.[136] Norbrook also offers a cogent analysis of how Hutchinson changed her earlier manuscript account of John Hutchinson's activities into a more measured (but no less radically committed) narrative.[137] While announcing his fidelity to the manuscript, Julius Hutchinson made numerous changes, and in particular cut many passages; however, his edition was enormously successful, being reprinted ten times in the nineteenth century, and achieving a French translation by François Guizot in 1823. This enormous popularity was given scholarly weight by C. H. Firth's 1885 edition, which was revised and reissued in 1906, and by the popularity in the twentieth century of the Everyman edition, which was first printed in 1908 and was finally re-edited from the original manuscript by N. H. Keeble in 1995.

Hutchinson's account of her husband was seen as a valuable piece of historical evidence, particularly after the imprimatur of a respected historian like C. H. Firth attested to its worth. And in the course of the nineteenth century, as we have already seen, Hutchinson was acclaimed in a number of popular works as a significant figure. Jane Williams, in her 1861 *Literary Women of England*, singled out the *Memoirs* as 'the most perfect piece of biography ever written by a woman', and offers eleven pages of extracts.[138] This might well seem to be a slightly backhanded compliment, confirming Hutchinson as a secondary figure: a dutiful chronicler, not an independent writer. But over the last ten years, thanks to the efforts of David Norbrook, Hutchinson has been revealed as a major seventeenth-century poet, and in this final area of her writing to be considered, she can be seen to have in some ways outshone her 'rival' Margaret Cavendish.

---

[134] Page references to Lucy Hutchinson, *Memoirs of Colonel Hutchinson*, ed. Rev. Julius Hutchinson (Dutton: Everyman, 1908).

[135] David Norbrook, ' "But a Copie": Textual Authority and Gender in Editions of "The Life of John Hutchinson" ', in W. Speed Hill, ed., *New Ways of Looking at Old Texts III* (Tempe: Arizona Center for Medieval and Renaissance Studies, 2004), 110.

[136] Ibid.      [137] Ibid. 112–14.

[138] Jane Williams, *The Literary Ladies of England* (London: Saunder, Otley and Co., 1861), 92.

## HUTCHINSON AS POET

Hutchinson was always drawn to poetry, noting in her fragmentary autobiographical essay in the *Memoirs* that 'I thought it not sin to learn or hear witty songs and amorous sonnets or poems, and twenty things of that kind, wherein I was so apt that I became the confidant in all the loves that were managed among my mother's young women' (15). In later life, as well as the earlier example of the Lucretius translation, Hutchinson wrote secular poetry, including a series of twenty-three elegies, one of which was published in Julius Hutchinson's edition of the *Memoirs* (and in succeeding editions). These elegies, as David Norbrook has explained in his edition of them, bear a close relationship to the *Memoirs* in so far as they share some common themes, but they reveal Hutchinson's personal, poetic voice.[139] The sequence is also notable for Hutchinson's powerful and consistent vision, combining her religious and political beliefs, and a stoical response to her personal situation after her husband's death. As depicted in the elegies, the figure of John Hutchinson, named as 'a greate Patriot' (516), symbolizes all that was best in the Republican cause, but unlike her approach in the *Memoirs*, in these deeply personal poems Hutchinson offers a stringent critique of the Restoration settlement.[140] For example, in the third poem Hutchinson attacks the restored monarchical order through a fierce account of the 'immodest Sun', which is characterized as associated with 'Violence briberry & oppression' (492). Read as a whole, the sequence is a skilled and moving intertwining of Hutchinson's personal and political position.[141]

But in 1679, taking what we can only speculate to have been a difficult and perhaps strategic decision, Hutchinson published the first five cantos of an extremely ambitious religious poem. *Order and Disorder* was published anonymously, so Hutchinson was certainly cautious about her first (and last) venture into print. The poem also circulated in manuscript and was known within the extended family. A manuscript of the entire poem was owned (and corrected) by Hutchinson's cousin Anne Wilmot, Countess Rochester, mother of the infamous John Wilmot. Anne Wilmot was rumoured to be Lucy Hutchinson's brother Sir Allen Apsley's mistress, and *Order and Disorder* was actually attributed to Apsley by Anthony à Wood—an attribution which remained until it was corrected by David Norbrook in 1999. Given Hutchinson's death in 1681, it is impossible to know if she planned to publish

---

[139] David Norbrook, 'Lucy Hutchinson's "Elegies" and the Situation of the Republican Woman Writer', *ELR* 27 (1997), 468–521; further references in parentheses.

[140] For another example of, this time, more direct political satire aimed at the Protectorate, although the attribution is not definitive, see Hutchinson's stanza by stanza attack on Waller's 'Panegyric' to Cromwell: David Norbrook, 'Lucy Hutchinson versus Edmund Waller: An Unpublished Reply to Waller's A Panegyrick to my Lord Protector', *Seventeenth Century*, 11 (1996), 61–86.

[141] It is worth noting that the manuscript of the elegies is not authorial and is in a different scribal hand to those found in other Hutchinson manuscripts: see Norbrook, 'Elegies', 485.

the entire poem, or if for some reason publication of the first five cantos met with a response that increased her caution. Certainly, as Norbrook points out, publishing the poem at a moment when the Exclusion Crisis was coming to a head was a daring move, even if on the surface its religious content might have seem uncontroversial (p. xx).[142] In fact, Hutchinson's version of Genesis was far from being politically neutral, and, in Norbrook's words, 'again and again she suggests that the existing political order is far from reflecting the divine order' (p. xxxvi).

In her preface to the published *Order and Disorder*, Hutchinson clearly reveals her identity to those who knew her translation of Lucretius by offering this religious poem as almost an act of penance for the translation:

These Meditations were not at first design'd for publick view, but fix'd upon to reclaim a busie roving thought from wandring in the pernicious and perplex'd maze of humane inventions; whereinto the vain curiosity of youth had drawn me to consider and translate the account some old Poets and Philosophers give of the original of things: which though I found it, blasphemously against God, and brutishly below the reason of a man, set forth by some, erroniously, imperfectly, and uncertainly, by the best; yet had it fill'd my brain with such foolish fancies, that I found it necessary to have recourse to the fountain of Truth, to wash out all ugly wild impressions . . . . Lest that arrive my misadventure, which never shall by my consent, that any of the pudled water, my wanton youth drew from the prophane Helicon of ancient Poets, should be sprinkled about the world, I have for prevention sent forth this Essay.[143]

For her divine poem, in contrast to Milton in *Paradise Lost*, Hutchinson stuck with the rhymed couplets she had used for the Lucretius translation. There is no doubt that, as *Order and Disorder* becomes better known, and especially after the authoritative Oxford edition of Hutchinson is available, the comparison with Milton will be explored in more detail.[144] Hutchinson offers an intriguing account of Eve that can be contrasted with Milton's depiction. Perhaps the most original aspect of this depiction is Hutchinson's vivid description of the tribulations of childbirth and child-rearing:

> How painfully the fruit within them grows,
> What tortures do their ripened births disclose,
> How great, how various, how uneasie are
> The breeding sicknesses, pangs that prepare
> The violent openings of lifes narrow door,
> Whose fatal issues we as oft deplore!
> What weaknesses, what languishments ensue,
> Scattering dead Lillies where fresh Roses grew.

---

[142] References in parentheses to Lucy Hutchinson, *Order and Disorder*, ed. David Norbrook (Oxford: Blackwell, 2001).

[143] *Order and Disorder; or the World Made and Undone* (1679), A1–A1v.

[144] See some interesting suggestions by David Norbrook, *TLS*, 19 March 1999.

What broken rest afflicts the careful nurse,
Extending to the breasts the mothers-curse
Which ceases not when there her milk she dries,
The froward child draws new streams from her eyes.[145]

In his detailed study of the texts of *Order and Disorder*, David Norbrook notes that there must have been at least three part or whole manuscripts of the poem in circulation during Hutchinson's lifetime, a situation which means that she must be seen as a significant example of a devoted adherent to the radical cause who, far from falling silent in the difficult years of the Restoration and the imprisonment and death of her husband, was an ambitious writer who demanded an audience.[146] In recent years, Hutchinson's achievement has been overshadowed by the sustained attention paid to Margret Cavendish (who, after all, has her own Society), but these two impressive women are certain to be on a more even footing now that *Order and Disorder* is readily available and scholars are beginning to pay more sustained attention both to it and to the elegies.

---

[145] *Order and Disorder*, 61–2.
[146] David Norbrook, 'Lucy Hutchinson and *Order and Disorder*', *English Manuscript Studies 1100–1700*, 9 (2000), 264 and *passim*.

# 7

# Saint and Sinner: Katherine Philips
## and Aphra Behn

In many ways, this chapter overlaps with the previous one, in so far as it deals
with two self-conscious writers who were engaged with a variety of literary genres.
Katherine Philips's career began just before Margaret Cavendish published her
first works. Philips shares Cavendish's Royalist politics, and they have a glancing association with the same Royalist artistic circle that gathered around Henry
Lawes (the most prominent Caroline composer/musician).[1] At the same time,
Philips constructed a very different literary image and career to that of Cavendish,
combining the carefully controlled circulation of her poetry in manuscript with
the late publicity and fame associated with the performance of her translation
of Corneille's *Pompey* in Dublin in 1663.[2] Aphra Behn established herself on
the professional stage from 1670, and from late in the seventeenth century Behn
and Philips were often seen as a contrasting pair of writers, especially during the
eighteenth century, when the comparison began to work to Behn's detriment.
While both Behn and Philips can be seen as Royalist writers, their engagement
with politics was very different and needs to be examined in some detail as part
of any assessment of the reception of their writing and later attitudes towards
them.

## KATHERINE PHILIPS AND LITERARY CONTROL

Katherine Philips began to develop her poetic persona at a very early age. She was
educated at a girls' boarding school run by a Mrs Salmon, and there she began
writing poetry, cultivated an interest in drama by Cavalier figures like William
Cartwright, and began an association with two girls who helped to establish her

---

[1] Cavendish visited Lawes's music circle a number of time with her brother-in-law when they were
in London; see Katie Whitaker, *Mad Madge: Margaret Cavendish, Duchess of Newcastle* (London:
Chatto and Windus, 2003), 136–7; Hero Chalmers offers a convincing argument that the artistic
activities undertaken by women in the Lawes circle 'must surely have helped galvanize Cavendish's
publication', *Royalist Women Writers 1650–1689* (Oxford: Clarendon Press, 2004), 19.

[2] Peter Beal astutely speculates that the scorn Cavendish attracted from people like Dorothy
Osborne must have served to make Philips cautious about her public image and the publication
of her poetry, see *In Praise of Scribes: Manuscripts and their Makers in Seventeenth-Century England*
(Oxford: Clarendon Press, 1998), 151.

literary coterie: Mary Aubrey, who was given the coterie name Rosania, and Mary Harvey, who was later to marry Sir Edward Dering (Silvander).[3] At the age of 16, Philips married Colonel James Philips, a cousin of her stepfather. While there was, as in the Cavendish marriage, a considerable age difference, there was also a political divide to overcome, as Colonel Philips was a Parliamentary commissioner in Wales, and a supporter of Cromwell. Katherine Philips's proven Royalist credentials (and connections) saved her husband from prosecution after the Restoration.

Testimony to Philips's precocious poetic talent is demonstrated by her first appearance in print in 1651. Philips was the only female contributor to the fifty-four commendatory poems that prefaced the posthumous collection of William Cartwright's plays and poetry, a collection that has been recognized by scholars as a Royalist touchstone.[4] Philips's poem specifically uses images that decry the present political situation and anticipate (albeit via a literary figure) a promised Restoration: 'Such horrid ignorance benights the times, | That wit and honour are become our crimes' moves to a vision of 'The splendour of restored Poetry' (143).[5] It is, at first sight, quite extraordinary that Philips's poem should be the first poem encountered in this extensive collection of prefatory praise for Cartwright, which marks out Royalist sentiment at a point when the Royalist cause was at a particularly low ebb. It is true that Philips's poem is signed only by her initials, K.P., and her identity would only have been known to those in her immediate circle. But recent studies of Philips, most notably the work of Carol Barash, Hero Chalmers, James Loxley, and Catharine Gray, have began to refocus attention from the 'private' poetry of friendship, and (in an increasing number of readings) erotic female to female desire, towards an acknowledgement of Philips as a political and politically aware poet.[6] Gray specifically addresses

---

[3] This Edward Dering was the son of the Edward Dering discussed in relation to Wroth in Ch. 3; for biographical information, see Philip Webster Souers, *The Matchless Orinda* (Cambridge, Mass.: Harvard University Press, 1931); Patrick Thomas, i *Katherine Philips* (Cardiff: University of Wales Press, 1988), and *The Collected Works of Katherine Philips*, ed. Patrick Thomas, i (Saffron Walden: Stump Cross, 1990).

[4] William Cartwright, *Comedies, Tragi-Comedies, with other Poems* (1651).

[5] Unless otherwise noted, for convenience I quote Philips's poems from Thomas's edition.

[6] See Carol Barash, *English Women's Poetry 1649–1714* (Oxford: Clarendon Press, 1996), ch. 2; Chalmers, *Royalist Women Writers*, ch. 2; James Loxley, ' Unfettered Organs: This Polemical Voices of Katherine Philips', in Danielle Clarke and Elizabeth Clarke, eds., *This Double Voice: Gendered Writing in Early Modern England* (New York: St Martin's Press, 2000), 230–48; Catharine Gray, 'Katherine Philips and the Post-Courtly Coterie', *ELR* 32 (2002), 426–51; see the pioneering work on Philips as a 'lesbian poet' by Harriet Andreadis, 'The Sappho-Platonics of Katherine Philips', *Signs*, 15 (1989), 34–60; Elaine Hobby, 'Katherine Philips: Seventeenth-Century Lesbian Poet', in Elaine Hobby and Chris White, eds., *What Lesbians Do in Books* (London, Women's Press, 1991); and for sophisticated readings of the implications of desire in Philips, see Kate Lilley, 'Dear Object: Katherine Philips's Love Elegies and their Readers', in Jo Wallwork and Paul Salzman, eds., *Women Writing 1550–1750* (Bundoora: Meridian, 2001), 163–78, Bronwen Price, 'A Rhetoric of Innocence: The Poetry of Katherine Philips, "The Matchless Orinda" ', in Barbara Smith and Ursula Appelt, eds., *Write or Be Written* (Aldershot: Ashgate, 2001), 223–46, and, as part of her

the publication of the poem to Cartwright in an essay which underlines Philips's associations with a group of moderate Royalists, and which reads many of Philips's poems as 'part of a public, poetic performance ... that circulated in a complex system of compliment, cross-gender identification and political affiliation' (430). Gray explains that the Cartwright volume serves to gather together a coterie of poets who are indirectly celebrating/mourning Charles I (433). In this particular respect, Gray's account can be linked to Carol Barash's complex reading of Philips's fascination with 'friendship and death' as 'emblems of the dismembered body of Charles I and the absent body of Charles II'.[7]

Gray speculates that placing Philips's poem at the beginning of the Cartwright volume may have been an attempt to gain, not so much the favour of Philips herself, but of her husband. That seems to me to be unlikely, given that only a few of the contributors would have come into direct contact with Colonel Philips in Wales. Gray also suggests that poetry by a woman was able to be given such prominence because the Royalist male contributors were removed from the homosocial milieu of Oxford to the 'margins of defeated Royalism in Wales and London' (435). In the absence of any clear evidence, it might also be worth speculating that one or two figures who saw Philips's precocious talent at close hand (Dering, Lawes) took the chance to display her worth to a wider audience. From this point on, as Gray herself notes (as do a number of scholars who have examined Philips as a consummate coterie poet, who constantly engineers a position of authority for herself), Philips begins to reel in her chosen band of influential friends (439).[8] This is a process not just directed, in her more famous poems, to women like Mary Aubrey (Rosania) and Anne Owen (Lucasia), but also to men, via early poems written to Dering, John Berkenhead (editor of the Royalist newsletter *Mercurius Aulicus* during the Civil War), Henry Vaughan, Henry Lawes (who was to write music for a number of Philips's lyrics), and Francis Finch. These manuscript poems from the early 1650s weave these men, as well as a number of women, into Philips's carefully controlled coterie, and into her linkage of the personal imagery of friendship and its political implications in the Interregnum. It is therefore worth looking briefly at the details of these poems and their subjects, and in doing so one can see how Philips constructed an intertwined network of 'friends' through her poetry.

formidable account of the entire period, see Valerie Traub's incisive reading of Philips in relation to the nexus between 'lesbian' desire and traditions of female friendship in *The Renaissance of Lesbianism in Early Modern England* (Cambridge: Cambridge University Press, 2002), 295–308, and 341–2.

[7] Barash, *English Women's Poetry*, 100.

[8] On Philips as coterie poet see esp. Mary Louise Coolahan, who argues against some of the biographical and historical approaches discussed here by stressing the malleable and occasional nature of much of Philips's poetry, in ' "We live by chance and slip into Events": Occasionality and the Manuscript Verse of Katherine Philips', *Eighteenth-Century Ireland*, 18 (2003), 9–23; see also Paul Tolander and Zeynep Tenger, 'Katherine Philips and Coterie Critical Practices', *Eighteenth-Century Studies*, 37 (2004), 367–87.

This process involved Philips's concept of friendship, which is in part an adaptation of the ideas about Platonic relationships that had circulated in Henrietta Maria's court, in part an English version of fashionable French *précieuses* culture, and in part Philips's own unique approach to friendship as simultaneously a way to express same-sex desire, and a way to establish a Royalist ideology that would compensate for recent defeat.[9] Philips, as Carol Barash points out, participates in debates 'about the shifting nature and structure of political authority', in part through the notion of friendship as transcending political and gender divides.[10] As Catharine Gray notes, at this earlier stage of Philips's career, her poetry 'is busy filling up the empty space left by Royalist defeat not with present debate and political experiment, but with the cultural and political artifacts and idealized identities of her Royalist friends' (443). Gray also offers an integrative reading of the poems to Rosania and Lucasia, seeing them as offering, through their homoerotic retreat from the world, a political critique of current events that extends even to Calvinist ideas about marriage (446). This reading complements Valerie Traub's extended account of what she sums up, in relation to Philips's poetry, as 'a symptomatic hinge between the rhetoric of innocuous chaste friendship, which governed understandings of female—female desire in the Renaissance, and the rhetoric of suspect intimacies, which became a primary mode of intelligibility by the late eighteenth century'.[11]

The early poems addressed to men also reveal how rapidly Philips established herself as a central figure within an active coterie, as the men concerned not only circulated and promoted Philips's own poems, but also wrote back to her and took up her themes. Thus 'To the Noble Palaemon on his incomparable discourse of Friendship' is directed to Francis Finch, who wrote a treatise on friendship in 1653 which was dedicated to Anne Owen, and which addresses 'Lucasia-Orinda', therefore illustrating the way Philips established the inseparable nature of her relationship with Owen. In his edition of Philips, Patrick Thomas explains how, prior to the discovery of the sole surviving copy of Finch's book, this poem was mistakenly thought to be part of Philips's response to the later, famous treatise on friendship published by Jeremy Taylor in 1657 in response to a letter written to him by Philips. It is worth noting here that, by 1657, Philips had established her identity as a poet and, one might say, a kind of philosopher, sufficiently for Taylor's treatise to address her ideas directly and in print.[12] Philips does remain identified by her initials on Taylor's title page (M.K.P.), so again this

---

[9] Here I follow the detailed account of the connections between these sources for Philips's treatment of friendship in Chalmers, *Royalist Women Writers*, 74–8; see also the valuable essay by Mark Llewellyn on the philosophical and literary contexts for Philips's views, 'Katherine Philips, Friendship, Poetry and Neo-Platonic Thought in Seventeenth Century England', *PQ* 81 (2002), 441–68; and see Traub's account of the relationship between friendship and 'lesbian' desire, *Renaissance of Lesbianism*, 295–308.

[10] Barash, *English Women's Poetry*, 61.     [11] Traub, *Renaissance of Lesbianism*, 341.

[12] Thus, for example, Peter Beal notes that Sarah Jinner in her 1658 almanac knows that Philips was the author of the poem in the Cartwright volume, *In Praise of Scribes*, 153–4.

identification is for the initiated, but by 1657 those aware of her identity were growing in number as her manuscript distribution of her poems increased like ripples across a pond. Taylor addresses Philips as 'you who are so eminent in friendships'.[13] In her account of the close connections between Philips's concept of friendship and the general confluence of concepts of friendship and Royalist ideology in the Interregnum, Hero Chalmers notes how friendship is a form of 'political bonding', and that 'Philips was entirely conscious of the royalist import of the writing on friendship which she fostered'.[14]

An early poem to Edward Dering provides a fascinating example of the literary exchanges within Philips's coterie. In 1651 Dering wrote a poem in which he imagined 'Orinda preferring Rosania before Salomons traffique to Ophir'.[15] (The rather daring biblical reference is to 1 Kings 9, describing the gold that Solomon's servants brought back from Ophir.) Philips's poem to Dering plays with this compliment to her attachment to Rosania; Philips writes: 'My thoughts with such advantage you express, | I hardly know them in this charming dress' (86). Philips places Dering in the role of 'great Orator' addressing Rosania on her behalf, but of course during this period, before Rosania's great betrayal when she married William Montagu in 1652, Philips herself was a far greater orator, writing, in poems like '19 Sept. Rosania shaddow'd whilest Mrs M. Awbrey 1651', of Rosania's erotic power: 'Not her least glance but sets all hearts on fire' (118).

Henry Vaughan cannot be seen as a member of Philips's coterie, but their exchange of poems is, once again, an interesting marker of Philips's rising fortunes in the seventeenth century. Philips wrote an admiring poem to Vaughan specifically praising the poetry he published in 1646.[16] Philips singles out, not just the love poems directed to 'Amoret', but also Vaughan's translation of Juvenal: 'Then Juvenal revived by thee declares | How flat man's Joys are, and how mean his cares' (96). Philips's poem remained in manuscript circulation until the unauthorized publication of her poems in 1664, although the original manuscript sent to Vaughan has not yet been traced.[17] Vaughan returned the compliment in print in a poem entitled 'To the most excellently accomplish'd, Mrs K. Philips', which he published in *Olor Iscanus* in 1651.[18] Vaughan identifies

---

[13]  Jeremy Taylor, *A Discourse of the Nature, Offices and Measures of Friendship* (1657), 2.

[14]  Chalmers, *Royalist Women Writers*, 68 and 70; and see ch. 2 *passim*.

[15]  This is the title in Dering's autograph manuscript of poems by Philips (University of Texas, Austin; Thomas's MS D).

[16]  Henry Vaughan, *Poems with the Tenth Satire of Juvenal Englished* (1646); Philips's poem is 'To mr Henry Vaughan, Silurist, on his Poems' (96–7).

[17]  Jonathan Nauman argues that the poem must have been intended to be published as part of Vaughan's *Silex Scintillans* (1650), but that Vaughan did not include it as he was already breaking away from the literary process of commendatory poems: see 'The Publication of *Thalia Rediviva* and the Literary Reputation of Katherine Philips', *HLQ* 61 (1998), 88–9.

[18]  The complex publishing history of *Olor Iscanus*, which was first prepared for publication in 1646 but then delayed and censored, is not directly relevant to my discussion here: see the summary account in Nauman, 'Publication', 81.

Philips by name, rather than by her initials, addressing her as 'wittie fair one'. Vaughan stresses Philips's femininity, yet at the same time praises her verse as masculine: 'The poem smooth, and in each line | Soft as your selfe, yet Masculine'.[19] Jonathan Nauman has speculated that Philips's poem was caught up in Vaughan's rejection of both the process of commendatory poetry and the ideology of the Royalist coterie.[20] But in a curious twist of fate, by 1678, when Vaughan's *Thalia Rediviva* appeared, Philips's posthumous poetic reputation was at its height, and Vaughan's was in decline, so Vaughan belatedly republished Philips's poem at the beginning of the volume.

Henry Lawes is the last male figure I will discuss here, and his relationship to Philips's early reputation is more significant than that of Finch, Dering, or Vaughan. Mary Harvey studied music with Lawes while she was at Mrs Salmon's School. Lawes's *Second Book of Ayres and Dialogues* was published in 1655 and was dedicated to Mary, now Lady Dering. Lawes also included three of Mary's own musical settings of her husband's lyrics. This fairly short volume opens, after an address to lovers of music, with Philips's commendatory poem 'To the much honoured Mr Henry Lawes, On His Excellent Compositions in Musick'.[21] It is significant that in her poetic contribution to this collection of lyrics by, once again, Royalist writers (including John Berkenhead), Philips compares harmony in music to a King 'conqu'ring what was his own'. The poem is signed with Philips's full name, and Lawes in return includes a setting of one of Philips's Lucasia poems, 'Friendship's Mysteries', which is titled 'Mutuall Affection Between Orinda and Lucasia' in the songbook.[22]

By 1655, when Lawes's setting was published, not only was Philips's poetry more visible in print, but her manuscript poetry was in increasing circulation, as she wrote a series of poems to and about Rosania and Lucasia, as well as other poems. At this point it is worth noting Marie-Louise Coolahan's strictures against the impulse to read Philips's poems as windows into a fixed biographical narrative that is focused solely on her erotic verse.[23] Coolahan, like other recent critics who have integrated Philips's 'personal' lyrics with her political context, notes that the contemporary manuscript evidence points to the shifting alignments of individual poems in changing situations. Kate Lilley, in a characteristically sophisticated essay, argues against the trajectory that sees Philips as moving from erotic verse to political verse.[24] In her discussion of Philips's

[19] Henry Vaughan, *Olor Iscanus* (1651), 28.     [20] See Nauman, 'Publication', *passim*.

[21] Henry Lawes, *Second Book of Ayres and Dialogues* (1655), b.

[22] Ibid. 46; Lawes's setting of Philips's 'On the Death of my First and dearest Child, Hector Philips' has recently been identified in a manuscript of his songs: see Joan Applegate, 'Katherine Philips's "Orinda Upon Little Hector": An Unrecorded Musical Setting by Henry Lawes', *English Manuscript Studies*, 4 (1993), 272–80.

[23] Coolahan, 'Occasionality', *passim*; see also Kate Lilley, 'Fruits of Sodom', paper delivered at ANZAMEMS, Auckland, February, 2005, and Gray, 'Katherine Philips', *passim*.

[24] Lilley, ' Dear Object', *passim*.

love elegies, Lilley notes how Philips's poetic drive in her lyrics written to and about women 'functions to prohibit reply'.[25] In Lilley's view, Philips is constantly engaged in negotiating a powerful position for herself through what might be viewed as a potentially restrictive liminality: 'Her interest in the inherent intricacy and instability of interpersonal and textual exchange is continually played out in the oscillation between coterie and proper names, the permeability of manuscript and print; the criss-cross of author and reader, private and public, personal and political.'[26] Accordingly, at this point in my discussion I want to outline the manuscript transmission of the great variety of poetry produced by Philips in the 1650s, taking into account the nature of some individual poems, but of necessity working back through the major manuscript collections of Philips's verse.

As Elizabeth Hageman and Andrea Sununu (editors of the much anticipated authoritative edition of Philips) note, 'Philips provides a near-perfect case study of a mid-seventeenth-century coterie poet whose work suited, or was made to suit, a wide range of literary tastes.'[27] It is also important to stress that Philips's poetic output is much more varied than the frequently anthologized friendship poems suggest; as well as the poems to men discussed above, Philips wrote a series of philosophical poems on abstract topics such as 'Death' or 'The Soul'; a number of songs (including those that formed part of her translation of *Pompey*); directly political poems, such as 'On the Double Murder of K. Charles' or 'To my Lord Duke of Ormond, Lord Lieutenant of Ireland, on the discovery of the late Plot'; what might be called genre poems, such as 'A Country Life'; epitaphs on the death not just of her own child ('On the Death of my First and Dearest Child, Hector Philips'), but on certain friends and acquaintances; and the more famous poems on Rosania, Lucasia, and Regina. Philips also, in a sense, had two literary careers: the first saw her controlling her Society, circulating poems widely within her coterie, and having them circulated by her friends, with an occasional appearance in print as discussed above; the second followed the sudden, much more public fame achieved by the performance of *Pompey* in Dublin, followed by literary success in London, and the unauthorized 1664 publication of her work—all this entangled with the need to protect her husband from the political consequences of the Restoration. After her death, Philips's fame continued, marked by the 1667 folio and numerous imitations and circulation of her writing.

---

[25] Lilley, ' Dear Object', 172.          [26] Ibid. 168.

[27] Elizabeth H. Hageman and Andrea Sununu, ' "More Copies of it abroad than I could have imagin'd": Further Manuscript Texts of Katherine Philips, "the Matchless Orinda" ', *English Manuscript Studies*, 5 (1995), 127; in this article and in 'New Manuscript Texts of Katherine Philips, the 'Matchless Orinda', *English Manuscript Studies*, 4 (1993), 174–219; Hageman and Sununu offer an invaluable account of the complex manuscript transmission of Philips's writing; I have also drawn on Peter Beal's insightful chapter in *In Praise of Scribes*, ch. 5.; also useful is the summarizing article by Claudia A. Limbert, 'The Poetry of Katherine Philips: Holographs, Manuscripts, and Early Printed Texts', *PQ* 70 (1994), 181–97.

## PHILIPS AND MANUSCRIPT TRANSMISSION

Manuscript traces of Philips's poetry are still being discovered, but the current situation can be outlined following Hageman and Sununu, as well as the information gathered together by Peter Beal.[28] The manuscript dissemination of Philips's poetry involved the collections compiled by Philips herself, and those close to her; sequences of Philips's poetry in various manuscript miscellanies; and individual poems that circulated in a variety of ways. After the publication of the 1664 and 1667 collected editions, poetry continued to circulate extensively in manuscript (often using the printed texts as a source), as well as being anthologized in a variety of ways in print, as will be detailed below. Accordingly, Philips offers a perfect illustration of the continuance of scribal publication during the seventeenth century, as described in the work of scholars like Harold Love, Arthur Marotti, and Margaret Ezell, and as I have discussed in earlier chapters of this book.[29]

The most important manuscript of Philips's poetry is the autograph Tutin Manuscript (National Library of Wales 775B), which contains about half of all her poetry. Philips compiled this collection some time in the 1650s, as the latest poem in it dates from 1658. It seems likely that this manuscript was put together over time by Philips as a book of fair copies of her poems (as evidenced by a few titles to poems which were not transcribed onto the blank pages below them).[30] Two poems were at some stage torn out of this volume, one of which, 'A Sea Voyage', has been located by Hageman and Sununu at the University of Kentucky.[31] Apart from the textual authority it provides, given that these are essentially Philips's fair copies of a large body of her Interregnum poems, the Tutin Manuscript is also a themed anthology, though its exact nature has been contested. In particular, Marie-Louise Coolahan has used this manuscript to argue against those who read an orderly biographical narrative back into the Rosania and Lucasia poems, instead seeing the poetry as thematically coherent

---

[28] See Peter Beal, *Index of English Literary Manuscripts* (London, 1993), ii.

[29] See esp. Harold Love, *Scribal Publication in Seventeenth-Century England* (Oxford: Clarendon Press, 1993); Margaret Ezell, *The Patriarch's Wife: Literary Evidence and the History of the Family* (Chapel Hill: University of North Carolina Press, 1987) and *Social Authorship and the Advent of Print* (Baltimore: Johns Hopkins University Press, 1999); Arthur Marotti, *Manuscript, Print, and the English Renaissance Lyric* (Ithaca, NY: Cornell University Press, 1995); Ezell, in *Social Authorship*, uses Philips as a perfect example of the continued use of manuscript transmission through the whole seventeenth century—and indeed into the eighteenth, see *passim*, and esp. 52–4; Harold Love's edition of Rochester's poetry also provides a fascinating illustration of this process at work and the complex editorial decisions required to deal with the ways in which poetry was transmitted and (often) transformed in manuscript in the Restoration: *The Works of John Wilmot Earl of Rochester* (Oxford: Oxford University Press, 1999).

[30] As argued by Thomas Philips, *Collected Works*, 42; Limbert, 'Poetry of Katherine Philips', 183.

[31] See 'New Manuscript Texts', 175–80.

but 'occasional', and also mutable in various ways.[32] Reading this manuscript can initially be a disorienting experience, especially for those unacquainted with seventeenth-century verse miscellanies, because the volume has poems transcribed from both 'front' and 'back': that is, the volume can, like some modern 'double-header' books for children, be read in two directions, and in each case the reader encounters poems that are 'upside down' coming from the opposite direction. This might simply be explained as a way of keeping different grouped themes separate from each other, but, as Marie-Louise Coolahan notes, such an arrangement 'disrupts any linear, chronological reading of the autograph manuscript in a very graphic fashion'.[33] One might also ask what reader Philips had in mind in arranging the poems in this way, given that we cannot know if this volume was purely intended for Philips's own use, or if it was intended eventually to be some sort of presentation volume (the fact that it contains no post-1660 poems makes this even harder to determine). Read as an anthology assembled by Philips, it is difficult to avoid seeing the largest number of poems as marking the 'front' of the book, and the smaller group of poems (eighteen out of fifty-five) as the 'back'. If one does read it this way, the volume certainly provides a sense of moving through a specific sequence which is then interrupted by the reversed poems. From this perspective, the volume begins with Philips's poem to her husband, 'To My Dearest Antenor, on his Parting', then two epitaphs, and the poems to Cartwright and Francis Finch discussed above, before moving on to a number of Rosania and Lucasia poems.

While Carol Barash's interpretation of this sequence as a shift from domesticity to 'an alternative community' is an interesting speculation, the first few poems (if they are to be considered the 'first') can also simply be seen as coming first because they are early poems—for instance, the epitaph on Hector Philips would fit Barash's narrative better than the epitaphs on little Regina Collier and John Collier, but the Collier epigraphs are there, I assume, because they date from 1649–50, while the Hector Philips epigraph dates from 1655.[34] This is not to say that the whole volume is arranged chronologically, but that the first few poems seem to be there because they are early poems, rather than for any clear, thematic purpose. It is worth noting that Philips includes in this volume the Collier epitaphs, but also the fierce condemnation of the widowed Regina Collier, mother of 'little' Regina, for refusing to marry (it would seem) the man preferred for her by Philips. John Collier was a cousin of Philips's father, and the admiration Philips expresses in her epitaph for him ('the worlds epitomy') seems heartfelt.[35] Philips was keen to control the marriages of her female friends, a situation that became particularly fraught when she supported Charles Cotterell's courtship of Anne

---

[32] Coolahan specifically argues against Barash's reading of the manuscript ('Occasionality', 14), but it seems to me that Barash too notes the heterogeneous nature of the manuscript.

[33] Ibid.      [34] Barash, *English Women's Poetry*, 68–9.

[35] In my discussion of the autograph volume, I quote directly from National Library of Wales MS 775B, but for convenient reference, page numbers refer to the Thomas edn.

Owen in 1662. (Owen/Lucasia ended up marrying Marcus Trevor, Viscount Dungannon, and the disgruntled Philips insisted on accompanying the newly-weds to Ireland, which at least had the positive effect of introducing her to the Lord Lieutenant Roger Boyle's literary circle, and to her translation of Corneille's *Pompey* with Boyle's encouragement.)

After the poem addressed to Finch (as Palaemon), Philips places six Rosania poems. While these do not provide an exact biographical narrative (whatever that might look like), they trace out a pattern of attachment and betrayal, given that they begin with 'L'Amitié', dated in the manuscript '6 April 1651', a poem that begins with an address to Mary Aubrey as 'Soule of my soule!' (142), but end with three poems lamenting Aubrey's marriage, beginning with 'Rosania's Private Marriage'.[36] It is, I think, worth making the point here that, regardless of whether one reads the Rosania and Lucasia poems as autobiography, staged erotic drama, an establishment of female friendship with political overtones, or whatever else, moving from the conventional (if accomplished) lines of the pre-ceding poems to 'L'Amitié' and 'To Mrs M.A, Upon Absence', and the poems that follow, means encountering truly powerful poetry of a level of achievement unsurpassed in the Restoration. After the sequence of Rosania poems, Philips mixes up a number of Lucasia poems, and various other occasional poems; once again, it is the Lucasia poems that stand out as particularly powerful. Kate Lilley makes the astute observation that 'The passionate poems addressed to Rosania, Lucasia and, to some extent, Regina, blur into each other (and yet stand apart from the other less affect-laden female addressees).'[37]

It is perhaps sheer coincidence that when we reach 'Friendship in Emblem' in the Tutin Manuscript, we also reach the first of the 'reversed' poems, which is 'To My Lucasia in Defence of Declared Friendship'. On the other hand, it is hard to resist the idea that Philips deliberately 'centred' her collection with the criss-crossing of two key Lucasia poems. This idea of deliberately group-ing poems in the Tutin Manuscript forms part of Elizabeth Hagemen's discus-sion of the relationship of the major Philips manuscripts to the publication of the 1664 edition of Philips's work.[38] Hageman sees the Tutin Manuscript as having a 'personal' section, and a philosophical section, and she stresses that there is no reason to favour one half over the other as the beginning of the book.[39]

In 'Friendship in Emblem', Philips reworks John Donne's compass image from 'A Valediction: Forbidding Mourning':

---

[36] I assume 'Injuria Amici' to be about Rosania's betrayal.          [37] Lilley, 'Dear Object', 171.

[38] Elizabeth Hageman, 'Treacherous Accidents and the Abominable Printing of Katherine Philips's 1664 Poems', in W. Speed Hill, ed., *New Ways of Looking at Old Texts III* (Tempe: Arizona Center for Medieval and Renaissance Studies, 2004), 89–90.

[39] Ibid. 89, and I have also benefited from hearing Prof. Hageman elaborate this argument in her plenary address at 'Still Kissing the Rod? Early Modern Women's Writing', St Hilda's College, Oxford, 2 July 2005.

> The compasses that stand above
> Express this great immortall Love;.
> For friends like them can prove this true,
> They are, and yet they are not two. (107)

In this poem, as Carol Barash has noted, 'It is almost as if Philips's speaker is addressing her partner from inside Francis Finch's emblem of the fused couple, Orinda-Lucasia.'[40] Although the poem is a statement about the general ideals of friendship, it is at heart a paean to the Orinda/Lucasia relationship:

> But as there is degrees of bliss
> So there's no friendship meant by this
> But such as will transmit to fame
> Lucasia's and Orinda's name. (108)

In the manuscript, the two names are written in much larger letters than the rest of the poem, underlining the power of their association (and ultimately of the poet who creates both the association and the fame). The crossing poem, 'To My Lucasia in Defence of Declared Friendship', because of its length, also crosses with a third Lucasia poem: 'To Lucasia' ('Let dull Philosophers enquire no more')—this is a poem with similar themes to the other two. 'To My Lucasia in Defence of Declared Friendship' is a triumphant and celebratory poem, which demands that the love between Orinda and Lucasia should be on display (as indeed it is in Philips's poems): 'O! My Lucasia let us speak our Love' (153).

From this point on in the volume, it is possible to keep reading from the 'front', in which case one has to change gear abruptly with 'On the Death of my First and Dearest Child Hector Philips', which is, strictly speaking, not an 'Orinda' poem, but rather a deeply personal lament for Philips's son, who died in 1655. This is not a permanent change of theme, however, as two poems on there is another Lucasia poem, 'Parting With Lucasia', followed by 'Against Pleasure': poems in a far less celebratory mood, especially 'Against Pleasure', a song which sounds the cynical note typical of Restoration wits like Rochester (and indeed the voice of the poem might as easily be that of a male poet like Rochester as Philips). After this poem, there is only the 'Epitaph on Mr John Lloyd', and the title, but not the poem, 'To The Right Honourable the Lady E.C.', so that at this point the reader will most likely turn the book around and start from the other end, therefore following a sequence of abstract, philosophical poems. The sequence begins on a torn page with a poem that was later titled 'God' in the Dering Manuscript, but here is headed only 'Out of Mr More's'—this is identified in later texts as 'Out of Mr More's Cup Conf': that is, a meditation on a passage from Henry More's *Cupid's Conflict* (1646). This is followed by 'On Controversies in Religion' (still on a torn page), and, most disconcertingly, by an interposed poem

---

[40] Barash, *English Women's Poetry*, 96.

in a later hand (present on other blank pages in the manuscript) entitled 'Ode to a Lincolnshire Pud', containing the immortal phrase 'O pudding! pudding!!' Philips's own poetry resumes, in a continuation of this philosophical sequence, with 'Happiness', 'Death', 'The World', 'The Soul', and 'L'Accord du Bien'. The following poems are a combination of more personal occasional poems ('Invitation to the Country'), overtly political poems ('On the 3rd September 1651'—a poem about the defeat of Charles II at Worcester), and further philosophical poems ('God Was in Christ Reconciled', 'La Grandeur d'Esprit').

This thematic ordering of the Tutin Manuscript had, as Elizabeth Hageman has argued, a profound influence on later manuscript collections of Philips's poetry, but these later manuscripts form part of the next stage of Philips's career, after the performance of *Pompey* produced a radical increase in her visibility as an author.[41]

## *POMPEY*, FAME, AND THE TRANSMISSION OF PHILIPS'S WORK

Philips was in London when Charles II made his triumphant return, and she wrote celebratory poems not just in the King's honour, but addressed to various members of the royal family. Around this time, Philips became friendly with Charles Cotterell, Master of Ceremonies in Charles II's court, to whom she gave the name Poliarchus. Philips's extensive correspondence with Cotterell was published (her letters having been edited by Cotterell) in 1705, and the letters cover the last few years of Philips's life.[42] After Cotterell's unsuccessful courtship of Anne Owen, Philips, when she followed Lucasia and her new husband, Marcus Trevor, to Ireland, consoled Cotterell with negative comments about Trevor. At the same time, she also documented her activities within the literary circle gathered around the Lord Lieutenant of Ireland. Roger Boyle, Earl of Orrery, the author of a number of plays, and *Parthenissa*, a long romance written in the style of the French heroic romances that Philips admired, suggested that Philips should translate the whole of Corneille's *La Mort de Pompé*, after looking over a scene which Philips had shown him. Philips completed the translation late in 1662, and it immediately circulated in manuscript in Dublin, and later, partly through Cotterell's obaining a copy which Anne Owen had transcribed for Mary Aubrey, in London.[43] *Pompey* was then performed in Dublin in early 1663, and from this point on Philips entered the public arena, and her writing had a general currency that took it out of her direct control, even before her untimely death in June 1664. The immediate response was, as Philips states in a letter to Cotterell, 'many Letters and Copies of Verses sent me, some from my Acquaintance, and

[41] Hageman, 'Treacherous Accidents', 89–93.
[42] For a detailed account, see Souers, *Matchless Orinda*, ch. 5.
[43] Ibid. 173 and again for a detailed account of Philips's time in Ireland, see ch. 6.

some from Strangers, to compliment me upon Pompey' (ii. 78). Philips goes on to say that 'One of them, who pretends to be a Woman, writes very well, but I cannot imagine who the author is' (ibid.). This poem was by someone calling herself 'Philo-Philippa', and it was eventually printed, together with other commendatory verses, in the 1667 posthumous folio of Philips's works. The Philo-Philippa poem marks an important symbolic moment in Philips's public profile, as the poet specifically hails Philips as an inspiration for women writers, describing her as a female counterweight to the male literary tradition: 'Let the male Poets their male Phoebus chuse, | Thee I invoke, Orinda, for my Muse'.[44] Philo-Philippa goes on to describe this liberation of female writers as a force that might well scare men: 'From these thy more than masculine Pen hath rear'd | Our Sex; first to be prais'd, next to be fear'd' (C4v). This poem, as well as paying lengthy tribute to the translation of *Pompey*, praises Philips's original verse as well.

Word of *Pompey*'s success led to a demand for manuscript copies of the play, as noted above.[45] In November 1662 Philips wrote to Cotterell that 'There are, tho' much against my Will, more Copies of it abroad than I could have imagined' (ii. 60). As Catharine Mambretti has noted, Philips's translation can be seen as part of her attempts to rehabilitate her husband: 'Orinda realized that the play could admirably represent her and James Philips's interests to the royal family, since it depicts not only the just punishment of treachery but pleads for kingly mercy.'[46] Philips made arrangements with Cotterell for her translation to be presented to the Duchess of York—she was particularly anxious that the rival translation, by Waller and other court wits, should not overshadow hers. Ultimately, the play was not just presented to the Duchess, but to the King, and interestingly, it was the printed text that Cotterell delivered to Charles, under Philips's instructions: 'I have sent you a packet of printed Pompeys to dispose of as you think fit. Be pleas'd to get one bound and present it to the Dutchess; and if you think the King will allow such a Trifle a place in his Closet, let him have another' (ii. 77). Given the play's public performance under the authorization of Ormonde and Orrery, and the ensuing demand, it is not surprising that a printed edition was arranged. The play was published first in Dublin by the King's Printer, John Crooke. Philips offers an interesting account of the printing in her next letter to Cotterell:

I wish I could have sent you more copies of Pompey, but there being in all but five hundred printed, I could not get as many as I had occasion to dispose of. Mr Herringman

---

[44] Katherine Philips, *Poems* (1667), C4.

[45] National Library of Wales MS 21867B is a manuscript of *Pompey* with corrections and emendations in Philips's hand; in their account of it, Hageman and Sununu describe it as probably completed before the first performance, and they also explain how its many variants indicate that the printed texts represent Philips's later version of the translation, see 'New Manuscript Texts', 187–94.

[46] Catharine Mambretti, 'Orinda on the Restoration Stage', *Comparative Literature*, 37 (1985), 243.

had written to me to give him leave to reprint it at London, and I have ordered my Brother Philips to treat with him about it. (ii. 79)

In fact, Crooke also printed the London edition of *Pompey*, while Herringman, despite attempts to secure the rights, printed the 'rival' *Pompey* translation, which had been acted by the Duke of York's company, although Herringman did end up as the printer of the 1667 folio.[47] The London edition of *Pompey* marks the next stage in the rapid increase in Philips's visibility as a writer, and Philips's correspondence with Cotterell shows how concerned she was over minor emendations and the printing and distribution process itself.

At this point in her career, Philips was poised between a careful acceptance of the increasing fame that the successful performance of *Pompey* guaranteed, and a residual reluctance to allow her works to circulate. This situation came to a head, after Philips had returned to Wales in July 1663, with the publication by Richard Marriot in 1664 of an unauthorized collection of her poetry. Marriott advertised this volume on 14 January 1664, but withdrew it from sale four days later, printing an apology for his actions. Philips wrote a number of letters complaining about the appearance of this volume, including one to Dorothy Temple (née Osborne), in which she states:

some most dishonest person hath got some collection of my Rimes as I heare, & hath delivered them to a printer who I understand is Just upon putting them out, & this hath so extreamly disturb'd me, both to have my private follys so unhandomly exposd, & ye belief yt I beleive the most part of ye world are apt enough to have, yt Iconniv'd at this ugly accident, that I have been on a Rack ever since I heard it. (ii. 142)

Philips actually wrote a special letter to Cotterell designed to be circulated publicly, in which she renounced the volume, decried the fact that her writing would be exposed to 'all the rabble', and lamented the injury it had done to her reputation (ii. 128–31). The appearance of this volume is clear testimony to the cultural capital represented by Philips's work at this stage of her career. While Germaine Greer has offered an ingenious argument to the effect that Philips's protests are disingenuous, and that she contrived the publication, Peter Beal and Elizabeth Hageman have offered convincing refutations of this idea.[48] Hageman has, in fact, used the surviving manuscript collections of Philips's poetry to piece together an account of the 'imperfect' manuscript (no longer extant) that served as Marriot's copy-text.[49] Given that Philips was prepared to authorize publication of *Pompey*, it is hard to ignore her desperate protests about the unauthorized publication of her much more personal poetry. This is not to say that Philips wanted her writing to be kept 'private', and during the last months of her life,

[47] See the detailed account in Souers, *Matchless Orinda*, 190–4.
[48] See Germaine Greer, *Slip-Shod Sybils: Recognition, Rejection and the Woman Poet* (London: Viking, 1995), 154–64; Beal, *In Praise of Scribes*, 163–5; Hageman, 'Treacherous Accidents', *passim*.
[49] Hageman, Treacherous Accidents', 88–95.

for example, she wrote a poem on the Queen's illness which was presented to the King (and received his approbation).[50] Inspired by the success of *Pompey*, Philips began translating a second Corneille play, *Horace*, which was left incomplete at her death.

During this time Philips also monitored her literary reputation, expressing, for example, considerable anxiety over the opinions of Waller, her rival in the translation of *Pompey*, and even, as it turned out, in a poem on the Queen's illness. Philips illustrates her anxiety by recounting an anecdote in which Waller purportedly said that he would have given up all his own compositions in order to have written Margaret Cavendish's poem 'The Hunting of the Stag', and on being charged with insincerity, explained that he meant 'that he could do no less in Gallantry than be willing to devote all his own Papers to save the Reputation of a Lady, and keep her from the Disgrace of having written anything so ill' (ii. 119–20). Waller refrained from any such criticism of Philips—perhaps because her poetry is so clearly accomplished in the very mode that Waller made his own, just as Philips's *Pompey* is manifestly superior to its rival. At this time, Philips also exchanged poetic compliments with Cowley.

We will never know what next step Philips might have taken to secure even further her poetic reputation, because she died suddenly in June 1664 from an attack of smallpox. From this point on her poetic reputation grew even more rapidly, but without her oversight.

## POSTHUMOUS CIRCULATION: MANUSCRIPT AND PRINT

After her death, the circulation of Philips's writing perfectly illustrates the way that, even during the last part of the seventeenth century, manuscript culture continued to flourish alongside print culture.[51] Philips's writing was gathered together in a number of manuscript collections, individual poems continued to circulate in manuscript, and single poems and groups of poems appeared in numerous manuscript anthologies. Within manuscript culture, the poems were also revised, adapted, and rewritten in a variety of ways. At the same time, an impressive folio publication superseded Marriot's 1664 edition of Philips, and the printed text in turn moved back into manuscript culture, as well as contributing, by the eighteenth century, to numerous printed examples of poems in collections. Given the complexity of this situation and the continuing discoveries by Philips's editors, I can offer here only a brief account in order to illustrate the general transmission of Philips's work. Perhaps the most fascinating aspect of this is the way that Philips was so thoroughly absorbed into a literary milieu that

---

[50] Souers, *Matchless Orinda*, 224–5.
[51] See esp. the detailed discussions in Love, *Scribal Publication*, and in Ezell, *Social Authorship*.

was still overwhelmingly masculine, despite the increasing visibility of writers like Margaret Cavendish, Aphra Behn, Anne Killigrew, Anne Finch, and a number of other late seventeenth-century women writers.

The most significant manuscript compilation of Philips's poetry (next to her autograph manuscript, discussed above), is the Rosania Manuscript, a collection of 96 poems, *Pompey*, and *Horace*, prefaced with a dedication to Rosania by someone (who remains unidentified) signing himself Polexander.[52] As Hageman and Sununu have explained, this commemorative volume is bound in black like a mourning bible or prayer book, and the preface stresses this purpose: 'Orinda though withdrawn is not from you'.[53] As a memorial volume compiled for Rosania, who, Polexander explains, nursed Philips in her last illness, this book will literally contain Orinda's memorial: 'Enjoy these dear Remains'.[54] The volume itself begins with *Pompey*, other translations (from Saint-Amant, Scudéry, and Corneille), and *Horace*, then, after a series of blank pages, ninety poems, arranged in a different order to the poems in the Tutin Manuscript.[55] So the Rosania poems begin with the tart 'To the Queen of Inconstancy Regina Collier', rather than with the Antenor poem that begins the Tutin Manuscript.[56] Two Lucasia poems precede the first Rosania poem, indicating, I think, that even in this volume prepared specifically for Rosania, the erotic/friendship poems are seen as allied, rather than opposed, regardless of which woman is being addressed. As opposed to the six Rosania poems placed early on in the Tutin Manuscript, discussed above, the first Rosania poem in the Rosania Manuscript is 'To Rosania' ('As men that are with visions grac'd'), the poem which mourns the loss of Rosania when she married:

> Diuided Riuers loose their name,
> And so our too unequall flame.
> Parted, will passion be in me,
> And an indifference in thee.[57]

One can only speculate on the reasons for offering this melancholy view of the relationship as the first of the Rosania poems—even though it is the case, as Peter Beal points out, that the more stringent 'On Rosania's Apostasy and Lucasia's Friendship' has been omitted.[58] But, as I have noted, there is no clear sequence of Rosania poems in this manuscript (the next poem is the song 'To My Lord Birons Tune of Adieu Phillis'), nor are the poems placed in anything like the order of their composition. There are still thematic sequences (for example, 'The

---

[52] National Library of Wales MS 776B.    [53] Ibid. 1.    [54] Ibid.

[55] It is worth noting here that, unless I misunderstand him, the order of poems in the Rosania manuscript does not tally with the list in Thomas, i. 65–9. Germaine Greer has speculated that the texts of the Rosania manuscript poems represent Philips's revisions, but this cannot be proven one way or another, and the 'authority' of the texts is less important to my discussion than the nature of their transmission; *Slip-Shod Sibyls*, 167–70.

[56] National Library of Wales MS 776B, 232.    [57] Ibid. 239.    [58] Beal, *Index*, 129.

World', 'The Soul', 'The Enquiry', and 'Good Friday' are grouped together, as are a number of the poems addressed to the royal family) but, taken as a whole, this manuscript reads much more like a collection designed to showcase Philips's versatility, and to preserve virtually all of her work.

In contrast, Edward Dering compiled a more personal anthology of Philips's poems, most probably, as Peter Beal suggests, during the time he and Philips co-incided in Dublin (July 1662 to July 1663).[59] Dering remained close to Philips from the time of his marriage to Mary Harvey until Philips's death. While in Dublin, he wrote the epilogue to *Pompey*. The Dering anthology is transcribed by Dering himself and, as Hageman and Sununu note, its contents closely resemble the poems in the Tutin Manuscript, beginning as it does with 'To Antenor', and moving through similar sequences of poems, including the philosophical poems, but (reflecting its later date) also including a selection of the post-Restoration poems to members of the royal family.

The final manuscript in this group is the so-called Clarke manuscript, a rather more mysterious volume compiled by someone with a less intimate relationship to Philips than Dering. This manuscript begins with seventy-three Philips poems, but then moves through a series of poems by other writers transcribed, as Peter Beal notes, by a number of late seventeenth- and early eighteenth-century hands.[60] Once again, as Elizabeth Hageman notes, this collection groups poems similarly to the Tutin manuscript, though, like the Dering Manuscript, it contains the post-Restoration poems (and was probably compiled around the same time).[61]

While these are the main manuscript sources of interest to editors, groups of Philips's poems, as well as individual examples, appeared in a wide variety of more general manuscript miscellanies, many of them deriving, not from earlier manuscript sources, but from the printed editions of Philips's work. This process is marked by the publication in 1667 of the folio collection of Philips's writing, an event of considerable importance in the history of the publication of women's writing, in so far as, unlike the earlier folios of Mary Wroth or Margaret Cavendish, Philips's volume is directly supported by members of the (male) literary establishment. The publication of Philips's work was eagerly anticipated, as testified to by Pepys, who wrote on 10 August 1667: 'to the New Exchange to the bookseller's there, where I hear of several new books coming out—Mr. Pratt's history of the Royal Society and Mrs. Phillips's poems.'[62] By 16 September Pepys read the volume in Henry Herringman's bookshop: 'at the New Exchange, where I stayed reading Mrs. Philips's poems'.[63] The very title page of the folio signals Philips's status, and enshrines her coterie name: *Poems by the most deservedly Admired Mrs Katherine Philips The Matchless Orinda*. This

[59] Beal, *Index*, 130.     [60] Ibid.     [61] 'Treacherous Accidents', 90–1.
[62] Samuel Pepys, *Diary*, ed. Robert Latham and William Matthews (London: Bell, 1983), viii. 370.
[63] Ibid. 439.

is followed by an engraving of Philips as a classical bust, again with the name 'Orinda' inscribed on the base. The volume was prefaced by an explanation that it replaces the 'false' edition of 1664. The editor prints in full the letter Philips wrote decrying the earlier edition, and then takes the opportunity to praise her letters as 'worth the reading'—and Cotterell did go on to publish Philips's letters to him in 1705. The editor praises Philips for 'her Verses and her Vertues both', stating that she might have been called 'the English Sappho' except that she had taken on the name of Orinda. Cowley goes on to make the same general point in his second dedicatory poem (there are also poems by Orrery, Roscommon, Philo-Philippa, James Tyrrel, and Thomas Flatman). The folio includes 121 poems as well as *Pompey* and *Horace*. This impressive volume was reprinted in 1669, 1678, and 1710. From its first appearance, as noted above, it helped to escalate Philips's status, and her influence is evident in both manuscript and print collections from this point on, often in quite surprising contexts. A number of the manuscript miscellanies that continued to flourish in this period featured groups of Philips's poems. For example, Bodleian Library MS Rawlinson poet. 65 is a collection of various poems that includes twenty-one by Philips. In this collection, put together by a member of St John's College, Oxford, the pages which contain Phillips's poem are headed 'K P. O.' (i.e. Katherine Philips. Orinda), again testifying to Philips's recognized status by this stage (the texts are all derived from the printed sources).[64] The compiler favoured poems like 'Death', 'Submission', 'Controversy in Religion', and chose none of the Lucasia, Rosania, or Regina poems. A similar Oxford manuscript, Rawlinson poet. 90, a compilation entitled 'A Collection of Verses, Fancyes and Poems, Morall and Devine', offers a slightly different selection, by including some of the more general friendship poems: 'A Retir'd Friendship', 'Friendship', 'A Friend', as well as the Lucasia poem 'Content'.[65]

Using Peter Beal's *Index*, it is possible to trace both Philips's general popularity in manuscript compilations, and also the popularity of individual poems.[66] While numerous poems appear in at least five manuscripts, seven poems appear in ten or more manuscripts: 'Against Pleasure', 'A Country Life', 'Happiness', 'In memory of . . . Mrs Mary Lloyd', the translation 'La Solitude de St Amant', 'To Mrs Mary Aubrey at Parting', and 'The Virgin'. Again this list contains only one personal friendship poem, and the most popular poem of all is 'A Country Life'. The more overtly political poems (which headed up the 1667 folio) are also absent from this list. It is clear that many of the manuscript compilers were drawn to Philips's less personal lyrics and genre poems, but a large number of poems had at least some manuscript circulation in the seventeenth and early eighteenth centuries.

---

[64] See Thomas's collation, which points to the 1667 folio as the source.

[65] For the fullest description of Philips's representation in manuscript miscellanies, see Beal, *Index*.

[66] It is perhaps worth noting that Beal's list is still being added to by new discoveries.

## REWRITING, REPUTATION, AND TRANSMISSION

Two unusual manuscript representations of Philips testify to her status, but also to the way that, while some forms of manuscript transmission pay testimony to the original writer by concerted attempts at accurate representation, such transmission often means that material is rewritten to suit the 'new owner' of the texts. In the first case, David Norbrook has scrutinized a manuscript produced by Robert Overton, a Puritan who was close to Milton and Marvell, and who managed to be imprisoned by both Cromwell and Charles II.[67] The manuscript is a memorial to Overton's wife, and, as Norbrook explains, it consists of adaptations of poetry and prose by Donne, Herbert, Quarles, Wither, and Philips. Norbrook notes how Overton was especially drawn to Philips's reworkings of Donne, so that 'The manuscript offers us not just Overton reading Donne but Overton reading Philips reading Donne' (237). In contrast to the manuscript compilers noted above, Overton was particularly drawn to the friendship poems, but, as Norbrook explains, he worked his way extensively through poems from the 1667 folio, changing them, often line by line, to suit his subject matter, his politics, and his temperament.

An even more dramatic testimony to Philips's cultural capital is provided by the Duke of Monmouth, who, as Hageman and Sununu explain, adapted 'A Country Life' and 'A Retir'd Friendship'.[68] Both poems are in the notebook taken from Monmouth after his capture at the Battle of Sedgemoor in 1685. Monmouth adapted some of Philips's lines, but he (or someone else) also provided music for them, and they are both headed 'Song' in the notebook.

By the 1670s and 1680s, Philips was widely acknowledged as a major poetic presence and influence. Edward Phillips, in *Theatrum Poetarum* (1674), states that Philips was: 'the most applauded, at this time, Poetess of our nation, either of the present or former Ages, and not without reason, since both her Fame is of a fresh and lively date from the but late publisht Volume of her Poetical works, and those also of a style suitable to the humour and Genius of these times' (257). While this only claims her as first among women, John Oldham, in his pastoral 'Bion', published in 1684, praises a series of contemporary poets, including Milton and Waller, and alongside them notes 'Orinda, whose bright shining name | Stands next great *Sappho*'s in the ranks of fame'.[69] As Hageman and Sununu point out, Philips's reputation had a significant influence on a whole group of women writers who followed her: they note in particular Anne Killigrew, Mary Chudleigh, Mary Astell, Anne Finch, Jane Barker, Elizabeth Rowe, Mary

---

[67] David Norbrook, '"This blushing tribute of a borrowed muse": Robert Overton and his Overturning of the Poetic Canon', *English Manuscript Studies*, 4 (1993), 220–66; further references in parentheses.

[68] 'New Manuscript Texts', 209–14.

[69] John Oldham, *Some New Pieces Never Before Published* (1684), 82.

Barber, and Mary Masters—many of whom had careers that stretched into the eighteenth century.[70] Anne Killigrew is a particularly apt example, because Dryden's support for her writing underlines Philips's position. In the Ode he wrote to preface the posthumous edition of Killigrew's poems, Dryden's refrain is that Killigrew's 'unsoil'd' poetry will atone for the lubricious writing that surrounded her. Killigrew, like Philips, died of smallpox, and they form a pair of martyrs in Dryden's poem: 'Heav'n, by the same Disease, did both translate, | As equal were their Souls, so equal was their fate'.[71] Carol Barash points out that Killigrew herself was far from being the pious ingénue described by Dryden; Killigrew compares herself to Philips in her poem 'Upon the saying that my verses were made by another', in a passionate defence of her authorship, which uses Philips's established position to defend her own:

> Orinda (*Albions* and her Sexes Grace)
> Ow'd not her Glory to a Beauteous Face,
> It was her Radiant Soul that shon With-in,
> Which struck a Lustre through her Outward Skin;
> That did her Lips and Cheeks with Roses dy,
> Advanc't her Height, and Sparkled in her Eye.
> Nor did her Sex at all obstruct her Fame,
> But higher 'mong the Stars it fixt her Name;
> What she did write, not only all allow'd,
> But ev'ry Laurel, to her Laurel, bow'd![72]

It is also worth citing, at this point, Aphra Behn's tribute to Philips, spoken as an 'aside' in her translation of Book Six of Cowley's *De Plantarum*, where Behn writes:

> Let me with *Sappho* and *Orinda* be
> Oh ever sacred nymph, adorn'd by thee;
> And give my Verses immortality.[73]

The general sense of Philips being above compare was common at this time, and while her example may have paved the way for the writers noted above, the idea of her unique virtue could also count against other women writers. For example, Mary Evelyn compares Philips unfavourably with the 'empty, whimsicall and rambling' Margaret Cavendish:

---

[70] 'More Copies', 159; one might add the still unidentified 'Ephelia' to this list; she praises Philips in her *Female Poems on Several Occasions* (1679); Warren Chernaik offers a bracing critique of those who assume that Ephelia *can* be identified in 'Ephelia's Voice: The Authorship of *Female Poems* (1679)', *PQ* 74 (1995), 151–73.

[71] Anne Killigrew, *Poems* (1686), b1v.

[72] Ibid. 46; see Barash, *English Women's Poetry*, 162–74; perhaps Killigrew's lines on Philips's true beauty have greater resonance if we recall John Aubrey's description of Philips as 'pretty fat; not tall; read pumpled face [red, pimpled]', *Brief Lives*, ed. Oliver Lawson-Dick (London: Mandarin, 1992), 242.

[73] Janet Todd, ed., *The Works of Aphra Behn* (London: Pickering, 1992), i. 325.

What contrary miracles does this Age produce.... This Lady and Mrs Philips, the one transported [*sic*] with the shadow of reason the other possessed of the substance and insensible of her treasure, and yet men who passe for learned and wise not only put them both in equall balance but make the greatnesse of the one weigh downe the certaine and reall worth of the other'.[74]

There were exceptions to these comparisons. Perhaps because her plays, rather than her poems, were the subject of the comparison, Gerard Langbaine, in his *Lives and Characters of English Dramatick Poets* (1699) has a clear preference for Aphra Behn: 'I must confess, I cannot but prefer Mrs. Behn infinitely before her; she seems to be a very cold Writer, while you may find in Aphra Behn both Fire and Easiness, which Mrs. Philips wanted' (110–11). Jeslyn Medoff has noted how the 'daughters of Behn' found it comparatively easy to publish in the late seventeenth century, but as time passed, Behn's legacy became a two-edged sword.[75]

By the early eighteenth century, as noted above, the 1710 edition of her collected works, and the 1705 edition of *Familiar Letters*, kept Philips's work highly visible. While the letters were reissued in 1729, the collected works did not reappear until the beginning of the twentieth century. The poems did remain popular in anthologies, however. Coleman and Thornton's *Poems by Eminent Ladies* (1755) contained eleven poems by Philips—a selection that ignores the political poems, and the more highly charged friendship poems, and that represents Philips in a way that endured into the nineteenth century.[76] George Ballard offers a judicious account in his *Memoirs of Several Ladies of Great Britain* (1752), drawing on Aubrey. Ballard describes Philips as 'the celebrated Orinda'.[77] She fits perfectly Ballard's notion of female decorum—'She proved a most excellent wife'—and Ballard praises 'Her remarkable humility, good nature and agreeable conversation' (269). He does also praise her literary gifts, and is prepared to quote at some length an anonymous letter (originally quoted by the Duke of Wharton) praising 'her solid masculine thoughts, in no feminine expression', and specifically singling out 'A Country Life' for praise (274).

As this quotation indicates, it is at this point in time that 'approved' women writers were largely being positioned on one side of an artificially constructed divide. Carol Barash offers a convincing argument that poets like Philips, Behn, Killigrew, Barker, and Finch created 'the possibility of an English women's poetic

---

[74] Quoted in Hageman and Sununu, 'More Copies', 160; Mary's husband, the diarist John Evelyn, referred to 'the virtuous Mrs Philips' in his entry on the court performance of *Horace* in 1668, ibid.

[75] Jeslyn Medoff, 'The Daughters of Behn and the problem of Reputation', in Isobel Grundy and Susan Wiseman, eds., *Women, Writing, History 1640–1740* (London: Batsford, 1992), 33–54.

[76] The poems are: 'Content', 'To the Queen of Inconstancy Regina Collier', 'Against Pleasure', 'The Enquiry', 'A Country Life', 'To Lady Elizabeth Boyle', 'On the Welsh Language', 'The Virgin', 'Against Love', 'To My Antenor', and 'Tendres Desirs'.

[77] George Ballard, *Memoirs of Several ladies of Great Britain*, ed. Ruth Perry (Detroit: Wayne State University Press, 1985), 268, further references in parentheses.

tradition', but, with the publication of Finch's poems in 1714, that tradition
was a divided one, feeding into an ideological gulf between the approved private
poetry of the domestic and respectable woman, and what Barash terms 'her
revolutionary double'.[78] In many eyes, in the eighteenth century, this became
symbolized by the contrast between the respectable Katherine Philips and the
disreputable Aphra Behn, although the contrast is not quite so simple, as will be
discussed below. In Paula Backscheider's memorable formulation, 'By 1696,
Philips was firmly established as what men wanted in a woman writer.'[79] Backscheider also explains how what she terms Philips's 'author function' was increasingly distanced from Philips's actual ambitions as a writer, as the image of Philips
as a specifically unthreatening woman was ever more firmly established.[80]

In the course of the eighteenth century, Philips became far less visible, but, as
Patrick Thomas notes, those who did comment on her poetry either followed
Ballard's lead in seeing her in terms of a feminine ideal, or, following Wharton's lead, praised the masculine qualities in her work (i. 39). The emphasis on
her poetry helped to narrow ideas about Philips's work—an emphasis which has
changed only with very recent criticism. After the 1710 edition of Philips's complete works, there was no further publication of *Pompey* (or *Horace*), and there
appear to have been no stage productions in the eighteenth century. Even the
poetry lost ground in anthologies later in the eighteenth century. It is a telling
irony that Samuel Johnson wrote lives of John Phillips and Ambrose Philips, but
not of Katherine Philips; just as Bell's 109-volume *Poets of Great Britain* series,
published from 1776 to 1782, included the poetry of both John and Ambrose,
but not of Katherine.[81]

Philips's position in Alexander Dyce's *Specimens of British Poetesses* (1825) is
a good indication of the diminution of her status by the early nineteenth century. Dyce trots out Ballard's notion of Philips discharging her domestic duties
in an exemplary manner, and sums her up, cosily, as an 'amiable woman' (76).
However amiable she might have been, Dyce does not rate her poetry very highly:
'The verses of Orinda appear to have been hastily composed; if they do not frequently gleam with poetry, they are generally impregnated with thought' (76).
Dyce reduced Colman and Thornton's eleven poems to four: 'Against Pleasure',
'To Lady Elizabeth Boyle', 'To My Antenor', and 'A Country Life'. (There were,
of course, exceptions to Dyce's judgement, the most notable being Keats, who, in
a letter to J. H. Reynolds in 1817 enthuses over Philips, and includes the full text

---

[78]  Barash, *English Women's Poetry*, 289 and 290.

[79]  Paula Backscheider, *Spectacular Politics: Theatrical Power and Mass Culture in Early Modern England* (Baltimore: Johns Hopkins University Press, 1993), 74; Backscheider's informative study also offers a significant account of how Behn remained a powerful writer in the eighteenth century, as well as a demonized figure.

[80]  Ibid. 79–81.

[81]  For an important account of the Bell series and its relationship to Johnson's *Lives*, see Thomas F. Bonnell, 'Poets of Great Britain: the "Little Trifling Edition" Revisited', *MP* 85 (1987), 128–52.

of 'To Mrs Mary Awbrey at Parting'.[82]) George Bethune's mid-century *British Female Poets* (1848) also offered only three poems, and an extract from a fourth, with 'Against Pleasure' and 'A Country Life' featuring again. By the end of the nineteenth century, Philips would have been virtually invisible except that the enthusiasm of a few admirers revived interest in her. In 1883, Edmund Gosse wrote a sympathetic treatment of her as part of his volume *Seventeenth Century Studies*. Gosse is quick to say that he does not value Philips's poetry very highly, and that from a literary point of view she was surpassed, in different ways, by Behn, Cavendish, and Catherine Trotter, but she is worthy of attention because of her 'pure and reasonable' muse.[83] A little later in the century, Philips attracted the admiration of two American writers: the fiction writer Sarah Orne Jewett, and the poet and scholar Louise Imogen Guiney. Jewett, together with her close companion Annie Fields, had a sustained interest in Philips. Jewett owned a number of Philips first editions, and annotated her copy of the 1669 edition with the comment that Philips 'was the first to dignify the love and friendship of women for each other'.[84] Guiney was a member of Jewett and Fields's Boston literary circle before she settled in Oxford in 1901.[85] Guiney wrote a brief but perceptive introduction to the selection of poems by Philips edited by the Hull bookseller and publisher John Ramsden Tutin. Tutin published, in small, limited editions, a wide range of poetry by early modern authors such as Crashaw and Donne. After his acquisition of the autograph manuscript that was purchased by the National Library of Wales on his death in 1913, and now goes under his name (the Tutin Manuscript), Tutin in 1904 published a selection of twenty-five poems from the 1667 edition prefaced by Guiney's introduction; in 1905 he printed a selection of fifteen poems from the manuscript; and in 1908 he published a smaller selection of six poems as part of a selection from Philips, Behn, Cavendish, and Winchelsea.[86] In her 'appreciatory note' to the selection from the 1667 edition, Guiney notes how little known Philips had become (though she acknowledges Gosse's essay as an exception to this neglect). Guiney sees Philips as an engaging amateur whose poetry is now of interest to those who want to understand an obscure literary period: 'The time is at hand when no one who would study the history of English intellectual development on the spindle side, or the intimate temper of the great century which altered England, will forbear some measure of acquaintance with "Orinda", queen of those virtuous poets who were among the public successes of the not-yet-understood Restoration' (8). Of

---

[82] *Letters of John Keats*, ed. Robert Gittings (Oxford: Oxford University Press, 1979), 21–2.

[83] Edmund Gosse, *Seventeenth Century Studies* (1883: rpt. London: William Heinemann, 1914), 230.

[84] Noted by Rachelle Trefousse as quoted in Hageman and Sununu, 'More Copies', 168.

[85] See E. M. Tenison, *Louise Imogen Guiney: Her Life and Works* (London: Macmillan, 1923).

[86] Katherine Philips 'The Matchless Orinda', *Selected Poems* (Cottingham near Hull: J. R. Tutin, 1904); Katherine Philips (Orinda), *Selected Poems* (Hull: J. R. Tutin, 1905); *Four Early English Poetesses* (Hull: J. R. Tutin, 1908).

course this early twentieth-century process of rediscovering the Restoration also involved rescuing the unvirtuous Aphra Behn from Victorian disapproval.

Coincidentally, at the same time as Tutin's obscure pamphlets championed Philips's poetry, she was given a more prominent and prestigious reprinting by Oxford University Press as part of George Saintsbury's multi-volume edition *Minor Poets of the Caroline Period*.[87] Published in 1905, Saintsbury's first volume contained a reprint of all the poems and also the songs from *Pompey* (but not the plays) from the 1678 edition. The other poets in the volume are Chamberlayne, Benlowes, and Patrick Hannay—and the continuing obscurity of the male poets is an interesting pointer to Philips's rising stocks in recent years. The indefatigable Saintsbury was, of course, a champion of an enormous range of minor literature, arguing in the general preface to this series that knowledge of such writers is vital to the strength of literary history. In the introduction to Philips, Saintsbury acknowledges Guiney's essay, and proceeds to offer fairly lukewarm admiration for Philips: 'her intrinsic interest, though mild, is by no mean insignificant' (486). Saintsbury compares Philips unfavourably with Winchelsea; he praises Philips's technique, but implies that her ideas and themes could be bracketed out of any assessment. Setting Saintsbury's views aside, this edition had the enormous advantage of reproducing all the published poetry, and so offering critics interested in a more thoroughgoing reassessment of Philips a fairly reliable, conservatively modernized text.

However, as I have already noted, it was the apparently bohemian Aphra Behn who appealed to those in the early twentieth century who were in search of early modern women writers, rather than the apparently staid Katherine Philips. And while there were limitations to the interest in Behn, much of it obsessively biographical, the enormous range of Behn's writing, especially her dramatic output, ensured that she has remained far more prominent than Philips over the last century. Philips's poetry has come back into vogue recently because of the rereading of her as a pioneering lesbian poet—and however much that definition has become sophisticated and refined in recent theoretical work on Philips, a debt is certainly owed to earlier critics like Harriete Andreadis and Elaine Hobby for revitalizing approaches to Philips, and seeing her as part of a living tradition.[88]


## APHRA BEHN: PROFESSIONAL WRITER

In September 1670 Aphra Behn's first play, *The Forc'd Marriage*, was performed by the Duke's Company. Katherine Philips had provided an example of a successful play produced by a woman, but *Pompey* was, after all, a translation, and following its success there was little direct movement by women towards the

---

[87] George Saintsbury, ed., *Minor Poets of the Caroline Period* (Oxford: Clarendon Press, 1905).
[88] See Andreadis, 'Sappho Platonics' and Hobby, 'Lesbian Poet'.

professional stage in London. Only two women playwrights who achieved productions (as opposed to Cavendish's many unstaged plays) seem to have preceded
Behn: Frances Boothby's *Marcelia* and Elizabeth Polwhele's *The Faithful Virgins*
and *The Frolicks* were all apparently performed sometime in 1669.[89] But Behn
went on to make an extremely successful career for herself in the theatre during
the 1670s. Prior to the commencement of her literary career, Behn had already
had a remarkable life, although biographical details are still often very sketchy,
especially for her childhood.[90] The entanglement of Behn's life and her works
became acute after the publication of *Oroonoko* in 1688, because it purported to
be a true account of her experiences in Surinam in the early 1660s, and debate
over the 'authenticity' of *Oroonoko* has continued through to the present day.
Given the thesis of this book, my interest is more in the fevered biographical
speculation itself, rather than in determining the exact details of Behn's early life,
and biographical material on Behn began as early as 1696 with the memoir that
formed part of a collection of her fiction.[91]

Behn seems to have had a very humble background: her father was probably
Bartholomew Johnson, a barber, and her mother apparently acted as a wet-nurse
for Thomas Colepepper, which did give Behn connections to a variety of aristocratic families, and therefore, as Janet Todd speculates, the connections that later
led to her activities as both spy and dramatist.[92] On balance, it seems likely that
Behn went to Surinam (though probably not in the elevated role she constructed
for herself in *Oroonoko*).[93] When she returned to London around 1664, she had
apparently married the shadowy Mr Behn, who seems to have been on the scene
for an extremely short period of time. In 1666 Behn set out on a spying mission
to the Netherlands, at which point we do finally have considerable documentary
evidence for her activities, as she wrote a series of letters back to London outlining
her discoveries.[94] Behn provided good information, but was left perilously short
of funds, and returned to London early in 1667 heavily in debt. Behn petitioned
Thomas Killigrew for funds; Killigrew was initially responsible for her engagement as a spy—he was also a playwright, and he ran the King's theatre company,

[89]  Derek Hughes, *The Theatre of Aphra Behn* (Houndmills: Palgrave, 2001), 5.

[90]  Despite the efforts of three very impressive biographers, details of Behn's birth and early life
remain largely speculative: see Maureen Duffy, *The Passionate Shepherdess: Aphra Behn 1640–89*
(2nd edn, London: Methuen, 1989); Angeline Goreau, *Reconstructing Aphra: A Social Biography of
Aphra Behn* (New York: Dial, 1980); Janet Todd, *The Secret Life of Aphra Behn* (London: André
Deutsch, 1996); I have drawn on all three, but rely most upon Todd.

[91]  *The Histories and Novels of the Late Ingenious Mrs Behn* (London: Samuel Briscoe, 1696).

[92]  See Todd, *Secret Life*, ch. 2, and see also Jane Jones, 'New Light on the Background and Early
Life of Aphra Behn', in Janet Todd, ed., *Aphra Behn Studies* (Cambridge: Cambridge University
Press, 1996), 310–20.

[93]  Again, see Todd's judicious and detailed account, *Secret Life*, ch. 3.

[94]  Behn's main target was William Scot, with whom she was said to have had an affair in
Surinam, though evidence for this is inconclusive; Behn's letters written during her spying mission
are in the Public Records Office, but transcripts and a useful account of her activities can be found
in W. J. Cameron, *New Light on Aphra Behn* (Auckland: University of Auckland, 1961).

one of two licensed by Charles at the beginning of the Restoration. When she managed to clear her debts, Behn began her literary career in earnest. While her initial theatrical contact must have been Killigrew, Behn's plays were performed by the rival Duke's Company, managed by Sir William Davenant. (This may have been due to the Duke's Company's greater need for new plays.) As Derek Hughes explains in his analysis of Behn's drama, Behn began by writing in the tragicomedy genre that was popular during the first decade of the Restoration theatre.[95] While *The Forc'd Marriage* was the first play by Behn to be performed, the first to be written was *The Young King*, although it was not performed until 1679. Behn also wrote *The Amorous Prince* in the same tragicomic mode around this time, and it became the second of her plays to be performed, in 1671.

In terms of Behn's self-representation and reception, perhaps the most interesting aspect of *The Forc'd Marriage* is its prologue. In the prologue, Behn uses imagery that evokes her career as a spy, marking her arrival as a female playwright. Initially this foray is announced by a male actor:

> Today one of their party ventures out,
> Not with design to Conquer, but to Scout:
> Discourage but this first attempt, and then,
> They'le hardly dare to sally out again. (v. 7)[96]

Behn plays games with images of conquest and seduction, and this is increased when an actress joins the actor, and proclaims that men have nothing to fear:

> Can any see that glorious sight, and say, [Woman pointing to the Ladies]
> A Woman shall not Victor prove to day: (v. 8)

A woman was a victor, in so far as *The Forc'd Marriage* had a run of six days (vital because the author received the takings from every third day of a run), and it was also published in 1671.[97] Following the success of *The Forc'd Marriage*, *The Amorous Prince* was performed early in 1671 and published in the same year. In the space of twelve months, Behn had achieved a high profile, and at least some financial, as well as critical, success.[98] Behn wrote the commendatory poem to Edward Howard's play *The Six Days' Adventure* (1671): a play in Jonson's mode that failed on stage in the same season as *The Amorous Prince*. The fact that Howard, who provided a defensive preface to his play, commissioned (or was offered) Behn's poem underlines her success at this time in establishing herself as a dramatist. Behn's tragicomedies were mocked in *The Rehearsal*, a satirical play

---

[95] Hughes, *Theatre*, 15, and see ch. 2 *passim*.

[96] References in parentheses are to Janet Todd, ed., *The Works of Aphra Behn*, 7 vols. (London: Pickering, 1992–6).

[97] See Todd, *Secret Life*, 145.

[98] Todd cautions that it was difficult to make a great deal of money from playwriting, ibid. 145–6, and Germaine Greer offers a speculative biographical account that particularly stresses the hand to mouth existence that Behn must have led for much of her writing life, *Slip-Shod Sybils*, ch. 6.

by the Duke of Buckingham, and various other wits, directed mostly at Dryden, but while, as Janet Todd suggests, this may have been why Behn did not stage *The Young King* at this time, is also marks Behn's status as a playwright worth the mocking.[99] Behn's next play, *The Dutch Lover*, was not performed until 1673 (and it was a failure on the stage). But in the meantime she continued to consolidate her presence in the London literary scene, almost certainly editing *Covent Garden Drollery* in 1672, a miscellany which included five of her own lyrics.[100]

When Behn published *The Dutch Lover* in 1673, provoked by its failure in the theatre, she added a preface sarcastically addressed to the 'Good, Sweet, Honey, Sugar-candied reader' (v. 160). The tone of this preface, which scorns any notion that plays might have a fundamental didactic purpose, while at the same time arguing that the pleasure they provide is completely justified, marks Behn's assumption of the style and attitude of the Restoration wit. Her boldness was then reflected in the shift of her plays towards sexual comedy (with the exception of *Abdelazar*), and this resulted both in her successful literary career, and the accusations of immorality levelled at her. In the preface, Behn describes a supposed wit who said 'they were to expect a woful Play, God damn him, for it was a womans' (v. 162). Behn defends her position as female playwright particularly by noting that drama does not require the kind of learning that other branches of literature may rely upon, and that many women lack; at the same time she ridicules the ignorance of anyone making such an accusation against women.

Behn's next play was not performed until 1676, and it was her only tragedy: *Abdelazar*. Derek Hughes has argued that at this time Behn was still experimenting with different dramatic forms, before soon settling on the type of comedy that became her forte.[101] *Abdelazar* was a moderate success, but Behn was clearly uncomfortable with the genre, and she turned to comedy for her next play. By the mid-1670s, Behn was a highly visible writer, and she was the subject of a number of satirical allusions. Behn's appearance in the mock epic 'Session of the Poets', probably written around 1676, might well have been seen as more compliment than critique:

> Next poetess Afra then showed her sweet face,
> And swore by her poetry and her black Ace
> The laurels by a double right were her own,
> For the poems she had writ, and the conquests she'd won.[102]

---

[99]  Todd, *Secret Life*, 153.

[100]  Behn's authorship seems fairly certain, but see Paul Hammond, 'The Prologue and Epilogue to Dryden's *Marriage A-la-Mode* and the Problem of *Covent Garden Drollery*', *PBSA* 81 (1987), 155–72; see also consideration in Mary Ann O'Donnell, *Aphra Behn: A Bibliography of Primary and Secondary Sources*, 2nd edn (Aldershot: Ashgate, 2004), item BA 1.1a.

[101]  Hughes, *Theatre*, 57.

[102]  'A Session of the Poets' as quoted in Jane Spencer, *Aphra Behn's Afterlife* (Oxford: Oxford University Press, 2000), 8.

It was in 1676 that Behn, with *The Town Fopp*, initiated a series of popular comedies, including Behn's most successful play, *The Rover*, which was first performed in March 1677. When *The Rover* was published, Behn's name did not appear on the title page, but this was remedied in the third issue of the first edition, which also acknowledged the author's sex in an emended version of the Postscript, which contains Behn's defence against the charge that the play was plagiarized from Thomas Killigrew's unperformed Interregnum play, *Thomaso*.[103] *The Rover* was, indeed, an adaptation of *Thomaso*, but Behn turned an over-long closet drama into a play that appealed to the nostalgia for an age of, as the subtitle proclaims, 'The banished Cavaliers', while at the same time capitalizing on the vogue for the modern witty and sympathetic rakish hero (Willmore, in this play). As both Jane Spencer and Nancy Copeland have noted, the success of *The Rover* is testified to by its numerous revivals, and also by its popularity in court performance, as requested not just by Charles II but also by James II and William and Mary.[104] Indeed, such was the play's popularity that Behn produced a sequel (again adapted from material in *Thomaso*) in 1681. On the other hand, as Derek Hughes explains, *Sir Patient Fancy*, which followed *The Rover* in 1678, was a failure, and from this point on the theatre seasons became more hazardous for playwrights, partly because of the political crises stemming from Whig–Tory conflict, and the frenzy of the Popish Plot.[105] This comedy, despite the audience reaction, shows Behn at the height of her dramatic powers, and her tart epilogue signals her self-confidence and her scorn for those who persist in condemning her for being a female playwright:

> I Here, and there, o'erheard a Coxcomb Cry
> A Rott it—'tis a Womans Comedy,
> One, who because she lately chanc't to please us,
> With her Damn'd stuff will never cease to teaze us.
> What has poor Woman done that she must be,
> Debar'd from Sense and Sacred Poetrie?
> Why in this Age has Heaven allow'd you more,
> And Women less of Wit than heretofore?
> We once were fam'd in Story and cou'd write
> Equall to men; cou'd Govern, nay cou'd Fight. (vi. 79)

Behn's next play, *The Feign'd Curtizans* (1679), was also a failure on the stage, and suffered from the general fallout of the Plot. Behn dedicated the printed text to Nell Gwyn—a moderately fawning dedication, typical for the time, but which Samuel Johnson was to single out in his life of Dryden as an especially egregious

---

[103] For the play's complex publication history see O'Donnell's bibliography, items A 6.1a, b, and c.

[104] See Spencer, *Afterlife*, ch. 5 and Nancy Copeland, *Staging Gender in Behn and Centlivre* (Aldershot: Ashgate, 2004), ch. 3.

[105] See Hughes, *Theatre*, 108–9.

example of offensive flattery. By the end of the 1670s, Behn was simultaneously a prominent, popular dramatist, but also faced with a more uncertain future, in so far as the theatre was proving less successful and profitable for her. Her status was acknowledged when Dryden asked her to join a group of translators to produce an English version of Ovid's *Epistles*. In his preface, which included his careful general account of the principles of translation, Dryden conveyed Behn's apology for not knowing Latin: 'I was desir'd to say that the Authour who is of the Fair Sex understood not Latine. But if she does not, I am afraid she has given us occasion to be asham'd who do.'[106]

This was the beginning of a successful series of translations by Behn, the majority of them from French (which she did know) rather than Latin, including prose fiction and poetry.[107] Much of the translation, along with Behn's original fiction, was written and published towards the end of her life, in the later 1680s, when her straitened financial circumstances seem to have spurred her on to new literary ventures in a variety of genres.

## BEHN, ROCHESTER, AND LITERARY REPUTATION

At this point in her career, Behn's literary reception can be analysed through a brief consideration of her association with Rochester, particularly following Rochester's death in 1680. After his death, Behn claimed a literary association with Rochester that was probably exaggerated: she stated that he had praised her poetry and helped her to improve it, although there is no direct evidence for this stemming from Rochester himself.[108] Rochester's allure, wit, and notoriety made him the most compelling of the Restoration rakes, and it has often been suggested that he was the model for the character of Willmore in *The Rover*. Behn wrote a commemorative poem, 'On the Death of the Late Earl of Rochester', which prompted a poem in reply from Rochester's niece Anne Wharton: 'To Mrs A. Behn on What She Writ of the Earl of Rochester'.[109] Wharton claims in her poem that Behn is her inspiration, but she also implicitly cautions Behn against what, by this stage of Behn's career, was a clear association with licentiousness: 'May yours excel the Matchless Sappho's name; | May you have all her Wit, without her Shame', and asking Behn to 'Scorn meaner Theams, declining low desire, | And bid your Muse maintain a vestal Fire' (243–4). Behn's response, 'To Mrs W. On her Excellent verses (Writ in Praise of Some I

106 *Ovid's Epistles Translated by Several hands* (1680), a4.
107 For an interesting account of Behn's translations see Elizabeth Spearing, 'Aphra Behn: The Politics of Translation', in Janet Todd, ed., *Aphra Behn Studies* (Cambridge: Cambridge University Press, 1996), 154–77.
108 For a full account, see Todd, *Secret Life*, 192–201.
109 Behn's poem was published in an anthology entitled *Miscellany* (1685); Wharton's was published in *A Collection of Poems by Several Hands* (1693), 242–4.

had made on the Earl of Rochester)', is a lurid evocation of the spirit of Rochester which essentially acts (via a compliment to Wharton) to endorse Behn's own poetic standing. Behn included part of this exchange in her miscellany *Lycidus* (1688), which, as Anne Russell suggests, was carefully designed to reinforce for the reader Behn's connections with Rochester and his niece.[110]

From Wharton's point of view, the fallout of this exchange was a tussle over propriety with Gilbert Burnet, who had extracted a conversion from Rochester on his deathbed, and who saw himself as moral arbiter of Rochester's memory, and of his surviving relatives. Burnet was horrified at the idea of Wharton exchanging poems and advice with the dissolute Behn: 'Some of Mrs Behn's songs are very tender; but she is so abominably vile a woman, and rallies not only all Religion but all vertue in so odious and obscene a manner, that I am . . . heartily sorry she had writ any thing in your commendation.'[111] Wharton's own literary career was cut short by her illness and early death, but Behn could be said to have had the victory over Burnet in this particular instance. At the same time, Behn was caught up in Rochester's currency in an even more interesting fashion when three substantial poems by her were printed in 'Rochester's' *Poems On Several Occasions* (1680). As a volume exploiting Rochester's posthumous reputation, this collection contained many poems misattributed (or cynically attributed) to him, and it could be seen as a further consolidation of Behn's reputation that 'The Disappointment', 'On a Juniper Tree', and 'On the Death of Mr Greenhill' were printed in the volume.[112] While it now seems obvious that 'The Disappointment' is a clever, female-centred version of the popular Restoration impotence poem, as written by misogynistic libertines like Rochester, it is understandable that a poem on such a subject could be attributed to Rochester because of its subject matter. When read as part of the 'Rochester' anthology, with a knowledge of Behn's authorship, it comes across as a knowing, wry commentary on masculine sexual pretensions such as those expressed in Rochester's own 'The Imperfect Enjoyment'. The volume also contains Rochester's 'Letter from Artemisia in Town to Chloe in the Country', with its casual put-down of women poets: '*Whore*, is scarce a more reproachful name | Than *Poetess*' (20).[113] Behn's three poems are placed about three-quarters of the way through the volume, and their more refined language certainly contrasts with the sexual explicitness and crude language, not to mention the misogyny, of most of the preceding poems (92–103). A version of 'A Session of the Poets' appears a few pages after Behn's poems, with, as noted above, at least an acknowledgement of Behn's literary achievements, even as it pokes fun at her faded charms (113).

[110] See Anne Russell, 'Aphra Behn's Miscellanies: The Politics and Poetics of Editing', *PQ* 77 (1998), 316–17.

[111] Gilbert Burnet, quoted in Todd, *Secret Life*, 263.

[112] See O'Donnell, *Bibliography*, BB4.1a.

[113] References to John Wilmot, *Poems On Several Occasions by the Right Honourable the E. of R——* ('Antwerp', 1680).

The success of the Rochester miscellany may well have prompted Behn to enter this promising marketplace with her own volume, using virtually the same title, *Poems Upon Several Occasions*, which she published in 1684. This was a substantial octavo volume that staked a strong claim for Behn's literary status, unlike the individual publication of the plays, a number of which were fairly poorly printed. *Poems Upon Several Occasions* has a quite sober, engraved portrait of Behn as its frontispiece. Behn dedicated the volume to the young James Cecil, Earl of Salisbury, clearly in the hope that she would gain something from him financially. As Janet Todd explains, this dedication provoked a satirical response from the anonymous author of 'A Satyre Against the Poets':

> Astrea with her soft gay Sighing Swains
> And rural virgins on the flowery Plains
> The lavish *Peers* profuseness may reprove
> Who gave her Guineas for the Isle of Love.[114]

The volume included Behn's fairly free translation of Tallemant's *Voyage de l'Isle d'Amour* (1663), which turned Tallemant's prose into verse. Given Behn's poverty at this time, it is notable that a letter from her to Jacob Tonson, the publisher of *Poems Upon Several Occasions*, has survived, in which she pleads for the value of her poetry ('I shou'd really have thought 'em worth thirty pound'), and begs for at least an extra five: 'good deare Mr. Tonson, let it be 5 pound more . . . I have been without getting so long that I am just upon the poynt of breaking, especially since a body has no credit at the Playhouse as we used to have, fifty or 60 deep.'[115] We do not know if Tonson was moved by this letter, and tossed an extra five pounds Behn's way. Tonson himself wrote one of the dedicatory poems to *Poems Upon Several Occasions*, along with ten others, most of them by unknown authors. The volume then contains forty-five of Behn's poems, including the three which had been published as Rochester's in the 1680 *Poems On Several Occasions*.


BEHN IN THE 1680S

By 1684 Behn's career in the theatre had, as her letter to Tonson makes clear, ceased to be profitable, although it was not at a complete end, mainly because there was now only one theatre company in London, and so the demand for new plays was diminished. *The Second Part of the Rover* was performed early in 1681 at a time of political uncertainty during the exclusion crisis, with James in exile, and Monmouth gaining in confidence. Behn threw in her lot with James, dedicating the play to him on its publication, and attacking the Whigs in her epilogue.[116]

---

[114] Todd, *Secret Life*, 326.      [115] Ibid. 324–5.

[116] For two important accounts of Behn's writing and views during this period, see Alison Shell, 'Popish Plots: *The Feign'd Courtizans* in Context', and Ros Ballaster, 'Fiction Feigning Femininity: False Counts and Pageant Kings in Aphra Behn's Popish Plot Writings', both in Todd, *Aphra Behn Studies*, 30–65.

Two of the four plays that Behn produced in 1681 and 1682 were more overtly political, and supported the Tory cause: *The Roundheads*, and *The City Heiress*. *The City Heiress* was particularly successful, and has been described by Derek Hughes as 'one of the masterpieces of restoration comedy'.[117] As Janet Todd notes, the success of *The City Heiress* provoked a number of (envious) satirical references to Behn, which tended to stress the sexually explicit nature of that play in particular, and relate that to Behn's supposedly dissolute character.[118] Robert Gould, in his fierce satire 'The Play House', holds Behn up to sarcastic ridicule, noting: 'that clean piece of wit, | The *City Heiress*, by *chast Sappho* writ, | Where the lewd *widow* comes, with brazen face, | Just reeking from a *Stallion*'s rank embrace'.[119]

Behn's turn to prose fiction was provoked, not by satire like Gould's, but by the continuing need to find new sources of revenue. At the same time, Behn was also clearly influenced by the vogue for fashionable French forms of prose fiction, and by the associated fascination with fiction as a means for representing current scandals. Paula Backscheider points out that Behn's attraction to fiction involved a political engagement, as well as an interest in a new form of literary expression.[120] In 1684 Behn wrote a novel in letters entitled *Love Letters between a Nobleman and his Sister*, which was based on a scandal involving Monmouth's supporter Lord Grey, who ran off with his sister-in-law, Lady Henrietta Berkeley. Grey was later implicated in the Rye House Plot, a pro-Monmouth plot to assassinate King Charles and his brother James. Janet Todd argues that Behn was commissioned to write *Love Letters*, but it is just as likely that she seized the chance to explore a new genre, cash in on a scandal, and contribute some timely propaganda for a probable reward.[121] Behn thinly disguised the origins of the story by setting it in France, but the relationship of her narrative to the details of the Grey scandal was crystal clear, and *Love Letters* was an immediate success. As well as the scandal, the appeal of the narrative stemmed from its erotic power; Behn is particularly adept at depicting Philander's passion for Silvia. Behn followed this volume up with a second part in 1685 and a third part, entitled *The Amours of Philander and Silvia*, in 1687. As Mary Ann O'Donnell explains, *Love Letters* was one of Behn's most popular works, running to eight editions by 1765.[122] Of course Behn did not benefit from the numerous posthumous editions of her work, and her increasing publication in a variety of genres underlines her desperate financial situation. She edited another anthology at this time, *Miscellany* (1685), which included ten of her own poems, and her translation of La Rochefoucauld, as well as a number of poems by 'marketable' figures like Rochester, Dorset, Etheredge, and Otway, as

[117] Hughes, *Theatre*, 147.
[118] See Todd, *Secret Life*, 287, citing in particular Wycherley's 'To the *Sappho* of the Age'.
[119] Robert Gould, *Poems* (1689), 173.
[120] See Backscheider's discussion of *Love Letters*, *Spectacular Politics*, 105–24.
[121] See Todd, *Secret Life*, 302.
[122] O'Donnell, *Bibliography*, 74.

well as poems by a number of women.[123] From a political perspective, the death of Charles and accession of James in 1685 led to a series of poems addressed to members of the royal family, a practice Behn continued through the turbulent events of the next few years, when finally, with the flight of James and the Glorious Revolution of 1688, she wrote a fascinating poem to Gilbert Burnet declining his suggestion that she should support the new regime with her pen.[124] Despite Behn's Tory credentials, and the poems she wrote to members of King James's household while he was on the throne, she seems not to have benefited materially in any substantial way from her loyalty.

Criticism of Behn's one successful play at this time, *The Lucky Chance*, which was performed in 1686, provoked her to write a much-quoted preface defending herself against the usual accusations of immorality and immodesty:

All I ask, is the priviledge for my Masculine Part the Poet in me (if any such you allow me) to tread in those successful Paths my Predecessors have so long thriv'd in . . . I am not content to write for a Third day only. I value Fame as much as if I had been born a *Hero* . . . (vii. 217)

Behn's confidence in her literary skills was undiminished, despite the uneven income provided by them. This is evident again in the preface to her translation of Fontenelle's *Entretiens sur la Pluralité des Mondes* (1686), published in 1688 as *A Discovery of New Worlds*. In the preface, Behn offers a detailed theory of prose translation, confidently explicates Fontenelle's scientific credentials, and satirically exposes the religious objections to Copernicus.[125] In the midst of the crisis of 1688, Behn published what was to be her most enduring work: *Oroonoko*. As noted above, Behn presents *Oroonoko* as an autobiographical account of her time in Surinam, but even if it is taken as based upon her experiences, the baroque tragedy of the enslaved Prince Oroonoko and his beloved Imoinda is an exemplary piece of fiction. Behn dedicated *Oroonoko* to Lord Maitland, a recent Catholic convert, and declared her own loyalty to the Catholic cause in a short passage which was quickly cancelled during the print-run, and which now exists only in a single copy in the Bodleian Library: 'Where is it amongst all our Nobility we shall find so great a Champion for the Catholick Church?'[126] The cancellation of this passage was a wise move, given that William of Orange was waiting in the wings for the chance to assume James's throne that was not long in coming. *Oroonoko* was a success, judging by its immediate reissue in the same year together with two other novellas, *The Fair Jilt* and *Agnes de Castro*, published as *Three Histories*.

When Behn died on 16 April, 1689, she had begun some sort of accommodation with the new regime with a congratulatory poem to Mary when she joined William

---

[123] See the discussion by Russell, 'Miscellanies', 310–15.
[124] *A Pindaric Poem to the Reverend Doctor Burnet* (1689).
[125] See the excellent account in Todd, *Secret Life*, 397–9.
[126] Quoted in O'Donnell, *Bibliography*, 130, *Oroonoko* (1688), A5v (Bodleian Library Vet.A.3. f.726).

in England. Some sense of her literary status is conveyed by her burial at Westminster Abbey, although it is worth pointing out that she was buried in the cloisters. Her simple memorial records only her date of death with the often-quoted couplet: 'Here lies a Proof that Wit can never be | Defence enough against Mortality'.

## BEHN'S POSTHUMOUS REPUTATION

Immediately following her death, Behn's literary reputation certainly made any unpublished works marketable, and 1690 saw the publication of *The Widdow Ranter*, a tragicomedy set at the time of Nathaniel Bacon's 1676 rebellion in Virginia, which had been performed in 1688. A number of earlier works were also reprinted at this time: *The Forc'd Marriage* in 1688 and 1690, *Abdelazar* in 1693, and *Love Letters* in 1693 and 1694. Behn's death was commemorated by a number of tributes. Dryden wrote a prologue and epilogue to *The Widdow Ranter*, which he had published separately. In the epilogue, Dryden offers some suggestive double entendres on the theme of the woman writer as object of sexual desire:

> Yet tho her Pen did to the Mark arrive,
> 'Twas common Praise, to please you, when alive;
> But of no other Woman, you have read.
> Except this one, to please you, now she's dead.[127]

A far more adulatory tribute was provided by a broadside elegy 'by a young lady of quality', which praises Behn as 'charming wise Astrea', and laments the death of the one woman who could outrank male writers:

> Our Sex for ever shall neglected lye;
> Aspiring Man has now regain'd the Sway
> To them we've left the Dismal Day:
> Astrea an equal Ballance held
> (Tho' she deserv'd it all).[128]

Whatever the worth of these tributes, Behn's stock rose most significantly when the dramatist Thomas Southerne turned to her fiction as a source for a series of successful plays. The search for plots led Restoration dramatists, including Behn herself, to find inspiration across a wide range of sources, a process which attracted the ire of Gerard Langbaine, who devoted a book to the practice: *Momus Triumphans: or, The Plagiaries of the English Stage* (1688). Southerne drew on *The Lucky Mistake* for his play *Sir Anthony Love* (1690), and then adapted *The History of the Nun* into *The Fatal Marriage* in 1694, but Southerne's greatest success was his adaptation of *Oroonoko* in 1695.[129] In his dedication,

[127] John Dryden, *The Prologue and Epilogue to the History of Bacon in Virginia* (1689), 4.

[128] *An Elegy Upon the death of Mrs. A. Behn* (1689).

[129] See Jacqueline Pearson's fascinating essay 'The History of *The History of the Nun*', in Heidi Hutner, ed., *Rereading Aphra Behn* (Charlottesville: University Press of Virginia, 1993), 234–52.

Southerne acknowledges his debt to Behn, and claims that her narrative should have been a play, so his actions in transforming her story are not merely justi-fied, but a worthy homage: 'She had a great Command of the Stage; and I have often wonder'd that she would bury her Favourite Hero in a Novel, when she might have reviv'd him in the Scene.'[130] Southerne goes on to imply that Behn's emotional involvement with Oroonoko meant that she was unable to do justice to his story: 'I have heard from a Friend of hers, That she always told his Story, more feelingly, than she writ it.'[131] Jane Spencer notes how this strategic move by Southerne establishes his 'rights' to Behn's story, especially given the signi-ficant changes he made to Behn's narrative—most particularly through making Imoinda white, rather than African.[132]

Paula Backscheider notes that the 1695–6 theatre season included plays by Delariviere Manley (two, in fact), Catherine Trotter, and Mary Pix, along with the first production of Behn's *The Younger Brother*.[133] Backscheider sees the plays by Pix, Manley, and Trotter as reflecting the lead Behn showed in writing for the stage, describing her as 'a shining signpost'.[134] Behn had become valued commer-cially as well at this time, which led to a series of collections of her work. These collections offer a range of very complex printings, reprintings, and rearrange-ments, and it is fortunate that Mary Ann O'Donnell has produced an exemplary bibliography for Behn which sorts out this complex textual history; while I will sum up the situation here, O'Donnell should be consulted for the full biblio-graphical picture.[135]

In 1696 Samuel Briscoe published a collection entitled *The Histories and Novels of the Late Ingenious Mrs Behn*. This collection consists of reissues of *Oroonoko*, *The Fair Jilt*, *Agnes de Castro*, and *The Lover's Watch*, but adds *The Lucky Mistake*, and a supposedly authentic series of love letters written by Behn. Much discus-sion has centred on the part played by Charles Gildon, Tom Brown, and Briscoe in the posthumous publication of fiction by Behn. Doubt has been cast on the authenticity of many of the posthumous works of fiction, with Germaine Greer

---

[130] Thomas Southerne, *Oroonoko* (1696), A2v; see also the edition of *Oroonoko*, ed. Maximillian E. Novak and David Rhodes (London: Edward Arnold, 1976), esp. pp. xxxvi–xlii.

[131] Southerne, A2v.

[132] Spencer, *Afterlife*, 131–3; as I will only be offering a brief account of the history of *Oroonoko*'s reception and transformations, it is worth noting here the growing body of critical material which looks at *Oroonoko* in a colonial context; as well as Spencer's invaluable account of *Oroonoko* in the eighteenth century (see ch. 6), see esp. Joyce Green MacDonald, 'The Disappearing African Woman: Imoinda in Oroonoko after Behn', *ELH* 66 (1999), 71–86; and perhaps the most sophisticated account in these terms is Margaret W. Ferguson's in *Dido's Daughters: Literacy, Gender, and Empire in Early Modern England and France* (Chicago: University of Chicago Press, 2003), ch. 7.

[133] Backscheider, *Spectacular Politics*, 71.

[134] Ibid. 82; see also the more detailed account of Behn's later image in Jacqueline Pearson, *The Prostituted Muse: Images of Women and Women Dramatists 1642–1737* (Brighton: Harvester, 1988).

[135] See O'Donnell, *Bibliography*, pt 1 *passim*.

in particular arguing for Gildon and Brown's authorship, while Behn's editor, Janet Todd, is more inclined to allow for Behn's possible authorship.[136] For my purposes here, the question of authenticity is not important, because what these collections represent is the exploitation of Behn's authorial signature, which had commercial value. This is why the Briscoe collections, as well as printing and reprinting material by Behn, also provide increasing biographical material (again, much of it of questionable authenticity) *about* Behn. This is underlined on the title page of the 1696 collection: 'Together with the life and memoirs of Mrs Behn written by one of the fair Sex'. As Robert Adams Day revealed in a careful disentanglement published in 1969, the 1696 biography was expanded in further reissues up until 1705, when a process of expansion that was largely fictional came to an end.[137] Again, the most interesting aspect of this situation, for my purposes, is not the accuracy of the biographical details, but the fact that Behn's editors saw that there was a market that would appreciate the maximum amount of biographical material—as well, of course, as appreciating the apparently expanding amount of new material written by Behn that was being unearthed (or provided). As Jeslyn Medoff explains, the biographical approach to Behn from 1696 to the early eighteenth century was tied to a key moment in the construction of the literary biography as a genre, as well as to a set of attitudes towards the 'marketing' of Behn as an author.[138]

The 1696 edition prints Behn's 'love letters' to Lycidus at the end of the volume, titled 'Love letters by Mrs A. Behn'. Once again, scholars are not in agreement about the authenticity of these letters, but they are significant because they offer the reader a supposedly intimate access to Behn's love life, given that Behn was seen as a sexually daring (not to say potentially scandalous and shocking) writer. In 1698 Gildon and Briscoe produced an expanded collection entitled *All the Histories and Novels*, and on the title page underlined the expanded material related to Behn's own love life: 'Together with the history of the life and memoirs of Mrs Behn. Never before printed. By one of the fair Sex. Intermix'd with Pleasant Love-Letters that pass'd betwixt her and Minheer van bruin, a Dutch Merchant; with her Character of the Country and Lover: And her Love-letters to a gentleman in England'.[139] Gildon wrote a new dedication (to Simon Scroop) for this expanded edition, citing his 'esteem' (A2) for Behn's memory as his motivation. In this edition, the biography, only eighteen pages in 1696, grows to sixty pages, and three new novellas are added.

---

[136] See Greer, *Slip-Shod Sibyls*, 196; Todd, *Secret Life*, 315–18; and the lively round table discussion from a 1999 Sorbonne conference on Behn, published as part of the conclusion to Mary Ann O'Donnell *et al.*, eds., *Aphra Behn (1640–1689): Identity, Alterity, Ambiguity* (Paris: L'Harmattan, 2000), 187–92.

[137] Robert Adams Day, 'Aphra Behn's First Biography', *Studies in Bibliography*, 22 (1969), 227–40.

[138] Jeslyn Medoff, ' "Very Like a Fiction": Some Early Biographies of Aphra Behn', in Smith and Appelt, *Write or be Written*, 247–69; see also Spencer, *Afterlife*, 32–43.

[139] This is O'Donnell, *Bibliography*, A40.3a.

Gildon had clearly hit upon the perfect formula to appeal to readers who were interested in Behn herself, and in her fiction. There were editions and reissues of the collection in 1699, 1700, 1705, 1718, 1732, 1735, and 1751. Briscoe also published a number of other small collections of Behn's fiction in the late 1690s, and these works were then reissued as part of the larger collections. At the same time, the success of Behn's fiction prompted the issue of collections of her plays as well, starting in 1702 with fifteen plays in two volumes published by Richard Wellington, with a second edition in 1716, and a third in 1724. In 1711 Wellington reissued this edition of the plays together with the 1705 edition of the histories and novels as *The Works of Mrs Behn*.[140]

Behn's poetry was also popular during this period. *Poems Upon Several Occasions* was reissued together with *Lycidus* in 1697. Colman and Thornton, in *Poems by Eminent Ladies* (1755), reprinted *A Voyage to the Island of Love* together with a large selection of Behn's poems from *Poems Upon Several Occasions*. As Margaret Ezell notes, later editions of Coleman and Thornton continued to offer this generous selection of Behn's poetry until, with the 1780 edition, the selection from Behn was cut to four poems only.[141]

Behn's general fortunes in the eighteenth century are the subject of Jane Spencer's fine study, *Aphra Behn's Afterlife*, and, given the detail in Spencer's study, I offer only the briefest of summaries here.[142] Spencer paints a much more complex picture of Behn's status in the eighteenth century than previous accounts, noting particularly how attitudes towards her intersected with realignments of women writers and notions of popular literature. The trajectory is different for each of Behn's major genres: poetry, drama, and fiction. In particular, Spencer explains that while Behn's fiction was increasingly despised as scandalous and outmoded, her plays, especially *The Rover*, were accorded much more respect, even when they were criticized (ch. 2). In publication terms, however, Spencer notes that the collections of Behn's fiction were unique (as opposed to collections of plays), and they clearly encouraged the marketing of other novelists in a similar fashion (89). *Love Letters* was also extremely popular in the eighteenth century, and was, Spencer notes, 'instrumental in establishing Behn in the eighteenth-century mind as an erotic novelist' (89). At the same time, eighteenth-century novelists, especially Richardson, sought to define themselves against their scandalous precursors, Behn, Manley, and Haywood.[143] By the end of the eighteenth century, as the novel established its respectability, Behn's fiction (with the exception of *Oroonoko*) had dropped out of the canon (96).

[140] See Spencer, *Afterlife*, 83.

[141] See Margaret Ezell, *Writing Women's Literary History* (Baltimore: Johns Hopkins University Press, 1993), 112–16.

[142] Spencer, *Afterlife, passim*, further references in parentheses; and see also Janet Todd, *The Critical Fortunes of Aphra Behn* (Columbia, Mo.: Camden House, 1998), ch. 3.

[143] See Ros Ballaster, *Seductive Forms: Women's Amatory Fiction from 1684 to 1740* (Oxford: Clarendon Press, 1992); William Warner, *Licensing Entertainment: The Elevation of Novel Reading in Britain 1684–1750* (Berkeley: University of California Press, 1998).

Spencer also explains how *The Rover*, while remaining a successful and popular part of the dramatic repertoire during the eighteenth century, was significantly altered as time went by, culminating in Kemble's 1790 version retitled *Love in Many Masks* (187–222). This process involved 'a male centred *Rover*, softening Behn's mocking view of her hero' (221); but while the process helped secure the play's success, by the time of Kemble's version, its long run finally ended, and it was not performed again until John Barton's Royal Shakespeare Company adaptation in 1986 (221). Parallel to *The Rover*, *Oroonoko* kept Behn visible, not only through performances of Southerne's dramatic adaptation, and through its associations with Behn's purported biography, but also through the use of *Oroonoko* by the abolitionist movement in various ways (223–5). Spencer explains how this association of *Oroonoko* with anti-slavery sentiment occurred at the expense of Behn's role as author and narrator. The 1745 French translation of *Oroonoko* was extremely popular throughout the eighteenth century, but, as Spencer explains, like Southerne, it was an adaptation that diminished the role of the narrator, made Imoinda white (or at least of mixed race), reduced the anti-slavery implications, and even provided a happy ending, with Oroonoko and Imoinda alive and reunited (240–3). In contrast, in England after 1760, adaptations of Southerne moved the dramatic version of *Oroonoko* back in the direction of anti-slavery sentiments (244).

In general, then, Behn remained a highly visible author in the eighteenth century, even if her literary reputation declined somewhat. Compared to most of the other early modern women writers discussed in this book, Behn remained visible throughout the nineteenth century, particularly thanks to the prominence of versions of *Oroonoko*. Behn retained some admirers, even as they had to deal with her ever more alienating Restoration literary conventions, and apparent licentiousness. Dyce notes the 'grossness' of Behn's plays, but praises the liveliness of her poetry, and includes eight poems, mostly lyrics from plays. Wordsworth had an intermittent correspondence with Dyce over his anthology, contrasting Dyce's volume with Colman and Thornton, with particular reference to Behn, 'from whose attempts they are miserably copious'—which implies that Dyce's eight poems were quite enough.[144] In contrast, Leigh Hunt admired Behn's poetry as he encountered it in Dyce, and began a tradition which reached as far as Virginia Woolf in singling out 'Love in Fantastic Triumph Sat' for special praise.[145]

By the mid-nineteenth century, Behn's poetry was generally seen as unfeminine. As Janet Todd outlines, Behn was excluded from Bethune's *The British Female Poets* (1848); on the other hand, Rowton's *Female Poets of Great Britain* (1848) includes a small selection and, despite Rowton's hesitation over Behn

---

[144] *Letters of William and Dorothy Wordsworth*, ed. Ernest de Selincourt, rev. Alan G. Hill (Oxford: Clarendon Press, 1979), v. 236 (Letter 521).
[145] Leigh Hunt, 'Specimens of British Poetesses', quoted in Todd, *Critical Fortunes*, 45.

as an individual, he finds a fair amount to praise in her poems, even if he also constantly underlines her coarseness and dubious morality.[146] Perhaps the most interesting account of Behn in the nineteenth century occurs in Julia Kavanagh's *English Women of Letters* (1863). Kavanagh devotes two chapters to Behn; the first is a sustained lament for Behn's coarseness and lack of refinement, and Kavanagh decries the waste of Behn's talents. However, as Janet Todd points out, 'Kavanagh is one of the few commentators of the Victorian age to note Behn's extraordinary range.'[147] As Todd notes, Kavanagh's second chapter, centred on *Oroonoko*, offers something of a vindication, praising *Oroonoko* as 'one of the first great works of English fiction' and offering copious illustrations from the text.[148] Kavanagh's conflicted view of Behn is not surprising, given her strong focus on the morality (from a Victorian perspective) of women writers, and Kavanagh's study certainly influenced later evaluations of Behn, including those set up in opposition to her, as we will see below with Vita Sackville-West.

Given the sheer quantity of Behn's literary output, it is worth noting how much more accessible her work has been in the nineteenth and twentieth centuries, in comparison to virtually all the others writers I have discussed so far. In 1871 an edition of Behn's works was published by John Pearson in six volumes. This Pearson edition was essentially a reproduction of the 1724 edition of the plays, and the 1735 edition of the prose, without the poetry, and without any new introduction or notes.[149] This edition was attacked as 'literary garbage' in the *Saturday Review*, and, albeit in slightly less extreme language, in *The Athenaeum*.[150] Pearson wrote letters in reply to both reviews and then in 1872 published a volume entitled *Two Centuries of Testimony in Favour of Mrs Aphra Behn*, which excerpts a series of favourable reflections from the seventeenth century through to Swinburne's 1868 praise of Behn's poetry in his study of William Blake.[151] Pearson may not have shifted Victorian opinion in Behn's favour, but he at least allowed those who were interested easy access to her work.

Pearson did not, on the other hand, offer an edition of Behn comparable to the many Victorian editions of 'minor' sixteenth- and seventeenth-century writers produced by figures such as Edmund Gosse. For such an edition, Behn had to wait until the early twentieth century, when Montague Summers edited her works in six volumes for Heinemann. Summers combined a fascination for Restoration drama with a fascination for the occult, and he marks a transition in culture where Behn's reputation for moral laxity became, at least for some groups of people, a drawcard rather than a drawback. Setting aside the fascinations of Summers's personal life, and exotic pursuits (a vivid picture of him is provided below by Vita Sackville-West), he produced an edition which remains useful, if at times

[146] Todd, *Critical Fortunes*, 45–7.     [147] Ibid. 49.     [148] Ibid. 50.
[149] O'Donnell, *Bibliography*, 154.
[150] Ibid. 155–9 and see the discussion in Todd, *Critical Fortunes*, 57–8.
[151] O'Donnell, *Bibliography*, 149.

eccentric.[152] Summers offered a partial collation of Behn's texts, and some limited annotation, providing an edition far in advance of anything enjoyed by the other writers discussed here so early in the twentieth century. Summers also produced his edition at the very moment when Behn criticism came to be dominated by questions of biography, stimulated by Ernest Bernbaum's 1913 *PMLA* article, 'Mrs Behn's Biography a Fiction'. Bernbaum disputed Behn's stay in Surinam, and responses to this and other biographical issues have threatened to overwhelm treatments of Behn's work until very recently—Behn has been the subject of no fewer than three twentieth-century biographies, which until a fairly short time ago outnumbered critical books on her writing. Summers does offer a biographical introduction to his edition, but also judiciously places Behn's plays in the context of other Restoration drama. Summers offers what was to become a familiar turn of phrase in describing Behn's literary efforts: 'We cannot but admire the courage of this lonely woman, who, poor and friendless, was the first in England to turn to the pen for her livelihood, and not only won herself bread but no mean position in the world of her day and English literature of all time.'[153]

## BEHN AND BLOOMSBURY

In Chapter 4 I outlined the way that Vita Sackville-West responded to the early diary of her ancestor, Anne Clifford, and in turn aroused Virginia Woolf's interest in Clifford. Sackville-West's engagement with the work of Aphra Behn produced a more complicated relationship with Woolf's literary interests. Woolf's most famous statement about Behn, made in *A Room of One's Own*, was: 'All women together ought to let flowers fall upon the tomb of Aphra Behn, which is, most scandalously but rather appropriately, in Westminster Abbey, for it was she who earned them the right to speak their minds.'[154] However, Woolf saw Behn, not really as a writer, but as a pathfinder, as she makes clear in the earlier backhanded compliment that:

She made, by working very hard, enough to live on. The importance of that fact outweighs anything she actually wrote, even the splendid 'A thousand Martyrs I have made', or 'Love in Fantastic Triumph sat', for here begins the freedom of the mind.[155]

Here Woolf is echoing Sackville-West's summation of Behn in the study of her she wrote in 1927.[156] Sackville-West's words are: 'The fact that she wrote

---

[152] For Summers's literary and personal interests, see Frederick S. Frank, *Montague Summers: A Bibliographical Portrait* (Metuchen: Scarecrow Press, 1988), and Timothy D'Arch Smith, *The Books of the Beast* (London: Crucible, 1987).

[153] *The Works of Aphra Behn*, ed. Montague Summers (1915; repr. New York: Phaeton, 1967), i, p. lvii.

[154] Virginia Woolf, *A Room of One's Own* (Harmondsworth: Penguin, 1928; rpt. 1972), 66.

[155] Ibid. 64.

[156] I am very grateful to Sophie Tomlinson for drawing the echo to my attention. Sackville-West wrote her study of Behn between June and August, 1927 and it was published in September; Woolf

is much more important than the quality of what she wrote. The importance of
Aphra Behn is that she was the first woman in England to earn her living by her
pen.'[157] It is significant that Woolf's comment singles out two of Behn's lyrics,
ignoring her career as a dramatist. Behn's writing and Behn's character did not
appeal to Woolf, but they raised Sackville-West's admiration and, once again, a
certain identification. In a letter written to Woolf on 4 August 1927, Sackville-
West wrote: 'A course of Mrs A.B. has turned me into the complete ruffling rake.
No more than Mrs A.B. do I relish, or approve of, chastity.'[158]

    Sackville-West wrote a book on Aphra Behn as part of a series entitled 'Repres-
entative Women', edited by Francis Birrell. The series included an eclectic mix of
subjects, ranging from Lady Hester Stanhope to Mary Shelley. As the statement
to Virginia Woolf makes clear, Sackville-West revelled in Behn's dubious reputation, beginning her book with a quotation emphasizing Behn's sexual allure: 'with
her neck and breasts bare' (13). Behn is seductive; Sackville-West is a 'ruffling
rake' who is clearly attracted to her. Sackville-West visited Montague Summers
for advice on Behn, and records her reaction in a letter to Harold Nicolson:

I went to lunch with the priest. Talk about Clive [Bell] having a Restoration appearance!
It is nothing to the Rev. Summers. Dressed in black, hung with amethyst crosses and
bits of jet, black suede shoes, fat white hands, a fat dimpled face, oiled black curls, very
carefully disposed—he is just like a Lely. He gave me a very good lunch and lots of
information, then when I asked him to tell me the way, he said he would come to the end
of the street, and put on a top-hat with a curly brim, and black silk gloves. You never saw
such an old sod in all your life.[159]

    A suggestive intersection is set up between the alluring but morally dubious
Aphra Behn, and her 'old sod' of an editor. But it is also important to point
out that Sackville-West's book on Behn is not just a subjective and impression-
istic appreciation, but is, in fact, an impressive study, especially when placed in
its historical context. For example, Sackville-West tackles the obsession with the
'authenticity' of *Oroonoko* with excellent judgement, arguing specifically that it is

---

delivered the Cambridge lectures on which she based *A Room of One's Own* in October 1928. Woolf
had suggested to Sackville-West on 22 Aug. 1927 that she would review Sackville-West's book, and,
while no review seems to have been written, it seems likely that Woolf read the book some time
in 1927; see *A Change of Perspective: Letters of Virginia Woolf*, iii. *1923–1929*, ed. Nigel Nicolson
(London: Hogarth Press, 1977), 411. In the first draft of *A Room*, written between March and April
1929, Woolf acknowledges the prior statement of the idea without naming Sackville-West: 'she was,
it is said, the first woman to make money by her writing', see Virginia Woolf, *Women & Fiction:
The Manuscript Versions of A Room of One's Own*, ed. S. P. Rosenbaum (Oxford: Shakespeare Head
Press, 1992), 97; Rosenbaum notes Sackville-West as a source, see 211.

[157] Vita Sackville-West, *Aphra Behn* (London: Gerald Howe, 1927), 12, further references in
parentheses.

[158] Victoria Glendinning, *Vita: The Life of V. Sackville-West* (London: Weidenfeld and Nicolson,
1988), 169, dates this letter Nov. 1926; it is dated 1927 in Louise de Salvo and Mitchell Leaska,
eds., *The Letters of Vita Sackville-West to Virginia Woolf* (London: Hutchinson, 1984).

[159] Nigel Nicolson, ed., *Vita and Harold: The Letters of Vita Sackville-West and Harold Nicolson*
(Stroud: Phoenix, 1992), 237.

surely worth considering a *via media* on the Surinam question by accepting the evidence that Behn went there, but at the same time seeing the actual narrative of Oroonoko's deeds as largely a fiction. Sackville-West astutely notes the parallels between the establishment of verisimilitude in *Oroonoko* and in *The Fair Jilt*, and sees how Behn creates an autobiographical voice in much of her fiction (45–6).

No stranger to exotic settings, thanks in particular to her trips to Harold Nicolson's diplomatic postings in Constantinople and Tehran, Sackville-West appreciated Behn's treatment of Surinam. Sackville-West's evocation of Oroonoko and Imoinda might seem as alien to current sensibilities as Behn's depiction of them, but she attempts to position Behn's use of romance in relation to some sense of a colonial past—she also points out how it is misleading to try to read *Oroonoko* as an anti-slavery text.

Sackville-West offers a similarly vivid account of Behn's return to London in 1667 after her spying mission to the Netherlands. At this pivotal point in her life, when Behn 'chooses' 'Pleasure and Poetry' as her vocation, Sackville-West is wholly sympathetic:

Sensible Astrea. Miss Julia Kavanagh, writing in 1863, thought otherwise. But Astrea, living in 1670, knew that her two great assets were her charm and her pen, and she had no scruples about using both to procure for herself the comfort, fun, and popularity that she desired. (83)

Sackville-West saw 1928 as being more like 1670 than it was like 1863, and her own semi-rebellious life demonstrated this. Accordingly, for Sackville-West, Behn represented a certain kind of sexual freedom: 'She prized freedom, and constantly and gaily advocated that the heart should bestow itself where it listed' (84). But Sackville-West is adamant in her defence of Behn against narrow-minded critics who accuse her of immorality, and she distinguishes carefully between Behn's sexuality and what she calls her 'fundamental honesty and idealism' (91). Here again one can detect considerable identification on Sackville-West's part, as she constructs a complex portrait of Behn as, at a certain level, 'dissolute' and even 'pornographic', but also 'an exceedingly moral and idealistic writer' (92). Sackville-West particularly admires Behn's honesty and her attacks on hypocrisy.

However, like Woolf, Sackville-West has a fairly low opinion of Behn's writing: 'given her natural talent, [she] prodigally wasted her opportunities' (138). At the heart of this criticism is an impatience with some of the conventions of Restoration fiction, and Sackville-West laments the absence of a realist narrative that few Restoration readers desired; at least Sackville-West's formulation of this is memorable: 'We might have had the mother of Moll Flanders, and all we get is the bastard of Mademoiselle de Scudéry' (139). At the end of her study, Sackville-West frankly (and characteristically) admits :

She is an example, we conclude, of those writers who perversely mistake their vocation. So be it. In the course of these three months spent in her company, it is Aphra the woman of whom I have grown fond, to the extent of forgiving Aphra the writer the tedious hours she has compelled me to spend over her volumes. (163)

When Virginia Woolf searched through her sources to find women who might be precursors, she did so deliberately, and ultimately in order to make tough-minded use of them as examples within her general argument. Sackville-West may have agreed with Woolf that Behn's writing did not really stand up to close scrutiny, but she was prepared to immerse herself in Behn's writing, and she emerged as a fervent admirer of Behn as a woman with whom she identified in many ways. The synergy between Woolf and Sackville-West was particularly manifested in relation to both Behn, and, as we have seen in Chapter 4, Anne Clifford, who were certainly seen by Sackville-West as alter egos. Indeed, I would go so far as to argue that Sackville-West's study of Behn was something of a gauntlet flung down before Woolf at a particularly difficult moment in their relationship: just as she was telling Woolf that Behn had turned her into a rake, Woolf was warning Sackville-West 'you'll be tired of me one of these days (I'm so much older) and so I have to take my little precautions', and going on to assess Sackville-West as ultimately unresponsive: 'There's something that doesn't vibrate in you.'[160] Sackville-West certainly vibrated to Aphra Behn, and it is frustrating that we have no evidence of Woolf's response to Sackville-West's book on Behn. It seems to me that the book was, indirectly, a reply to Woolf's accusation.


## SINNER AND SAINT

Sackville-West's view of Behn in the 1920s begins a process of recuperation that valued, rather than denigrated, Behn's sexuality. But on the whole, the critical response to Behn in recent years has been concerned to establish her serious political credentials, while placing less emphasis on her erotic writing, which in itself now seems far from challenging.[161] In parallel to this process, criticism of Katherine Philips has tended to emphasize the erotic nature of the friendship poems, though it too has tackled Philips as a political writer. It seems to me that for some time now many critics have preferred early modern women writers to be sinners, rather than saints.[162] I want to return to the issue of historical perspective in my conclusion.

[160] Glendinning, *Vita*, 169.
[161] See e.g. Chalmers, *Royalist Women Writers*, ch. 4: '"Secret Instructions": Aphra Behn's Negotiations of the Political Marketplace'; for an overview of the history of Behn criticism, see Todd, *Critical Fortunes, passim*.
[162] *Pace* Jonathan Goldberg's claim in *Desiring Women Writing: Renaissance Examples* (Stanford, Calif.: Stanford University Press, 1997); see my detailed discussion of Goldberg in the Introduction.

# Conclusion

I have explored three key aspects of early modern women's writing in this book. In my first chapter, I attempted an overview of women's writing from around 1550 to 1700. This overview was intended to orient the reader, and at the same time explore just how diverse both the writing, and the women who produced it, were. While not intended to be a history as such, that chapter did analyse how interactions between women writers changed over time, and it emphasized not only the range of the writing itself, but also the intersections of print and manuscript circulation.

The case studies following Chapter 1 illustrate both how early modern women's writing was produced, circulated, and responded to at the time it was written, and also how it was reproduced, recirculated, and commented on by succeeding generations of readers, editors, and scholars. My case studies underline the great range of writing and writers mentioned in Chapter 1, including genres as diverse as prophecies, family histories, and poetry, and writers ranging in status from Queen Elizabeth 'down' as far as Anna Trapnel or Aphra Behn. My inspiration for this approach has been the recent interest in the history of reading. In early modern studies, this has resulted in books from the perspective of historical approaches, such as Kevin Sharpe's in *Reading Revolutions*, through to studies of specific works or authors, such as Lori Humphrey Newcomb's history of Robert Greene's *Pandosto*, or Anna Beer's study of seventeenth-century readers of Walter Ralegh.[1] In this book, I have taken 'reading' in its widest possible sense to include elements of book history, bibliography, and cultural and critical history.

All such recuperative histories of reading press against a history of forgetting. This is particularly acute in relation to the different strands of early modern women's writing, where in some cases feminist scholarship really did recover an author or text from centuries of silence (for example, Isabella Whitney), but in many cases, there has been a tendency to project forgetfulness onto the reception history. I believe that this occurs, not simply when we overlook the life this writing had in the seventeenth, eighteenth, and nineteenth centuries, but also when we dismiss the supposed limitations of the commentary, annotation, marginalia, and remarks of earlier generations. For example, in my last chapter, I quoted

---

[1] Kevin Sharpe, *Reading Revolutions: The Politics of Reading in Early Modern England* (New Haven: Yale University Press, 2000); Anna R. Beer, *Sir Walter Ralegh and his Readers in the Seventeenth Century* (London: Macmillan, 1997); Lori Humphrey Newcomb, *Reading Popular Romance in Early Modern England* (New York: Columbia University Press, 2002).

Vita Sackville-West's dismissal of Julia Kavanagh's opinion of Aphra Behn. Ironically, Sackville-West's own study of Behn is now largely ignored. It is easy to
show one's apparent superiority to Kavanagh's Victorian account of Behn, or
indeed to Sackville-West's 1920s book. I have tried to avoid scoring easy points
at the expense of earlier writers, and instead I have endeavoured to underline the
fact that, for many early modern women writers, there has been a rich and diverse
history of reception and transmission across succeeding generations.

So, to return to the question I asked in my preface: were they that name?
That is, is it possible to approach early modern women's writing without falling
into either a monolithic notion of fixed identity or, alternatively, an overwhelm-
ing sense of inchoate and unconnected texts? Is early modern women's writing
simply a heuristic category? The answer varies according to the context of both
time, and the nature of the writers, but it is certainly true to say that in the course
of the seventeenth century more and more women saw themselves as 'women
writers'. At the same time, as scholars unearth still increasing amounts of manuscript material, it is clear that early modern women's writing had an enormous
range of projected and actual readers, from immediate family members through
to the powerful women whose patronage was sought by a writer like Aemilia
Lanyer. As my case studies have shown, readers varied from small circles of initiates, such as Anna Trapnel's followers towards the end of the 1660s, to the wider
(and suitably scandalized) public that read Mary Wroth's *Urania*. Some writers,
like Anne Clifford, attempted to exert maximum control over their readers; others were prepared to publish and let the market decide. Some manuscript material
had wide circulation, while some remained within the confines of the writer's
family. We may read these works with a difference, but there were always readers for early modern women's writing, and by 1679 Ephelia could claim, with
something approaching insouciance,

> To see such things flow from a Womans Pen,
> As might be Envy'd by the wittiest Men[2]

----

[2] *Female Poems on Several Occasions* (1679), 72.

# Bibliography

## 1. EARLY MODERN WOMEN'S WRITING

### A. Manuscripts

Beineke Library, Yale University, Osborn MS b. 233: Elizabeth Brackley and Jane Cheney, 'Concealed Fancies'.

Bodleian Library MS Ballard 74.

Bodleian Library MS Digby 138.

Bodleian Library MS Rawlinson D78 (Diary of Elizabeth Delavel).

Bodleian Library MS Rawlinson D1262 and D1263 (Diary of Anne Bathurst).

Bodleian Library MS Rawlinson Poet. 16: Elizabeth Brackley and Jane Cheney, 'Poems'.

Bodleian Library MSS Rawlinson Poet. 65, 90, 108.

British Library Additional MS 27351–5 (Diary of Mary Rich).

British Library MS Royal 15Aix.

British Library MSS Harley 6177, 6933, 7392.

Cumbrian Records Office, Kendal, WD/Hoth, Hothfield Manuscripts.

Folger Library MS V.b.317.

Huntington Library MS HM 600.

Inner Temple Library MS Petyt 538, vol .10.

Leeds University, Brotherton Library MS Lt q 32: Hester Poulter, 'Poems Breathed Forth by the Nobel Hadassas'.

Longleat House, Portland Papers MS vol .23.

National Library of Wales MS 21867B.

National Library of Wales MS 775B (Tutin Manuscript).

National Library of Wales MS 776B (Rosania Manuscript).

University of Texas, Austin, Dering MS.


### B. Printed Sources

ASTELL, MARY, *A Serious Proposal to the Ladies* (1694).

BARKER, JANE, *Poetical Recreations: Consisting of Original Poems, Songs, Odes, &c. with Several New Translations* (1688).

———, *The Galesia Trilogy and Selected Manuscript Poems of Jane Barker*, ed. Carol Shiner Wilson (New York: Oxford University Press, 1997).

BATHURST, ELIZABETH, *An Expository Appeal to the Professors of Christianity* (1678).

BEAUMONT, AGNES, *The Narrative of the Persecutions of Agnes Beaumont*, ed. Vera J. Camden (East Lansing, Mich.: Colleagues Press, 1992).

BEHN, APHRA, *A Discovery of New Worlds* (1688).

———, *Love Letters Between a Nobleman and his Sister* (1684, part two, 1685, *Amours of Philander and Sylvia*, 1687).

———, *Lycidus* (1688).

———, *Oroonoko* (1688).

———, *Poems Upon Several Occasions* (1684).

BEHN, APHRA, *The Histories and Novels of the Late Ingenious Mrs Behn* (London: Samuel Briscoe, 1696).

_____, *The Works of Aphra Behn*, ed. Montague Summers, 6 vols. (London: Heinemann, 1915).

_____, *The Works of Aphra Behn*, ed. Janet Todd, 7 vols. (London: Pickering, 1992–6).

BIDDLE, HESTER, *Woe to the Town of Cambridge* (1655).

_____, *Woe to Thee City of Oxford* (1655).

BRACKLEY, ELIZABETH [Egerton], *Subordination and Authorship in Early Modern England: The Case of Elizabeth Cavendish Egerton and her 'Loose Papers'*, ed. Betty S. Travitsky (Tempe: Arizona Center for Medieval and Renaissance Studies, 1999).

BRADSTREET, ANNE, *The Tenth Muse* (1650).

_____, *The Poems of Mrs Anne Bradstreet*, ed. Frank E. Hopkins (New York: Duodecimo, 1897).

_____, *The Works of Anne Bradstreet*, ed. Jeannine Hensley (Cambridge, Mass.: Harvard University Press, 1967).

_____, *The Works of Anne Bradstreet in Prose and Verse*, ed. John Harvard Ellis (Charleston, SC: Abram E. Cutter, 1867).

_____, *The Complete Works of Anne Bradstreet*, ed. Joseph McElrath and Allan Robb (Boston: Twayne, 1981).

CARY, ELIZABETH, *The Tragedy of Mariam* (1613); see editions by A. C. Dunstan and W. W. Greg (London: Malone Society, 1914); Diane Purkiss (London: Pickering, 1994); Barry Weller and Margaret W. Ferguson (Berkeley: University of California Press, 1994); and Stephanie Wright (Keele: Keele University Press, 1996).

CAVENDISH, MARGARET, *De Vita et Rebus Gestis Nobilissimi Illustrissimique Principis Guilielmi Ducis*, trans. Walter Charleton (1668).

_____, *Grounds of Natural Philosophy* (1668).

_____, *Life of . . . William Cavendish* (1667); ed. C. H. Firth (1886, 2nd edn., 1916).

_____, *Nature's Pictures Drawn by Fancy's Pencil To The Life* (1656).

_____, *Observations Upon Experimental Philosophy* (1666).

_____, *Orations* (1662).

_____, *Philosophical and Physical Opinions* (1655).

_____, *Philosophical Opinions* (1653).

_____, *Plays* (1662).

_____, *Poems and Fancies* (1653).

_____, *Sociable Letters*, ed. James Fitzmaurice (Toronto: Broadview, 2004).

_____, *A True Relation*, ed. Egerton Brydges (Lee Priory, 1814).

_____, *The World's Olio* (1655).

_____, *The Convent of Pleasure and Other Plays*, ed. Anne Shaver (Baltimore: Johns Hopkins University Press, 1999).

_____, *Bell in Campo and The Sociable Companions*, ed. Alexandra G. Bennett (Peterborough: Broadview Press, 2002).

_____, *Selected Poems of Margaret Cavendish Duchess of Newcastle*, ed. Egerton Brydges (Lee Priory, 1813).

CERASANO, S. P., and WYNNE-DAVIES, MARION, eds., *Renaissance Drama by Women: Texts and Documents* (London: Routledge, 1996).

CLIFFORD, ANNE, *The Diary of Anne Clifford 1616–1619: A Critical Edition*, ed. Katherine O. Acheson (New York: Garland, 1995).

_____ , *The Diaries of Anne Clifford*, ed. D. J. H. Clifford (Stroud: Sutton, 1990).

CLINTON, ELIZABETH, *The Countesse of Lincoln's Nursery* (1622).

*Collection of Letters and Poems, A* (1678).

*A Collection of Poems by Several Hands* (1693).

COLLINS, AN, *Divine Songs* (1653).

COTTON, PRISCILLA, and COLE, MARY, *To the Priests and People of England* (1655).

DAVIES, ELEANOR, *Prophetic Writings of Lady Eleanor Davies*, ed. Esther S. Cope (New York: Oxford University Press, 1995).

DOWRICHE, ANNE, *The French History* (1589).

ELIZABETH I, *Elizabeth's Glass*, ed. Marc Shell (Lincoln: University of Nebraska Press, 1993).

_____ , *The Poems of Queen Elizabeth I*, ed. Leicester Bradner (Providence, RI: Brown University Press, 1964).

'EPHELIA', *Female Poems on Several Occasions* (1679/1682).

_____ , *Female Poems on Several Occasions*, ed. Maureen Mulvihill (Delmar, NY: Scholars' Facsimiles, 1992).

_____ , *Poems*, ed. Maureen Mulvihill, The Early Modern Englishwoman series, 2 (Aldershot: Ashgate, 2003).

EVANS, KATHERINE, and CHEEVERS, SARAH, *A Brief History of the Voyage of Katherine Evans and Sarah Cheevers* (1715).

FELL, MARGARET, *A Brief Collection* (1710).

_____ , *The Daughter of Sion Awakened* (1677).

_____ , *Women's Speaking Justified* (1666).

FOWLER, CONSTANCE ASTON, *The Verse Miscellany of Constance Aston Fowler*, ed. Deborah Aldrich-Watson (Tempe, Ariz.: Medieval and Renaissance Texts and Studies, 2000).

FREKE, ELIZABETH, *The Remembrances of Elizabeth Freke 1671–1714*, ed. Raymond A. Anselment (Cambridge: Cambridge University Press, 2001).

GRYMESTONE, ELIZABETH, *Miscellanea. Meditations. Memoratives* (1604).

HARLEY, BRILLIANA, *Letters of the Lady Brilliana Harley*, ed. Thomas Taylor Lewis (London: Camden Society, 1854).

HOBY, MARGARET, *The Private Life of an Elizabethan Lady: The Diary of Margaret Hoby*, ed. Joanna Moody (Stroud: Sutton, 1998).

HUGHEY, RUTH, ed., *The Arundel Harington Manuscript of Tudor Poetry*, 2 vols. (Columbus: Ohio State University Press, 1960).

HUTCHINSON, LUCY, *Lucy Hutchinson's Translation of Lucretius, De rerum natura*, ed. Hugh de Quehen (London: Duckworth, 1996).

_____ , *Memoirs of Colonel Hutchinson*, ed. Revd. Julius Hutchinson (London: Dutton Everyman, 1908).

_____ , *Order and Disorder*, ed. David Norbrook (Oxford: Blackwell, 2001).

JOSELIN, ELIZABETH, *The Mothers Legacie to her Unborne Childe* (1624).

KILLIGREW, ANNE, *Poems* (1686).

LANYER, AEMILIA, *Salve Deus Rex Judaeorum* (1611).

LANYER, AEMILIA, *The Poems of Aemilia Lanyer*, ed. Susanne Woods (New York: Oxford University Press, 1993).

LEAD, JANE, *A Fountain of Gardens* (1696–1701).

LEIGH, DOROTHY, *A Mothers Blessing* (1616).

LOCK, ANNE, *The Collected Works of Anne Vaughan Lock*, ed. Susan M. Felch (Tempe, Ariz.: Renaissance English Text Society, 1999).

MAKIN, BATHSUA, *An Essay to Revive the Ancient Education of Gentlewomen* (1673).

*The Nine Muses, or, Poems Written by Nine Severall ladies Upon the Death of the Late Famous John Dryden Esq.*(1700).

OSBORNE, DOROTHY, *Letters to William Temple 1652–54*, ed. Kenneth Parker (Aldershot: Ashgate, 2002).

PALMER, JULIA, *The 'Centuries' of Julia Palmer*, ed. Victoria Burke and Elizabeth Clarke (Nottingham: Trent Editions, 2001).

PARR, KATHERINE, *Prayers or Meditacyons* (1545).

PHILIPS, KATHERINE (Orinda), *Selected Poems* (Hull: J. R. Tutin, 1905).

———, 'The Matchless Orinda', *Selected Poems* (Cottingham near Hull: J. R. Tutin, 1904).

———, *Poems* (1664).

———, *Poems* (1667).

———, *The Collected Works of Katherine Philips*, ed. Patrick Thomas, 3 vols. (Saffron Walden: Stump Cross, 1990–3).

SHARP, JANE, *The Midwives Book*, ed. Elaine Hobby (New York: Oxford University Press, 1999).

SIDNEY, MARY, *The Countess of Pembroke's Antonie*, ed. Alice Luce (Weimar, 1897).

———, *Psalmes of David*, ed. Samuel W. Singer (London: Chiswick Press, 1823).

———, *The Collected Works of Mary Sidney Herbert*, ed. Margaret P. Hannay *et al.* (Oxford: Clarendon Press, 1998).

SOUTHWELL, ANNE, *The Southwell–Sibthorpe Commonplace Book, Folger MS V.b.198*, ed. Jean Klene (Tempe, Ariz.: Medieval and Renaissance Texts and Studies, 1997).

SPEGHT, RACHEL, *Polemics and Poems*, ed. Barbara K. Lewalski (New York: Oxford University Press, 1996).

STUART, ARBELLA, *Letters of Lady Arbella Stuart,* ed. Sara Jayne Steen (New York: Oxford University Press, 1994).

SUTCLIFFE, ALICE, *Meditations of Man's Mortalities* (1634).

THYNNE, JOAN, and THYNNE, MARIA, *Two Elizabethan Women: Correspondence of Joan and Maria Thynne 1571–1611*, ed. Alison D. Wall (Devizes: Wiltshire Record Society vol. 38, 1983).

TRAPNEL, ANNA, *The Cry of a Stone*, ed. Hilary Hinds (Tempe: Arizona Center for Medieval and Renaissance Studies, 2000).

———, *A Legacy for Saints* (1654).

———, *A Lively Voice for the King of Saints and Nations* (1657).

———, *Anna Trapnel's Report and Plea* (1654).

———, *Strange and Wonderful News From Whitehall* (1654).

———, Untitled folio (?1658), Bodleian Library Arch.Ac.16.

———, *Choice Experiences of the Kind Dealings of God* (1653).

VAUGHAN, HENRY, *Olor Iscanus* (1651).

———, *Poems with the Tenth Satire of Juvenal Englished* (1646).

_____, *Thalia Rediviva* (1678).

WENTWORTH, ANNE, *A Vindication of Anne Wentworth* (1677).

_____, *The Revelation of Jesus Christ* (1679).

WHITNEY, ISABELLA, *A Sweet Nosegay* (1573).

_____, *The Floures of Philosophie by Sir Hugh Plat,* ed. Richard Panofsky (New York: Scholars' Facsimiles, 1982).

WOOLLEY, HANNAH, *The Queen-Like Closet* (1670).

_____, *A Supplement to the Queen-Like Closet* (1674).

WROTH, MARY, *The First Part of the Countess of Montgomery's Urania*, ed. Josephine Roberts (Binghampton: Medieval and Renaissance Texts and Studies, 1995).

_____, *Lady Mary Wroth's Love's Victory: The Penshurst Manuscript*, ed. Michael Brennan (London: Roxburghe Club, 1988).

_____, *The Poems of Lady Mary Wroth*, ed. Josephine Roberts (Baton Rouge: Louisiana State University Press, 1983).

_____, *The Second Part of The Countess of Montgomery's Urania*, ed. Josephine Roberts with Suzanne Gossett and Janel Mueller (Tempe, Ariz.: Renaissance English Text Society, 1999).

_____, *Urania*, ed. Josephine Roberts, Early Modern Englishwoman series, Series 1 vol. 10 (Aldershot: Ashgate, 1996).

## 2. COMMENTARY ON EARLY MODERN WOMEN'S WRITING 1550–1970

BALLARD, GEORGE, *Memoirs of Several Ladies of Great Britain who have been celebrated for their writings or skill in the learned languages, arts and sciences*, ed. Ruth Perry (Detroit: Wayne State University Press, 1985).

BENTLEY, THOMAS, *The Monument of Matrones* (1582).

BERNBAUM, ERNEST, 'Mrs Behn's Biography a Fiction', *PMLA* 28 (1913), 432–53.

BETHAM, MATILDA, *A Biographical Dictionary of the Celebrated Women of Every Age and Country* (Philadelphia, 1804).

BETHUNE, GEORGE, *The British Female Poets* (Philadelphia, 1848).

BULLEN, A. H., *Poems Chiefly Lyrical from Romances and Prose Tracts of the Elizabethan Age* (London: Nimmo, 1890).

CARTWRIGHT, WILLIAM, *Comedies, Tragi-Comedies, with other Poems* (1651).

CHAMBERLAIN, JOHN, *Letters of John Chamberlain*, ed. Norman McClure (Philadelphia: American Philosophical Society, 1939).

CIBBER, THEOPHILUS, *Lives of the Poets of Great Britain and Ireland* (1753).

CLIFFORD, ARTHUR, ed., *Tixall Poetry* (Edinburgh: Longman, 1813).

_____, ed., *Tixall Letters* (London: Longman, 1815).

COLERIDGE, HARTLEY, *Lives of Northern Worthies*, ed. Derwent Coleridge (London: Edward Moxon, 1852).

COLMAN, GEORGE, and THORNTON, BONNELL, *Poems by the Most Eminent Ladies of Great Britain and Ireland* (1755).

COSTELLO, LOUISA STUART, *Memoirs of Eminent Englishwomen* (London: Richard Bentley, 1844).

DRYDEN, JOHN, *Ovid's Epistles Translated by Several hands* (1680).

DRYDEN, JOHN, *The Prologue and Epilogue to the History of Bacon in Virginia* (1689).

DYCE, ALEXANDER, *Specimens of British Poetesses* (1825).

*An Elegy Upon the death of Mrs. A. Behn* (1689).

ELLIS, HENRY, *Three Collections of English Poetry of the Latter Part of the Sixteenth Century* (1845).

FULLERTON, LADY GEORGIANA, *The Life of Elisabeth Lady Falkland 1585–1639* (London: Burns and Oates, 1883).

GOSSE, EDMUND, *Seventeenth Century Studies* (1883; rpt. London: William Heinemann, 1914).

GOULD, ROBERT, *Poems* (1689).

HARINGTON, HENRY, *Nugae Antiquae* (London: W. Frederick, 1769).

HAYS, MARY, *Female Biography* (London, 1803).

HEYWOOD, THOMAS, *Gynaikeion; or Nine Bookes of Various History Concerning Women* (1624).

JACOB, G., *An Historical Account of the Lives and Writings of Our Most Considerable English Poets* (1719).

JENKINS, EDWARD, ed., *The Cavalier and his Lady* (London: Macmillan, 1872).

KAVANAGH, JULIA, *English Women of Letters* (1863).

LAMB, CHARLES, *Elia* (London, 1823).

——, *Last Essays of Elia* (London, 1833).

LANGBAINE, GERARD, *An Account of the English Dramatick Poets* (1691).

LAW, WILLIAM, *Serious Call to a Devout Life* (1726).

LAWES, HENRY, *Second Book of Ayres and Dialogues* (1655).

*Letters and Poems in Honour of the Incomparable Princess, Margaret, Duchess of Newcastle* (1676).

LOWER, MARK ANTHONY, ed., *The Lives of William Cavendish . . . and of his Wife Margaret* (London: John Russell Smith, 1872).

MATHER, COTTON, *Magnalia Christi Americana* (1702), ed. Kenneth B. Murdock (Cambridge Mass.: Belknap Press, 1977).

NICOL, ALEXANDER, *Poems on Several Subjects Both Comical and Serious* (Edinburgh, 1766).

OLDHAM, JOHN, *Some New Pieces Never Before Published* (1684).

PEARSON, JOHN, ed., *Two Centuries of Testimony in Favour of Mrs Aphra Behn* (1872).

PERCY, THOMAS, *Reliques of Ancient English Poetry* (1765).

PHILLIPS, EDWARD, *Theatrum Poetarum, or A Compleat Collection of the Poets* (1675).

PUTTENHAM, GEORGE, *The Arte of English Poesie*, ed. Gladys Willcock and Alice Walker (Cambridge: Cambridge University Press, 1936).

REYNOLDS, MYRA, *The Learned Lady in England* (Boston: Houghton Mifflin, 1920).

ROBERTSON, ERIC, *English Poetesses* (1886).

ROWTON, FREDERIC, *The Female Poets of Great Britain* (1848).

RUSKIN, JOHN, *Rock Honeycomb* [Sidney Psalter], in *The Works of John Ruskin*, ed. E. T. Cook and Alexander Wedderburn (London: George Allen, 1907), vol. xxxi.

SACKVILLE-WEST, VITA, *Knole and the Sackvilles* (Tonbridge: Ernest Benn, 1922; rpt. 1984).

——, ed., *The Diary of the Lady Anne Clifford* (London: William Heinemann, 1923).

——, *Aphra Behn* (London: Gerald Howe, 1927).

SAINTSBURY, GEORGE, ed., *Minor Poets of the Caroline Period* (Oxford: Clarendon Press, 1905).

SEWARD, WILLIAM, *Anecdotes of Some Distinguished Persons* (London: T. Cadell, 1795).

SIDNEY, MARY, *Penshurst* (Tunbridge Wells: Goulden and Curry, 1931).

SOUTHERNE, THOMAS, *Oroonoko* (1696).

TAYLOR, JEREMY, *A Discourse of the Nature, Offices and Measures of Friendship* (1657).

WALPOLE, HORACE, *Catalogue of Royal and Noble Authors* (Strawberry Hill Press, 1758).

——, *A Catalogue of the Royal and Noble Authors of England, Scotland, and Ireland ... enlarged and continued to the present time by Thomas Park*, 5 vols. (London: John Scott, 1806).

WILLIAMS, JANE, *The Literary Ladies of England* (London: Saunder, Otley and Co., 1861).

WILMOT, JOHN, *Poems On Several Occasions by the Right Honourable the E. of R*___ ('Antwerp', 1680).

——, *The Works of John Wilmot Earl of Rochester*, ed. Harold Love (Oxford: Oxford University Press, 1999).

WOOLF, VIRGINIA, *The Common Reader* (London: Hogarth Press, 1925).

——, *Women & Fiction: The Manuscript Versions of A Room of One's Own*, ed. S. P. Rosenbaum (Oxford: Shakespeare Head Press, 1992).

——, *Collected Essays*, iv, ed. Andrew McNeillie (London: Hogarth Press, 1994).

## 3. MODERN CRITICAL WORKS CITED

ANDREADIS, HARRIET, 'The Sappho-Platonics of Katherine Philips', *Signs*, 15 (1989), 34–60.

APPLEGATE, JOAN, 'Katherine Philips's "Orinda Upon Little Hector": An Unrecorded Musical Setting by Henry Lawes', *English Manuscript Studies*, 4 (1993), 272–80.

ATKINSON, COLIN, and ATKINSON, JO, 'The Identity and Life of Thomas Bentley, Compiler of *The Monument of Matrones* (1582)', *Sixteenth Century Journal*, 31 (2000), 323–48.

BACKSCHEIDER, PAULA, *Spectacular Politics: Theatrical Power and Mass Culture in Early Modern England* (Baltimore: Johns Hopkins University Press, 1993).

BALLASTER, ROS, *Seductive Forms: Women's Amatory Fiction from 1684 to 1740* (Oxford: Clarendon Press, 1992).

——, 'Fiction Feigning Femininity: False Counts and Pageant Kings in Aphra Behn's Popish Plot Writings', in Janet Todd, ed., *Aphra Behn Studies* (Cambridge: Cambridge University Press, 1996), 50–65.

BARASH CAROL, *English Women's Poetry 1649–1714* (Oxford: Clarendon Press, 1996).

BARKER, NICOLAS, *The Publications of the Roxburghe Club 1814–1962* (Cambridge: Roxburghe Club, 1964).

BATTIGELLI, ANNA, *Margaret Cavendish and the Exiles of the Mind* (Lexington: University of Kentucky Press, 1998).

BAUMAN, RICHARD, *Let Your Words Be Few: Symbolism of Speaking and Silence among Seventeenth-Century Quakers* (Cambridge: Cambridge University Press, 1983).

BEAL, PETER, *Index of English Literary Manuscripts* (London, 1993).

——, *In Praise of Scribes: Manuscripts and their Makers in Seventeenth-Century England* (Oxford: Clarendon Press, 1998).

BEER, ANNA R., *Sir Walter Ralegh and his Readers in the Seventeenth Century* (London: Macmillan, 1997).

BEILIN, ELAINE, *Redeeming Eve: Women Writers of the English Renaissance* (Princeton: Princeton University Press, 1987).

BELL, MAUREEN, *et al.*, eds., *English Women Writers 1580–1720* (Brighton: Harvester, 1990).

BENNETT, ALEXANDRA G., 'Female Performativity in *The Tragedy of Mariam*', *SEL* 40 (2000), 293–309.

——, 'Fantastic Realism: Margaret Cavendish and the Possibilities of Drama', in Line Cottegnies and Nancy Weitz, eds., *Authorial Conquests: Essays on Genre in the Writings of Margaret Cavendish* (Madison: Associated University Presses, 2003), 179–94.

BINGHAM, CLIVE, *The Roxburghe Club: Its History and its Members, 1812–1927* (Oxford: Oxford University Press, 1928).

BONNELL, THOMAS F., 'Poets of Great Britain: the "Little Trifling Edition" Revisited', *MP* 85 (1987), 128–52.

BOTONAKIS, EFFIE, 'Seventeenth-Century Englishwomen's Spiritual Diaries: Self-Examination, Covenanting, and Account Keeping', *Sixteenth Century Journal*, 30 (1999), 3–19.

BRENNAN, MICHAEL, 'Creating Female Authorship in the Early Seventeenth Century: Ben Jonson and Lady Mary Wroth', in George Justice and Nathan Tinker, eds., *Women's Writing and the Circulation of Ideas* (Cambridge: Cambridge University Press, 2002), 73–93.

BURKE, VICTORIA E., 'Medium and Meaning in the Manuscripts of Anne, Lady Southwell', in Justice and Tinker, *Women's Writing and the Circulation of Ideas* [see Brennan above], 94–120.

——, and GIBSON, JONATHAN, eds., *Early Modern Women's Manuscript Writing* (Aldershot: Ashgate, 2004).

CAMERON, W. J., *New Light on Aphra Behn* (Auckland: University of Auckland, 1961).

CAPP, BERNARD, *The Fifth Monarchy Men* (London: Faber, 1972).

CATTY, JOCELYN, *Writing Rape, Writing Women in Early Modern England* (Houndmills: Macmillan, 1999).

CAVANAGH, SHEILA T., *Cherished Torment: The Emotional Geography of Lady Mary Wroth's Urania* (Pittsburgh: Duquesne University Press, 2001).

CERASANO, S. P., and WYNNE-DAVIES, MARION., eds., *Renaissance Drama by Women: Texts and Documents* (London: Routledge, 1996).

—— ——, eds., *Readings in Renaissance Women's Drama* (London: Routledge, 1998).

CHALMERS, HERO, *Royalist Women Writers 1650–1689* (Oxford: Clarendon Press, 2004).

CHERNAIK, WARREN, 'Ephelia's Voice: The Authorship of *Female Poems* (1679)', *PQ* 74 (1995), 151–73.

CLARKE, DANIELLE, *The Politics of Early Modern Women's Writing* (Harlow: Pearson, 2001).

CLARKE, ELIZABETH, 'Anne Southwell and the Pamphlet Debate', in Cristina Malcomson and Mihoko Suzuki, eds., *Debating Gender in Early Modern England, 1500–1700* (Houndmills: Palgrave, 2002), 37–53.

CLIFFORD, HUGH, *The House of Clifford* (Chichester: Phillimore, 1987).

CLUCAS, STEPHEN, 'The Atomism of the Cavendish Circle: A Reappraisal', *Seventeenth Century*, 9 (1994), 247–73.

COOLAHAN, MARIE-LOUISE, '"We live by chance and slip into Events": Occasionality and the Manuscript Verse of Katherine Philips', *Eighteenth-Century Ireland*, 18 (2003), 9–23.

COPE, ESTHER S., *Handmaid of the Holy Spirit: Dame Eleanor Davies: Never Soe mad a Ladie* (Ann Arbor: University of Michigan Press, 1992).

COPELAND, NANCY, *Staging Gender in Behn and Centlivre* (Aldershot: Ashgate, 2004).

COWELL, PATTIE, 'The Early Distribution of Anne Bradstreet's Poems', in Pattie Cowell and Ann Stanford, eds., *Critical Essays on Anne Bradstreet* (Boston: G. K. Hall, 1983), 270–9.

CRAWFORD, PATRICIA, *Women and Religion in England 1500–1720* (London: Routledge, 1993).

DAVIES, ADRIAN, *The Quakers in English Society 1655–1725* (Oxford: Clarendon Press, 2000).

DAY, ROBERT ADAMS, 'Aphra Behn's First Biography', *Studies in Bibliography*, 22 (1969), 227–40.

DAYBELL, JAMES, ed., *Early Modern Women's Letter Writing, 1450–1700* (Houndmills: Palgrave, 2001).

DE QUEHEN, HUGH, 'Ease and Flow in Lucy Hutchinson's Lucretius', *SP* 93 (1996).

DUFFY, MAUREEN, *The Passionate Shepherdess: Aphra Behn 1640–89* (2nd edn, London: Methuen, 1989).

DUNCAN-JONES, KATHERINE, 'Philip Sidney's Toys', in Dennis Kay, ed., *Sir Philip Sidney* (Oxford: Clarendon Press, 1987), 61–80.

DUSINBERRE, JULIET, *Virginia Woolf's Renaissance* (London: Macmillan, 1997).

EZELL, MARGARET, *The Patriarch's Wife: Literary Evidence and the History of the Family* (Chapel Hill: University of North Carolina Press, 1987).

——, '"To Be Your Daughter in Your Pen": The Social Functions of Literature in the Writings of Lady Elizabeth Brackley and Lady Jane Cavendish', *HLQ* 51 (1988), 281–96.

——, *Social Authorship and the Advent of Print* (Baltimore: Johns Hopkins University Press, 1999).

——, *Writing Women's Literary History* (Baltimore: Johns Hopkins University Press, 1993).

FEHRENBACH, R. J., 'Isabella Whitney, Sir Hugh Plat, Geoffrey Whitney, and "Sister Eldershae"', *ELN* 21 (1983).

FERGUSON, MARGARET W., 'Running On with Almost Public Voice: The Case of E.C.', in Florence Howe, ed., *Tradition and the Talents of Women* (Urbana: University of Illinois Press, 1991), 37–67.

——, *Dido's Daughters: Literacy, Gender and Empire in Early Modern Europe and France* (Chicago: University of Chicago Press, 2003).

FINDLAY, ALISON, '"Upon the World's Stage": The Civil War and Interregnum', in Alison Findlay and Stephanie Hodgson-Wright, eds., *Women and Dramatic Production 1550–1700* (Harlow: Longman, 2000), 68–94.

FITZMAURICE, JAMES, 'Margaret Cavendish on her Own Writing: Evidence from Revision and Handmade Correction', *PBSA* 85 (1991), 297–307.

FITZMAURICE, JAMES, 'Front Matter and the Physical Make-up of *Nature's Pictures*', *Women's Writing*, 4 (1997), 353–67.

FOX, ALICE, *Virginia Woolf and the Literature of the English Renaissance* (Oxford: Clarendon Press, 1990).

FREEMAN, ARTHUR, '*Love's Victory*: A Supplementary Note,' *Library*, 19 (1997), 252–4.

FRIEDMAN, ALICE T., 'Portrait of a Marriage: The Willoughby Letters of 1585–6', *Signs*, 11 (1986), 542–55.

GALLAGHER, CATHERINE, 'Embracing the Absolute: The Politics of the Female Subject in Seventeenth Century England', *Genders*, 1 (1988), 24–39.

GIBBONS, B. J., *Gender in Mystical and Occult Thought: Behmenism and its Development in England* (Cambridge: Cambridge University Press, 1996).

GILSON, J. P., ed., *Lives of Lady Anne Clifford* (London: Roxburghe Club, 1916).

GLENDINNING, VICTORIA, *Vita: The Life of V. Sackville-West* (London: Weidenfeld and Nicolson, 1983).

GOLDBERG, JONATHAN, *Desiring Women Writing: Renaissance Examples* (Stanford, Calif.: Stanford University Press, 1997).

GOREAU, ANGELINE, *Reconstructing Aphra: A Social Biography of Aphra Behn* (New York, Dial, 1980).

——, *The Whole Duty of a Woman* (New York: Dial Press, 1985).

GRAHAM, ELSPETH, *et al.*, eds., *Her Own Life: Autobiographical Writings by Seventeenth-Century Englishwomen* (London: Routledge, 1989).

GRAY, CATHERINE, '"Feeding on the Seed of the Woman": Dorothy Leigh and the Figure of Maternal Dissent', *ELH* 68 (2001).

——, 'Katherine Philips and the Post-Courtly Coterie', *ELR*, 32 (2002), 426–51.

GREER, GERMAINE, *Slip-Shod Sibyls* (London: Viking, 1995).

——, *et al.*, eds., *Kissing the Rod* (London: Virago, 1988).

HACKETT, HELEN, *Women and Romance Fiction in the English Renaissance* (Cambridge: Cambridge University Press, 2000).

HAGEMAN, ELIZABETH, 'Treacherous Accidents and the Abominable Printing of Katherine Philips's 1664 Poems', in W. Speed Hill, ed., *New Ways of Looking at Old Texts III* (Tempe: Arizona Center for Medieval and Renaissance Studies, 2004), 89–90.

——, and SUNUNU, ANDREA, 'New Manuscript Texts of Katherine Philips, the "Matchless Orinda"', *English Manuscript Studies*, 4 (1993), 174–219.

—— ——, '"More Copies of it abroad than I could have imagin'd": Further Manuscript Texts of Katherine Philips, the "Matchless Orinda"', *English Manuscript Studies*, 5 (1995).

HALLETT, NICKY, 'Anne Clifford as Orlando: Virginia Woolf's Feminist Historiology and Women's Biography', *Women's History Review*, 4/4 (1995).

HALLIWELL, JAMES ORCHARD, *A Brief Description of the Ancient and Modern Manuscripts Preserved in the Public Library, Plymouth* (London: 1853).

HAMMOND, PAUL, 'The Prologue and Epilogue to Dryden's *Marriage A-la-Mode* and the Problem of *Covent Garden Drollery*', *PBSA* 81 (1987), 155–72.

HANNAY, MARGARET P., *Philip's Phoenix: Mary Sidney, Countess of Pembroke* (New York: Oxford University Press, 1990).

HARVEY, ELIZABETH, *Ventriloquized Voices: Feminist Theory and English Renaissance Texts* (London: Routledge, 1992).

HERMAN, PETER C., ed., *Reading Monarch's Writing* (Tempe, Ariz.: Medieval and Renaissance Texts and Studies, 2002).

HIGGINS, PATRICIA, 'The Reactions of Women, with Special Reference to Women Petitioners', in Brian Manning, ed., *Politics, Religion and the English Civil War* (London: Edward Arnold, 1973), 179–222.

HILL, CHRISTOPHER, *The World Turned Upside Down* (Harmondsworth: Penguin, 1975).

HINDS, HILARY, *God's Englishwomen: Seventeenth Century Radical Sectarian Writing and Feminist Criticism* (Manchester: Manchester University Press, 1996).

HOBBS, MARY, *Early Seventeenth Century Verse Miscellany Manuscripts* (London: Scolar Press, 1992).

HOBBY, ELAINE, *Virtue of Necessity: English Women's Writing 1649–1688* (London: Virago, 1988).

——, 'Katherine Philips: Seventeenth-Century Lesbian Poet', in Elaine Hobby and Chris White, eds., *What Lesbians Do in Books* (London: Women's Press, 1991).

——, 'Handmaids of the Lord and Mothers in Israel: Early Vindications of Quaker Women's Prophecy', in Thomas N. Corns and David Loewenstein, eds., *The Emergence of Quaker Writing* (London: Frank Cass, 1995), 88–98.

——, 'The Politics of Women's Prophecy in the English Revolution', in Helen Wilcox et al., eds., *Sacred and Profane: Secular and Devotional Interplay in Early Modern British Literature* (Amsterdam: VU University Press, 1996).

HODGSON-WRIGHT, STEPHANIE, 'Jane Lumley's Iphigenia at Aulis', in S. P. Cerasano and Marion Wynne-Davies, eds., *Readings in Renaissance Women's Drama* (London: Routledge, 1998), 129–41.

HOLSTUN, JAMES, *Ehud's Dagger: Class Struggle in the English Revolution* (London: Verso, 2000).

HUGHES, DEREK, *The Theatre of Aphra Behn* (Houndmills: Palgrave, 2001).

HUGHEY, RUTH, 'Cultural Interests of Women in England from 1524 to 1640', Cornell University Ph.D. diss., 1932.

HUTTON, SARAH, 'In Dialogue with Thomas Hobbes: Margaret Cavendish's Natural Philosophy', *Women's Writing*, 4 (1997).

——, 'Margaret Cavendish and Henry More', in Stephen Clucas, ed., *Princely Brave Woman* (Aldershot: Ashgate, 2003), 185–98.

INGRAM, RANDALL, 'First Words and Second Thoughts: Margaret Cavendish, Humphrey Moseley, and "the Book"', *Journal of Medieval and Early Modern Studies*, 30 (2000), 101–24.

JONES, ANN ROSALIND, *The Currency of Eros* (Bloomington: University of Indiana Press, 1990).

——, 'Maidservants of London', in Susan Frye and Karen Robertson, eds., *Maids and Mistresses, Cousins and Queens: Women's Alliances in Early Modern England* (New York: Oxford University Press, 1999), 21–32.

JONES, JANE, 'New Light on the Background and Early Life of Aphra Behn', in Janet Todd, ed., *Aphra Behn Studies* (Cambridge: Cambridge University Press, 1996), 310–20.

JUSSERAND, J. J., *The English Novel in the Time of Shakespeare* (1890; repr. London: Ernest Benn, 1966),

KAHN, VICTORIA, 'Margaret Cavendish and the Romance of Contract', *RQ* 50 (1997).

KEEBLE, N. H., *The Cultural Identity of Seventeenth Century Woman* (London: Rout-ledge, 1994).

KING, KATHRYN R., 'Jane Barker, *Poetical Recreations*, and the Sociable Text', *ELH* 61 (1994), 551–70.

——, and MEDOFF, JESLYN, 'Jane Barker Her Life: The Documentary Record', *Eighteenth Century Life*, 21 (1997), 16–38.

KOHLER, CHARLOTTE, 'The Elizabethan Woman of Letters', University of Virginia Ph.D. diss., 1936.

KRONTIRIS, TINA, *Oppositional Voices* (London: Routledge, 1993).

KUNIN, AARON, 'From the Desk of Anne Clifford', *ELH* 71 (2004), 587–608.

KUNZE, BONNELYN YOUNG, *Margaret Fell and the Rise of Quakerism* (London: Macmillan, 1994).

LAMB, MARY ELLEN, 'The Cooke Sisters: Attitudes towards Learned Women in the Renaissance', in Margaret Patterson Hannay, *Silent but for the Word: Tudor Women as Patrons, Translators, and Writers of Religious Works* (Kent: Kent State University Press, 1985), 107–25.

——, *Gender and Authorship in the Sidney Circle* (Madison: University of Wisconsin Press, 1990).

——, 'Women Readers in Mary Wroth's *Urania*', in Naomi Miller and Gary Waller, eds., *Reading Mary Wroth* (Knoxville: University of Tennessee Press, 1991).

——, 'The Biopolitics of Romance in Mary Wroth's *The Countess of Montgomery's Urania*', *ELR* 31 (2001).

——, 'The Agency of the Split Subject: Lady Anne Clifford and the Uses of Reading', *ELR* 22 (1992), 347–68.

LENNAM, T. N. S., 'Sir Edward Dering's Collection of Playbooks, 1619–1624,' *SQ* 16 (1965), 145–53.

LETHBRIDGE, B., 'Anthological Reading and Writing in Tudor England', in Barbara Korte *et al.*, eds., *Anthologies of British Poetry: Critical Perspectives from Literary and Cultural Studies* (Amsterdam: Rodopi, 2000).

LEWALSKI, BARBARA, *Writing Women in Jacobean England* (Cambridge Mass.: Harvard University Press, 1993).

LILLEY, KATE, 'Dear Object: Katherine Philips's Love Elegies and Their Readers', in Jo Wallwork and Paul Salzman, eds., *Women Writing 1550–1750* (Bundoora: Meridian, 2001), 163–78.

LIMBERT, CLAUDIA A., 'The Poetry of Katherine Philips: Holographs, Manuscripts, and Early Printed Texts', *PQ* 70 (1994), 181–97.

LLEWELLYN, MARK, 'Katherine Philips, Friendship, Poetry and Neo-Platonic Thought in Seventeenth Century England', *PQ* 81 (2002), 441–68.

LONGFELLOW, ERICA, 'Lady Anne Southwell's Indictment of Adam', in Victoria Burke and Jonathan Gibson, eds., *Early Modern Women's Manuscript Writing* (Aldershot: Ashgate, 2004), 111–33.

——, *Women and Religious Writing in Early Modern England* (Cambridge: Cambridge University Press, 2004).

LOVE, HAROLD, *Scribal Publication in Seventeenth-Century England* (Oxford: Clarendon Press, 1993).

LOXLEY, JAMES, 'Unfettered Organs: The Polemical Voices of Katherine Philips', in Danielle Clarke and Elizabeth Clarke, eds., *This Double Voice: Gendered Writing in Early Modern England* (New York: St Martin's Press, 2000), 230–48.

MACCARTHY, B. G., *Women Writers: Their Contribution to the English Novel* (Cork: Cork University Press, 1944).

MACDONALD, JOYCE GREEN, 'The Disappearing African Woman: Imoinda in Oroonoko after Behn', *ELH*, 66 (1999), 71–86.

MCDOWELL, PAULA, 'Tace and Andrew Sowle', in James K. Bracken and Joel Silver, eds., *The British Literary Book Trade 1474–1700* (Detroit: Gale, 1996), 249–57.

——, *The Women of Grub Street* (Oxford: Oxford University Press, 1998).

——, 'Enlightenment Enthusiasms and the Spectacular Failure of the Philadelphian Society', *Eighteenth-Century Studies*, 35 (2002).

MACK, PHYLLIS, *Visionary Women: Ecstatic Prophecy in Seventeenth-Century England* (Berkeley: University of California Press, 1992).

MAGRO, MARIA, 'Spiritual Autobiography and Radical Sectarian Women's Discourse: Anna Trapnel and the Bad Girls of the English Revolution', *Journal of Medieval and Early Modern Studies*, 34 (2004), 405–37.

MALCOMSON, CRISTINA, and SUZUKI, MIHOKO, eds., *Debating Gender in Early Modern England* (Houndmills: Palgrave, 2002).

MAMBRETTI, CATHARINE, 'Orinda on the Restoration Stage', *Comparative Literature*, 37 (1985), 233–51.

MARCUS, LEAH, 'Elizabeth I as Public and Private Poet', in Peter C. Herman, ed., *Reading Monarch's Writing* (Tempe, Ariz.: Medieval and Renaissance Texts and Studies, 2002).

MAROTTI, ARTHUR F., *Manuscript, Print, and the English Renaissance Lyric* (Ithaca, NY: Cornell University Press, 1995).

MARTIN, RANDALL, 'Isabella Whitney's "Lamentation upon the death of William Gruffith"', *Early Modern Literary Studies*, 3 (1997).

MASTEN, JEFF, '"Shall I turne blabb": Circulation, Gender and Subjectivity in Mary Wroth's Sonnets', in Naomi Miller and Gary Waller, eds., *Reading Mary Wroth* (Knoxville: University of Tennessee Press, 1991).

——, 'Margaret Cavendish: Paper, Performance, "Sociable Virginity"', *MLQ* 65 (2004).

MATCHINSKE, MEGAN, *Writing, Gender and the State in Early Modern England* (Cambridge: Cambridge University Press, 1998).

MCELRATH, JOSEPH, 'The Text of Anne Bradstreet: Biographical and Critical Consequences', *Seventeenth Century News* (Summer 1976).

MEDOFF, JESLYN, 'The Daughters of Behn and the Problem of Reputation', in Isobel Grundy and Susan Wiseman, eds., *Women, Writing, History 1640–1740* (London: Batsford, 1992), 33–54.

——, '"Very Like a Fiction": Some Early Biographies of Aphra Behn', in Barbara Smith and Ursula Appelt, eds., *Write or Be Written* (Aldershot: Ashgate, 2001), 247–69.

MENDELSON, SARA HELLER, 'Stuart Women's Diaries and Occasional Memoirs', in Mary Prior, ed., *Women in English Society 1500–1800* (London: Methuen, 1985), 181–210.

——, *The Mental World of Stuart Women* (Brighton: Harvester, 1987).

MILLER, NAOMI J., *Changing the Subject: Mary Wroth and Figurations of Gender in Early Modern England* (Lexington: University Press of Kentucky, 1996).

MILLER, NAOMI J., and WALLER, G., eds., *Reading Mary Wroth* (Knoxville: University of Tennessee Press, 1991).

MILLMAN, JILL SEAL, and WRIGHT, GILLIAN, eds., *Early Modern Women's Manuscript Verse* (Manchester: Manchester University Press, 2005).

MORRISSEY, MARY, 'Narrative Authority in Spiritual Life Writing: The Example of Dionys Fitzherbert (fl .1608–41)', *Seventeenth Century*, 15 (2000), 1–17.

NAUMAN, JONATHAN, 'The Publication of *Thalia Rediviva* and the Literary Reputation of Katherine Philips', *HLQ* 61 (1998).

NEALE, J. E., *Queen Elizabeth* (London: Jonathan Cape, 1934).

NEWCOMB, LORI HUMPHREY, *Reading Popular Romance in Early Modern England* (New York: Columbia University Press, 2002).

NIXON, SCOTT, 'The Manuscript Sources of Thomas Carew's Poetry', *English Manuscript Studies*, 8 (2000).

NORBROOK, DAVID, ' "This blushing tribute of a borrowed muse": Robert Overton and his Overturning of the Poetic Canon', *English Manuscript Studies*, 4 (1993), 220–66.

——, 'Lucy Hutchinson versus Edmund Waller: An Unpublished Reply to Waller's A Panegyrick to my Lord Protector', *Seventeenth Century*, 11 (1996), 61–86.

——, 'Lucy Hutchinson's "Elegies" and the Situation of the Republican Woman Writer', *ELR* 27 (1997), 468–521.

——, 'Lucy Hutchinson and *Order and Disorder*', *English Manuscript Studies 1100–1700*, 9 (2000).

——, 'Margaret Cavendish and Lucy Hutchinson: Identity, Ideology and Politics', *In-Between*, 9 (2000), 179–203.

——, ' "But a Copie": Textual Authority and Gender in Editions of "The Life of John Hutchinson" ', in W. Speed Hill, ed., *New Ways of Looking at Old Texts III* (Tempe: Arizona Center for Medieval and Renaissance Studies, 2004).

——, 'Women, the Republic of Letters, and the Public Sphere in the Mid-Seventeenth Century', *Criticism*, 46 (2004).

O'CALLAGHAN, MICHELLE, *The 'shepheards nation', Jacobean Spenserians and Early Stuart Political Culture* (Oxford: Clarendon Press, 2000).

O'DONNELL, MARY ANN, *Aphra Behn: A Bibliography of Primary and Secondary Sources*, 2nd edn. (Aldershot: Ashgate, 2004).

——, *et al.*, eds., *Aphra Behn (1640–1689): Identity, Alterity, Ambiguity* (Paris: L'Harmattan, 2000).

OTTEN, CHARLOTTE, *English Women's Voices 1540–1700* (Miami: Florida International University Press, 1992).

PEARSON, JACQUELINE, *The Prostituted Muse: Images of Women and Women Dramatists 1642–1737* (Brighton: Harvester, 1988).

——, 'The History of *The History of the Nun*', in Heidi Hutner, ed., *Rereading Aphra Behn* (Charlottesville: University Press of Virginia, 1993), 234–52.

PENDER, PATRICIA, 'Disciplining the Imperial Mother: Anne Bradstreet's "A Dialogue between Old England and New" ', in Jo Wallwork and Paul Salzman, eds., *Women Writing 1550–1750* (Bundoora: Meridian, 2001), 115–31.

PETERS, KATE, *Print Culture and the Early Quakers* (Cambridge: Cambridge University Press, 2005).

POLLOCK, LINDA, *With Faith and Physic: The Life of a Tudor Gentlewoman, Lady Grace Mildmay 1552–1620* (London: Collins and Brown, 1993).

PRICE, BRONWEN, 'A Rhetoric of Innocence: The Poetry of Katherine Philips, "The Matchless Orinda" ', in Barbara Smith and Ursula Appelt, eds., *Write or Be Written* (Aldershot: Ashgate, 2001), 223–46.

PRINEAS, MATTHEW, 'The Discourse of Love and the Rhetoric of Apocalypse in Anna Trapnel's Folio Songs', *Comitatus*, 28 (1997), 90–110.

PURKISS, DIANE, 'Material Girls: The Seventeenth-Century Woman Debate', in Clare Brant and Diane Purkiss, eds., *Women, Texts and Histories* (London: Routledge, 1992), 69–101.

_____ , 'Producing the Voice, Consuming the Body: Women Prophets of the Seventeenth Century', in Isobel Grundy and Susan Wiseman, eds., *Women, Writing, History: 1640–1740* (London: Batsford, 1992), 139–58.

_____ , *Three Tragedies by Renaissance Women* (Harmondsworth: Penguin, 1998).

QUILLIGAN, MAUREEN, 'Staging Gender', in James Grantham Turner, ed., *Sexuality and Gender in Early Modern Europe* (Cambridge: Cambridge University Press, 1993), 208–32.

RAYLOR, TIM, ' "Wits Recreations" Not by Sir John Mennes or James Smith', *Notes and Queries*, 230 (1985), 1–2.

RAYMOND, JOAD, *Pamphlets and Pamphleteering in Early Modern Britain* (Cambridge: Cambridge University Press, 2003).

REAY, BARRY, *The Quakers and the English Revolution* (London: Temple Smith, 1985).

REES, EMMA, *Margaret Cavendish: Gender, Genre, Exile* (Manchester: Manchester University Press, 2003).

RILEY, DENISE, *Am I That Name?: Feminism and the Category of 'Women' in History* (London: Macmillan, 1988).

ROBERTS, JOSEPHINE, 'The Huntington Library Manuscript of Lady Mary Wroth's Play *Loves Victorie*,' *HLQ* 46 (1983), 156–74.

_____ , 'Deciphering Women's Pastoral: Coded Language in Wroth's *Love's Victory*', in Claude Summers and Ted-Larry Pebworth, eds., *Representing Women in Renaissance England* (Columbia: University of Missouri Press, 1997), 163–74.

ROSE, MARY BETH, *Gender and Authorship in the Sidney Circle* (Madison: University of Wisconsin Press, 1990).

ROSS, ISABEL, *Margaret Fell: Mother of Quakerism* (London: Longmans, Green and Co., 1949).

ROWSE, A. L., *Shakespeare the Man* (London: Macmillan, 1973).

_____ , *Shakespeare's Sonnets: The Problems Solved*, 2nd edn. (London: Macmillan, 1973).

_____ , *The Poems of Shakespeare's Dark Lady* (London: Jonathan Cape, 1978).

RUSSELL, ANNE, 'Aphra Behn's Miscellanies: The Politics and Poetics of Editing', *PQ* 77 (1998).

SALZMAN, PAUL, ed., *Early Modern Women's Writing: An Anthology 1560–1700*, World's Classics (Oxford: Oxford University Press, 2000).

_____ , 'Early Modern (Aristocratic) Women and Textual Property', in Nancy E. Wright *et al.*, *Women, Property and the Letters of the Law in Early Modern England* (Toronto: University of Toronto Press, 2004).

SALZMAN, PAUL, *Literary Culture in Jacobean England: Reading 1621* (Houndmills: Palgrave/Macmillan, 2002).

SANDERS, JULIE, '"A Woman Write a Play?" Jonsonian Strategies and the Dramatic Writings of Margaret Cavendish', in S. P. Cerasano and Marion Wynne-Davies, eds., *Readings in Renaissance Women's Drama* (London: Routledge, 1998), 293–305.

SCHLEINER, LOUISE, *Tudor and Stuart Women Writers* (Bloomington: Indiana University Press, 1994).

SCHOENBAUM, SAMUEL, *Shakespeare and Others* (Washington: Folger Books, 1985).

SHANNON, LAURIE J., '*The Tragedy of Mariam*: Cary's Critique of the Terms of Founding Discourses', *ELR* 24 (1994), 135–53.

SHARPE, KEVIN, *Reading Revolutions: The Politics of Reading in Early Modern England* (New Haven: Yale University Press, 2000).

SHELL, ALISON, 'Popish Plots: *The Feign'd Courtizans* in Context', in Janet Todd, ed., *Aphra Behn Studies* (Cambridge: Cambridge University Press, 1996), 30–49.

SHERBO, ARTHUR, *Isaac Reed, Editorial Factotum* (University of Victoria: English Literary Studies, 1989).

SILVER, BRENDA R., '"Anon" and "the Reader": Virginia Woolf's Last Essays', *Twentieth Century Literature: A Scholarly and Critical Journal*, 25/3-4 (1979).

SMITH, CATHERINE F., 'Jane Lead: Mysticism and the Woman Cloathed with the Sun', in Sandra Gilbert and Susan Gubar, eds., *Shakespeare's Sisters* (Bloomington: Indiana University Press, 1979), 3–18.

——, 'Jane Lead: The Feminist Mind and Art of a Seventeenth-Century Protestant Mystic', in Rosemary Ruether and Eleanor McLaughlin, eds., *Women of Spirit* (New York: Simon and Schuster, 1979), 183–203.

SMITH, NIGEL, *Perfection Proclaimed: Language and Literature in English Radical Religion 1640–1660* (Oxford: Clarendon Press, 1989).

SMITH, ROSALIND, 'Lady Mary Wroth's *Pamphilia to Amphilanthus*: The Politics of Withdrawal', *ELR* 30 (2000).

——, '"In a Mirrour clere": Protestantism and Politics in Anne Lock's Miserere mei Deus', in Danielle Clarke and Elizabeth Clarke, eds., *'This Double Voice': Gendered Writing in Early Modern England* (Basingstoke: Macmillan, 2000), 41–60.

SOUERS, PHILIP WEBSTER, *The Matchless Orinda* (Cambridge, Mass.: Harvard University Press, 1931).

SPEARING, ELIZABETH, 'Aphra Behn: The Politics of Translation', in Janet Todd, ed., *Aphra Behn Studies* (Cambridge: Cambridge University Press, 1996), 154–77.

SPENCE, RICHARD T., *Lady Anne Clifford* (Stroud: Sutton, 1997).

SPENCER, JANE, *Aphra Behn's Afterlife* (Oxford: Oxford University Press, 2000).

STANFORD, ANN, ed., *The Women Poets in English: An Anthology* (New York: McGraw Hill, 1972).

STEVENSON, JANE, 'Women, Writing and Scribal Publication in the Sixteenth Century', *English Manuscript Studies*, 9 (2000).

——, and DAVIDSON, PETER, eds., *Early Modern Women Poets* (Oxford: Oxford University Press, 2001).

STEVENSON, JAY, 'The Mechanist-Vitalist Soul of Margaret Cavendish', *SEL* 36 (1996), 527–43.

STRAZNICKY, MARTA, 'Reading the Stage: Margaret Cavendish and Commonwealth Closet Drama', *Criticism*, 37 (1995), 355–90.

SUMMIT, JENNIFER, ' "The Arte of a Ladies Penne": Elizabeth I and the Poetics of Queenship', in Peter C. Herman, ed., *Reading Monarch's Writing* (Tempe, Ariz.: Medieval and Renaissance Texts and Studies, 2002).

SUZUKI, MIHOKO, 'Anne Clifford and the Gendering of History', *Clio*, 30 (2001), 195–230.

——, *Subordinate Subjects: Gender, the Political Nation, and Literary Form in England 1588–1688* (Aldershot: Ashgate, 2003).

SWIFT, CAROLYN RUTH, 'Feminine Self-Definition in Lady Mary Wroth's *Love's Victorie*', *ELR* 19 (1989), 171–88.

TENISON, E. M., *Louise Imogen Guiney: Her Life and Works* (London: Macmillan, 1923).

THOMAS, PATRICK, *Katherine Philips* (Cardiff: University of Wales Press, 1988).

THUNE, NILS, *The Behmenists and the Philadelphians* (Uppsala, 1943).

TODD, JANET, *The Secret Life of Aphra Behn* (London: André Deutsch, 1996).

——, *The Critical Fortunes of Aphra Behn* (Columbia, Mo.: Camden House, 1998).

TOLANDER, PAUL, and TENGER, ZEYNEP, 'Katherine Philips and Coterie Critical Practices', *Eighteenth-Century Studies*, 37 (2004), 367–87.

TOMLINSON, SOPHIE, ' "My brain the stage": Margaret Cavendish and the Fantasy of Female Performance', in Clare Brant and Diane Purkiss, eds., *Women, Texts and Histories, 1575–1760* (London: Routledge, 1992).

——, 'Too Theatrical? Female Subjectivity in Caroline and Interregnum Drama', *Women's Writing*, 6 (1999).

——, *Women on Stage in Stuart Drama* (Cambridge: Cambridge University Press, 2005).

TRAUB, VALERIE, *The Renaissance of Lesbianism in Early Modern England* (Cambridge: Cambridge University Press, 2002).

TRAVITSKY, BETTY S., and PRESCOTT, ANNE LAKE, eds., *Female and Male Voices in Early Modern England* (New York: Columbia University Press, 2000).

VAN LENNEP, WILLIAM, ed., *The London Stage 1660–1800* (Carbondale: Northern Illinois University Press, 1965).

WALKER, KIM, *Women Writers of the English Renaissance* (New York: Twayne, 1996).

WALL, WENDY, 'Isabella Whitney and the Female Legacy', *ELH* 58 (1991).

——, *The Imprint of Gender: Authorship and Publication in the Renaissance* (Ithaca, NY: Cornell University Press, 1993).

WALLER, GARY, *The Sidney Family Romance: Mary Wroth, William Herbert, and the Early Modern Construction of Gender* (Detroit: Wayne State University Press, 1993).

WARNER, WILLIAM, *Licensing Entertainment: The Elevation of Novel Reading in Britain 1684–1750* (Berkeley: University of California Press, 1998).

WATT, DIANE, *Secretaries of God: Women Prophets in Late Medieval and Early Modern England* (Cambridge: Brewer, 1997).

WHITAKER, KATIE, *Mad Madge: Margaret Cavendish, Duchess of Newcastle* (London: Chatto and Windus, 2003).

WHITE, ELIZABETH WADE, *Anne Bradstreet* (New York: Oxford University Press, 1971).

WHITE, MICHELINE, 'Renaissance Englishwomen and Religious Translations: The Case of Anne Lock's *Of the Markes of the Children of God* (1590)', *ELR* 29 (1999), 375–400.

WILLIAMS, GWENO, '"No Silent Woman": The Plays of Margaret Cavendish, Duchess of Newcastle', in Alison Findlay and Stephanie Hodgson-Wright, eds., *Women and Dramatic Production 1550–1700* (Harlow: Longman, 2000), 95–122.

——, 'Translating the Text, Performing the Self', in Alison Findlay and Stephanie Hodgson-Wright, eds., *Women and Dramatic Production 1550–1700* (Harlow: Longman, 2000), 15–41.

WILLIAMSON, GEORGE C., *Lady Anne Clifford* (Kendal: Titus Wilson and Son, 1922).

WISEMAN, SUSAN, 'Unsilent Instruments and the Devil's Cushions: Authority in Seventeenth-Century Women's Prophetic Discourse', in Isobel Armstrong, ed., *New Feminist Discourses* (London: Routledge, 1992), 176–96.

——, *Drama and Politics in the English Civil War* (Cambridge: Cambridge University Press, 1998).

——, 'Knowing Her Place: Anne Clifford and the Politics of Retreat', in Philippa Berry and Margaret Trudeau-Clayton, eds., *Textures of Renaissance Knowledge* (Manchester: Manchester University Press, 2003).

——, *Conspiracy and Virtue: Women, Writing, and Politics in Seventeenth-Century England* (Oxford: Oxford University Press, 2006).

WOODS, SUSANNE, *Lanyer: A Renaissance Woman Poet* (New York: Oxford University Press, 1999).

WOOLRYCH, AUSTIN, *Commonwealth to Protectorate* (Oxford: Oxford University Press, 1982).

WORDEN, BLAIR, *The Sound of Virtue: Philip Sidney's Arcadia and Elizabethan Politics* (New Haven: Yale University Press, 1996).

WOUDHUYSEN, H. R, *Sir Philip Sidney and the Circulation of Manuscripts 1558–1640* (Oxford: Clarendon Press, 1996).

WRAY, RAMONA, 'Anthologising the Early Modern Female Voice', in Andrew Murphy, ed., *The Renaissance Text* (Manchester: Manchester University Press, 2000), 55–72.

WYNNE-DAVIES, MARION, '"My Seeled Chamber and Dark Parlour Room": The English Country House and Renaissance Women Dramatists', in S. P. Ceresano and Marion Wynne-Davies, eds., *Readings in Renaissance Women's Drama* (London: Routledge, 1998), 60–8.

——, ed., *Women Poets of the Renaissance* (London: Dent, 1998).

——, '"Here is a sport will well befit this time and place": Allusion and Delusion in Mary Wroth's *Love's Victory*', *Women's Writing*, 6 (1999), 47–63.

——, '"For *Worth*, Not Weakness, Makes in Use but One": Literary Dialogues in an English Renaissance Family', in Danielle Clarke and Elizabeth Clarke, eds., *'This Double Voice': Gendered Writing in Early Modern England* (Houndmills: Macmillan, 2000), 164–84.

# Index